POSTCOLONIAL SOCIOLOGIES:
A READER

POLITICAL POWER AND SOCIAL THEORY

Series Editor: Julian Go

Recent Volumes:

POLITICAL POWER AND SOCIAL THEORY   VOLUME 31

POSTCOLONIAL SOCIOLOGIES: A READER

EDITED BY

JULIAN GO

Boston University, Boston, MA, USA

United Kingdom – North America – Japan
India – Malaysia – China

Emerald Group Publishing Limited
Howard House, Wagon Lane, Bingley BD16 1WA, UK

First edition 2016

British Library Cataloguing in Publication Data
A catalogue record for this book is available from the British Library

ISBN: 978-1-78635-326-9
ISSN: 0198-8719 (Series)

ISOQAR certified
Management System,
awarded to Emerald
for adherence to
Environmental
standard
ISO 14001:2004.

Certificate Number 1985
ISO 14001

INVESTOR IN PEOPLE

CONTENTS

LIST OF CONTRIBUTORS

Gurminder K. Bhambra	Department of Sociology, Warwick University, Coventry, UK
Manuela Boatcă	Sociology & Institute for Latin American Studies, Freie Universität Berlin, Berlin, Germany
Claire Laurier Decoteau	Department of Sociology, University of Illinois at Chicago, Chicago, IL, USA
Julian Go	Department of Sociology, Boston University, Boston, MA, USA
Fatma Müge Göçek	Department of Sociology, University of Michigan, Ann Arbor, MI, USA
Manu Goswami	Department of History, New York University, New York, NY, USA
Jeffrey Guhin	Department of Sociology, Yale University, New Haven, CT, USA
Zine Magubane	Department of Sociology, Boston College, Boston, MA, USA
Steven Seidman	Department of Sociology, State University of New York-Albany, Albany, NY, USA
George Steinmetz	Department of Sociology, University of Michigan, Ann Arbor, MI, USA
Jonathan Wyrtzen	Department of Sociology, Yale University, New Haven, CT, USA

SENIOR EDITORIAL BOARD

STUDENT EDITORIAL BOARD

EDITORIAL STATEMENT

Political Power and Social Theory is a peer-reviewed annual journal committed to advancing the interdisciplinary understanding of the linkages between political power, social relations, and historical development. The journal welcomes both empirical and theoretical work and is willing to consider papers of substantial length. Publication decisions are made by the editor in consultation with members of the editorial board and anonymous reviewers. For information on submissions, please see the journal website at www.emeraldgrouppublishing.com/tk/ppst

INTRODUCTION: SOCIOLOGY AND POSTCOLONIALITY

Julian Go

ABSTRACT

The study of postcoloniality has taken on the form of "postcolonial theory" in the humanities, sociology's approach to postcolonial issues has been comparably muted. This essay considers postcolonial theory in the humanities and its potential utility for reorienting sociological theory and research. After sketching the historical background and context of postcolonial studies, three broad areas of contribution to sociology are highlighted: reconsiderations of agency, the injunction to overcome analytic bifurcations, and a recognition of sociology's imperial standpoint.

Consider two monumental events of the past century. The first is the violent imperial expansion of the European and Anglo-American states. Beginning in the late nineteenth and through the early twentieth century, powerful states like England, France, Germany, the United States, Belgium, Italy, and others mounted new territorial assaults upon Africa and Asia, creating what has become known as the period of "high

Postcolonial Sociologies: A Reader
Political Power and Social Theory, Volume 31, 1−30
Copyright © 2016 by Emerald Group Publishing Limited
All rights of reproduction in any form reserved
ISSN: 0198-8719/doi:10.1108/S0198-871920160000031001

imperialism." Soon enough, modern colonial empires encompassed nearly all of the globe. The second, starting roughly in the wake of the Second World War and continuing through the 1960s, was imperial retrenchment and decline: the dismantling of those very same colonial empires that had been expanding previously. A multitude of independent nation-states appeared; new postcolonial states hoping to throw off the legacy of their colonial past and embark upon promising developmental paths. If the first process was a staggering display of metropolitan political power, the second marked the dramatic disintegration of that very same power. The colonial empires passed away. Nation-states replaced them. And for the millions upon millions of postcolonial peoples, hope was in the air.

What does this have to do with sociology? On the one hand, disciplinary sociology as we know it today was founded exactly during the first moment – the age of high imperialism – in the late nineteenth and early twentieth centuries. And sociology directly engaged it. In Europe and the United States, founding sociologists either criticized imperialism, affirmed it, or reproduced the imperial gaze in their thinking. Their data often depended upon the knowledge of the Other culled from imperial expansion. Many of the issues they thought about were directly connected to the new imperialism unleashed around them (Connell, 1997; Go, 2013b). When Franklin Giddings, President of the American Sociological Society who had previously been given the first full professorship in Sociology in the United States, gave a speech in 1910 listing "the questions that vex us" and which sociology should address, the first was the question "of territorial expansion and of rule over alien peoples" (Giddings, 1911, p. 580). On the other hand, sociology's engagement with the issues surrounding the second moment of postcoloniality remains obscure. Sociology responded to the new imperialism, but it is not yet clear how, if at all, sociology has responded to decolonization and postcolonialism. So what about sociology and *post*coloniality? How *might* sociology engage questions associated with the postcolonial era? This is the underlying problematic of the present volume.

"POSTCOLONIAL THEORY" AND SOCIOLOGY

Other academic disciplines besides sociology have surely responded to the postcolonial era. Beginning around the early 1980s, something called "postcolonial theory" and its cognate "postcolonial studies" swept over literature departments in American universities. This intellectual movement was mounted upon what we might call the "first wave" of postcolonial studies in the 1950s and 1960s: writers such as W. E. B. DuBois, Frantz Fanon, Aimé Césaire, and Amilcar Cabral among many others (Young, 2001). Influenced by these writers (and other theoretical movements like poststructuralism and subaltern studies), Edward Said, Homi Bhabha, Gayatri Spivak, and others produced a range of texts that fell under the rubric of "postcolonial theory."[1] These works were quickly devoured by young scholars and dazzled students. Other disciplines soon fell: history, anthropology, linguistics, philosophy, and even art and architecture (e.g., Loomba et al., 2006). By the late 1990s, the revolution had not been televised but it did appear the popular press: in 1995, *The New York Times* observed that the term "postcolonial" had become "the latest catchall term to dazzle the academic mind" (Jacoby, 1995). A few years later, Leela Gandhi, scholar and granddaughter of the late Mahatma Gandhi, observed that "postcolonialism has taken its place with theories such as poststructuralism, psychoanalysis and feminism as a major critical discourse in the humanities" (Gandhi, 1998, p. viii).

This body of work was varied but it shared overarching themes, all of which arose in response to the historical process of decolonization in the mid to late twentieth century and the new condition of postcoloniality. Disappointment was part of that context. The political decolonization of Asia, the Middle East and Africa, or in other parts of the world had been promising. National independence portended a blessed future − a future whereby colonial exploitation would be replaced with economic "development" and social "progress." For some, this would come in the form of socialism or adjacent ideologies; for others it would come from neoliberal markets, enabling the postcolonial world to "catch up" with the status of their former metropolitan masters. But in reality, the post-independence years were marked by continued exploitation, violence and global inequality. Furthermore, political decolonization did not herald the end of the West's power over the globe. While colonial relations of power officially receded, the older power relations simply took on more subtle, insidious, and even more potent forms, variously called "neo-imperialism" or "neo-colonialism." Nor did decolonization in the political sphere bring a decolonization of consciousness or culture. Racialized forms of thought persisted among ex-colonizers and ex-colonized alike; as did self-negation, cultural annihilation, and feelings of marginalization among postcolonial peoples. The "West" was no longer the center of traditional colonial power but it surely retained its cultural power, beckoning the ex-colonized to be *like it*. The cultures of imperialism seemed to persist into the present period. And they contributed to and helped sustain global inequalities and power discrepancies between the global South and North. "We live," Gayatri Spivak famously declared, "in a postcolonial neo-colonized world" (Spivak & Harasym, 1990, p. 166).

Postcolonial theory in the humanities — a sort of "second wave" of postcolonial studies — intellectually grappled with these persistent relations of power and the cultures of imperialism that underpinned them. The overarching idea was that, as the cultures of imperialism persist, new and different sorts of knowledge must be produced to help decolonize consciousness. Accordingly, second wave postcolonial theory analytically attended to colonialism and its legacies. It sought representations and forms of knowledge that would not fall prey to colonialist knowledge's misrepresentations and epistemic violence. This is why it was labeled *post*colonial theory. It is not just that it was interested in societies that emerged from colonialism. More broadly, this intellectual movement sought theories, ways of representing the world, and histories that critique rather than authorize or sustain imperialistic ways of knowing. Postcolonial theory elaborated "theoretical structures that contest the previous dominant western ways of seeing things" (Young, 2003, p. 4). This is probably why postcolonial theorists like Homi Bhabha turned to first wave postcolonial thinkers like Frantz Fanon, who offered sustained critiques of the psychological impact of colonialism while also crafting visions of a truly postcolonial world. It is also why one early incarnation of postcolonial studies in the humanities was "Commonwealth Studies": the study and promotion of literary texts from the Caribbean or Africa to highlight non-Western voices and perspectives (Ashcroft, Griffiths, & Tiffin, 2002). Meanwhile, Edward Said's *Orientalism* revealed the discursive operations of imperial power, tending to the representations of the Other that imperialism created and which nonetheless persisted into the postcolonial period (Said, 1979). All of these early works challenged the deep systems of knowledge, identity, and culture that had enabled colonialism and which needed to be overcome for a truly postcolonial era to be inaugurated.

The second wave of postcolonial thought joined but also surmounted Marxist critiques of imperialism (e.g., Brewer, 1990). It was partly inspired by traditional Marxism but it was also critical of it on at least two major grounds. The first is traditional Marxism's universalism. Marxist thought formulated a critique and theory of capitalism, but generated them Eurocentrically; that is, by making capitalism as it appeared in Europe the only model (Robinson, 2000). When traditional Marxist thought analyzed colonies, slavery, primitive accumulation in the Global South, or racial domination, it marginalized their importance, seeing them as outcomes or add-ons to more fundamental dynamics modeled upon social dynamics in Europe – not as constitutive of those dynamics (cf. Anderson, 2010). The first wave directed this sort of critique against the Marxism of the Communist party – a critique exemplified by Aime Césaire's resignation letter from the party (and carried on by Bhabha and Said in their own ways). Césaire wrote that conventional Marxism had been reluctant to deal with the specificity of the colonial situation, instead absorbing it into its homogenizing categories:

> The colonial question, cannot be treated as a subsidiary part of some more important global matter, as part over which deals can be arranged or upon which others patch up compromises they think they have a right to seek in the name of an overall situation which they retain the exclusive right to interpret ... our colonialism, the struggle of coloured people against racism, is much more complex, indeed, it is of a totally different nature than the struggle of the French workers against French capitalism, and cannot in any case be considered a part, as a fragment, of that struggle (Césaire, 2010 [1956], p. 147)

Postcolonial thinkers, secondly, also took Marxism to task for overemphasizing the economic relations of imperialism and colonialism and thus overlooking the racialized, gendered, psychological, cultural and semiotic dimensions and legacies of imperial power. This was one of the distinct contributions of postcolonial theory: to go beyond economic determinism and unearth various types of discourses, *epistemes*, cultural schemas, representations, and ideologies that were part and parcel of Western imperialism – whether embodied in everyday discourse, novels, works of art, scientific tracts, or ethnographies. Where Marxist critiques did not, postcolonial studies mounted an assault upon the entire culture of western global dominance – or as Said put it in a different context, upon all the "impressive ideological formations" and "forms of knowledge affiliated with [colonial domination]" (Said, 1993, p. 9).

Given this emphasis on culture, and the critique of Marxist universalism, it is probably appropriate that postcolonial studies took root and proliferated in the humanities; and that postcolonial theory was seen as, and partly drew from, the poststructuralist and postmodern turns. Said's *Orientalism* famously owes its origins to Foucault's theory of discourse and power/ knowledge (Foucault, 1972, 1979). Other sectors of postcolonial studies adopted the postmodern critique of the Enlightenment and its grand narratives, totalizing schemas, and identitarian thinking to critique imperialism. Just as Lyotard's critique of grand narratives worries about Western knowledge's universalizing gestures – or "overcoming" (*dépassement*) – at

the expense of particularity, so did postcolonial studies "join postmodernism in an attempt to analyse and to resist this *dépassement*" (Gandhi, 1998,
p. 41). Postcolonial studies of colonial discourse (typically known as "colonial discourse analysis") critiqued the essentializing representations in
colonizers' imaginations and speech but also treated this critique not as
a "specialized activity only for minorities or for historians of imperialism
and colonialism" but rather as a starting point for questioning all of
"Western knowledge's categories and assumptions" (Young, 1990, p. 11).
Postcolonial studies thereby echoed the postmodern claim "that all knowledge may be variously contaminated, implicated in its very formal or
'objective' structures" (Young, 1990, p. 11).

   While the humanities have indeed responded to the historical condition
of postcoloniality – and with a vehemently verbose vigor – the same cannot be said of sociology. Though it had been entangled with imperialism
earlier in the century, it has been more hesitant to engage with postcoloniality. This is seen in the fact that the theories and thinkers that launched
postcolonial studies in other disciplines simply have not resonated to the
same degree in sociology. References in the major sociological journals to
postcolonial texts and thinkers like Said or Bhabha are minimal at best
compared with humanities and history journals (Go, 2013). None of the
five best-selling introductory textbooks in sociology have sections on postcolonialism or have postcolonialism or postcolonial theory in their indices
(even though they have entries on "postmodernism"). None list Edward
Said's *Orientalism* in their bibliography or include Edward Said in their
indices; nor do they include other postcolonial thinkers like Homi Bhabha
or Frantz Fanon. Texts and readers on contemporary theory, which would
seem the natural candidates for discussions of postcolonial theory, are also
lacking. The best-selling top five contemporary theory readers devote
lengthy separate sections to "Feminist Theory," "Postmodern Theory," or
"The Body" but they have no comparable sections on postcolonial theories
and thinkers (Go, 2013). And while courses on "postcolonialism," "postcolonial literature," or "postcolonial theory" could be found in most literature, language, and history departments, parallel courses in sociology are
relatively absent. Postcolonialism is another one of sociology's "missing
revolutions" (Bhambra, 2007a).

   Not that sociology has completely failed to analytically engage the
dilemmas of decolonization and postcoloniality. But when it has engaged,
it has done so through suspect lenses – or at least lenses very different
from those deployed by postcolonial studies in the humanities. In the
1960s, as the dilemmas about nation-building in the postcolonial world

proliferated, sociologists joined political scientists, and economists in promulgating modernization theory, the dominant variant of "development" theory. This body of work indeed addressed concerns about postcolonial states but its linear and universal template rendered it a conservative rather than a critical theory. It did not abjure the intellectual legacies of colonialism, it reinscribed them: a neo-colonial intervention rather than a postcolonial one.

Dependency theory and world-systems analysis, which offered a powerful critique of modernization-development paradigms, merit consideration here. Their critique of modernization theory, their rigorous account of imperialism, and their concern for continued inequalities between the so-called "core" ("metropole") and "periphery" ("satellite") make them parallel to postcolonial theory in the humanities. They stand, in a sense, as sociology's best answer. And a booming, loud and vibrant one at that. Still, we must not neglect the stark differences between postcolonial theory in the humanities and dependency/world-systems theory. One is that dependency/world-systems, as indeed a form of Marxist thought, focused upon economic structures while postcolonial theory has been concerned with the cultural, psychological, discursive, epistemic or representational or textual dimensions of colonialism.[2] Another difference is that while dependency theory and world-systems analyses tend to reduce colonialism and racialized processes to economic class – or even conflate them – postcolonial scholarship theorizes racial, ethnic, gender or cultural relations and grants them more autonomy. This difference is important. Colonial formations of power were surely about economic exploitation, but they were also about racial difference, religious chauvinism, masculine domination, and attendant cultural or semiotic processes which world-systems theory relegates to analytic irrelevance. At issue, then, is traditional Marxism's universalism, and its attendant refusal to allow difference to trouble its analytical architecture. World-systems theory runs the risk of keeping this universalism intact. The critique from Said encapsulates the point: Marxist narratives such as world-systems analysis produce only "universalising and self-validating" histories that depend "on a homogenizing and incorporating world historical scheme that assimilated non-synchronous developments, histories, cultures, and peoples to it" (Said, 2000, p. 210). Postcolonial theory thereby entails a *critique* of world-systems theory just as it does of Marxism, however sympathetic that critique is.[3]

In these and other respects, sociology's analytic engagement with postcoloniality warrants reconsideration, critical rearticulation, and generative expansion.[4] Might the humanities' engagement with postcoloniality also help? What might social scientists learn from the sorts of theory and research found in interdisciplinary postcolonial studies? In other words, what exactly might sociology take from "postcolonial theory" to better address the dilemmas and dynamics of the world's postcolonial malaise? All of these questions raise an overarching and perhaps more difficult one: can there even *be* a postcolonial sociology?

ENGAGING POSTCOLONIAL THEORY

The premise of this volume is that engaging postcolonial studies – either for inspiration, for theories, concepts and methods, or even to critique – would be productive for social science. Exactly, what from post-colonial studies, how it might be incorporated, and the implications for sociology: these are open questions, and each of the contributions to this volume entails their own ideas and proposals. What follows are some preliminary summary thoughts.

It helps to begin by clarifying what postcolonial theory does *not* mean for sociology. Foremost, it does not mean a valorization of the "colo-nized," "the East" or "Global South" in romanticized opposition to "the colonizer," the "West" or the "Global North." Postcolonial theory should not just be about countering Eurocentrism with an Asian-centrism or African-centrism; this would only prioritize the dialectical opposite of its object of critique. "Afrocentrism, I believe," Said asserted, "is as flawed as Eurocentrism." (Said, 2003). Postcolonial theory, for it to be *truly* post-colonial, must move beyond colonial knowledge structures entirely, hence it must strive to transcend the very oppositions between Europe and the Rest, or the West and the East, which colonialism inscribed in our theories. To think that postcolonial theory only means studying the non-West or the non-European the world would be an egregious and unfortunate misunder-standing. For another thing, postcolonial theory does not only offer sociol-ogy an injunction to examine colonialism. While examining colonialism, understanding its operations, and tracking its legacies should be a part of any postcolonial knowledge project, and while it should be the starting point of a postcolonial theory, there remains the risk of reducing colonial-ism to yet another "variable" that we add to our otherwise conventional accounts. Postcolonial theory offers more besides.

But what exactly? Something of what postcolonial theory offers has already been noted: a serious analytic engagement with the racialized, cultural, discursive, and epistemic aspects of global inequalities which conventional sociology (including traditional world-systems theory) has only partially addressed. But related to this are three areas of potential contribution in particular: (1) reconsiderations of agency, (2) an injunction to overcome analytic bifurcations, and (3) a recognition of sociology's imperial standpoint.

Letting the Subaltern Speak

One contribution is to remind us of the agency of colonized and postcolonial subjects and hence the possible limits of metropolitan (i.e., imperial or colonial) power. Admittedly, from a certain standpoint, to say that postcolonial theory emphasizes subaltern agency might induce confusion. Did not Gayatri Spivak famously question whether the subaltern can be represented, hence upending any attempt to render them "agentic" in our historical or social scientific models (Spivak, 1988a)? And does not Edward Said's *Orientalism* forsake any agency on the part of colonized peoples for the voice and discourses of the Western Orientalists? But postcolonial theory *does* offer insights into questions of agency. After all, it is in part a sympathetic response to decolonization, the anticolonial movements that exploded around the world in the early twentieth century, and the dilemmas of postcolonial nation-building. Embedded in its very founding, then, is an attempt to grapple with the potential for postcolonial peoples to take control of their destiny in the face of perpetual Western power, as well as to ponder seriously the possible limits of any such projects.

Yet, rather than any naïve romanticization of subaltern agency, it is the *problematic* of agency which postcolonial theory places on the grid. Two different strands of postcolonial theory's genealogy remind us of this. One is postcolonial literature. Reacting to the proliferation of literature in the postcolonial world, and their occlusion in the Western academy, some scholars in the United Kingdom promoted the field of "Commonwealth Studies," which meant to recover and promote literary texts from the Caribbean or Africa (and in particular parts or former parts of the British Commonwealth). In literary studies, this was one of the initial forms that "postcolonial studies" took, and it was all about excavating non-Western voices and perspectives so as to give voice to voices which had been previously repressed or ignored (Ashcroft et al., 2002).

Another strand originates in the "subaltern studies" project.[5] Partly inspired by traditional Marxist problematics (why didn't the Indian working class adopt a revolutionary consciousness?) and the related "history from below" approach to social history pronounced by E. P. Thompson, subaltern studies raised the issue of agency first and foremost. It took aim at the Cambridge School of Indian history and conventional anticolonial nationalistic historiography, both of which focused solely on elite history. The problem was that these existing histories never analyzed "the contributions by people, *on their* own, that is, independent of the elite" (Guha, 1988, p. 39). Founding member Ranajit Guha explained: "We are indeed opposed to much of the prevailing academic practice in historiography ... for its failure to acknowledge the subaltern as the maker of his own destiny. This critique lies at the very heart of our project" (Guha, 1984, p. vii). But more than simply adding in the subaltern or transplanting Thompson's histories from below to India, subaltern studies also insisted upon disentangling historiography from the "universalist histories of capital" and the nation-form which narrated the peasant/subaltern as premodern figures (Chakrabarty, 2002, p. 8). Subaltern Studies thereby adopted Marxism but also implicitly and explicitly at times offered a critique of it, expressing a need to analytically respect difference and highlight the very particularity marked by the figure of the subaltern. Refusing to reduce difference to historical time (i.e., rendering peasants "backwards") or Orientalist categories (the peasant as "irrational"), it sought alternative ways of thinking about, and representing, subaltern subjects.[6]

It is by now well known that Gayatri Spivak's "Can the Subaltern Speak" was inspired by and was meant as a direct engagement with the subaltern studies project (Chakrabarty, 2002, p. 17; Spivak, 1988a). Spivak famously critiqued the idea of representing the subaltern. Still, Spivak's critique did not suggest that our narrative or theories should ignore the subaltern. It was instead meant to disclose how truths are produced and render visible the *limits of the West's own agency* in representing the subaltern, hence by implication revealing the limits of Western agency, knowledge and power. Spivak's notion of "strategic essentialism" − a "strategic use of positivist essentialism" − followed: the subaltern must be analyzed and textually treated as an actor to serve as a critical counterpoint to Orientalist discourse (Spivak, 1988b, p. 205).[7] Homi Bhabha's analysis of "mimicry" and "hybridity" also followed: rather than purporting to capture a true native voice, Bhabha examined colonizers' texts to show their limits, attending to the traces of the colonized's ability to disrupt colonial representations and hence the colonizers' power to control the meaning of their own texts (Bhabha, 1994, pp. 85−92).[8]

Can the "subaltern speak"? Can the subaltern be represented? If so, what does that do to our conventional narratives? If not, by what conceptual or textual means, methods and modes might we capture the traces of agency? Does it matter at all? How is the figure of the subaltern, or any presumed truth about essential identities and agency, produced? Postcolonial theory does not cohere around any single answer to these complicated questions. It does, however, bring them to the fore.

Here sociology has something to learn. Sociological research on social movements or ethnographic studies of urban and minority populations are probably the only traditional subfields of sociology where the actions, practices, and agency of peripheralized groups are analyzed in any sustained manner. And in these areas, too, questions about reflexivity such as those raised in postcolonial studies have surfaced (e.g., Wacquant, 2002). Alternatively, most meso-level and macro-level sociology, and indeed much of social theory, has been more silent on the agency of non-elite subjects. This is true even for the sociological subfields where one might expect marginalized groups and actors to be most relevant, such as political sociology, comparative-historical sociology, or studies of globalization.

To take one example, consider studies of global culture. Most of these studies focus their theory and research on global diffusion, tracing the adoption of modern ideas, political forms, policies, and practices by postcolonial states. In this work, the subjectivity, perceptions, or actions of postcolonial "adopters" are treated as unproblematic. There is no interaction; hence no action much less agency among the adopters. It may very well be that our modern notion of human rights emerges from key discourses and events in the West and that the concept of rights has diffused to other parts of the world. But what would not be captured in existing sociological theories of diffusion is how the notion of rights has been able to diffuse partly as a dialectical response to western imperial domination; or that the very reason it has been able to resonate with non-Western peoples (and therefore more easily diffuse) is because non-Western peoples *already* have their own indigenous or preexisting local discourses of rights from which to work. Also occluded is how the ostensibly diffused modern thing itself has a history that belies notions of European originality. Theories of world society insist that documents like the US constitution spread to non-Western societies that unconsciously mimic it but those theories are blind to how the US constitution itself was partly modeled upon and inspired by Native-American political forms (Grinde & Johansen, 1991). The problematic assumption, reflected in the theory, is that diffusion always and only happens when it is from the West to the Rest; a uni-linear flow.

Historical sociological work on revolutions, surprisingly, is the same; not because they overlook subaltern groups but because when they restrict their focus to revolutions in Europe, they fail to consider how those events may have been shaped by events elsewhere in the world — not least in the colonial and postcolonial world. Skocpol's *States and Social Revolutions* incorporated China but steadfastly refused to include anticolonial revolutions — as if those revolutions (which traversed the globe) were irrelevant in the French revolution (Skocpol, 1979). Nor did she offer ways of thinking about how "peripheral" revolutions might have shaped or impacted metropolitan ones. Hence, from historical sociologists we read much about the French revolution and the attendant Eurocentric claim that the French revolution was the originator of liberal political modernity (and, according to Skocpol, the first "modern social revolution") (Skocpol & Kestnbaum, 1990). But we read next to nothing about how France in the wake of its supposedly seminal declaration of liberty, equality and fraternity proceeded to extend its violent imperial hand overseas. Nor do we read about the other significant revolution at the time that in some ways facilitated France's own revolution: that is, the Haitian revolution (Magubane, 2005, pp. 101–2). To be sure, as CLR James highlighted, key events of the French revolution were responses to and shaped by the slave revolt in Haiti (James, 1989). It was not from the minds of valiant French thinkers that the question of universal rights was put on the agenda of the French revolutionaries' debates, it was the resistance of the slaves in Haiti (Dubois, 2004). While the US constitution carries the traces of Native-American ingenuity, so too does the French revolution carry the traces of the Haitian revolt. But we would not know from this sociological theory and research, nor has sociological theory and research let such issues trouble its theoretical or conceptual apparatus.

While a number of social scientists have partially remedied the European-focus by paying attention to imperialism and colonialism, most of this work nonetheless runs the risk of reinscribing the problems it ostensibly seeks to transcend (Go, 2009; Pitts, 2010; Steinmetz, 2013, 2014). Much of it, for instance, focuses upon what the imperialists and colonizers do without reference to their embeddedness in interactive local environments. This otherwise promising literature examines the causes of imperialism, the policies of colonial states, or the political-economic legacies of colonialism but the explanatory "factors" are rarely if ever the actions of colonized groups. Said's *Orientalism* in part prefaced this sort of analysis — eliding completely the voices and actions of non-Europeans for an examination of how they were represented — as if "colonial discourse" was not in fact a discourse but a one-way discussion. Still, Said's subsequent and other work indeed took a turn and paid greater attention to subaltern writing and texts — a lesson from which historical sociologists can and should learn (Said, 1993, 1999, 2000). For the problematic of agency in postcolonial theory is not about demarcating a space absent from power relations or somehow distinct from them — this is more so the approach in conventional social theory, where questions of agency are subsumed into universalizing and abstract categories like "agency versus structure" or pragmatist reflexivity.[9] Rather, the problematic of agency is about attending to what even traditional sociology should attend to: *interactions*. It is about recognizing the lesson imprinted by founding postcolonial theorists like Fanon (1968[1961]) or Memmi (1965[1957]) — viz., that colonizer and colonized are mutually constituted, that the history of European states or any powerful metropolitan states is not separable from the history of their so-called Others, and that power is always exercised in concrete setting and in turn refracted or reflected by those whom it seeks to control — hence it has limits. It is about, in short, *relationality* (Go, 2013a). Even Said's *Orientalism*, with its focus upon the voices of Orientalists (i.e., Europeans), intimated this relationality, for Said's illumination of the West's representations of the "Orient" implied not only that the West discursively constructs the Orient but also that, in so doing, it constructs its self-understanding at the same time.

Overcoming Analytic Bifurcations

This brings us to the other potential contribution of postcolonial theory to social theory and sociological research. As noted, postcolonial theory registers its interest in agency by recognizing the entanglements and relations between colonizer and colonized, metropole and colony, center and periphery and by disclosing how identities, institutions, spaces, or places that might be deemed separate were in fact connected, intertwined and mutually constituted. This has implications for thinking about agency, but it also has implications much wider in scope. Put simply, postcolonial theory can alert us to and perhaps help us overcome sociology's *analytic bifurcations*. By this I mean the analytic abstraction or separation of social objects from their wider constitutive relations (Go, 2013a). Of course, any social scientific conceptualization entails some form of separation. The problem is fetishism: mistaking the conceptual abstraction for a real abstraction. A particular pernicious form of this operation, for example, is the analytic bifurcation of "Europe" from the "Rest" and variants thereof, such as the bifurcation between the "inside" of nations versus the "outside" of nations; or "the domestic" from the "foreign."

This bifurcation is seen in sociology's long-standing theorization of modernity. Sociology as we know it originated in an attempt to apprehend the constitution, formation, and reproduction of modernity. As Adams, Clemens, and Orloff (2005) poignantly remind us, one of the questions driving sociology has long been: "How did societies come to be recognizably 'modern'?" (Adams et al., 2005, p. 3). But conventional sociology's account of modernity has long fallen prey to the myth of separation, or analytic bifurcation, of spaces and places around the world. As critics like Bhambra and Boatcâ and Costa stress, sociology's standard accounts of modernity suppress the history of colonialism and imperialism and thereby impede an understanding of the West's entanglements with subject peoples (Bhambra, 2007b; Boatcâ & Costa, 2010). Seidman notes (2016), for example, that while Karl Marx, Max Weber, and Emile Durkheim addressed questions of empire, none of them saw imperialism or colonialism as independent forces in their own right, nor as constitutive features of European society. Imperialism figures either as an abnormality or a result of an already formed European modernity or capitalism. Likewise, the founders of disciplinary sociology in the United States responded to the high imperialism of their times but most often, their approach to imperialism was to support it or see it as an evolutionary theory of racial expansion; in either case imperialism was treated as an outgrowth of modernity rather than constitutive of it (Go, 2013b).[10]

More recent social theories also fall prey. Consider Foucault. Even as postcolonial theorists draw from Foucault's critical approach to power/ knowledge, his actual historical narratives and genealogies are problematic from the postcolonial standpoint (e.g., Stoler, 1995). In *Discipline and Punish*, Foucault argues that the spectacle attendant with punishment in the *ancien regime* "disappears" and is replaced by the prison (Foucault, 1979, pp. 7–8). Foucault restricts this "transformation" (in his words) to Europe, but the realities of imperial history upend his characterization and this reflective spatial qualifier. The British colonial state in India did not respond to the "Indian Mutiny" with a panopticon but with public brutality that involved executions, "hangings and floggings" and spectacles such as "blowing rebels from the cannon's mouth" (Connell, 2006, p. 261). France's colonies from Saigon to Senegal to Algeria saw spectacular

violence too. As Rosalind Morris points out, "if it is true that the 'slacken-
ing of the hold on the body' and the 'decline of spectacle' marked the nineteenth and twentieth centuries in Europe ... it remained profoundly central
to colonial regimes" (Morris, 2002, p. 265). While Foucault qualifies his
narrative spatially to Europe, this gesture itself gets at the heart of the
issue: his theory arbitrarily cuts "Europe" off from its colonies – as if
imperial and colonial history *were not also Europe's history*. Such separation or bifurcation may render the theoretical categories themselves inadequate. In Foucault's analytic, exactly when, where, and for whom does
"disciplinary power" as opposed to the spectacle dominate?

The reigning master works in historical sociology do not escape the trap
of bifurcation either. Charles Tilly's *Coercion, Capital, and European States*
is an exemplary work in historical sociology for it seeks, as the best historical sociology does, to illuminate a prominent feature of modernity: the
national state (Tilly, 1990). We would think that this book would make
empires crucial to the analysis. Indeed, Tilly's entire point is to explain how
the national state came to become the dominant form over other possible
sociopolitical forms, including city-states and – yes indeed – *empires*! But
where is empire in his story? In fact, Tilly relegates them to the margins.
He defines *national states* as "states governing contiguous regions and their
cities by means of centralized, differentiated, and autonomous structures"
(p. 2). He argues that the national state form exemplified in Britain and
France won out over other forms, including empires, in the nineteenth century Europe and that they later spread throughout the world. But those
key "national states" in Europe were never properly *national* as he defines
it nor were they only *in Europe* only. They were *empire-states*: coercion
wielding organizations governing expansive regions and cities with a hierarchy of citizen/subject at the core of the form (Cooper & Burbank, 2010). In
the 1920s and 1930s, the British empire-state was at its territorial highpoint,
encompassing more than 33 million miles of territory around the world,
structured by various hierarchical political divisions and fragmented sover-
eignties. The French empire encompassed over 12 million miles around the
same time. These states only became truly national states after Second
World War, not the nineteenth century.

The problem is that Tilly's analysis analytic bifurcates states from
empires. Tilly admits that France and England, and other European countries, constructed empires but he treats their empires as an externality. He
notes that just as national states in Europe were emerging, they were also
"creating empires *beyond* Europe, in the Americas, Africa, Asia and the
Pacific." He refers to these as "external empires" (167). In other words,

Tilly approach posits an "internal" national state ostensibly inside Europe separate from an "external" empire putatively "outside Europe." There is a "European" national state and then there is imperialism and an overseas "empire"; there is a national state *in* Europe, exerting sovereignty over parts of Europe, and then there is, *over there*, an "empire"; as if the latter were an appendage irrelevant to the constitution of the former, as if the model of sovereignty had not been already forged in and by interactions with the periphery *out there*; as if there could realistically be such an easy distinct between "inside" and "outside."

Yet, national states did not develop their ideas and practices about sovereignty first "in Europe" and then transpose them outward; they developed them amidst sixteenth century colonial claims and disputes between empires about overseas territory (Branch, 2012). And the so-called "external" colonies of Britain were not "outside" Britain: they *were* British. They were declared subject to the sovereignty of Britain, just as France's so-called "external" colonies were subject to the sovereignty of France – hence fully inside it. This is why the English crown fought, so hard and so often, to keep colonies within itself, suppressing the American revolution in the 1770s or, for that matter, violently suppressing the Mau-Mau rebellion in the 1950s. And France's colonies likewise were not "outside" of France: they *were* French. Hence France fought the bloody Algerian war in the 1950s to "keep Algeria French." That was the mantra after all. Tilly's model analytically bifurcates into distinct domains the "national state" and "empire" – 'internal' and 'external', 'inside' and 'outside' – that were never really separated in practice.[11]

Sociology's Standpoint and the Limits of Knowledge

Mainstream sociology's suppression of postcolonial peoples' agency and its analytic bifurcations attest to another issue that postcolonial theory can help problematize: sociology's metropolitan standpoint. At stake here are two interrelated issues. The first is the knowledge/power complex. Postcolonial theory has been especially vocal on this issue. Said's *Orientalism* famously revealed the previously hidden relationship between Orientalist knowledge and imperial power. Categories, discourses, and silent assumptions about the Orient were not a sideshow to imperial domination but constitutive of it – part of an entire culture of dominance. In this, Said extended the Foucauldian tradition. Foucault had already exposed the relationships between power/knowledge, not least the relationships between knowledge, governmentality, and disciplinary power. Feminist theory, and later queer theory, also disclosed the knowledge/ power nexus, which is why postcolonial theory is often seen as adjacent or parallel with these other theoretical formations. But building upon Said's work, postcolonial theory has also expressed a more specific interest in the knowledge/power relation: that is, in exposing and understanding the culture of *imperial dominance*, in particular. This culture includes popular representations and their racialized subtexts; hence, the insights of some of Spivak's (1986) readings of Victorian texts. But it also includes putatively objective "expert" knowledge. While Said examines Orientalism, for instance, the noted postcolonial historian Dipesh Chakrabarty takes the postcolonial task to the discipline of "history," while others like Gyan Prakash have examined science, in general (Chakrabarty, 2000; Prakash, 1999). Postcolonial theory is thus interested in the epistemic violence entailed in all of these representations − whether in novels or in social scientific categories.

The second issue follows. In interrogating Orientalist knowledge, Said also, however implicitly, put his finger on the idea of an *imperial standpoint of knowledge*. In other words, Said's examination not only revealed that Orientalist knowledge is biased for its essentializing and homogenizing operations; it also disclosed that the bias was but the natural by-product of the very positionality of the knower in the geopolitical hierarchy. This was the standpoint of the Western imperialist: the type of knowledge produced by Orientalism followed from the Western imperial states' history, institutions, politico-economic interests and global position. Foucault had in fact registered a similar point about discipline: classificatory schemes deployed by the prison complex, the school, or military were not only enlisted for disciplinary power but produced *for* it, thus expressing the standpoint of power itself. And postcolonial studies and adjacent intellectual movements have long been interested in the same issue. Fanon criticized colonial psychiatry in French Algeria for normalizing subjects rather than addressing structural inequalities that produced the disorders in the first place: psychiatric knowledge reflected the interests of French colonial regime (Fanon, 1968 [1961]). Similarly, the Subaltern Studies project's methodological innovation was to read between the lines of the colonial archive. This was based upon the assumption that the colonial archive narrowly reflected the standpoint of colonial administrators; that is, was merely the "discourse of power" (Guha, 1983, p. 11).

Sociology has yet to fully take stock of these issues regarding knowledge, power, and standpoint. Feminist critiques, critical race theory, and queer studies have all emerged within disciplinary sociology to question sociology's white male hetereonormative standpoint, but as yet sociology's particular geopolitical-imperialistic standpoint has only begun to be problematized.[12] Postcolonial theory can help here. Specifically, it can help sociology question its tendency toward *metrocentrism*. By this I mean sociology's assumption that its particular knowledge, rooted in specific understandings of Europe and the rest of the world, is universal. This can be traced to the founding work of Weber, Marx, or Durkheim. Their social theories posited presumably universal templates of development and general theoretical categories based upon Europe's experience. They operated from Orientalist assumptions and reduced cultural and spatial difference to temporal difference (Bhambra, 2007b; Connell, 2007). "Since its institutional beginnings in the nineteenth century," Boatcă, Costa, and Rodriguez point out, "sociology, self-defined as a science of the modern (Western) world, has conceptualized modernity endogenously by taking the social norms, structures, and values characterizing the so-called Western societies as a universal parameter for defining what modern societies are and the processes of their emergence as the path to be followed by other, modernizing countries" (Boatcâ, Costa, & Rodríguez, 2010, p. 1). This metrocentrism was reproduced and paralleled in American sociology. Early US sociology, when not drawing from European's concerns, was aimed at understanding industrialization, class conflict, ethnic relations, and urbanization in early twentieth century America. It primarily worked from Spencerian themes, hence applying socioevolutionary categories to the entire world (Breslau, 2007), especially but not restricted to when it discussed imperialism. The standpoint of the metropole persisted (Go, 2013b).

Sociology as we know it today thus emerged at a specific time and place. It was concerned largely with European modernity, and in particular modernity conceived as separated from and superior to the rest of the world's presumed "backwards-ness." Just as positivist epistemology was a response to the decaying foundations of religious certainty in the wake of the Reformation, so too was sociology as we know it was forged in a specific local context. This, along with its connection with Western imperialism, highlights that sociology has provincial origins; or in Connell's (2007) terms, it has "Northern" origins. It comes from an imperialist standpoint. Yet much of sociological theory and research masks this provincial standpoint with global pretentions. Warranted with the premises of positivism, and readily applying its specific categories to all times and places — including to its colonized and postcolonial Others — it covers up its particularity with claims to universality. The rest of the world, outside

Europe and North America, appears as a blank slate onto which to project our otherwise provincial categories.

Can sociology overcome this problem? One strand of the postcolonial critique would say no. In this view, sociology's European origins, its positivism and conceptual abstractions are inherently violent or, at the very least, woefully insufficient. The reproach, which as noted earlier joins the postmodern and poststructuralist critique of sociology, is unsettling: within the inherited positivist terms of social science, there is no way out. This would make sociology and postcolonialism fundamentally incompatible. In as much as sociology is inherently positivist and as postcolonial studies insists on equating positivism with the imperialist standpoint, there can be no rapprochement (Seth, 2009). As Goswami (2016) notes, this makes postcolonial studies "appear as among sociology's more non-sociological, even stridently post-sociological, 'others'," while fueling "postcolonial suspicion of sociology." Or as McLennan puts it, the sociological project is merely part of the "*problem* for postcolonialism, not part of the solution" (McLennan, 2003, p. 72).

On the other hand, we need not accept this view.[13] While any claims sociologists make must entail some form of universality and some minimal of epistemological positivism, even a postcolonial critique of sociology's Eurocentrism, and hence its metrocentrism, itself relies upon a minimal epistemological positivism. Otherwise there would be no basis for claiming that sociology is Eurocentric or that it emerged at a specific time and place to manage particular European concerns (Go, 2016; McLennan, 2013). Furthermore, just because sociology has presumably European origins, this does not in itself negate the validity of its knowledge. The scientists who discovered the law of gravity did so in a particular time and place but this does not mean there is no law of gravity. Finally, disciplinary sociology is not intrinsically positivist, as various post-positivist methods and epistemologies proliferate within its parameters. These include standpoint theory itself (Harding, 2005), certain forms of realism and its variants like critical realism (Steinmetz, 1998, 2004); forms of descriptive historical sociology (Abbott, 2001); or recent articulations of interpretative social science that align with postcolonial theory's emphasis upon subjectivity and meaning (Reed, 2008). It follows that sociology and postcolonial theory are not intrinsically opposed. As Chakrabarty puts it in another context, there is a "simultaneous indispensability and inadequacy of social science thought" (Chakrabarty, 2000, p. 6).

Perhaps the key is neither to uncritically accept sociology or reject it entirely but to acknowledge its origins, its standpoint, and its limitations so as to push ahead. In other words, while sociology may have provincial origins, this fact does not invalidate its knowledge project altogether. It merely calls for reflexivity, a recognition that the knowledge produced might be limited, and invites us to search for new methods, concepts, theories – or redeployments of established ones – so as to meet the postcolonial challenge. This would be the larger task of a postcolonial sociology.

THE PRESENT COLLECTION

A nascent but growing literature loosely connected with or under the rubric of disciplinary sociology has already begun to consider the questions invoked by postcolonial theory. Some work, partly emerging from the world-systems paradigms but looking beyond it, has taken an interest in the cultural and epistemic aspects of coloniality and postcoloniality, excavating "indigenous" social science knowledges that transcend the "captive mind" created by Western domination (Alatas, 2006a, 2006b; Connell, 2007; Patel, 2010; Sitas, 2006). Furthermore, sociologists located in Europe and the United Kingdom have begun to increasingly employ postcolonial frameworks (Bhambra, 2007a, 2007b; Gutiérrez Rodríguez, Boatcâ, & Costa, 2010; Patel, 2006).[14] The present volume contributes to this growing movement by taking up the question: *how*? How to "do" postcolonial sociology?[15]

The essays in this collection open up some possible routes to take. One approach is to *reconsider and reconstruct sociological thought's history* – not least by identifying the silences and omissions of the so-called canonical sociological texts or thinkers. Seidman's essay reveals that the "classic" thinkers (Marx, Weber, and Durkheim) were aware of empire and wrote about it but failed to let empire fundamentally alter their theoretical systems. As their engagement with empire was shaped by their "Orientalist assumptions," they did not treat empire "as a discrete, independent social and political process." Marx subsumed the logics of empire under those of capital; Durkheim treated imperialism as an abnormality; Weber treated empire as incidental rather than fundamental to Occidental modernity. Sociology's so-called founding theorists thus analytically engaged imperialism but then relegated it to the theoretical margins.

The essays by Manuela Boatcă and Zine Magubane also follow this route of reconsideration and reconstruction. Boatcă's analysis of Max Weber's views on race and ethnicity reveals that not only did Weber repress the history of slavery and colonialism in his theory of race but also that his overarching views were underwritten by nationalist undercurrents. It is as if the nationalist jingoism driving European and US imperialism at the time (the early twentieth century) also shaped Weber's sociological categories. Magubane's essay addresses a similar theme in the thought of American sociologist Robert A. Park (who, like Weber, had wrote about the Tuskegee Institute). Magubane shows how Park initially incorporated colonialism into his analysis of race, thereby connecting the so-called "race problem" in the United States with racial issues attendant with colonialism in Africa, but his later work dropped the connection. The sociology of race has never recovered.[16]

Attendant with these critical investigations of the history of sociological thought lies another approach for doing postcolonial sociology: to *systematically analyze the relations between knowledge and power.* Investigating such relations has been a dominant approach in postcolonial studies in the humanities. As noted, Said's *Orientalism* was seminal in this regard. But a social scientific approach to studying knowledge and power would also be fruitful. It might, for instance, offer systematic studies of how institutions generate knowledge and the precise links between these institutions and the operations of imperial or colonial power. Said draws upon Foucault, who in turn had highlighted the notion that knowledge *is* power, but a postcolonial sociology would ask more precisely: *is it really?* Is all knowledge power? Under what conditions do certain types of knowledge articulate with power, and how exactly?

Such questions are evinced by existing postcolonial scholarship but not always explored to their fullest extent. Two of the contributions here address them. Guhin and Wyrtzen's contribution deftly articulates them with the sociology of knowledge. Building upon Said's *Orientalism,* they offer a typology of epistemic violence and show how the different forms operate in different contexts. In this way, their essay not only reveals how sociology might be enlightened by postcolonial theory but also reveals how postcolonial theory might be advanced by sociology; that is, by the sociological tools of rigorous classification and empirical analysis. Just as they draw upon Said to explore the relationship between imperial power and knowledge, their typology of epistemic violence complexifies postcolonial theory's otherwise unproblematized approach to the relationship between them. Finally, Guhin and Wyrtzen suggest that a postcolonial sociology should practice "post-orientalist reflexivity," one that is alert to the violence of categories. While Bourdieu has called for a "reflexive sociology" (Bourdieu, 1990a), Guhin and Wyrtzen suggest that social scientific knowledge should not only consider the difference that sociological knowledge might make but also, as they put it, "the *sort* of difference our work makes" (emphasis added).

While Guhin and Wyrtzen explore the power-knowledge nexus by typologizing relations, Steinmetz's contribution takes a deep historical look at a specific case: German sociologists and empire. Steinmetz frames the matter in terms of Pierre Bourdieu's concept of "autonomy": to what extent can intellectuals be autonomous from imperial power? Steinmetz here implicitly connects Pierre Bourdieu's sociology with Edward Said's postcolonial theory – even though the latter criticized the former for occluding colonialism in his work (Go, 2013c). The move is generative. By deploying Bourdieu's autonomy concept, Steinmetz is directed to ask whether sociological knowledge is connected to imperialism rather than assume it always is. He examines two German sociologists, each of whom represents two extremes of autonomy and dependence: Max Weber (here extending the discussions of Seidman and Boatcǎ) and Richard Thurnwald. Steinmetz thus offers a novel examination of some of the ways in which sociological thought has been, or has not been, entangled with empire.

Both of these approaches – reconsidering the history of sociological thought and problematizing the relationship between sociological knowledge and power – offer ways to critically reassess sociology's standpoint and the limits of knowledge. The essay by Manu Goswami contributes to this project, too, but by a different approach: *excavating sociological thought from the colonial and postcolonial world.*[17] Goswami recovers the thought of Benoy Kumar Sarkar (1887–1949), a "dissident colonial intellectual" in India. Sarkar was one of the founders of comparative and historically oriented sociology in India, but unlike his European or North American counterparts his sociology was critical of abstractions and developmental historicism. It challenged the orientalism and metrocentrism of European sociology and, drawing upon and rearticulating indigenous concepts like *vishwa* and *shakti*, theorized histories and societies as interconnected rather than independent. In this and other ways richly described by Goswami, Sarkar offered a novel comparative if not cosmopolitan sociology that escapes the traps of analytic bifurcation, metrocentrism, and European-centered historicism.

The contributions from Decocteau and Bhambra offer a third approach for doing postcolonial sociology: *deploying concepts from postcolonial theory for social analysis.* In so doing, they also offer sociological analyses that highlight colonial agency. Decocteau's contribution uses Homi Bhabha's concept of hybridity to analyze responses to AIDS in the Global South, and puts that concept into conversation with Bourdieu's sociology. As AIDS continues to plague Africa, and as the Northern medical-humanitarian complex continues to try to manage it, Decoteau shows how South Africans negotiate it all. Decoteau reveals that conventional categories from medical sociology as well as Bourdieu's concept of habitus would have a hard time apprehending South Africans' complex response to the imposition of modern medicines like antiretrovirals. Needed, Decoteau suggests, is Bhabha's concept of "hybridity." On the other hand, Decoteau enlists Bourdieu's theory of fields to better situate hybrid practices in wider relations of power and systems of interaction – the very sort of social analysis that Bhabha's conceptual apparatus does not in itself offer up. Decoteau thus puts postcolonial and conventional sociological categories to work, and in a way that emphasizes rather than occludes the agency of colonized and postcolonial peoples.

Bhambra's essay takes us to another arena of social analysis that she enlightens using postcolonial concepts: global sociology. A number of pro-minent sociologists – from Ulrich Beck to Michael Burawoy – have made passionate pleas for sociology to be more "global." They and others have introduced various new concepts to do so: from "cosmopolitanism" to "multiple modernities." But as Bhambra demonstrates, missing from these pleas is a postcolonial perspective that takes seriously the histories of colo-nialism and slavery in the making of modernity. Rather than seeing the global as a flat space, Bhambra insists that we must recognize the "*colonial* global." This, she insists, is not just about adding colonialism or slavery into our categories but rather rethinking those categories altogether. The lesson is as relevant for a proper postcolonial sociology as it is for global sociology: we need to reconstruct our existing accounts and categories rather than simply throw new variables into them. And if new accounts and categories such as "the global" are to be cultivated and used at all, they need to carry within them the recognition of colonialism's enduring past. While postcolonial thought has used the concept "colonialism" to reconstruct knowledge in the humanities, Bhambra's essay thus shows how social scientists might use it to better understand global dynamics – and in a way that reveals the agency of colonialism upon the global present.

This then is the challenge – if not the irony – of a *postcolonial* sociol-ogy. Postcolonial sociology, like postcolonial theory, seeks to go beyond the epistemic legacies of colonialism. But it cannot do so without keeping colonialism in full view. But what, then, of contexts that are not "colonial" in the conventional sense? Gocek's contribution raises this question in her discussion of the Ottoman empire. Gocek reminds us that postcolonial theory emerged in response to Western European colonialism, in which case how might it translate to understand empires such as the Ottoman empire, or for that matter, the Chinese or Russian empires? And would translating postcolonial theory to these contexts merely be another form of metrocentrism? Gocek's contribution recognizes the limits of applying post-colonial analytic categories to these cases, while also extracting from some utility from those categories.

Gocek's piece makes for a salutary conclusion, for it reminds us that postcolonial theory must be aware of its tendency toward universalization but, like the sociology which it would critique, this does not mean it must be dispatched entirely. The key is to recognize its limits as well as its utility, to work with knowledge's power and also its limits — a recognition which is itself in the guiding spirit of postcolonial critique.

NOTES

1. This literature is far too massive to effectively cite but good readers and over-views include Ashcroft, Griffiths, and Tiffin (2006), Gandhi (1998), Loomba, Kaul, Bunzl, and Burton (2006), Loomba (1998), Moore-Gilbert (1997), and Young (1990).

2. More recent work by Wallerstein (1997) offers a critique of Eurocentrism, while other scholars working in the world-systems tradition have applied the world-systems critique to the global hierarchy of academia and Western domination therein (Alatas, 2000).

3. There is of course the Marxist-inspired critique of postcolonial studies, famously leveled by Ahmad (1994) and continued in part by Chibber (2013), though both of these side-step the postcolonial critique by insisting upon the universality of Marxist categories rather than accepting the theoretical pluralism implied by post-colonial theory (Go, 2016).

4. One other area where sociology has addressed postcolonial concerns is in cri-tical and global race studies, partly rooted in the early work of sociologists like WEB Dubois (Du Bois, 1993; Gilroy, 1993; Weiner, 2012). This is a rich body of work but for the most part it has been marginalized, as mainstream sociological approaches to race have fallen prey to methodological nationalism and have thus neglected global hierarchies of race or the study of connections between racial hier-archies in metropoles and those constructed in the post-colony (Winant, 2007).

5. Dipesh Chakrabarty, one of the founders of subaltern studies and also a major postcolonial theorist in history today, describes subaltern studies as a "post-colonial project" and "in conversation with postcolonial studies" (Chakrabarty, 2002, pp. 3, 16).

6. Postcolonial theory thereby both draws upon and parallels this project, for entailed in this attempt to redraw the agency of the subaltern was a sustained inves-tigation into the relationship between power and knowledge — both colonial

knowledge and related historiographical knowledge. Edward Said's introduction to the subaltern studies project thus referred to it as "intellectually insurrectionary." For this see (Chakrabarty, 2002, pp. 8, 16–19).

7. In an interview published in 1993, Spivak said that her two most misunderstood ideas were "Can the Subaltern Speak" and "strategic essentialism" (Spivak, Danius, & Jonsson, 1993, pp. 35–36).

8. See also Edward Said's discussion of representing the "colonized" and the occlusion of "the native point of view" and "voices on the outside" (Said, 1989, p. 219).

9. Sociologists and social theorists are no strangers to questions of agency. The "agency-structure" problematic discussed in Giddens or Bourdieu and a host of related concepts have long been a part of the sociological theoretical apparatus (Bourdieu, 1990b; Giddens, 1986). Pragmatism in sociology also grapples with agency (Emirbayer & Mische, 1998). But this approach to agency is specific to questions about how social actors negotiate and reproduce structures in the abstract — universalizing theories meant to capture processes acontextually — while the agency problematic raised in postcolonial theory is less about these theoretical abstractions and more about concretely analyzing how subject or marginalized populations specifically negotiate power relations and the intertwined histories of metropolitan and subaltern actors. For a more context-specific discussion of agency, see Adams (2011).

10. On German sociology see Steinmetz (2016).

11. Note too that while Tilly places much emphasis on the role of "war-making" for state-making, most of the wars he pinpoints were imperial wars or wars of conquest overseas, occurring either outside Europe or as wars for territory outside "Europe" (165–181). Tilly's demarcation of his theory to national states "in Europe" is thereby questionable, for they never really occurred "in Europe." For a different approach to European empires where events in the periphery are not "external" but constitutive, see Adams (2007).

12. Exceptions include voices from outside the North American academy, such as Alatas (2000) and Connell (2006).

13. As Steinmetz (2004) highlights, there is a danger in conflating the violence of abstraction in social practice with the violence of conceptual abstraction. On the other hand, this difference should not excuse the violence of conceptual abstraction. Just because theories might not translate into practical violence does not mean we should continue to utilize them without reflection or modification.

14. In North American sociology, works that discuss or incorporate postcolonial theory include Go (2013a, 2016), Kempel and Mawani (2009), Magubane (2005), Ray (2012), and Steinmetz (2007).

15. I offer a more extensive discussion of postcolonial thought and its implications for social science in Go (2016).

16. For a recent reconsideration of W. E. B. DuBois and American Sociology, see Morris (2015).

17. This approach is best exemplified also in the work of Connell (2007).

REFERENCES

Abbott, A. (2001). *Time matters: On theory and method*. Chicago, IL: University of Chicago Press.

Adams, J. (2007). *The familial state: Ruling families and merchant captialism in early modern Europe*. Ithaca, NY: Cornell University Press.

Adams, J. (2011). 1-800-how-am-I-drving? Agency in social science history. *Social Science History*, *35*(1), 1–17.

Adams, J., Clemens, E. S., & Orloff, A. S. (2005). Introduction: Social theory, modernity, and the three waves of historical sociology. In J. Adams, E. S. Clemens, & A. S. Orloff (Eds.), *Remaking modernity* (pp. 1–73). Durham, NC: Duke University Press.

Ahmad, A. (1994). *In theory: Nations, classes, literature*. London: Verso.

Alatas, S. F. (2006a). *Alternative discourses in Asian social science: Responses to Eurocentrism*. New Delhi: Sage.

Alatas, S. F. (2006b). A khaldunian exemplar for a historical sociology for the south. *Current Sociology*, *54*(3), 397–411.

Alatas, S. H. (2000). Intelllectual imperialism: Definition, traits and problems. *Southeast Asian Journal of Social Science*, *28*(1), 23–45.

Anderson, K. B. (2010). *Marx at the margins*. Chicago, IL: University of Chicago Press.

Ashcroft, B., Griffiths, G., & Tiffin, H. (2002). *The empire writes back: Theory and practice in post-colonial literatures*. London: Routledge.

Ashcroft, B., Griffiths, G., & Tiffin, H. (Eds.). (2006). *The post-colonial studies reader*. New York, NY: Routledge.

Bhabha, H. K. (1994). *The location of culture*. London: Routledge.

Bhambra, G. (2007a). Sociology and postcolonialism: Another 'missing' revolution? *Sociology*, *41*(5), 871–884.

Bhambra, G. (2007b). *Rethinking modernity: Postcolonialism and the sociological imagination*. Basingstoke: Palgrave-Macmillan.

Bhambra, G. (2011). Talking among themselves? Weberian and marxist historical sociologies as dialogues without 'others'. *Millenium – Journal of International Studies*, *39*, 667–681.

Boatcâ, M., & Costa, S. (2010). Postcolonial sociology: A research agenda. In E. G. Rodríguez, M. Boatcâ, & S. Costa (Eds.), *Decolonizing European sociology: Transdisciplinary approaches* (pp. 13–32). Burlington: Ashgate.

Boatcâ, M., Costa, S., & Rodríguez, E. G. (2010). Decolonizing European sociology: Different paths towards a pending project. In E. G. Rodríguez, M. Boatcâ, & S. Costa (Eds.), *Decolonizing European sociology: Transdisciplinary approaches* (pp. 1–10). Burlington: Ashgate.

Bourdieu, P. (1990a). *In other words: Essays towards a reflexive sociology*. Stanford, CA: Stanford University Press.

Bourdieu, P. (1990b). *The logic of practice*. Palo Alto, CA: Stanford University Press.

Branch, J. (2012). 'Colonial reflection' and territoriality: The peripheral origins of sovereign statehood. *European Journal of International Relations*, *18*(2), 277–297.

Breslau, D. (2007). The American spencerians: Theorizing a new science. In C. Calhoun (Ed.), *Sociology in America: A history* (pp. 39–62). Chicago, IL: University of Chicago Press.

Brewer, A. (1990). *Marxist theories of imperialism: A critical survey*. New York, NY: Routledge.

Césaire, A. (2010 [1956]). Letter to Maurice Thorez. *Social Text, 28*(2), 145–152.

Chakrabarty, D. (2000). *Provincializing Europe: Postcolonial thought and historical difference.* Princeton, NJ: Princeton University Press.

Chakrabarty, D. (2002). *Habitations of modernity: Essays in the wake of subaltern studies.* Chicago, IL: University of Chicago Press.

Chibber, V. (2013). *Postcolonial theory and the specter of capital.* New York, NY: Verso.

Connell, R. (2006). Northern theory: The political geography of general social theory. *Theory and Society, 35*(2), 237–264.

Connell, R. (2007). *Southern theory.* Cambridge: Polity Press.

Connell, R. W. (1997). Why is classical theory classical? *American Journal of Sociology, 102*(6), 1511–1557.

Cooper, F., & Burbank, J. (2010). *Empires in world history: Power and the politics of difference.* Princeton, NJ: Princeton University Press.

Du Bois, W. E. B. (1993). *The souls of black folk.* New York, NY: Knopf: Distributed by Random House.

Dubois, L. (2004). *A colony of citizens: Revolution and slave emancipation in the French Caribbean, 1787–1804.* Chapel Hill, NC: University of North Carolina Press.

Emirbayer, M., & Mische, A. (1998). What is agency? *American Journal of Sociology, 103*, 962–1023.

Fanon, F. (1968 [1961]). *The wretched of the earth.* New York, NY: Grove Press.

Foucault, M. (1972). *The archaeology of knowledge.* London: Tavistock Publications.

Foucault, M. (1979). *Discipline and punish: The birth of the prison.* New York, NY: Vintage Books.

Gandhi, L. (1998). *Postcolonial theory.* New York, NY: Columbia University Press.

Giddens, A. (1986). *The constitution of society: Outline of the theory of structuration.* Berkeley, CA: University of California Press.

Giddings, F. H. (1911). The relation of social theory to public policy. *The American Journal of Sociology, 16*(5), 577–592.

Gilroy, P. (1993). *The black Atlantic.* London: Verso.

Go, J. (2009). The 'new' sociology of empire and colonialism. *Sociology Compass, 3*(5), 775–788.

Go, J. (2013). Decolonizing Bourdieu: Colonial and postcolonial theory in Pierre Bourdieu's early work. *Sociological Theory, 31*, 49–73.

Go, J. (2013a). For a postcolonial sociology. *Theory & Society, 42*(1), 25–55.

Go, J. (2013b). Sociology's imperial unconscious: The emergence of American sociology in the context of empire. In G. Steinmetz (Ed.), *Sociology and empire.* Durham, NC: Duke University Press.

Go, J. (2016). *Postcolonial thought and social theory.* New York, NY: Oxford University Press.

Goswami, M. (2016). Provincializing sociology: The case of a premature postcolonial sociologist. In J. Go (Ed.), *Postcolonial sociologies: A reader* (Vol. 31). Political Power and Social Theory. Bingley, UK: Emerald Group Publishing Limited.

Grinde, D. A., & Johansen, B. E. (1991). *Exemplar of liberty: Native America and the evolution of democracy.* Los Angeles, CA: University of California Press.

Guha, R. (1983). *Elementary aspects of peasant insurgency in colonial India.* Delhi: Oxford.

Guha, R. (1984). Preface. In R. Guha (Ed.), Subaltern studies III: Writings on Indian *history* and society (pp. vii–viii). Delhi: Oxford University Press.

Guha, R. (1988). On some aspects of the historiography of colonial India. In R. Guha (Ed.), *Selected Subaltern studies* (pp. 37–44). New York, NY: Oxford University Press.

Gutiérrez Rodríguez, E., Boatcâ, M., & Costa, S. (Eds.). (2010). *Decolonizing European sociology: Transdisciplinary approaches*. Burlington: Ashgate.

Harding, S. (2005). Negotiating with the positivist legacy: New social justice movements and a standpoint politics of method. In G. Steinmetz (Ed.), *The politics of method in the human sciences* (pp. 346–365). Durham, NC: Duke University Press.

Jacoby, R. (1995). Marginal returns: The trouble with post-colonial theory. *Lingua Franca*, *September/October*, 30–37.

James, C. L. R. (1989). *The Black Jacobins*. New York, NY: Vintage.

Kempel, T., & Mawani, R. (2009). The sociological imagination and its imperial shadows. *Theory, Culture, and Society*, *26*, 7–8.

Krishnan, S. (2009). The place of India in postcolonial studies: Chatterjee, Chakrabarty, Spivak. *New Literary History*, *40*(2), 265–280.

Loomba, A. (1998). *Colonialism/postcolonialism: The new critical idiom*. London: Routledge.

Loomba, A., Kaul, S., Bunzl, M., & Burton, A. (Eds.). (2006). *Postcolonial studies and beyond*. Durham, NC: Duke University Press.

Magubane, Z. (2005). Overlapping territories and intertwined histories: Historical sociology's global imagination. In J. Adams, E. S. Clemens, & A. S. Orloff (Eds.), *Remaking modernity: Politics, history, sociology* (pp. 92–108). Durham, NC: Duke University Press.

McLennan, G. (2003). Sociology, eurocentrism and postcolonial theory. *European Journal of Social Theory*, *6*(1), 69–86.

McLennan, G. (2013). Postcolonial critique: The necessity of sociology. *Political Power and Social Theory*, *24*, 119–144.

Memmi, A. (1965 [1957]). *The colonizer and the colonized*. Boston, MA: Beacon Press.

Moore-Gilbert, B. (1997). *Postcolonial theory: Contexts, practices, politics*. London: Verso.

Morris, A. (2015). *The scholar denied: W.E.B. Dubois and the birth of modern sociology*. Berkeley, CA: University of California Press.

Morris, R. (2002). Theses on the questions of war: History, media, terror. *Social Text*, *20*(3), 146–175.

Patel, S. (2006). Beyond binaries: A case for self-reflexive sociologies. *Current Sociology*, *54*(3), 381–395.

Patel, S. (2010). *The ISA handbook of diverse sociological traditions*. Los Angeles, CA: Sage.

Pitts, J. (2010). Political theory of empire and imperialism. *Annual Review of Political Science*, *13*, 211–235.

Prakash, G. (1999). *Another reason: Science and the imagination of modern India*. Princeton, NJ: Princeton University Press.

Ray, R. (2012). Reconcilable differences: Sociology and the study of the postcolonial. Paper Presented at the Annual Meeting of the Social Science History Association, Vancouver.

Reed, I. A. (2008). Justifying sociological knowledge: From realism to interpretation. *Sociological Theory*, *26*(2), 101–129.

Robinson, C. (2000). *Black Marxism: The making of the black radical tradition*. Chapel Hill, NC: University of North Carolina Press.

Said, E. (1979). *Orientalism*. New York, NY: Vintage Books.

Said, E. (1989). Representing the colonized: Anthropology's interloctors. *Critical Inquiry*, *15*, 205–225.

Said, E. (1999). Travelling theory reconsidered. In N. C. Gibson (Ed.), *Rethinking fanon* (pp. 197–214). New York, NY: Humanity Books.

Said, E. (2000). *Reflections on exile and other essays*. Cambridge, MA: Harvard University Press.

Said, E. (2003). Always on top. *London Review of Books*, *25*(6), 3–6.

Said, E. W. (1993). *Culture and imperialism*. New York, NY: Knopf: Distributed by Random House.

Seidman, S. (2016). The colonial unconscious of classical sociology. In J. Go (Ed.), *Postcolonial sociologies: A reader* (Vol. 31). Political Power and Social Theory. Bingley, UK: Emerald Group Publishing Limited.

Seth, S. (2009). Historical sociology and postcolonial theory: Two strategies for challenging eurocentrism. *International Political Sociology*, *3*(3), 334–338.

Sitas, A. (2006). The African renassiance challenge and sociological reclamations in the south. *Current Sociology*, *54*(3), 357–380.

Skocpol, T. (1979). *States and social revolutions*. Cambridge: Cambridge University Press.

Skocpol, T., & Kestnbaum, M. (1990). Mars unshackled: The French revolution in world-historical perspective. In F. Fehér (Ed.), *The French revolution and the birth of modernity* (pp. 13–29). Berkeley, CA: University of California Press.

Spivak, G. C. (1986). Three women's texts and a critique of imperialism. In H. L. Gates, Jr. (Ed.), *"Race," writing, and difference* (pp. 262–280). Chicago, IL: University of Chicago Press.

Spivak, G. C. (1988a). Can the Subaltern speak. In C. Nelson & L. Grossberg (Eds.), *Marxism and the interpretation of culture* (pp. 271–313). London: Macmillan.

Spivak, G. C. (1988b). *In other worlds: Essays in cultural politics*. New York, NY: Routledge.

Spivak, G. C., Danius, S., & Jonsson, S. (1993). An interview with Gayatri Spivak. *Boundary 2*, *20*(2), 24–50.

Spivak, G. C., & Harasym, S. (1990). *The post-colonial critic: Interviews, strategies, dialogues*. New York, NY: Routledge.

Steinmetz, G. (1998). Critical realism and historical sociology: A review article. *Comparative Studies in Society and History*, *39*(4), 170–186.

Steinmetz, G. (2004). Odious comparisons: Incommensurability, the case study, and 'small N's' in sociology. *Sociological Theory*, *22*(3), 371–400.

Steinmetz, G. (2007). *The devil's handwriting: Precoloniality and the German colonial state in Qingdao, Samoa, and Southwest Africa*. Chicago, IL: University of Chicago Press.

Steinmetz, G. (Ed.). (2013). *Sociology and empire*. Durham, NC: Duke University Press.

Steinmetz, G. (2014). The sociology of empires, colonies, and postcolonialism. *Annual Review of Sociology*, *40*, 77–103.

Steinmetz, G. (2016). Neo-Bourdieusian theory and the question of scientific autonomy: German sociologists and empire, 1890s–1940s. In J. Go (Ed.), *Postcolonial sociologies: A reader* (Vol. 31). Political Power and Social Theory. Bingley, UK: Emerald Group Publishing Limited.

Stoler, A. L. (1995). *Race and the education of desire: Foucault's history of sexuality and the colonial order of things*. Durham, NC: Duke University Press.

Tilly, C. (1990). *Coercion, capital and European states, AD 990-1992*. Oxford: Blackwell Publishers.

Wacquant, L. (2002). Scrutinizing the street: Poverty, morality, and the pitfalls of urban ethnography. *American Journal of Sociology*, *107*(6), 1468–1532.

Wallerstein, I. (1997). Eurocentrism and its avatars. *New Left Review*, *1*(226), 93–107.

Weiner, M. F. (2012). Towards a critical global race theory. *Sociology Compass*, *6*(4), 332–350.

Winant, H. (2007). The dark side of the force: One hundred years of the sociology of race. In C. Calhoun (Ed.), *Sociology in America: A history* (pp. 535–571). Chicago, IL: University of Chicago Press.

Young, R. (1990). *White mythologies: Writing history and the west*. London: Routledge.

Young, R. (2001). *Postcolonialism: An historical introduction*. Malden, MA: Blackwell Publishing.

Young, R. (2003). *Postcolonialism: A very short introduction*. Oxford: Oxford University Press.

THE COLONIAL UNCONSCIOUS OF CLASSICAL SOCIOLOGY ☆

Steven Seidman

ABSTRACT

So-called classical sociology took shape during perhaps the high point of a world dominated by imperial states. In the "west" the British, French, and German empires, along with a surging America, claimed political and sometimes territorial control over wide stretches of the globe. Beyond Europe and the United States, while the Ottoman and Qing empires were in there last days, new states were staking out their imperial claims such as Japan and Russia. The tension between a reality of empire and an ideal of sovereign nation-states eventually exploded in WWI. Curiously, much of this dynamic, especially the global power of empire, went theoretically unnoticed by the makers of modern sociology. This chapter explores this theme through a sketch of the failure of this theoretical reckoning in Marx, Weber, and Durkheim.

Sociologists have often interpreted the French Revolution as symbolizing the transition from a traditional to an industrial-scientific or modern

☆Reprinted from *Postcolonial Sociology*, Political Power and Social Theory, Volume 24, 2013, pp. 35–54.

Postcolonial Sociology
Political Power and Social Theory, Volume 24, 31–50
ISSN: 0198-8719/doi:10.1108/S0198-8719(2013)0000024008

31

society. In this great transformation monarchies and empires would be replaced by nation-states. This canonized account of social change suffers however from a certain historical amnesia: the successor to Revolutionary France was Napoleon's imperial state. *Emperor* Napoleon was inspired less by the liberal nationalism of the Treaty of Westphalia than by the dreams of Alexander and Charlemagne to create a united European empire which would be the core of a world empire (Cooper, 2005, pp. 168–172; Fontana, 2002; Padgen, 2003, pp. 134–136). Although Napoleon was defeated by the alliance of the British and Russians, the dream of empire was not vanquished. In 1815, as the great powers convened in Vienna, it was unclear whether Europe would be organized as nations or empires. What was clear though is that the dream of empire continued to inspire Great Britain, Russia, Prussia, France, and Austria-Hungary. And what should have also been clear to contemporary social thinkers was that a world organized by imperial states and empires persisted well into the early twentieth century (Burbank & Cooper, 2010; Fieldhouse, 1967; Hobsbawm, 1989)

An undeniable but curiously unremarked upon reality has informed most accounts of sociology's origins, namely, classical sociology emerged in the context of imperial states aspiring to world empires. By the late nineteenth century major state powers such as Great Britain, France, Germany, Russia, China, Japan, and the Ottomans, were imperial rivals operating on a global playing field. The shape of nations was inextricably linked to the fate of these imperial states. Moreover, the very period of the institutionalization of sociology (1890–1920) coincided with the establishment of Anglo-European world dominance. By the early twentieth century, the Ottomans were an empire on paper only; the Chinese empire (Qing) was crumbling in the face of a wave of European assaults; only the Russian empire, and perhaps an ambitious imperial Japan, presented a serious rival to the Europeans. By World War I. European and Anglo-American imperial states exercised dominion over most of Africa, Australasia, Asia, and many of the islands in the Caribbean, Indian Ocean and the Pacific, and had already left a deep colonial footprint across the Americas (Ferguson, 2004; Fieldhouse, 1967, p. 178; Kennedy, 1987, pp. 148–149; Padgen, 2003, p. 157).

Yet, curiously, these imperial realities, and the very idea of empire, were peripheral to classical sociology. The historical sociology of "modernity" proposed by Marx, Weber, Simmel, Durkheim, Spencer, Ward, and other important social thinkers of the time was not formed by a *theoretical reckoning* with the realities of empire (Magubane, 2005).[1] In this essay,

I address the following contradiction. The contemporary realities of empire were recognized by all the major nineteenth century sociologists; many were in fact critics or advocates of imperial state agendas. Moreover, as the fog of post-imperial Whiggish histories, including those of classical sociology, have been lifted, there is little doubt that empire was at the very heart of the making and organization of modernity (Cooper, 2005, pp. 156, 171, 182; Dirks, 1992; McClintock, 1995, p. 5; Pomeranz, 2000; Silverblatt, 2004, p. 220; Steinmetz, 2005, p. 358; Veer, 2001, pp. 7–8; Wilder, 2005): So, how could these publicly engaged social thinkers avoid a conceptual and analytical consideration of the realities of empire in their critical accounts of the present? What assumptions about world history and social change prevented classical sociologists from making empire integral to their historical sociology of modernity?

To explore this contradiction I restrict the scope of my analysis to the canonized figures of Marx, Weber, and Durkheim. I offer the outlines of an account, which is all that is possible in these few pages. Despite being keenly aware of imperial dynamics, I aim to make a plausible case that these thinkers did not incorporate the dynamics of empire into their historical sociology of contemporary societies. I underscore the role of *Orientalist* assumptions to explain this missing connection between empire and modernity in classical sociology. I conclude by considering the classical sociological "discourse of modernity" as rhetoric or, if you will, ideology from the vantage point of imperial realities.

CLASSICAL SOCIOLOGY AND EMPIRE

The classical sociologists were keenly aware of the realities of empire. However, they did not conceptually integrate empire into their historical sociology of contemporary societies. The great social changes of the time associated with industrial capitalism, the making of a world market, state bureaucratization, mass democracy, rational law, secularism, institutional differentiation, and a culture of individualism and citizenship, were assumed to be the product of internal societal processes. In this section, I review their broad approach to empire in both their occasional writing (political and social commentary or advocacy] and in their academic work. I aim to underscore the point that in their sociological and theoretical studies there is a systemic *neglect or absence* of imperial dynamics as a discrete, independent social and political process.

Marx

As is well known, the greater part of Marx's intellectual life was spent in political exile. After short periods in Belgium and France, Marx settled in Great Britain, the very heartland of nineteenth-century capitalism and imperialism. Indeed, Marx earned a livelihood through much of the 1850s and 1860s by analyzing the politics of the British Empire.

In his political writings, Marx distinguished between empires that existed before and after industrial capitalism. "Asiatic" empires (Persia, the Ottomans, India, and China) were understood as paradigmatic of precapitalist empires. Such empires were said to undergo political but not social change. Marx cited the histories of successive dynasties, emperors, and military rulers in China and India prior to British intervention. One ruler succeeds another but social life barely changes. Marx believed that the social roots of the unchanging character of the Asiatic type is the socially autonomous village. Geographically isolated and economically self-sufficient, the continuity of village life rests ultimately on the collective ownership of property. The means of production could not be individually owned or sold because it was attached, for eternity, to the village. Historically, then, the rise and decline of political rulers in Asiatic empires did not alter village social life (Marx, 1968, pp. 125, 418; Marx & Engels, 1942, p. 70).

By contrast, Marx argued that contemporary imperial states such as Great Britain and France are driven by capitalist political economies. In these societies, a dynamic political economy drives social change. Contemporary imperialism is fundamentally about preparing the ground for a global transformation. Becoming a colony under conditions of global capitalism meant transforming workers into wage labor, making labor, land, and resources into commodities, turning landowners into capitalists, villages into commercial centers, and a local into a nation- centered and world-centered social life. Marx's favorite example of the transformative meaning of imperialism was India. For centuries, India witnessed a succession of political rulers but its village-centered social order was unaltered. British imperialism however destroyed India's autonomous village life by linking the local economy to a world market. India was transformed as common property was replaced by private property, as a kin and caste-based social order gave way to a social world organized around individualism, competition, and commercialization, and as parochialism led to a social world oriented toward national and global horizons (Marx, 1968, pp. 37, 85–89, 130–131). Marx leaves no doubt about the engine of world change: bourgeois capitalism (Marx, 1974a, pp. 70–71).

What is the role of colonialism in the dynamics of capitalism? Marx's chief claim was that colonialism is significant as a means to create the conditions of a world capitalist order (Marx & Engels, 1942, p. 439). Imperial states will sweep away the dead weight of centuries-old social traditions and fossilized forms of social life (Marx, 1968, pp. 124–131). As capital becomes global every society will be compelled to accommodate to the market principle, or else suffer stagnation or worse. If imperialism is driven by capital, if its role is to serve as a historical vehicle for universalizing capital, the specific dynamics of colonial organization and rule are incidental to the defining logic of capitalism.

Marx argued that imperialism is a necessary but transitional moment in the development of capitalism. It helps create the social conditions for world capitalism. Yet, colonialism inevitability brings war which impedes capitalist development; it interferes with the transformative power of capital by obstructing the workings of the free market. Marx never wavered from believing that, left to its own logic, the endpoint of capital is a *postcapitalist and postimperial order*. Marx may have brought empire into the drama of modern life but the chief story, from beginning to end, is the revolutionary social logic of capital. Marx folded colonialism into the history and sociology of capital.

In *Capital*, Marx revealed capital to be a story of the political economy of exploitation, market expansion, capital concentration, and class conflict. Imperialism was but a brief historical phase in the internationalization of capitalism. Unfortunately, but perhaps tellingly, Marx had very little to say about imperialism in his successive drafts of the critique of political economy. Nevertheless, his theory of capitalism underscored a sociological logic that connected capital and colonialism. The dynamic of capital is expansion – of profit, of capital (i.e., concentration and centralization), and of capitalisms territorial reach. Initially, capital expands by enlarging the domestic market. Eventually, the rationalization of capital and escalating national rivalries compels capital to expand its playing field from the nation to the globe. The imperial state does the work of freeing capital from territorial restrictions. It was of course left to Marx's heirs – most notably, Lenin and Luxembourg – to sketch a full-blown economic theory of imperialism.

Durkheim

The invasion of Algiers (1830) and eventual conquest of Algeria (1882) launched France as a world empire. Driven by domestic politics, geopolitical competition, and a civilizing mission, France established colonies through-out Africa, the islands in the Pacific and Indian Ocean, Southeast Asia (Vietnam, Laos Cambodia), as well as secured garrisons and trading posts in India and China. In contrast to the British, the French aspired to centralized state control over its colonies. In principle, the French state was to extend from Paris to the provinces and the colonies. "Greater France" would be unified by Republican egalitarian ideals. Natives were to be remade in the image of the ideal French citizen. Such hopes were quickly dashed in Algeria (Ruedy, 1992), and effectively put to rest as the French established its dominion in Southeast Asia.

French imperialism stirred up a robust public debate, especially during the Third Republic. Critics reasoned that it was unthinkable that the nation which defended the Principles of 1789 would deny liberty to other peoples. The brutal conquest of Algeria and fierce native resistance raised grave doubts about the idea of a universal French Republic. Yet, advocates of colonialism were equally vocal and often better organized. By the late nineteenth century, a loose network of scientists, geographers, explorers, public officials, and colonialists called the *parti colonial* was one of the first organizations advocating imperial state policies. By the end of the nineteenth century, colonial advocacy organizations emerged in almost every social sector. For example, the French Colonial Union represented big business while the *groupe colonial* represented pro-colonial members of the Chamber of Deputies. In addition, academic committees were created to promote knowledge of the French colonies, for example, the Committee for French Asia or the Committee for French Morocco. These organizations aggressively supported an imperial state. They sponsored public lectures and exhibitions, lobbied Paris, published work celebrating enlightened coloni-alism, and provided the images of the backward native that would help rationalize and guide colonial policy (Aldrich, 1996, pp. 100–101; on ethnography and colonialism, see Rabinow, 1989, Chap. 5; Wilder, 2005, Chap. 3).

French imperialism was as much an event of the metropole as the colonies. Despite efforts to maintain a rigid division between French nationals and colonial natives, people, ideas and goods circulated between the metropole and colony. Colonial culture was brought into France. For example, memoirs of colonial experience, newspaper accounts of colonial triumphs and heroic stories of the encounters between the enlightened French colonist and the backward native circulated widely in French metropole culture. Academic organizations were formed to study colonial geography, history, language, and culture. Each colonial expedition was followed by a wave of researchers flooding into the colonies. New academic societies were formed around the study of Morocco (the Institute for Advanced Moroccan Studies) or the Pacific islands and Southeast Asia. Museums were established (e.g., Museum of Man became the Ethnography Museum) to house the artifacts collected from colonial expeditions. Distinguished academic Chairs in colonial studies, a Colonial Studies Centre, schools of colonial medicine and agronomy, and even an Association of Colonial Scientists were established (Aldrich, 1996, pp. 246–250; Wilder, 2005, Chap. 3). In short, representations of the native and colonial life shaped the culture of the metropole.

As best I can tell, Durkheim was neither a public advocate nor critic of French imperialism. However, during World War I, he sketched a sociological critique of German imperialism (Durkheim, 1986). Durkheim rejected the idea that imperialism was an inevitable outcome of the current rivalry of national powers. Instead, he considered German militarism and imperialism to be an "abnormal" social condition. His ideas about contemporary imperialism were rooted in his sociology.

Durkheim argued that a political society only develops in collectivities that feature a "polysegmental" social structure or are composed of diverse social groupings. Given a certain stage of social structural complexity, authority structures emerge that are distinct from those who rule the individual segments or groupings (e.g., patriarchs, clan leaders, and religious figures). In other words, in political societies there is a distinction between a government and the governed. The governing authority, which is made up of officials, agencies, and councils, is the state. Durkheim believed that a territorially based state is unique to contemporary Europe (Durkheim, 1958, Chap. 4).

The state was said to be a specialized social institution. It has an "external" and "internal" role. In the former instance, the state has a military function: to protect society from outside threats. With regard to its latter role, the state is a moral agency. Composed of assemblies and parliamentary bodies, the state is a deliberative body that aspires to represent the collective values and interests of society. In its moral role, the state aims to promote civil order (Durkheim, 1958, pp. 69–72).

Durkheim argued that in the course of social evolution the role of the state changes. In general terms, states in premodern social formations had almost unlimited power (Durkheim, 1958, p. 72; 1933, p. 220). The premodern state was essentially a military and colonial state. "The principal task of the State was to increase the material power of a society, either by adding to its territory or by incorporating within it an ever-increasing

number of citizens. The sovereign was above all ... directed to rolling back
the frontiers or destroying ... neighboring countries ... . A prince ... is
above all the military leader; the army ... the organ of conquest" (Durkheim,
1986, pp. 47–48). By contrast, in contemporary European societies, the
military role of the state diminishes while its moral role becomes primary.
"Today a state of war has become the exception ... . Instead we see the
growth of deliberative assemblies, judiciary, legal codes, contractual
relations ... administrative bodies" (Durkheim, 1986, p. 49). The European
state is becoming a "civil organ of justice ..." (*ibid.*, p. 49).

In order to understand Durkheim's conviction that the shift from a
military to a moral function of the state was "normal" we need to turn to
The Division of Labor in Society (1933). Durkheim maintained that prior to
"organized" or modern type societies contact with foreign societies was
experienced as a threat to collective life. An aggressive, militaristic state
sought to protect collective borders. Durkheim believed that the state
continued to serve a primarily military role in the era of the great European
monarchies. To the extent that there were few moral restraints placed on a
militarized state, and a heightened anxiety about collective order and
borders, colonial conquest and wars were commonplace. Durkheim
concluded that the absolutist state was a militaristic and imperial institution
circumscribed only by the constraints of foreign powers (Durkheim, 1933,
pp. 150, 220–221).

In modern type societies, regular exchange between different groups and
societies is a "normal" social condition. Social differentiation and inter-
dependence between individuals, institutions and societies is a defining
condition of modern life (Durkheim, 1933, pp. 222, 281). Accordingly, the
moral role of the state expands as societies become modern (Durkheim,
1933, p. 221). However, the modern state does not become a moral entity in
the sense meant by Hegel and Pan-Germanism. Its deliberative civic role
expands as it takes on more responsibility for securing the moral conditions
of civic order and justice. At the same time, its military role diminishes as
an international order oriented toward civic peace places moral restraints
on all governments. Militaristic imperial states are then inconsistent
with a modern international order (Durkheim, 1933, p. 225). National
rivalries will remain a part of the modern world, but international conflicts
will "normally" be addressed through "negotiations, coalitions, treaties"
(Durkheim, 1933, p. 225). Whereas premodern societies struggle for
survival, modern societies aspire to a condition of justice. In the spirit of
Kant and the liberal Enlightenment, Durkheim anticipated a world of
nations regulated by an international moral order anchored in ideals of the

sacredness of the person, national sovereignty, and perpetual peace (Durkheim, 1958, pp. 69–75).

Durkheim's historical sociology assumed that it is "normal" for the modern state to become differentiated from civil society in order to be effective as a moral agency. And while the modern state is considerably more elaborated than in previous times, Durkheim expected it to be regulated by civil society and by an international order. From this historical perspective, Durkheim claimed that the German imperial state is an "abnormal" social development. It was the product of a unique civic culture (e.g., Pan-Germanism) which championed the state as the highest social and moral expression of the German nation. Moreover, to the extent that German civil society and the international community lacked the moral and social authority to impose constraints, the German state drove the nation into the militaristic and imperial pursuit of power.

Weber

Germany was a latecomer to nationhood. National unity was accomplished in 1871 under Bismarck, but the Chancellor was a reluctant imperialist. Establishing national unification and civic order under Prussian dominance was his overriding task. Bismarck worried that the cost of colonies would harm Germany's industrial take-off. He also wished to avoid a confrontation with either France or Britain, both world powers with mighty navy's and economies.

Yet, influential Germans believed that national prosperity in an era of imperial rivalry required that Germany become a world power. Business groups, Prussian elites, merchant associations, politicians, intellectuals, and colonial groups lobbied for an imperial state (Blackbourn, 1998, pp. 333, 428; Smith, 1978, Chap. 2). Without securing their own colonies for raw materials and as markets, German economic growth and its very national independence would, it was believed, be in jeopardy. Weak nations could not compete with powerful imperial states. Securing foreign markets meant establishing political and military control over foreign territories. An imperial policy was also defended on the grounds that Germany's rapid industrialization had forced many of its citizens to migrate in order to find work or land. Establishing German colonies would make it possible for citizens to leave the homeland but sustain their national loyalty.

From the early 1880s through World War I, Germany became a major force in the global field of imperial rivalry (Blackbourn, 1998, p. 332).

Beginning with the colonization of South West Africa in 1883–1884, Germany established African colonies in Togo, Cameroon, and east Africa, as well as securing an imperial presence in the Pacific, the most important being west Samoa (Mommsen, 1995; Steinmetz, 2002). By World War I Germany's colonial territory was exceeded only by the British and French.

Max Weber was a fairly conventional nationalist (Blackbourn, 1998, pp. 424–440). He believed that domestic and foreign policy should be guided by the interests of the nation-state. Specifically, he maintained that the defense of national culture and the expansion of national power should be the highest value guiding the state (Weber, 1994, p. 17). Like other liberal nationalists, Weber was convinced that the fate of the German nation hinged on securing foreign markets and resources. In his 1895 Freiberg address, Weber defended economic expansion as, at bottom, a form of rivalry between great powers. "The expanded economic community [i.e. international markets] is just another form of the struggle of the nations with each other ..." (Weber, 1994, p. 16). Tellingly, Weber reminded his contemporaries that future generations will judge current leaders by Germany's success as an imperial state. "Our successors will hold us answerable to history not primarily for the kind of economic organization we hand down to them, but for the amount of elbow-room in the world which we conquer and bequeath to them" (*ibid.*). It is hard to disagree with Mommsen's observation that Weber's political ideas were central to "the legitimation and development of a movement of liberal imperialism in late nineteenth century Germany" (Mommsen, 1984, p. 71).

Was empire also integral to Weber's sociology of modernity? Aside from his discussions of ancient empires in his early writings (Weber, 1976), it is only in *Economy and Society* (1968) that Weber directly engages the dynamics of imperialism.

Empire is associated with "patrimonial" rule, which is a form of the traditional legitimation of political authority. Patrimonialism involves a clear differentiation between ruler and subject, the notion that the property and resources of the patrimonial realm belong to or can be claimed by the ruler, and the development of an administrative staff that is either personally selected or drawn from the royal household and is loyal to the person of the patrimonial ruler (Weber, 1968, Vols. 1, 3). Weber introduced an important distinction between patrimonialism and feudalism, both forms of traditional domination. The former is personalistic, involves a sharp division between ruler and subject, and the concentration of legitimate authority; the latter is legalistic and distributes rights and authority.

Whereas patrimonialism, unchecked and unchallenged, tends toward empire, feudalism promotes the decentralization and distribution of power.

Weber argued that after the Roman Empire patrimonialism gave way to feudalism in the Occident. Although political power was eventually concentrated in the bureaucratization of the European state, it was a modern legal-rational form of political domination. In Ancient and "Oriental" civilizations, however, a patrimonial imperial state never evolved into feudalism or a legal-rational state. Weber contrasted the patrimonial–empire nexus of the "Orient" to the feudal–modern nexus of the "Occident."

In *The Economic Foundations of Imperialism* Weber further addressed the theme of empire, but this time with the aim of outlining a sociology of imperialism (Weber, 1968, Vol. 2, p. 914). Against Marxist and other economistic perspectives, Weber underscored the role of what he called "power-prestige" or "nationalism" in explaining imperialism. He argued that the expansion of national power is the driving force of imperialism. However, instead of applying this political notion of imperialism to contemporary European dynamics, Weber proceeded to sketch a typology of imperialism. In other words, Weber aimed to clarify the general concept of imperialism as part of producing a universal lexicon that could serve as a conceptual basis for a "general sociology." Although the aim of his interpretive sociology was to explain "successful" modernization in the West and its failure in the East, nowhere in *Economy and Society* does Weber consider the imperial context of Occidental modernization.

In his "Vorbemerkung" to *Gesammelte Aufsatze zur Religionssoziologie* (published as the "Author's Introduction" to the English translation of the *Protestant Ethic and the Spirit of Capitalism*), Weber framed his historical sociology as an account of the sociocultural uniqueness of Occidental civilization. "It is ... our first concern ... to explain ... the special peculiarity of Occidental rationalism, and within this field that of the modern Occidental form" (Weber, 1958, p. 26). Why, Weber asks, did bourgeois capitalism, rational law, monocratic bureaucracy, mathematical experimental science, ideas of citizenship and constitutionalism develop only in the Occident? And, what are the human consequences of a European-driven dynamic of global modernization? In the course of his wide-ranging studies of the histories of the Greeks and Romans, early Christianity and the Middle Ages, and the Renaissance and the Reformation, Weber proposed an internalist explanation of Occidental modernization. It was long-term developments within Occidental history such as the appearance of Roman law, autonomous urban communities, or Christian this-worldly activism that explain modernization in the West. The imperial context of these changes, the interconnection between metropole and colony, and the struggle between imperial states, were not written into his historical sociology.

To summarize this section, classical sociology developed in an era of British and European imperialism. Unlike the old empires, which were driven by military conquest and plunder, the emergence of national imperial states pursued world dominance through commerce and territorial control. Marx, Weber, and Durkheim developed their sociological ideas as citizens of imperial states. They were keenly aware of the realities of imperialism but did not incorporate imperial dynamics into their historical sociology of the contemporary world. Empire is neither theorized as a defining feature of the present nor is the interconnection of metropole and colony understood as a driving force of social change.

ORIENTALISM AND THE DISAVOWAL OF EMPIRE

Orientalist assumptions partly explain the failure of classical sociologists to incorporate the dynamics of colonialism into their historical sociology. Marx, Weber, and Durkheim assumed, as did their European predecessors and contemporaries, that a civilizational divide between the Occident and the Orient was at the foundation of world history. The Orient was imagined to have its historical roots in the ancient empires of the Mesopotamia, Egypt, Persia, and China. Oriental civilization was defined by a more or less fixed cluster of social traits: traditionalism, localism, social stagnation, and empire. By contrast, the historical origins of Occidental civilization could be traced to the Greek city-states and the Roman republic. Its defining features were social development, cosmopolitanism, the advance of reason, and human progress. Whereas the history of the Orient endlessly replayed a cyclical pattern of imperial rise and decline, the Occident revealed a pattern of development and progress culminating in the modern era. I will argue that the Orientalist presuppositions of classical sociology also meant that modernity and empire were understood as antithetical.

Marx conceptualized the Orient less as a geographical region (China, Russia, Central Asia, and the Middle East) then a type of society: the Asiatic. Such societies were village-centered, tradition-bound, rigidly hierarchical, based on collective property and sustained by an imperial or despotic state. Emperors and kings rise and fall, but the social world of villages and despotism has remained unchanged. "Oriental empires always show an unchanging social infrastructure coupled with unceasing change in the persons and tribes who manage to ascribe to themselves the political superstructure" (Marx, 1968, p. 9).

Marx's social typology is telling, in this regard. He classified social formations into four types: Asiatic, Ancient, Feudal, and Bourgeois. Driven by internal social dynamics, the West evolved from Ancient to Feudal to Bourgeois. Oriental societies however never developed beyond the Asiatic stage. Unless compelled to change by Western capitalism and imperialism, Asiatic societies do not evolve, as is evident, Marx thought, by the histories of China, India, Persia, the Middle East (Marx & Engels, 1942, p. 70; Marx, 1974b, pp. 325–326; Marx, 1968, p. 17; 88).

Like Marx, Durkheim proposed a typological approach to understand social change. In *The Division of Labor in Society*, he charted a path of social evolution from a "segmented" or "collective" social type to an organized or modern social type. Modern societies were dynamic because they are based on social differentiation and individualism. By contrast, collective social types are static as their common culture and repressive laws resist change. They evolve only when exposed to national disasters or foreign interventions or encounters.

All societies, past and present, can be placed somewhere along the continuum between collective and modern. Not all societies though evolve into the modern type. Many collective societies stagnate, decline, or are incorporated through conquest. Paralleling Marx's evolutionary theory, Durkheim argued that modernizing development has only occurred in the Occident. Non-Western societies such as contemporary China and Russia remain collective types – traditional, stagnant, and despotic (Durkheim, 1933, pp. 175, 159).

The Occident/Orient division played a foundational role in Weber's historical sociology. He sought to explain modernization in the Occident and its absence in the Orient. Weber relied on a version of Oriental despotism to explain failed modernization in the East. For example, in his study of China, Weber charts a dramatic shift from a social period of warring feudal lords to unification under the Qin dynasty in 221 B.C. Although there were many dynastic changes between the Qin and the Qing Dynasty (1644–1912), Weber assumed that the foundations of the Chinese social order remained unchanged for almost two millennia. The world of clan-based villages, rooted in patriarchal authority and ancestor worship, and enforced by a patrimonial imperial state impeded social development. Emperors triumphed and declined, but the social world of clans, villages, traditionalism, Confucianism, and state despotism barely changed. By contrast, the Occident exhibited a historical pattern of internally driven change that culminates in European modernity. In short, the core structures of China bound its people to the past; the inner dynamism of the Occident – its autonomous cities, independent class of jurists and merchants, and Christian this-worldly activism – propelled the modernization of the West.

Framing world history in terms of a civilizational divide between the Occident and Orient is at the heart of "Orientalism" (Said, 1978). Such discourses assume that the diverse social formations that make up world history can be classified into two civilizational types that neatly fold into the geographical regions of the West and the East. Orientalist representations stipulate that each civilization has a core social identity. For example, while the social organization of China and India vary in many specific ways, they are said to share a social core featuring traditionalism, localism, collective property, despotic rule, and cyclical development. Moreover, Orientalist representations understand the Occident and Orient as antithetical civilizational types. The Occident is not the Orient: it is not traditional and stagnant but dynamic and cosmopolitan, not collective but individual, and not locked into cyclical change but exhibits linear developmental.

Orientalism has been a prominent conceptual lens through which Europeans interpret world history. Scholars and writers may appeal to documents and observations to validate these binary civilizational categories, but they are fundamentally imaginative constructions – "world hypotheses," rhetorical and mythic. Orientalist representations emerge from European anxieties and fears toward non-Christian and non-white social worlds, and from a geopolitical interest in expanding their global power. Stated otherwise, Orientalism is part of the politics of the West's troubled relation to the non-West. Specifically, a history of threatening and challenging assertions of power from Arab-Islamic, Chinese, Persian, Russian, and Ottoman power over many centuries stretching well into the twentieth century.

Although Orientalism can be traced to the early history of the Greeks and Romans, it was institutionalized in the eighteenth and nineteenth centuries in academic disciplines, academies, and varied scientific organizations. It was during this time that the geopolitical dominance of Islam, China, Persia, and the Ottomans was giving way to the triumph of Christian Europe. With its representation of a civilizational division and hierarchy, Orientalism provided a rationale for European imperial states to assert their global power by claiming to serve a world historical project of driving social progress and human advancement. Classical sociology infused authority into Orientalism's civilizational binary by claiming to represent a postideological science of society and history (Chatterjee, 1993; Veer, 2001). As a theoretical standpoint, Orientalism is indefensible. By interpreting histories through the lens of a rigid totalizing civilizational binary, Orientalism misrepresents actual histories (Coronil, 1996; Said, 1979). Instead of a distinct historical accounts of diverse peoples and social formations, Orientalism substitutes a single drama – Oriental traditionalism and despotism juxtaposed to Occidental modernism and liberty (Chatterjee, 1993, pp. 29–32; Frank, 1998; Go, 2006; Hostetler, 2001; Pomeranz, 2000; Veer, 2001). In place of grounded histories and sociologies of social formations, Orientalism fashions polluted projections of the East and purifying constructions of the West. The West is imagined as the dramatic center of history, as the driving force of change, and as the agent of human freedom. Accordingly, representations of the West are purged of everything that might blur the boundaries between East and West. Orientalism projects the realities of Anglo-European localism, traditionalism, and authoritarianism either to its distant past or onto the Oriental. Orientalism is then as much a misrepresentation of the West as it is of the East. And, one of its key misrepresentations is that it disavows or resists a discourse that links empire and modernity.

TRADITION/MODERNITY REVISITED

Orientalism also helps to account for their investment in Western culture as unique, dynamic, postimperial, and as bearing global significance. In the context of European geopolitics between 1880 and 1920 such Eurocentric notions were inevitably implicated in the politics of European imperialism. By way of a conclusion, I want to briefly address the following question: to what extent did their positioning as citizens of imperial states shape classical sociology?

The coherence of classical sociology rests, as much as anything, on the claim that contemporary Europe was undergoing a momentous social transformation. Although these social thinkers differed in their interpretations of this change (capitalism, social differentiation, rationalization), they agreed that a new type of society and historical period was emerging. In this way, classical sociologists participated in creating a "discourse of modernity." From at least the eighteenth century, social changes occurring in Anglo-European territories were understood by the *philosophes* and their successors, as ushering in a new or modern social world; this epoch was

imagined as having world historical significance in that its core structures
and dynamics (science, formal law, the market, citizenship, secularism),
though initially appearing in Europe, would become global. As a universalizing process, modernity anticipated a world transformative and the
inauguration of an era of unending human and social progress.

However, much these sociologists aspired to legitimate the notion of
modernity in scientific terms, the totalizing character of this concept, and
their assumptions about its uniqueness, universality, and progressiveness,
contradicted the standards of social science. A discourse of modernity,
however, played a significant symbolic role. It marked off the present from
the past, and projected the world historical significance of contemporary
Europe. In other words, the coherence of the concept of modernity was
based on the presumed contrast to all past societies. Despite their
considerable differences, past societies were understood as tradition-bound
or governed by custom, ritual, and patterns of social repetition, for example
cycles of rise and decline. The classical discourse of modernity then created a
division between the "modern" and the "traditional," as two unitary,
bounded, antithetical objects of knowledge.

If it is plausible to interpret the modern/tradition dichotomy as a cultural
code that classifies, organizes, and establishes hierarchies, then we need to
ask: what are the social conditions that produced this code, and what is its
moral-political significance?

Unsurprisingly, I suggest that European imperialism formed an important
"background condition" for the production of the modern/tradition binary.
I am not saying that the Europeans discovered their modernity through
exposure to the traditionalism of native culture. They certainly encountered
social difference, but at issue is how they theorized difference. Europeans
frequently interpreted the native other as the antithesis of the modern.
If European modernity was individualistic, legal-rational, secular, and
dynamic, the non-Europeans encountered in their colonial projects
were conceived of as collectivist, ritualistic, guided by customary law, and
socially stagnant. In short, non-European cultures were understood as
"traditional"– the very opposite of what the Europeans were becoming,
"modern."

The modern/tradition binary functioned in European colonial culture as a
trope of difference and hierarchy. It marked off two distinct, unitary global
social types. The modern was understood as superior to the traditional. It
was dynamic, evolved, and world transformative. A discourse of modernity,
from the *philosophes* to Weber's *Vorbemerkung* to his studies of religion and
society, allowed Europeans to view themselves as world historical agents of

human progress. Imperial acts were transfigured into acts of sociohistorical redemption.

The modern/tradition code found a place in the very organization of colonial rule. For example, in the course of the nineteenth century the British insisted that colonial rule should preserve the core institutions and culture of native life. But what was the nature of native culture? As the British encountered nonwhite, non-Christian, and non-European cultures, they had little if any reliable knowledge about these peoples. However, to the extent that they were understood as signifying "the traditional," native culture was assumed to be custom bound, collectivist, religious, and authoritarian. Drawing on anthropological and popular sensationalist accounts of "ancient" and "primitive" societies, colonialists presumed that the central building blocks of native cultures were a relatively unchanging order of clans, tribes, villages, sheiks, tribal chiefs, and customary laws. In other words, colonial rule *traditionalized* native life and organized native peoples to reflect European ideas of traditional society.

Consider British colonial rule in Africa. In their initial exposure to "Africans" in the second half of the nineteenth century, the British did not encounter a uniform social order based on distinct, clearly bounded tribes and chiefs; instead, the continent exhibited a wide range of forms of social organization – from federations, kingdoms, and state regimes to ethnic communities and nomadic peoples. However, the British recognized only an indigenous order of tribes based on customary law and the rule of the chief. Importantly, the British enforced colonial rule by assigning every individual to a distinct tribe to be governed by its unique tribal customs and by a (British) appointed chief (Davidson, 1992; Mamdani, 1996). In other words, the British organized "African" peoples according to its idea of the traditional, and then cited native traditionalism as a justification for its civilizing mission (cf. Dodge, 2003, Veer, 2001).

Let me be clear on one point. The meaning and role of the modernity/tradition binary exceeds its imperial deployment. Yet, it cannot perhaps be thoroughly removed from this setting and this significance insofar as the conditions of Anglo-European world dominance continue to obtain. In any event, the affinity between a discourse of modernity in the eighteenth and nineteenth centuries and European imperialism is striking. The classical sociologists forged their perspectives in part through a far-reaching critique of the various currents of Enlightenment rationalism. Despite this, they rearticulated a discourse of modernity that left in place the modern/tradition, Occident/Orient cultural divisions that continued to nourish colonial ambitions. To the extent that the historical significance of empire is reconsidered (as it has been in the past two decades), and as Europe and the United States retreat from their recent historical world dominance, these binaries will likely lose credibility and cultural authority.

ACKNOWLEDGMENTS

Many thanks to Richard Lachmann, Jeff Alexander, Emily Erikson Linda Nicholson, George Steinmetz, Julia Adams, and Ron Jacobs for reading an earlier draft of this essay

NOTE

1. Since at least the eighteenth century, there has been a dominant Anglo-European 'discourse of modernity' which has assumed that the changes occurring in Europe, beginning roughly in the 16th century, signaled a new type of society and a new era of world history. While this discourse has become part of the life-world of peoples across the globe, it has been widely challenged in the past two decades. No one doubts there were significant changes during this time in Europe and elsewhere, but efforts to specify the configuration of changes and dynamics that mark a new social type and historical era have proven impossible and problematic (e.g., Cooper, 2005; Knauft, 2002; Yack...). Today, many scholars have simply abandoned all such efforts or prefer to speak of multiple modernities. In this essay, I have tried to avoid this term; at times, it was simply convenient to speak of modern societies or modernity to refer to a loose series of changes or dynamics which may or may not occur together and which does not presume a contrast to a "premodern" or "traditional" order.

REFERENCES

Aldrich, R. (1996). *Greater France*. New York, NY: St. Martin's Press.
Blackbourn, D. (1998). *The long nineteenth century*. New York, NY: Oxford University Press.
Burbank, R., & Cooper, F. (2010). *Empires in World History*. Princeton: Princeton University Press.
Chatterjee, P. (1993). *The nation and its fragments*. Princeton, NJ: Princeton University Press.
Cooper, F (2005). *Colonialism in question*. Berkeley, CA: University of California Press.
Coronil, F. (1996). Beyond occidentalism: Towards nonimperial geohistorical categories. *Cultural Anthropology, 11*(February), 51–87.
Davidson, B. (1992). *The black man's burden*. New York, NY: Random House.
Dirks, N. (1992). Introduction: Colonialism and culture. In N. Dirks (Ed.), *Colonialism and culture*. Ann Arbor, MI: University of Michigan Press.
Dodge, T. (2003). *Inventing Iraq*. New York, NY: Columbia University Press.

Durkheim, E. (1933). *The division of labor in society.* Glencoe, IL: Free Press.
Durkheim, E. (1958). *Professional ethics and civic morals.* Glencoe, IL: Free Press.
Durkheim, E. (1986). *Durkheim on politics and the state.* Stanford, CA: Stanford University Press.
Ferguson, N. (2004). *Empire.* New York, NY: Basic.
Fieldhouse, D. K. (1967). *The colonial empires.* New York, NY: Delacorte Press.
Fontana, B. (2002). The Napoleonic empire and the Europe of nations. In A. Padgen (Ed.), *The idea of Europe.* Cambridge: Cambridge University Press.
Frank, A. G. (1998). *Reorient: Global economy in the Asian age.* Berkeley, CA: University of California Press.
Go, J. (2006). Imperial power and its limits: America's colonial empire in the early twentieth century. In C. Calhoun (Ed.), *Lessons of empire.* New York, NY: The New Press.
Hobsbawm, E. (1989). *The age of empire 1875–1914.* New York, NY: Vintage.
Hostetler, L. (2001). *Qing colonial enterprise.* Chicago, IL: University of Chicago Press.
Kennedy, P. (1987). *The rise and fall of the great powers.* New York, NY: Random House.
Knauft, B. (Ed.). (2002). *Critically modern.* Bloomington, IN: Indiana University Press.
Magubane, Z. (2005). Overlapping territories and intertwined histories: Historical sociology's global imagination. In J. Adams (Ed.), *Remaking modernity.* Durham: Duke University Press.
Mamdani, M. (1996). *Citizen and subject: Contemporary Africa and the legacy of late colonialism.* Princeton, NJ: Princeton University Press.
Marx, K. (1968). In S. Avineri. (Ed.), *Karl Marx on colonialism and modernization.* Garden City, NY: Doubleday.
Marx, K. (1974a). *The revolutions of 1848.* New York, NY: Vintage.
Marx, K. (1974b). *Surveys from exile.* New York, NY: Vintage.
Marx, K., & Engels, F. (1942). *Selected correspondence 1846–1895.* New York, NY: International Publishers.
McClintock, A. (1995). *Imperial leather.* New York, NY: Routledge.
Mommsen, W. (1984). *Max Weber and German politics 1890–1920.* Chicago, IL: University of Chicago Press.
Mommsen, W. (1995). *Imperial Germany 1867–1918.* New York, NY: Oxford University Press.
Padgen, A. (2003). *Peoples and empires.* New York, NY: Random House.
Pomeranz, K. (2000). *The great divergence: China, Europe, and the making of the modern world economy.* Princeton, NJ: Princeton University Press.
Rabinow, P. (1989). *French modern.* Cambridge: MIT Press.
Ruedy, J. (1992). *Modern Algeria.* Bloomington, IN: Indiana University Press.
Said, E. (1978). *Orientalism.* New York, NY: Random House.
Said, E. (1979). *The Question of Palestine.* New York, NY: Vintage.
Silverblatt, I. (2004). *Modern Inquisitions: Peru and the colonial origins of the civilized world.* Durham: Duke University Press.
Smith, W. (1978). *The German colonial empire.* Chapel Hill, NC: University of North Carolina Press.
Steinmetz, G. (2002). Precoloniality and colonial subjectivity: Ethnographic discourse and native policy in German overseas imperialism, 1780s–1914. *Political Power and Social Theory, 15*, 135–228.

Steinmetz, G. (2005, December). Return to empire: The new US imperialism in comparative historical perspective. *Sociological Theory*, *23*(4), 339–367.

Veer, P. V. D. (2001). *Imperial encounters: Religion and modernity in India and Britain.* Princeton, NJ: Princeton University Press.

Weber, M. (1958). *Author's introduction. The protestant ethic and the spirit of capitalism.* New York, NY: Scribners.

Weber, M. (1968). *Economy and society* (3 Vols.). New York, NY: Bedminster Press.

Weber, M. (1976). *The agrarian sociology of ancient civilizations.* London: NLB.

Weber, M. (1994). *Political Writings.* Cambridge: Cambridge University Press.

Wilder, G. (2005). *The French imperial nation-state.* Chicago, IL: University of Chicago Press.

Yack, B. (1997). *The Fetishisms of Modernities.* Notre dame: University of Notre Dame Press.

"FROM THE STANDPOINT OF GERMANISM": A POSTCOLONIAL CRITIQUE OF WEBER'S THEORY OF RACE AND ETHNICITY ☆

Manuela Boatcă

ABSTRACT

Sociological conceptualizations of capitalism, modernity, and economic development as due only to factors endogenous to Western Europe have been prominent targets of postcolonial criticism. Instead of an over-the-board condemnation of classical sociology as a whole or of the work of one classic in particular, the present article zooms in on Max Weber's theory of ethnicity from a postcolonial perspective in order to pinpoint the absences, blind spots and gestures of exclusion that Weber's classical analysis has bequeathed to the sociology of social inequality more generally and to the sociology of race and ethnicity in particular. Through a reconstruction of Weber's conceptual and political take on race and ethnicity, the article links Weber's general social theory with his particular views on racial and ethnic matters and reveals both as historically and politically situated. To this end, it starts with a brief look

☆ Reprinted from *Postcolonial Sociology*, Political Power and Social Theory, Volume 24, 2013, pp. 55–80.

Postcolonial Sociology
Political Power and Social Theory, Volume 24, 51–76
Copyright © 2013 by Emerald Group Publishing Limited
ISSN: 0198-8719/doi:10.1108/S0198-8719(2013)0000024009

at Weber's theory of modernity as an indispensable prerequisite for an analysis of his approach to race and ethnicity and subsequently discusses his chapter on Ethnic Groups, his treatment of the "Polish question" in the 1890s and of the "Negro question" in the United States in the 1890s. Using Weber's canonical treatment of ethnicity as a test case, the article ends by suggesting that postcolonial critique can prove sociological theory more generally as built upon unwarranted overgeneralization from a particular standpoint constructed as universal.

Sociological conceptualizations of capitalism, modernity, and economic development as Western European phenomena emerged due only to factors endogenous to the region, such as the French Revolution, the Enlightenment, and the "industrial revolution," have been prominent targets of postcolonial criticism. The main charge – the systematic omission of exogenous factors such as colonial rule and imperial exploitation from social scientific explanations – has alternately been referred to as typical of the "gestures of exclusion" (Connell, 2007, p. 46) of metropolitan theory and as responsible for the "silences," "absences" (Santos, 2004, p. 14ff.) or "blind spots" (Hesse, 2007) of mainstream sociological analysis.

Against this background, Portuguese sociologist Boaventura de Sousa Santos (2004) coined the term "sociology of absences" – "an inquiry that aims to explain that what does not exist is in fact actively produced as nonexistent" – as a complement to which he advanced a "sociology of emergences" – "an inquiry into the alternatives that are contained in the horizon of concrete possibilities." Both become necessary in order to incorporate past and present experiences of the colonized world into general social theory and build collective futures. While postcolonial critique has charged sociological classics from Comte to Marx and from Durkheim to Weber collectively or individually with Eurocentrism, evolutionary determinism, and ignorance of non-Western contexts, it was with reference to Max Weber's thesis of the "uniqueness of the West" that the notion of a Western sociology actively producing absences was first formulated (Hirst, 1975, in Zubaida, 2005, p. 112). Famously, Weber substantiated his thesis by means of defining non-Western societies, especially China and India, but also Islamic societies, in terms of lacking the specific Occidental characteristics which had allowed the development of rational capitalism in the West.

Instead of an over-the-board condemnation of classical sociology as a whole or of the work of one classic in particular, the present article zooms in on Max Weber's theory of ethnicity in order to pinpoint the absences, blind spots and gestures of exclusion that Weber's classical analysis has bequeathed to the sociology of social inequality more generally and to the sociology of race and ethnicity in particular. Through a reconstruction of Weber's conceptual and political take on race and ethnicity, the article links Weber's general social theory with his particular views on racial and ethnic matters and reveals both as historically and politically situated in the local cultural context of imperial Germany as well as in Weber's specific nationalist outlook. As such, the present analysis aligns itself with Edward Said's now classic postcolonial critique, according to which Western academic knowledge has only been constructed as universal, generally valid, and unsituated by simultaneously demoting non-Western knowledges to the status of the local, particular, and therefore ungeneralizable (Said, 1978); and it seeks to contribute to a postcolonial sociology outlined elsewhere as a context-specific, history-sensitive sociology of power, the subject matter of which is not the Western world or its normative modernity, but the entanglements between Western and non-Western modernities emerged at the intersection of military power, capital expansion and enduring colonial structures of knowledge (Boatcă & Costa, 2010, p. 30).[1]

PRELUDE: MODERNITY AS MODERN WESTERN RATIONALISM

Rather than standing on their own as a theory, Weber's views on ethnicity, race and class are intimately tied to his larger notion of the rise of the modern world. A brief look at Weber's theory of modernity is therefore an indispensable prerequisite for any analysis of his approach to race and ethnicity.

Although he clearly placed great emphasis on modernity as a series of specifically Western achievements, Weber never used the term as such. Alongside terms such as "the modern West," "modern European culture," and especially "modern rationalism" that he used to describe the modern epoch, it was frequently "modern capitalism" and "the modern capitalist enterprise" that he employed as proxies for modernity. Unlike Marx, however, his primary concern was not capitalism itself, but the uniqueness of the West – of which modern capitalism was but one component – as well as the origin of this uniqueness. Thus, although he acknowledged that scientific inquiry had existed outside the Western world and had given rise to such highly sophisticated developments as Islamic theology, Chinese historiography, Babylonian astronomy, and Indian medicine, for Weber, systematic, rational science was unique to the West and could be traced back to "the Hellenic mind," that is, ancient Greece (Weber, 2005, p. 53). In his view, a series of innovations in music, architecture, and art, such as the rational use of linear and spatial perspective in painting, were unknown outside the West, as was the Western universities' "rational and systematic organization into scientific disciplines" and the Western modern state's "organization of specially trained civil servants" (2005, p. 55), only precursors of which could be found elsewhere. Similarly, only "rudimentary developments" of the state as a political institution operating on the basis of "a rationally enacted 'constitution' and rationally enacted laws" (*ibid.*) had crystallized outside the West, where these distinguishing features now characterized the modern state. The singularity of the West in all these regards could not be overstated, as Weber stresses in *General Economic History*:

> Only the Occident knows the *state in the modern sense*, with a constitution [*gesatzter Verfassung*], specialized officialdom, and the concept of citizenship. Beginnings of this institution in antiquity and in the Orient were never able to develop fully. Only the Occident knows *rational law*, made by jurists and rationally interpreted and planned, and only in the Occident is found the concept of *citizen* (*civis romanus, citoyen, bourgeois*) because only in the Occident does the *city* exist in the specific sense of the word. (Weber, 1961, p. 232)

In Weber's view, the same applied for capitalism. While the capitalist enterprise was a universal occurrence, having existed in all world civilizations from ancient China, India, and Egypt, through the Mediterranean and medieval Europe, modern Western capitalism alone was founded on "the rational-capitalist organization of legally *free labor*," which was either lacking in other regions of the globe or was present only in "preliminary development stages" there (2005, p. 58). According to Weber, the capitalist economic act in general, that is, universal capitalism, involved not only the pursuit of profit, but "an expectation of profit based on the utilization of opportunities for *exchange*; that is, of (formally) *peaceful* opportunities for acquisition[2]" (2005, p. 56). In practice, however, capitalists have financed

> above all wars, piracy and all types of shipping and construction projects; as entrepreneurs in the colonies they have served the international policy goals of nations, [...] have acquired plantations and operated them using slaves or (directly or indirectly) forced labor; they have leased land and the rights to use honorific titles; they have financed both the leaders of political parties standing for re-election and mercenaries for civil wars. (2005, p. 58)

Weber called this type of entrepreneurs "adventure capitalists" and saw them as the main agents of "promoter, adventure, colonial, and [...] modern financial capitalism" (*ibid.*), that is, capitalist enterprises of an irrational or speculative nature or of a violent character. These capitalists' use of coerced labor, Weber maintained, whether in the form of slavery, serfdom, cottage industries, or day labor, had only allowed for a very limited degree of rational organization of work when compared to that of free industrial labor in the West. Even while acknowledging that modern capitalism had emerged alongside adventure capitalism, Weber thus viewed the former as an entirely different type, characterized by "the rational organization of industrial companies and their orientation to *market* opportunities, rather than to political violence or to irrational speculation" (2005, p. 59). He therefore sharply dissociated Western capitalism from the colonial enterprise, and, ultimately, the emergence of modernity from the history of colonialism.

Despite tracing the rise of modernity back to the emergence of industrial capitalism in Europe, Weber however did not consider the question of capitalism as such to be the main factor in the explanation of the West's uniqueness. Rather, the central problem for him was that of accounting for the origin of the Western middle class and its particular economic ethos, supported as it was (only) in the West by the rational structure of law and administration (2005, p. 160). Hence, according to Weber, the common denominator of the unique modern technological developments, state-building processes, capitalist organization, calculable law and administration, and work ethic emerged in the West was the specific rationalism characterizing Western civilization as a whole.

In contrast with irrational and speculative capitalism as well as with the feudal economy, modern capitalism was therefore, for Weber, uniquely characterized by a maximum of rationality, efficiency, and the systematic, dispassionate pursuit of profit (Weber, 2005, p. 69ff.). This, however, entailed an increasing depersonalization and distancing from ethical norms and charitable orientations, the advancement of which went hand in hand with the expansion of bureaucratization.[3] Weber's "uniqueness of the West" thesis thereby constitutes a prime example of the active production of absences in an account of modernity that systematically strips it of colonial and imperial entanglements. The monopolization of terms such as modernity, rationality, and capitalism – or what Aníbal Quijano has termed "the European patent on modernity" (Quijano, 2000, p. 543) – would prompt postcolonial critics to ask how the thought of classical European sociologists was related to the place of their emergence, that is, was drawn

from particular intellectual and historical traditions, rather than reflecting
universally valid, transhistorical experience (Chakrabarty, 2007, p. xiii; see
also Mignolo, 2000).

A UNIVERSAL THEORY OF RACE AND ETHNICITY

On the other hand, the assumption that European thought is universally
valid has attracted Weber (to a somewhat lesser extent than Marx) charges
of having provided the wrong prognosis on the trajectory of social change.
Neither the massive bureaucratization, nor the reign of formal rationality,
nor social ossification came about as predicted in *The Protestant Ethic*
(Kalberg, in Weber, 2005, p. 37). Weber's assessment of race and ethnicity
as status categories [*Stände*][4] – that would disappear in the course of a
modern self-identification increasingly based on class has often been viewed
as belonging in the same category of wrong prognosis.

The source to which this interpretation is primarily traced back is the
chapter entitled "Ethnic Groups" in the English translation of *Economy and
Society*, which has long been considered to represent Weber's conclusive
stance on the issues of ethnicity and race alike[5]. Although it was made
available to an English-speaking public much later than Weber's sociology
of religion, especially the *Protestant Ethic*, and enjoyed much less attention
than the former for a considerable period of time, the chapter left an
indelible mark on both the sociology and the social anthropology of
ethnicity and race in the twentieth century (Fenton, 2003, p. 62).

Famously, for Weber, neither race nor ethnic membership by themselves
constitute communities (*Gemeinschaften*), but both can facilitate community-
building (*Vergemeinschaftung*), when subjectively *perceived* as common traits
on account of shared physical features, customs, or a shared past, which
included the "memories of colonization or migration."[6] Even in the absence
of an objective common descent, the belief in group affinity on the basis of
race or ethnic membership can thus lead to the formation of political
communities and may even persist after such communities disintegrate.
Likewise, the existence or absence of intermarriage between different "racial"
or "ethnic" groups is, more often than not, due to social closure around
"ethnic honor" – which Weber considered to be closely related to status
honor [*ständische Ehre*] – rather than to biological differences:

> Pure anthropological types are often a secondary consequence of such closure: examples
> are sects (as in India) as well as pariah peoples, that means, groups that are socially

despised yet wanted as neighbors because they have monopolized indispensable skills. (Weber, 1920, p. 386)

Similarities between membership in ethnic groups such as "pariah peoples" and racial groups such as "Negroes" in the United States are therefore more directly pertinent to Weber's thesis that group formation was contingent upon common subjective beliefs than are differences between the two. Weber therefore never distinguished between race and ethnic group, other than noting that excessively heterogeneous "racial qualities" of members of a group could effectively limit the belief in their common ethnicity. Instead, he stressed the importance of status stratification [*ständische Schichtung*] through honor, that he saw as underlying both ethnic and racial group formation, by using the example of the "one-drop rule" in the United States:

> In the United States the smallest admixture of Negro blood disqualifies a person unconditionally, whereas very considerable admixtures of Indian blood do not. Doubtlessly, it is important that Negroes appear esthetically even more alien than Indians, but it remains very significant that Negroes were slaves and hence disqualified in the status hierarchy [*Ständehierarchie*]. The conventional *connubium* is far less impeded by anthropological differences than by status differences, that means, differences due to socialization [*anerzogene Unterschiede*] and upbringing. (Weber, 1920, p. 386f.)

Despite this and other references to the influence of the former slave condition upon an individual's position in the modern status (i.e., racial) hierarchy, the relationship between racism, colonialism, and slavery does not enter into Weber's conceptualization of racial or ethnic communities. Instead, he illustrates the compelling notion that memories of colonization and migration underpin group formation either through the experience of the colonists or of voluntary migration that did not result in disqualification in the status hierarchy [*Ständehierarchie*], such as in the case of German-Americans – but not through the shared experience of being colonized or enslaved. Thus, Weber's examples bespeak merely one side in the power differential that gave rise to the status hierarchy: the white, European, male experience. As such, the notion of group formation through memories of colonization or migration remains unconnected to his argument that "racial antipathy" in the United States was socially determined by the whites' tendency to monopolize social power and status (Weber, 1920, p. 386). His focus therefore lies on supplying a *universally valid definition* of ethnic differentiation as a form of status stratification using examples from a variety of historical contexts rather than on offering a *historically informed analysis* of the emergence of specific racial and ethnic groups. This approach is therefore consistent both with his relegation of slaves to a *status group* [*Stand*] of low social honor (rather than to a lower *class*) and with his treatment of ethnic groups as characteristic of societies with a low degree of rationalization, as opposed to the rationally organized and potentially more class-based societies of the West: Thus, for Weber, "ethnic fictions" – group belief in a common ancestor – in the Greek city state were "a sign of the rather low degree of rationalization of Greek political life," while the loose connection between social subdivision and ethnic claims in ancient Rome was "a symptom of the greater rationalization" there (Weber, 1978, p. 389f.).

Consequently, the belief in common ethnicity belongs, together with irrational (or less rational) social action and the estate order [*Ständeordnung*], to traditional social arrangements and forms of authority. Weber's definition of ethnicity has accordingly been found in line both with his theory of social action and with his typology of forms of domination: Ethnic groups that engage primarily in *communal social action* based on feelings of belongingness are characteristic of the estate order under *traditional rule*, whereas class members who engage in *associative social action* grounded in rational economic interests are typical of forms of *rational rule* (Jackson, 1983, p. 10f.). Even though Weber defines *charismatic domination* based on *charismatic action* in opposition to both the traditional and the rational types of rule, he points out that the process of routinization of charisma into either one of the two leads to *charisma of office* (*Amtscharisma*) in the rational order and to *hereditary charisma* (*Erbcharisma*) in the traditional one, that is, to legitimacy through the holding of an office vs. legitimacy through the belief in the importance of blood relationship, respectively (Weber, 1920, p. 249ff.). While charisma of office allowed the bureaucratization of the Catholic Christian church by separating the powers of the office from the individual qualifications of the priest, Weber saw hereditary charisma as best illustrated by the Indian caste system, the Japanese lineage state before bureaucratization, and China before the rationalization in the territorial states, all of which replaced the principle of qualification through achievement by the one of qualification through descent (Weber, 1920, p. 253f.). Thus, despite Weber's repeated disavowal of a staged theory of social evolution with respect to forms of social stratification, types of social action, or of forms of legitimate domination, it is tribal and lineage states and their corresponding ethnic fictions, communal social action, and traditional or hereditary charismatic forms of rule that repeatedly feature as examples of pre-rational, premodern social contexts, that is, lend themselves to being associated with those aspects of Weber's theory that "emphasize the past" (Jackson, 1983, p. 11). Modernization theorists would later abstract from Weber's recurring historical examples the implicit contrast between modern Occidental rationality and its premodern counterparts within and outside the Western world and develop it into a clear-cut dichotomy between modern and traditional societies clearly located at different stages of development and moments in time, thus completing the active production of the non-West as absence from modernity.

THE POLISH QUESTION, THE NEGRO QUESTION, AND THE NATION

Weber's analysis of ethnic communities has been both hailed for explicitly opposing biological explanations of their origin and thus anticipating the later literature on race and ethnicity as social constructs, on the one hand, and criticized for insufficiently addressing the historical origins of group formation as well as for disregarding the importance of multiple group memberships for the cohesion of a community, on the other (Banton, 2007). Recognizing the text's limitations however did not prevent scholars from considering it the "canonical treatment of ethnicity" (Scaff, 1998, p. 89; Stender, 2000, p. 76) on which further research on the phenomenon can and should build.[7] Its prominence notwithstanding, the chapter is in fact far from exhausting Weber's views on race and ethnicity, as one of the earliest overviews convincingly shows (Manasse, 1947). Most scholarship in the latter half of the twentieth century has however tended to overlook the bulk of Weber's statements on the issue and to concentrate instead on its succinct treatment in *Economy and Society.*

That the entry on "ethnic groups" in the *Max Weber Dictionary* should point to the existence of diametrically opposed views in the work of Weber himself is therefore not self-explaining: "While Weber took a stance against anti-Semitism and racial prejudices in general, it is common to find ethnic slurs in his early social science writings on the role of the Poles in Germany" (Swedberg, 2005, p. 92). How are Weber's views in the chapter compatible with ethnic slurs in his early work?

At stake are the following landmark dates: In the 1890s, Weber delivered a series of papers on the agrarian economy of the German East, in which he described the growing immigration of Catholic Polish laborers to West Prussia as the demise of the more developed Protestant civilization of the

German peasants before the physically and mentally lesser "Slav race." In his conclusions, he called for a closing of the state frontier to immigration from the East as a means of preserving German culture (Weber, 1980). In 1904, shortly after having concluded the first part of *The Protestant Ethic and the Spirit of Capitalism,* Max Weber traveled to the United States, where he lectured on the topic of rural communities and modern economic development, arguing that, besides the economic contradictions occasioned by the advance of capitalism, the most pressing social problems of the U.S. South were "essentially ethnic" (4/8). Finally, in 1910, Max Weber challenged Alfred Ploetz and his biologically determinist theory of race at the meeting of the German Sociological Association in Frankfurt, using the example of the United States and arguing that race relations cannot be explained in terms of inborn racial qualities, but solely through cultural and economic factors.

Usually, the contradiction between the earlier and the later statements is resolved by Weber's biographers and reviewers by assessing his thought in terms of an evolution from an anti-Polish nationalism in the 1890s to a liberal and social pluralist antiracism by the early 1900s (Manasse, 1947; Tribe, 1980; Kalberg in Weber, 2005, p. 294n1). In particular, Weber's acquaintance with W. E. B. Du Bois during his trip to the United States and their subsequent exchanges, which included the publication of an article by Du Bois on racial prejudice as the "new spirit of caste" in the *Archiv für Sozialwissenschaft und Sozialpolitik,* are credited with having decisively influenced Weber's sociology of class, status [*Stand*], and caste (Manasse, 1947, p. 200; Scaff, 1998, p. 89). In the same vein, several authors have even assumed a "basic reversal" of Weber's political stance toward Poland, coupled with a move away from his early Social-Darwinist position on racial differences (Mommsen, 1984, p. 53; Roth, 1993, 2000, p. 129; Vernik, 2011, p. 178). In Japan, where research on Max Weber has been exceptionally prolific, the shift has even been interpreted as a full-fledged conversion from the racist Weber of power politics to a humanist, unemotional Weber (Konno, 2004, p. 22). Alternatively, a growing literature on the subject sees the evolution of Weber's thought as proceeding from a specific anti-Polish nationalism – which used religion as a proxy for race – in his early writings, to a cultural and economic racism cloaked as a comparative sociology of religion in his later work, especially as related to India and China (Abraham, 1991; Zimmerman, 2006, 2010; for China see Steinmetz, 2010).

That the works dealing with the questions of race and ethnicity in Weber should be (literally) few and far between, and that they should moreover span a wide range of interpretations, yields no more than an inconclusive picture of his views on the topic. Ernst Moritz Manasse's 1947 article "Max Weber and race" (Manasse, 1947), addressing the entire range of race-related issues in Weber's work, from early treatments of "the Polish question," to the turn-of-the-century statements on "the Negro question," up to the discussion of the Indian caste system and the development of postexilic Judaism, remained the reference treatment on the topic for several decades. As late as 1971, in the introduction to the first English-language translation of Weber's debate with Alfred Ploetz at the 1910 meeting of the German Sociological Association, Benjamin Nelson deplored the fact that Weber's contributions to discussions on the use of sociology in the formation of public policy had, "strangely enough... generally been ignored" (Weber, 1971, p. 30). Such statements were however only true for the U.S. context: In Germany, Wolfgang J. Mommsen's 1959 book *Max Weber and German Politics* (Mommsen, 1974), which argued that Weber had been at once an ardent liberal and an extreme nationalist, and that he had embraced imperialist views dangerously close to fascist ideologies, had sparked a vivid and decade-lasting controversy on the relationship between Weber's sociology and his power-politics. In England, Jacob Peter Mayer's equally devastating *Max Weber and German Politics: A Study in Political Sociology* (1944), which charged Weber with theoretical and ideological contributions to the rise of National Socialism, failed to attract the academic attention that Mommsen's work did within and outside of Germany, and, tellingly, was never translated into German. By the time Mommsen's book finally appeared in English (Mommsen, 1984) – with a new preface, in which the link to fascism was toned down – the prevalent notion in the United States was that Max Weber's politics was irrelevant to his sociology, and that the former was a "kind of anti-ideological Anglo-American liberalism" (Turner, 1986, p. 49). It is only in recent works in the ambit of racial and ethnic studies as well as postcolonial studies that Mommsen's theses on Max Weber's political stance have been systematically read in the context of his views on various racial issues. In the 1980s, Gary Abraham contended that the antipluralistic and assimilationist outlook reflected in Weber's writings on the Polish workers was replicated in his treatment of German Catholics as well as his later treatment of Jews and was as such no accident, but central to understanding Weber's thought as a whole (1991). More recently, Andrew Zimmerman denounced "the work of repression" that sociologists had undertaken in order to mobilize Weber's thought in support for liberal political and social scientific positions, and called instead for a "decolonization" of Weber through a detailed analysis of his approach to race and labor and of his theory of empire, seen as having paved the way for contemporary right-wing models (2006, p. 53).

A postcolonial critique of Weber's treatment of race and ethnicity is more in line with these later approaches, as it reveals both his analysis of Polish workers and of race relations in the United States to be informed by Weber's own geopolitical and historical location in turn-of-the-century Germany as well as by his upper middle-class position[8] – which he himself referred to as "the standpoint of Germanism." Revealing what counts as the canonical treatment on the topic to be neither universally valid social theory, nor legitimately generalizable knowledge is both an exercise in the particular task of "decolonizing Weber" and a possible step toward a "sociology of emergences" able to expand the range of alternative knowledges on the topic.

The 1890s: Suppressing "Polonism"

As an astute critic has noted, Weber constructed his model of inequality relations at the very moment that the rise of imperial Germany rendered many of them obsolete (Wenger, 1980, p. 373). The medieval estates were disappearing; industrialization attracted large flows of labor migrants from the European East, while the local labor force was ever more proletarianized. European colonialism in Africa prompted an increased awareness of "the other" that translated as the infamous anthropological distinction between European *Kulturvölker* (cultural peoples) and colonized *Naturvölker* (natural peoples), in turn associated with different degrees of humanity. Growing anti-Semitism was reflected in allegedly scientific support of racial concepts of German national identity as distinct from a Jewish race (Zimmerman, 2001, p. 242f.). With Germany's unification in 1871, existing anti-Catholic sentiment was institutionalized in Bismarck's *Kulturkampf* ("culture struggle") policies, meant to restrict the power of the Catholic Church and help define Germany as a secular state. As a result, the increasing presence of Catholic Poles in Eastern Germany was officially countered through the resettlement of German farmers in the region. The conservative *Verein für Sozialpolitik*, which Weber joined in 1888, had until then supported the Prussian state's resettlement policies only on class terms, that is, as a means of preventing the further proletarianization of German farmers and an impending social revolution. It was Max Weber whose work in the *Verein* first made ethnic and cultural explanations central to the discussions of the Prussian East and who warned of the "danger of assimilation" from the standpoint of "reason of state" rather than an economic one (Zimmerman, 2006, p. 61; 2010, p. 100ff.).

These views subsequently made the subject of other works during the same period. Central to Weber's controversial[9] inaugural lecture at the University of Freiburg (1895), entitled "Nationality in Economic Policy," was the question "What social strata are the repositories of Germanism (*Deutschtum*) and Polonism (*Polentum*) in the country districts?" (Weber, 1980, p. 429). The systematic land purchase by the German state, the settlement of German farmers on Polish-owned land, as well as the closing of the German frontier to Polish workers had been part of Bismarck's official program of "Germanization" of the Eastern provinces up to 1890, in which suppressing "Polonism" was an explicit goal. Weber was therefore employing known terms in order to address a known problem: the decline of the German landworker population in the face of Polish settlement on small farms and of the growing imports of cheap Polish labor on large estates. What was new, both with respect to the general discussion and to Weber's earlier treatments of the issue, was phrasing these *economic* developments in *ethnic* and *cultural* terms derived from each of the groups' religious affiliation: Since the census data available to him only differentiated by religion, not ethnicity, Weber interpreted the numbers indicating the decline of the Protestant population relative to the Catholic one to mean that it must be German day-laborers who move out of the estates on good soil, and it is Polish peasants who proliferate on low-quality land.[10] He traced this tendency back to "*a lower expectation of living standards*, in part physical, in part mental, which the Slav race either possesses as a gift from nature or has acquired through breeding in the course of its past history" (Weber, 1980, p. 432). Although the Polish peasants, unlike the seasonal migrant workers, were German citizens at the time, Weber described the situation as an economic struggle "between nationalities" (1980, p. 428), ultimately decided through a selection process in favor of the nationality with the greater "ability to adapt" itself to given economic and social conditions. From this perspective, the Polish peasants living off subsistence production, that is, not affected by price fluctuations on the market, were better adapted than the economically "more gifted" German farmers:

> The small Polish peasant in East Germany is a type far removed from the bustling peasant owner of a dwarf property, whom one may see here in the well-favored valley of the Rhine as he forges links with the towns via greenhouse cultivation and market-gardening. The small Polish peasant in East Germany gains more land because he as it were eats the very grass from off of it, he gains not *despite* but *on account of* the low level of his physical and intellectual habits of life. (Weber, 1980, p. 434)

Weber thus uses the Social Darwinist terminology of "adaptation," "selection process," and "race breeding" popular at the time in order to explain that a group's economic advance did not necessarily correlate with the "political maturity" needed in order to build up "the nation's power." Thus, in his view, Polish settlement and labor migration led to the rise of "unviable Slav hunger colonies" (1980, p. 435) and drove out German agricultural laborers, instead of steering in the direction of the emergence of a strong proletariat on the model of England. The wish to protect "the German character of the East" (1980, p. 437) from such tendencies in turn led Weber to formulate his policy demands "from the standpoint of Germanism" and uphold "a German standard of value" against the international standards of social justice he saw political economy as promoting:

> The science of political economy is a *political* science. It is a servant of politics, not the day-to-day politics of the individuals and classes who happen to be ruling at a particular time, but the lasting power-political interests of the nation. And for us the *national state* is not, as some people believe, an indeterminate entity [...], but the temporal power-organization of the nation, and in this national state the ultimate standard of value for economic policy is "reason of state." (Weber, 1980, p. 438)

Speaking at the close of the 19th century as a German economic theorist, a member of the bourgeois classes, and a son of a National Liberal member of the Prussian Diet,[11] Weber considered the "reason of state" in the case of German economic policy to be "the amount of elbowroom" conquered for the economic well-being of "the race of the future" (Weber, 1994, p. 16). He therefore called for the renewed closing of the Eastern frontier to Polish migrants, as under Bismarck, and for a state policy of systematic colonization by German peasants on suitable land as a means of preserving German culture.

The same logic underlies Weber's 1894 article on Argentina's rising cereal exports after the devaluation of the Argentinean peso in 1889/1890. In arguing both against the free trade doctrine and the "entirely unrealistic assumption of the international equality of cultures" (4/4, p. 302), Weber insisted that Argentina's low production costs could to a great extent be traced back to the very low wages and cheap food that planters offered the "nomadic barbarians" that they hired for seasonal work. According to this low living standard, these workers "appear when the time for demand comes and disappear afterwards or after having drunk away their wages," while "in terms of housing [they] only know clay huts" (p. 292). Economic competition with colonial economies such as the Argentinean one would therefore require *lowering* the level of German social organization and culture in order to match that of Argentina's "half-savage trash" (p. 129), a phenomenon Weber saw as occurring with the Polish immigration in East Elbia:

> Should we be able and willing to work just as "cheaply," our rural workers would have to approach this type as well, and we can indeed find the first manifestations of this change if we observe the itinerant workforce and the import of Poles in the East.

> Briefly, the fact is that we are an old sedentary civilized people (*Kulturvolk*) on densely populated land with an old, highly distinctive and therefore sensitive social organization and typical national cultural necessities, which make it impossible for us to compete with these economies. (44/299, p. 298f.)

Inherent in Weber's defense of the "standpoint of Germanism" in the 1890s is therefore a roundabout theory of ethnicity premised on the inequality of the cultural levels and the attitudes toward work of different "nationalities" that both reflects the views of his time and goes beyond them. His approach is thus closer to a political position – against any type of internationalism in general, and against socialism in particular – than to a full-fledged theoretical apparatus. As Guenther Roth (1993, p. 152) has noted, in arguing this position, Weber even turned against close collaborators: At the 1896 founding meeting of the National Social party, Weber cautioned its founder, Friedrich Naumann, that the new party's political platform required adopting a *national* stance with respect to the Polish question, instead of denouncing its promoters, as Naumann had done in *Die Zeit*.[12] On such occasions, his anti-Polish rhetoric went beyond mere Social Darwinistic overtones and acquired racist traits: "It has been said that we have degraded the Poles to second-class German citizens. The opposite is the case: We have turned them into human beings in the first place" (4/4, p. 622). Clearly, Weber is extrapolating here from the distinction between *Kulturvölker* as civilized humanity and *Naturvölker* as barbaric humanity that he had explicitly mobilized in reference to the German versus the Argentinean economies (and that was commonly used in 19th century German anthropology to refer to European and colonized peoples, respectively) in order to deny full humanity to populations within Europe. The modern, the civilized and the rational are thereby confined to an even more exclusive space within the European continent, which the imperial imaginary conceives as ending at Germany's eastern border and which I have elsewhere labeled "heroic Europe" (Boatcă, 2010).

The 1900s: The Problem of the Color Line

Weber's views on the matter had largely remained unchanged by the time he and Marianne Weber undertook their trip to the United States a few years later. Weber would put them to extensive use in his 1904 talk at the St. Louis World's Fair on the topic of rural society and modern economic development. While claiming that capitalism had different effects in old civilized countries with a dense population and strong rural traditions – such as Germany – than in new countries with vast amounts of land and no old aristocracy – such as the United States, Weber predicted that the same set of circumstances would eventually affect the latter as well. When that moment comes, Germany's experience could therefore be a valuable lesson for the United States, in particular as regards policies addressing the rural social question, which, according to Weber, "cannot be cut with the sword, as was the slave question" (4/8, p. 241). Expressed as an economic struggle between "two nations, Germans and Slavonians," Germany's rural social question was at the same time a cultural one:

> While thus under the pressure of conjuncture the frugal Slavonian small farmer gains territory from the German, the advance of culture toward the east, during the Middle Ages, founded upon the superiority of the older and higher culture, has changed completely to the contrary under the dominion of the capitalistic principle of the "cheaper hand." (4/8, p. 241f.)

That the absence of rural traditions and of an old aristocracy in the United States made the effects of capitalism stronger there than in Europe, did not, in Weber's view, prevent both American and German cultures from facing the same threat in the long run – economic competition from culturally unassimilable elements. As early as 1893, Weber had argued that migrant labor was less of a danger to German culture in the case of the importation of Chinese *coolies*, with whom Germans would not assimilate, than in the case of immigrant Polish workers. As he claimed in his Freiburg address soon thereafter, Poles tend to "soak up" national minorities, leading to the decline of Protestantism and the advance of Catholicism (Weber, 1980, p. 432). With respect to its effects on the standard of living of civilized countries, the "Negro question" in the United States therefore paralleled the "Polish question" in Germany and would accordingly be aggravated by Eastern European immigration to North America:

> [...] also the number of negro farms is growing and the migration from the country into the cities. If, thereby, the expansive power of the Anglo-Saxon-German settlement of the rural districts and, besides, the number of children of the old, inborn population are on

the wane and if, at the same time, the enormous immigration of uncivilized elements from eastern Europe grows, also here a rural population might arise which could not be assimilated by the historically transmitted culture of this country; this population would change forever the standard of the United States and would gradually form a community of a quite different type from the great creation of the Anglo-Saxon spirit. (4/8, p. 242)

In which direction Weber saw this "change of standard" to be pointing was spelt out in his 1906 article on the Russian Revolution, in which he spoke of how the "tremendous immigration of European, especially east European people into the United States, [...] erodes the old democratic traditions there" (4/10, p. 272). As late as 1906, Weber thus used similar racial stereotypes as in his early work on Polish laborers, only this time extrapolated to the entire European East, seen as lacking in both civilization and democratic tradition and as such closer to a colonized *Naturvolk* than to an European *Kulturvolk* in the imperial imaginary.

The parallel with the Negro question would in turn be detailed in his study of the "psychophysics of work" in the context of a larger project on industrial labor in Germany that the *Verein für Sozialpolitik* undertook in 1908/1909. The clearest proof of the relevance of "racial differences" for an assessment of the capacity to perform industrial work, Weber maintained, was the employment of Negroes in the North American textile industry (*"textilindustriellen Verwendung der Neger,"* MWG I/11, p. 110). That race should be the determining factor in such "extreme cases," however, did not mean that it could incontestably account for less conspicuous differences, such as those between ethnic and regional groups in Europe:

> The neurotic disqualification of American Negroes for certain tasks in the textile industry is easy to assess; but the infinitely finer, yet for the rentability of the respective workers decisive differences, which can be observed in European manufactures, are not. (MWG I/11, p. 238)[13]

Although he rejected the biological explanations that experimental psychology provided for the work capacities of various ethnic groups, Weber did not question the existence of differences as such. Indeed, he assumed they were the rule in the case of Blacks in the United States and he would later repeatedly mention "the Negroes'" alleged unsuitability for factory work as "one case in economic history where tangible racial distinctions are present" (Weber, 1923 in Manasse, 1947, p. 210n41). With respect to the "finer" distinctions within Europe, he instead argued that, rather than *hereditary differences*, the temperament, disciplinability, and psychic constitution necessary for manufacturing work should be analyzed as *differences of tradition*. Accordingly, whereas experimental psychology asked whether inherited or achieved characteristics were decisive for labor efficiency in general, economics, before taking into account any biological predispositions, inquired whether the characteristics that affected the different rentability of industrial workers could be traced back to the workers' social and cultural environment, tradition, and upbringing. In Wolfgang Schluchter's words, Weber thus counterposed the question of psychophysical *aptitude* to work to the one of cultural *attitude* to work (Schluchter, 2000, p. 75).

Again, this approach can be seen as thoroughly consistent with the rejection of biological racism and the plea for a cultural and economic explanation of racial inequalities that Weber espoused in the famous debate with Alfred Ploetz at the meeting of the German Sociological Association one year after completing the study on the psychophysics of labor. A physician, biologist, and staunch Social Darwinist, whose work would later prove one of the main sources for Nazi eugenic policies, Alfred Ploetz had recently founded the journal *Archiv für Rassen und Gesellschaftsbiologie und Gesellschaftshygiene* and the German Association for Racial Hygiene (*Deutsche Gesellschaft für Rassenhygiene*) and had joined the German Sociological Association following the invitation of Ferdinand Tönnies (Weindling, 1989, p. 140). Against Ploetz, Weber argued that no socio-logically relevant circumstances could be traced back to hereditary racial qualities, and gave the example of "the contrast between white and Negro in North America" 1971, p. 37). While hereditary qualities most likely were "strong factors at work," Weber insisted that the emergence of the unequal social standing of the two racial groups was primarily socially determined:

> [.] if it were possible for us today to impregnate persons from birth with black color, these persons – in a society of whites – would be constantly in a precarious and peculiar situation. (1971, p. 37f.)

At the same time, the equivalent view that Indians enjoyed a relatively higher social status in the United States than Blacks not because of superior innate characteristics, but because they had not been enslaved – a view which Weber would later express in *Economy and Society* – strikingly paralleled the logic of a group's "ability to adapt" to social and economic circumstances that Weber had used in his analysis of the Polish workers. Just like the Poles, and in keeping with the claim that they were not fit for industrial work, the "Negroes" were viewed as better adapted to lower forms of labor than Indians; as in the case of "the Slav race," Weber left open the question of whether this condition was a matter of biology or of cultural custom:

> [...] the reason constantly formulated by the whites for their different evaluation of the Indians is: "They did not submit to slavery" [...] Indeed, insofar as their specific qualities are the reason for their not having been slaves, it was their *inability to endure* the quantity of work demanded by the plantation capitalists – which the Negro could accomplish. Whether this was a consequence of purely hereditary peculiarities or of their traditions is doubtful. (Weber, 1971, p. 38, emphasis mine)

If, therefore, Weber wrote to W. E. B. Du Bois that "'the colour-line' problem will be the paramount problem of the time to come, here and everywhere in the world" (Weber, 1904 in Scaff, 1998, p. 90), apparently echoing Du Bois' own famous dictum that "the problem of the Twentieth Century is the problem of the color line," it is unlikely that they meant the same thing[14]. In light of the analogies Weber had repeatedly drawn to the situation of immigrant labor in Germany, his much-quoted statement about his 1904 visit to the United States – "the Americans are a wonderful people, and only the Negro question and the terrible immigration form the big black clouds" (quoted in Weber, 1988a, p. 302) seems a better indicator of his concerns: While Weber was an explicit and outspoken opponent of biological racism, his concern with "the power-political interests of the nation" consistently led him to check for economic and cultural "threats" to these national interests, such as immigrant workers and religious Others, and to treat them as culturally separate, unassimilable (and as such undesirable) social groups, thus using culturally racist arguments through-out. In the context of defining world power as "the power to determine the character of culture in the future" (Weber et al., 1994, p. 76) during World War I, what Weber had described in his Freiburg lecture as the "standpoint of Germanism" would be restated as "the standpoint of those cultural values that have been entrusted to a people" (1994, p. 75) and which is the duty of a *Machtstaat* to protect. Insofar as Weber considered other countries to be *Machtstaaten*, great military states with a cultural "responsibility before history," this standpoint equally applied to them. Seeing, as he did, the problem of the color line as paramount everywhere, was in this context an acknowledgment of the parallel threats that Weber saw both Germany and the United States as facing – not a plea for the social emancipation of Blacks in the United States, as formulated by W. E. B. Du Bois. Thus, it is precisely because the threat Weber perceived in both cases did not come from a biologically distinct race, but from a lowering of cultural standards, that he could dismiss as unfounded the "one-drop rule"

for determining race membership and condemn the anti-Black racism of the
poor whites in the U.S. South, yet refer to black plantation workers as lesser
humans in the same breath: On the one hand, the "numerous half-Negroes,
quarter-Negroes and one hundredth-part Negroes whom no non-American
can distinguish from whites" that he and Marianne Weber encountered at
the Tuskegee Institute were, for him, part of the "educated and often nine-
tenths white Negro upper class" (quoted in Marianne Weber, 1988b, p. 296).
On the other hand, what made the Negro question paramount was that, by
comparison, "The semi-apes one encounters on the plantations and in the
Negro huts of the 'Cotton Belt' afford a horrible contrast, but so does the
intellectual condition of the whites in the south" (idem). Clearly, Weber
considered the second grouping – both uneducated blacks and poor whites –
to have more in common with the Polish peasant's "low intellectual habits
of life" or the Argentinean seasonal worker's "semi-barbarian" existence in
clay huts than either with a Black intellectual like W. E. B. Du Bois (whom
he mentioned in the debate with Ploetz as "the most important sociological
scholar anywhere in the Southern States in America, with whom no white
scholar can compare" (Weber, 1971b, p. 312) – or with members of the
educated white upper class.

CODA: ON THE PERSISTENCE AND
PERVASIVENESS OF STANDPOINT

As late as 1917, Weber still championed the standpoint of Germanism
underlying the "reason of state" policy – all the more forcefully so given the
world war context. Placing the interests of Germanism (*Deutschtum*) above
the task of democratization, upholding both the privilege and the duty of
the "master race" (*Herrenvolk*) to engage in world politics[15], and protecting
the Fatherland against "Negroes, Ghurkas and all manner of barbarians
who have come from their hiding places all over the world and who are now
gathered at the borders of Germany, ready to lay waste to our country"
(Weber et al., 1994, p. 132) are statements characteristic of Weber's political
writings of the period. In the conclusion to his book on Weber and the
Polish question, Hajime Konno therefore noted that "observing and judging
people *from the vantage point of the West* seems to have been Weber's
lifelong method" (2004, p. 200, my translation).

Subsequent scholarship has however tended to differentiate between
Weber's political and his theoretical writings to the point of juxtaposing

his "nationalist politics" to his "cosmopolitan sociology" (Roth, 1993, p. 148), mostly on the basis of Weber's own postulate of value-freedom. However, in view of the particular (and particularistic) standpoint of Germanism that underlies both his theoretical and his political treatment of race and ethnicity – and at the same time belies his methodological postulate – Weber's sociology and politics can be shown to be closely intertwined. As Keith Tribe, calling for a reconstruction of Weber as a theoretician of power-politics, has noted in the 1980 introduction to the English translation of Weber's Freiburg address, "the question of power and the national state is one that retains a central importance until his death. The conditions under which this power is exercised, and the means adopted for the realization of a 'decisive national status' might alter, but the objects of this did not" (Tribe, 1980, p. 422f.). Accordingly, while Weber's approach to the Negro question in the United States might not derive in a straight line from his earlier treatment of the Polish question in Germany, one certainly is inextricable from the other, and an awareness of both is needed in order to understand his analysis of the nation (see also Chandler, 2007, p. 261).

That Weber's sociology should be so clearly indebted to narrowly defined and historically contingent cultural and political values underlying his notion of national identity has been alternatively seen as a reason for either discarding him as a classic (Abraham, 1992) or re-reading him as a neo-racist (Zimmerman, 2006). The use of a postcolonial sociology concerned with the blind spots of metropolitan theories might be of a more immediate practical nature: In revealing Weber's canonical treatment of ethnicity as not only culturally and historically contingent, but also politically committed to Germany's national interests and imperial designs, postcolonial critique proves sociological theory more generally as built upon unwarranted overgeneralization from a particular standpoint constructed as universal. The more obvious this becomes with regard to other canonized treatments of allegedly general – that is, unsituated, apolitical – social theory, the closer we are to a postcolonial sociology alert to both the structural absences and the potential emergences of necessarily situated knowledge.

ACKNOWLEDGMENT

This article was elaborated in the context of a book-length project on the postcolonial critique of classical inequality concepts (see Boatcă, 2013). I thank Julian Go and the two anonymous reviewers for their inspiring suggestions and comments on a previous version of this text.

NOTES

1. For a sociology of the shared histories of entangled modernities, see Randeria (1999), Randeria, Fuchs, and Linkenbach (2004) ; see also Bhambra (2007), Connell (2007), and Go (2009).

2. Unless otherwise indicated, the emphases in Weber's texts are found in the original.

3. However, Weber thought that the social dynamism instilled by the logic of market competition under capitalism could mitigate the tendency toward bureaucratization. This would in turn be more difficult under socialism, which promoted its own, even larger bureaucratic apparatus, thus placing the worker under the "dictatorship of the official" (Weber, 1994, p. 292). The emergence of a "closed caste" of functionaries, a fully rational, "organic social stratification," and social ossification might be the outcome, for "State bureaucracy would rule *alone* if private capitalism were eliminated" (Weber, 1994, p. 157).

4. Literally, "(medieval) estates." The discussion surrounding the inappropriate, but firmly established English translation of Weber's term *Stand* as "status group" is ongoing and too complex to be addressed here. For the sake of adequacy as well as consistency, I will however retain the German original throughout this text. For articles that deal with the wide-ranging implications of the historical decontextualization operated by the false translation, see, for example, Wenger (1980) and Böröcz (1997).

5. In light of recent scholarship on the manuscripts that Marianne Weber edited and published as *Economy and Society*, it has however been argued that it is improbable that Weber would have even agreed with its publication (Banton, 2007; Mommsen, 2005).

6. His definition of ethnic groups accordingly read: "We shall call 'ethnic groups' (*ethnische Gruppen*) those human groups that entertain a subjective belief in their common descent because of similarities of physical type or of customs or both, or because of memories of colonization or migration; this belief must be important for the propagation of group formation; conversely, it does not matter whether or not an objective blood relationship exists. Ethnic membership (*Gemeinsamkeit*) differs from the kinship group precisely by being a presumed identity, not a group with concrete social action (*Gemeinschaftshandeln*), like the latter" (Weber, 1920, p. 389, first and last German original added).

7. Weber himself neither coined nor ever used the word "ethnicity" (*Ethnizität*), which did not exist in his time, but referred instead to "ethnic commonality" (*Gemeinsamkeit*), "ethnic groups," and "ethnic communities," as explained above. In the English-language editions of his chapter on ethnic and race groups, first published in the late 1960s, these terms were nevertheless translated as "ethnicity," which not only confuses the term's history, but also obscures Weber's more differentiated treatment of the phenomena it encompassed. See also the entry on "ethnicity" in Swedberg, 2005, p. 92.

8. On the difficulty of pinpointing Weber's class habitus between the German bourgeoisie and the intelligentsia, see Steinmetz (2010, p. 243f).

9. Although Max Weber himself has later expressed misgivings about aspects of his lecture, they did not refer to his upholding of the German nation, which is the focus of the following summary (see Abraham, 1991, p. 47; Roth, 1993).

10. Weber was of course aware of the methodological short-circuit inherent in using religion as a proxy for nationality, but decided that "only approximate accuracy" is good enough in the case of West Prussia, where religious affiliation "coincides within a few percent with nationality" (1980, p. 429).

11. For an assessment of the significance of Weber's family history for a broader understanding of Weber's intellectual and political concerns, see Guenther Roth's 1993 review of volume 4 of the Max Weber Gesamtausgabe (Roth, 1993).

12. The same national political position would lead Weber to withdraw from the Pan-German League in 1899, arguing that its immigration-friendly policies toward Polish workers were subservient to agrarian capitalists (Roth 1993, p. 159, Zimmerman, 2006, p. 64).

13. For a detailed examination of Weber's views on cultural attitudes to work, see Schluchter (2000); for further examples of his treatment of the Negro question in this context, see Zimmerman (2006, p. 67f).

14. A detailed study of the possible intersections between Max Weber's and W. E. B. Du Bois' approaches on the Negro question against the background of Weber's early engagement with the Polish question in Germany has recently been undertaken by Chandler (2007).

15. Most commentators agree that Weber's use of the notion of *Herrenvolk* should not be mistaken for the National Socialists' subsequent misuse of Nietzsche's concept, even though it still has clear imperialist connotations. See the corresponding entry in Swedberg (2005, p. 111).

REFERENCES

Abraham, G. (1992). *Max Weber and the Jewish question. A study of the social outlook of his sociology*. Urbana, IL: University of Illinois Press.

Abraham, G. A. (1991). Max Weber: Modernist anti-pluralism and the polish question. *New German Critique, 53*, 33–66.

Abraham, G. (1992). *Max Weber and the Jewish question. A study of the social outlook of his sociology*. Urbana, IL: University of Illinois Press.

Banton, M. (2007). Max Weber on 'ethnic communities': A critique. *Nations and Nationalism, 13*(1), 19–35.

Bhambra, G. (2007). *Rethinking modernity. Postcolonialism and the sociological imagination*. Basingstoke: Palgrave Macmillan.

Boatcă, M. (2010). Multiple Europes and the politics of difference within. In H. Brunkhorst & G. Grözinger (Eds.), *The study of Europe* (pp. 49–64). Baden-Baden: Nomos.

Boatcă, M. (2013). Beyond classical concepts of social inequality. A postcolonial critique of global inequality and stratification, Farnham: Ashgate.

Boatcă, M., & Costa, S. (2010). Postcolonial sociology. A research agenda. In E. Gutiérrez Rodríguez, M. Boatcă & S. Costa (Eds.), *Decolonizing European sociology. Transdisciplinary approaches* (pp. 13–32). Farnham: Ashgate.

Böröcz, J. (1997). Stand reconstructed: Contingent closure and institutional change. *Sociological Theory, 15*(3), 215–248.

Chakrabarty, D. (2007). *Preface to the 2007 Edition: Provincializing Europe in global times* (pp. xi–xxi). *Provincializing Europe. Postcolonial thought and historical difference*. Princeton, NJ: Princeton University Press.

Chandler, N. D. (2007). The possible form of an interlocution: W. E. B. Du Bois and Max Weber in correspondence, 1904–1905. *The New Centennial Review*, 7(1), 213–272.

Connell, R. (2007). *Southern theory. The global dynamics of knowledge in social science*. Crows Nest: Allen & Unwin.

Fenton, S. (2003). *Ethnicity*. Oxford: Polity.

Go, J. (2009). The 'new' sociology of empire and colonialism. *Sociology Compass, 3,* 1–14.

Hesse, B. (2007). Racialized modernity: An analytics of white mythologies. *Ethnic and Racial Studies, 30*(4), 643–663.

Jackson, M. (1983). An analysis of Max Weber's theory of ethnicity. *Humboldt Journal of Social Relations, 10*(1), 4–18.

Konno, H. (2004). *Max Weber und die polnische Frage (1892–1920). Eine Betrachtung zum liberalen Nationalismus im wilhelminischen Deutschland*. Baden-Baden: Nomos.

Manasse, E. M. (1947). Max Weber on race. *Social Research, 14,* 191–221.

Mignolo, W. (2000). *Local Histories/Global designs. Coloniality, subaltern knowledges, and border thinking*Princeton, NJ: Princeton University Press.

Mommsen, W. (1974). *Max Weber und die deutsche politik 1890–1920*. Tübingen: Mohr/Siebeck.

Mommsen, W. (2005). Max Weber's "grand sociology": The origins and composition of Wirtschaft und gesellschaft. soziologie. In C. Camic, P. S. Gorski & D. M. Trubeck (Eds.), *Max Weber's economy and society: A critical companion* (pp. 70–97). Stanford, CA: Stanford University Press.

Mommsen, W. J. (1984). *Max Weber and German politics, 1890–1920*. Chicago, IL: University of Chicago Press.

MWG I/4. (1993). Landarbeiterfrage, Nationalstaat und Volkswirtschaftspolitik. Schriften und Reden 1892–1899. Herausgegeben von Wolfgang J. Mommsen in Zusammenarbeit mit Rita Aldenhoff 1. Halbband, XXI, 534 pp.

MWG I/8. (1998). Wirtschaft, Staat und Sozialpolitik. Schriften und Reden 1900–1912. Herausgegeben von Wolfgang Schluchter in Zusammenarbeit mit Peter Kurth und Birgitt Morgenbrod. XVII, 545 pp.

MWG I/10. (1989). Zur Russischen Revolution von 1905. Schriften 1905–1912. Herausgegeben von Wolfgang J. Mommsen in Zusammenarbeit mit Dittmar Dahlmann. XV, 855pp.

MWG I/11. (1995). Zur Psychophysik der industriellen Arbeit. Schriften und Reden 1908–1912. Herausgegeben von Wolfgang Schluchter in Zusammenarbeit mit Sabine Frommer. XII, 470 pp.

Quijano, A. (2000). Coloniality of power, eurocentrism, and Latin America. *Nepantla: Views from South, 1.3,* 533–574.

Randeria, S. (1999). Geteilte geschichte und verwobene moderne. In J. Rüsen (Ed.), *Zukunftsentwürfe. Ideen für eine kultur der veränderung* (pp. 87–96). Frankfurt a.M: Campus.

Randeria, S., Fuchs, M., & Linkenbach, A. (2004). Konfigurationen der moderne: Zur einleitung. In S. Randeria, M. Fuchs & A. Linkenbach (Eds.), *Diskurse zu Indien, sonderheft der "Sozialen welt"* (pp. 9–34). München: Nomos.

Roth, G. (1993). Between cosmopolitanism and eurocentrism: Max Weber in the nineties. *Telos, 96,* 148–162.

Roth, G. (2000). Global capitalism and multi-ethnicity. Max Weber then and now. In S. Turner (Ed.), *The Cambridge companion to Weber* (pp. 117–130). Cambridge: Cambridge University Press.

de Santos, B. S. (2004). A critique of the lazy reason: Against the waste of experience. In I. Wallerstein (Ed.), *The modern world-system in the longue durée* (pp. 157–197). Boulder, MA: Paradigm Publishers.

Said, E. (1978). *Orientalism.* New York, NY: Vintage Books.

Scaff, L. (1998). Weber's amerikabild and the African American experience. In D. McBride, L. Hopkins & C. Blackshire-Belay (Eds.), *Crosscurrents: African Americans, Africa, and Germany in the modern world* (pp. 82–96). Columbia: Camden House.

Schluchter, W. (2000). Psychophysics and culture. In S. Turner (Ed.), *The Cambridge companion to Weber* (pp. 59–80). Cambridge: Cambridge University Press.

Steinmetz, G. (2010). Feldtheorie, der deutsche kolonialstaat und der deutsche ethnographische diskurs 1880–1920. In M. Boatcă & W. Spohn (Eds.), *Globale, multiple und postkoloniale modernen* (pp. 219–261). Munich: Rainer Hampp Verlag.

Stender, W. (2000). Ethnische erweckungen. Zum funktionswandel von ethnizität in modernen gesellschaften-ein literaturbericht. *Mittelweg, 36*(4), 65–82.

Swedberg, R. (2005). *The Max Weber dictionary: key words and concepts.* Stanford, MA: Stanford University Press.

Tribe, K. (1980). Introduction to Weber. *Economy and Society, 9*(4), 420–427.

Turner, S. P. (1986). Weber agonistes. Review of Max Weber and German politics, 1890–1920. *Contemporary Sociology, 15*(1), 47–50.

Vernik, E. (2011). La cuestión polaca. Acerca del nacionalismo imperialista de Max Weber, Entramados y perspectivas. *Revista de la Carrera de Sociologia, 1*(1), 165–180.

Weber, M. (1920). Grundriss der Sozialökonomik, III. Abteilung. Wirtschaft und Gesellschaft, Tübingen: Mohr (Siebeck).

Weber, M. (1961). *General economic history.* New York, NY: Collier Books.

Weber, M. (1971). On race and society, translated by Jerome Gittleman, with an introduction by Benjamin Nelson. *Social Research, 38*(1), 30–41.

Weber, M. (1978). Economy and society. In G. Roth & C. Wittich, (Eds.), *An outline of interpretive sociology* (2 Vols.). Berkeley, CA: University of California Press.

Weber, M. (1980). The National state and economic policy (Freiburg address). *Economy and Society, 9*(4), 428–449.

Weber, M. (1988a). Die sozialen Gründe des untergangs der antiken kultur. In M. Weber (Ed.), *Max Weber: Gesammelte aufsätze zur sozial- und Wirtschaftsgeschichte.* Tübingen: Mohr (Siebeck).

Weber, M. (1988b). *Max Weber: A biography* (H. Zohn, Trans.) With an introduction by Guenther Roth. New Brunswick, NJ: Transaction Press.

Weber, M. (2005). In S. Kalberg (Ed.), *Readings and commentary on modernity.* Malden, MA: Blackwell.

Weber, M., Lassman, P., & Speirs, R. (Eds.). (1994). *Political writings.* Cambridge: Cambridge University Press.

Weindling, P. (1989). *Health, race and German politics between national unification and nazism, 1870–1945.* Cambridge: Cambridge University Press.

Wenger, M. G. (1980). The transmutation of Weber's Stand in American sociology and its social roots. *Current Perspectives in Social Theory, 1*, 357–378.

Zimmerman, A. (2001). *Anthropology and anti-humanism in imperial Germany*. Chicago, IL: University of Chicago Press.

Zimmerman, A. (2006). Decolonizing Weber. *Postcolonial Studies, 9*(1), 53–79.

Zimmerman, A. (2010). *Booker T. Washington, the German empire, and the globalization of the new south*. Princeton, NJ: Princeton University Press.

Zubaida, S. (2005). Max Weber's the city and the Islamic city. *Max Weber Studies, 5/6*, 111–118.

COMMON SKIES AND DIVIDED HORIZONS? SOCIOLOGY, RACE, AND POSTCOLONIAL STUDIES ☆

Zine Magubane

ABSTRACT

This essay uses the sociology of race in the United States (as it pertains to the study of African Americans) as point of entry into the larger problem of what implications and impact the body of theory known as "postcolonialism" has for American sociology. It assesses how American sociology has historically dealt with what the discipline (in its less enlightened moments) called the "Negro Problem" and in its more "enlightened moments" called "the sociology of race relations." The first half of the essay provides a sociological analysis of a hegemonic colonial institution – education – as a means of providing a partial history of how, why, and when American sociology shifted from a more "global" stance which placed the "Negro Problem" within the lager rubric of global difference and empire to a parochial sociology of "race relations" which expunged the history of colonialism from the discipline. The second half of the essay applies postcolonial literary theory to a series of texts written by the founder of the Chicago school of race relations, Robert Ezra Park, in order

☆Reprinted from *Postcolonial Sociology*, Political Power and Social Theory, Volume 24, 2013, pp. 81–116.

Postcolonial Sociology
Political Power and Social Theory, Volume 24, 77–112
ISSN: 0198-8719/doi:10.1108/S0198-8719(2013)0000024010

*to document Park's shift from analyzing Black Americans within a colonial
framework which saw the "Negro Problem" in America as an "aspect or
phase" of the "Native Problem" in Africa to an immigration/assimilation
paradigm that tenaciously avoided engaging with the fact that Black
resistance to conflict in America might be articulated in global terms.*

INTRODUCTION

Is a postcolonial sociology possible? Clearly, postcolonial theory has had a
profounder impact on literature, history, and anthropology than it has had
on sociology (Kemple & Mawani, 2009, p. 236). Why is this case? The
answers to this question are varied and complex, however, I see the
sociology of race as providing key insights into *why* it has been particularly
difficult for the perspectives of postcolonial criticism to penetrate into
American sociology as well as offering a point of entry for integrating those
perspectives into our discipline. Indeed, the lack of engagement between
postcolonial theory and race scholarship is particularly glaring. Christine
MacLeod concludes that "by and large, theorists and practitioners of
postcolonial criticism have tended to steer well-clear of African American
cultural politics" (1997, p. 51).

In this essay I use the sociology of race in the United States (as it pertains
to the study of African Americans) as point of entry into the larger
problematic of what implications and impact the body of theory known as
"postcolonialism" has for American sociology. Although all of the social
science disciplines have contributed to the collective body of knowledge on
race, it was only in sociology that studying race became "a full bodied
specialty" (McKee, 1993, p. 1). Given the centrality of race to postcolonial
studies it would seem that the sociology of race (particularly as it pertains
to African Americans) *should be* an obvious place where existing bodies
of sociological thought and research are compatible with postcolonial
theory. The ideas in DuBois' *The Souls of Black Folk* "fulfill the entire
definition of postcolonialism" (pp. 257, 268). Even more "mainstream" and
domestically focused African-American sociologists of race like E. Franklin
Frazier, Charles Johnson, and Horace Cayton or Robert Blauner's (1972)
idea of "internal colonialism" all carry strong postcolonial currents, as do
some contemporary sociologists of race. But the engagement between
critical race theory in sociology and postcolonial theory has been minimal
(Dorbin, 1999, pp. 117–118) and some have speculated that instead the

sociology of race has been "surpassed" by postcolonial studies (Henry, 1995, p. 650; see also Shohat, 1992, p. 108).

The sociology of race has not yet been surpassed by postcolonial studies but if it doesn't begin to take the insights of postcolonial theory more seriously, it might be. What, then, are the conditions of possibility for making the sociology of race "postcolonial"? A compelling place to begin bridging the divide between the sociology of race and postcolonial theory is by assessing how American sociology has historically dealt with what the discipline (in its less enlightened moments) called the "Negro Problem" and in its more "enlightened moments" called "the sociology of race relations." Indeed, the sociology of "race relations" would benefit from a postcolonial analysis of its own history – not unlike the one that R. W. Connell developed for the discipline at large in her pathbreaking article "Why is Classical Theory Classical."

Connell usefully divides the intellectual history of sociology into two discrete phases that are separated by an epistemic break. In the first, sociology was concerned with "global difference" and thus can be said to have been definitely "formed within the culture of imperialism and embodied a response to the colonial world." After the break, the concern with "global difference" was eclipsed by an obsession with "difference and disorder in the metropole" (1997, p. 1536). Yet, in the United States, after emancipation and prior to 1920, slaves and their descendents were *always already* simultaneously a "colonial problem" *and* the foremost examples of "difference and disorder in the metropole." After slavery was abolished and the established relationship between slaves and slave masters ruptured, Blacks moved to center stage in sociological thinking. The new social status of African Americans posed a unique set of theoretical circumstances on sociologists as they (along with America's political and civil leadership) began to give serious thought to the future of the four million emancipated slaves (McKee, 1993, p. 23). Blacks thus represented "the anomaly of an exclusion that was at once foundational to and located within the polity" (Singh, 2005, p. 22). In the first paper he ever published in the *American Journal of Sociology*, Robert E. Park included the text of a 1908 speech given in Richmond, Virginia where the author, Charles Francis Adams, said: "We are confronted by the obvious fact, as undeniable as it is hard, that the African will only partially assimilate and that he cannot be absorbed. He remains an alien element in the body politic. A foreign substance, he can be neither be assimilated nor thrown out" (Park, 1914, p. 610).

Park agreed with some of the points made by Holub and Adams but noted that in most colonies it was "possible to segregate the races and set them apart each in its own territory" whereas "in the United States the life of the Negro is so intimately interwoven with that of the white man that no such solution is possible" (1916, p. 305). Does this fact give American sociology's "cultural response" to the colonized world a different tenor? Did it alter the content or method of the newly emerging discipline? And what are the implications for how we understand the emergence of American sociology? For much of its history, Sociology "monopolized" empirical inquiry into the plight of African Americans. This empirical focus gave the discipline a distinct identity and legitimacy (Stanfield, 1985, p. 20). What is the significance, therefore, of the fact that in the 1920s, the time that Connell identifies with the epistemic shift, "sociology had established itself as the one among the social sciences most persistently committed to a social under-standing of race in American life" (McKee, 1993, p. 101)? Does this fact change how we think about this epistemic break? Does it alter how we conceive of how the American sociology of race fits into the making of the political culture of empire?

These questions can only be answered by marshalling the insights of postcolonial theory so as to do for sociology what Asad (1991, p. 315) called on his fellow anthropologists to do for their discipline: "Illuminate through [sociology] the aspects of the imperialist transformations of which this discipline was a small part." The bulk of this essay, therefore, is devoted to a sociological analysis of a hegemonic colonial institution – education – as a means of providing a partial history of how, why, and when American sociology shifted from a more "global" stance which placed the "Negro Problem" within the lager rubric of global difference and empire to a parochial sociology of "race relations" which expunged the history of colonialism from the discipline. If we understand how, why, and *when* the sociology of race began to suppress its transnational roots and "thrive analytically" on the "closure" provided by the nation state (Sassen, 2010, p. 3) we may also be able to discern how, when, and where the sociology of race began to delimit the study of African Americans in a ways that have helped to validate, produce, and reproduce the "exceptionalist premise" or the idea that United States' history can be neatly severed from any association with the world-systemic projects of racial and colonial domination.

Analyzing the writings and career of Robert E. Park, paying particular attention to the many years he spent working for and with Booker T. Washington, first at the Congo Reform Association (CRA) and later at Tuskegee Institute, provides an excellent entryway into thinking though these questions. We can easily document the epistemic shift that occurred within the sociology of race by tracing Park's career because, in many ways,

Park is *responsible* for the shift. Park began his career not only openly writing and speaking about the continuities between the race problem at home and colonialism abroad but he also played a role as a "consultant" to empire by building relationships between colonial officials from across the globe. Thus, he helped to create the conditions that his theory went on to describe. After arriving at the University of Chicago in 1914, however, Park stopped writing openly about his former "activist" life. Repudiating activism was a key part of the "distinction strategy" through which sociology marked its separation from social work and Park fully embraced it (Breslau, 1990). Indeed, as will be discussed below, Park successfully erased not only his own history of engagement with colonialism but that of the broader field of sociology as well.

EDUCATION, SOCIOLOGY, AND THE POLITICAL CULTURE OF EMPIRE, 1885–1914

Stocking (1991) uses the term "mythistorical archetypification" to describe how the scholarship produced about a discipline's "favored sons" and "founding fathers" divorces them from historical context so as to selectively suppress politically unpalatable aspects of their (and their disciplines') history. Many historians of sociology, when providing descriptions of Park's career and the path that led him to the University of Chicago, exhibit this tendency. Park is often given credit for having pioneered the use of empiricism in sociological race research and for the study of the city and race, as Park himself noted (Raushenbush, 1979). Lannoy, however, questions the dominant "narrative" about Park by asking: "Is it possible to see the ten years that Park spent in the rural South working for Booker T. Washington as a brief episode in Park's life to the point that [his writing] can be understood as a direct translation of his earlier journalist experience into sociological language" (2004, p. 37)? Park's own recollections seem to suggest otherwise. In an article published in *Social Forces* in 1941 Park reflected back on his long career. He unequivocally stated that "a man I knew longer and from whom I learned more than from any of my other teachers was Booker Washington" (1941, p. 40) Elsewhere Park remarked that, "I think I probably learned more about human nature and society, in the South under Booker Washington, than I learned elsewhere in all my previous studies" (quoted in Harlan, 1983, p. 291). Even those who see the importance of Park's relationship with Washington and time at the CRA and Tuskegee, disagree on how to interpret it: some see it as relevant and formative, others not (Connell, 1997, p. 1529; Matthews, 1973, p. 37; Steinberg, 2007, p. 55). What do we make of these competing claims?

Park, Liberal Imperialism, and the Congo Reform Association

Park began working for the American Congo Reform Association, of which Booker T. Washington was vice-president, in 1903. Washington subsequently hired Park as his publicist. Park eventually became a lecturer at Tuskegee. It might seem incongruous that a renowned conservative like Washington was involved in a protest organization of this type. However, as King (1971, p. 13) explains, "Washington's somewhat uncharacteristic approval of protest policies in Africa may largely be explained by his desire to show...that many classes of people, especially Negroes, were much worse off outside the United States." Park helped to publicize atrocities in the Congo "by enlisting the aid of prominent figures, lobbying with Congressmen for United States pressure on the Congo government, and writing a series of articles to be signed by notables" (Matthews, 1973, p. 38). Because Park denounced King Leopold's atrocities in the Congo many historians view him as a "radical" or at least very progressive. However, a closer analysis of what drew Park first to the Congo Reform Association and later to Tuskegee reveals that Park had a distinctively colonialist world view.

Park agreed with E. D. Morel, founder of the CRA, that there was "nothing inherently wrong with colonialism" (Hochschild, 1998, p. 213). Park criticized Leopold for being "hasty" and "ruthless" and expressed his regret that "the Congo native was treated as an alien in his own country and neither local spirit nor local custom was permitted to modify, mitigate, or humanize to any appreciable extent the stern logic of King Leopold's benevolent despotism" (1912a, p. 369). But he never suggested that colonialism itself was wrong. Indeed, in his paper, "Education by Cultural Groups," Park observed: "Africa must expect to serve a long and hard apprenticeship to Europe, an apprenticeship not unlike that which Negroes in America underwent in slavery" (1912a, p. 370). Just as Morel had suggested that the solution to the Congo atrocities was "not less colonialism, but more" (Zimmerman, 2010, p. 177), Park argued that "if the White man and his civilization is to rule the world his government must not be an oppression, the domination of mere stupidity and brute force but a control based on sympathy and understanding" (1906, p. 353).White rule in Africa would come in the form of a British and American led "civilizing mission" which "educated" rather than coerced Africans to labor. In this way Park was a firm proponent of "liberal exceptionalism" which "admits that the United States [is] an empire but insists that the empire [is] unique. While European empires were tyrannical and exploitative, American empire [is] beneficent and selfless" (Go, 2007, p. 75).

Morel contrasted "scientific colonialism" (which he saw Britain and the United States adopting) with "commercial colonialism" which he saw as characteristic of Belgian rule. Morel explained that the aim of "commercial colonialism" is the "rapid acquisition of the natural riches of the African tropics…by a combination of various forms of pressure which in the aggregate amount to compulsion" (1912, p. 355). Morel concluded that this type of economic compulsion was not only cruel to Africans, but more importantly, was economically inefficient and wasteful for European merchants (1912, pp. 358–359). The "scientific school" of colonialism, by contrast, was where colonizers embraced their "sacred obligation" to be economic and social "protectors and helpers" (1912, p. 361). Morel's firm belief that "what is morally right is economically sound" went hand in hand with his belief that Africans, despite being naturally lazy, were also the world's preferred workforce. He believed that blacks were natural workers who "because of inherent laziness needed outside force to realize their true natures" (Zimmerman, 2010, p. 168). His desire to see Africans educated, rather than coerced into manual labor, led him to appoint Booker T. Washington as vice-president of the CRA.

Park admired Cecil John Rhodes and considered going to South Africa to work for him before he accepted a position at the CRA. (Matthews, 1973). What did Park admire about Rhodes and what did he hope to do in South Africa? Park's own writings suggest that his interest in "native education" drew him to the CRA, Rhodes, and eventually Washington and Tuskegee.

> In the course of the campaign to arouse public opinion on the subject of the Congo natives, I sought out everyone in the United States who knew anything about the so-called Congo Free State and anyone else who could be interested in the fate of the natives there. It was in this way that I met Booker Washington. By the time I met him, however, I had become convinced that conditions in the Congo were not the result of mere administrative abuses. …I said something about my theory to Washington. I told him I believed the evils of Leopold's regime in the Congo were endemic, i.e., one of the more or less inevitable incidents of the civilizing process. He did not seem interested. His mind was essentially pragmatic and he was allergic to theories of any sort. When, however, I told him that I was thinking of going to Africa; that there was, I heard, an industrial school for natives, and that, if there was any solution of the Congo problem it would probably be some form of education, he invited me to come to Tuskegee. I went to Tuskegee to stay a few weeks, but I remained for seven years. (Park, 1941, p. 41)

What was the state of education for Africans in South Africa at this time
and what role did Rhodes play in providing it? The South African mission
school Lovedale Institute, which Park thought so highly of, was a strong
ally of Rhodes and threw its support behind his British South Africa
Company. The British South Africa Company was a chartered company
that enjoyed sweeping powers to govern large territories of illegally
expropriated African land. Rhodes was also the president of De Beers
Consolidated Mines and Consolidated Gold Fields, the largest corporation
in the world at the time. As Prime Minister of the Cape Colony Rhodes
authored the Glen Grey Act (1894) which established artificial chieftainships
and local "native authorities" to enforce colonial domination. The Act also
specified that Africans should be given "industrial training" as a way of not
only ensuring an adequate labor supply but also suppressing African
political dissent (Reilly, 1995, p. 107).

Rhodes' economic, political, and educational policies were interrelated.
He hoped to use industrial schools to create a small class of indigenous
rulers who were "not Westernized" but nevertheless sympathetic to colonial
rule. Their job would be to act as the indigenous arm of the colonial state
and clamp down on any "native dissent" (i.e., Indirect Rule) while teaching
Africans the "dignity" of labor by training them in the manual occupations
most suitable for the economic development of the colonial economy. On
July 30, 1894 during the second reading of the Act Rhodes gave a detailed
explanation of how differentiation in education would provide a steady
supply of African workers for the colonial labor force while also keeping a
check on their political aspirations:

> I propose to use the labour tax for industrial schools and training. I propose that the
> neglect of labour should provide a fund for instruction in labour. I have called them
> industrial schools, but I mean that they should be carried out under regulations to be
> framed by the Government. Why? I have travelled through the Transkei, and have found
> some excellent establishments where the natives are taught Latin and Greek.... There
> are Kaffir parsons everywhere – these institutions are turning them out by the dozen.
> They are turning out a dangerous class.... These Kaffir parsons would develop into
> agitators against the Government (Vindex 1900, p. 382).

In his speech, Rhodes references the full spectrum of issues that interested
Park, Morel, and Washington and captures the *raison d'être* of Hampton
Institute, Booker T. Washington's alma mater, as well as Tuskegee Institute,
the school Washington founded. Park believed that political domination
should be achieved through education of the colonized, rather than through
brute force. Since there was "no possibility of reversing this civilizing
process, and very little hope of slowing it up," Park concluded that

"education would prepare not merely the natives but the European invaders, as well, for the kind of world in which they were both inescapably destined to live" (Matthews, 1973, p. 41). What kind of world was that? Its main features were that it was segregated; Blacks were rural, rather than urban people; Blacks (in the colonies and at home) produced agricultural staples for export; Blacks should receive a special type of education which taught them simple handicrafts or farming; and rather than engage in political protest, Blacks should seek to "raise their standard of civilization" as a way of demonstrating their merit and earning the right to participate more fully in civil society.

Hampton and Tuskegee in the Political Culture of Empire

Mainstream historians of sociology tend to narrate its development with an often reverent posture to certain universities – Chicago, Columbia, Harvard, Wisconsin – which they credit with having developed and promoted our discipline. One of the key starting points for the construction of a postcolonial sociology lies in providing an alternative institutional history that demonstrates the role of segregated agricultural and industrial schools for Negroes in the South (the forerunners of contemporary Historically Black Colleges and Universities) in the evolution of our discipline. A number of insights from postcolonial theory are useful for recovering this hidden history. One is the idea that knowledge often circulates along imperial pathways. Imperial knowledge is located "not only within the bounds of nation states and in relationship to their subject colonized populations" but also travels "trans-nationally, across imperial centers" (Cooper & Stoler, 1997, p. 13). The education offered to the newly emancipated slaves in America clearly follows such a pattern. The degree to which the curriculum of Hampton and Tuskegee bore the influence of ideas about race, education, and citizenship that were developed in the wider colonial world makes them choice examples of what Sassen (2010, p. 4) calls "thick social environments that mix national and non-national elements." The type of education offered at Hampton and Tuskegee reflected the needs of an economic system that integrated Blacks into the lower levels of the economic structure while excluding them from exercising democratic privileges. Like other colonized people, African Americans had to be denied national status despite their central role in the national economy. As Williamson (1965, p. 276) explained: "separation was a means of securing the quasi-elimination of Negroes at home. It was, perhaps, a more

satisfactory solution than their demise or emigration since it might produce
many of the benefits of their disappearance without losing an advantageous,
indeed, a necessary supply of labor."

Hampton and Tuskegee were two of the first educational institutions in
America for emancipated slaves. Hampton was founded by Samuel
Chapman Armstrong, the son of Baptist missionaries. Armstrong's parents
began working in Hawaii in 1831 under the auspices of the American Board
of Commissioners for Foreign Missions. His father became minister of
public instruction in 1839 and Samuel often accompanied him on school
inspection rounds. Schools for indigenous people in Hawaii were run much
like schools for indigenous people in all the other colonies – manual labor,
simple agriculture, and religion were strongly emphasized for their civilizing
properties – and Armstrong was profoundly influenced by what he witnessed
there. At that time, the chief dilemma facing missionaries was this:
"How could [they] produce the needed indigenous leadership and technical
skills ... and at the same time avoid stimulating social, economic, and
political aspirations of upward mobility, urban migration, and assimilation
into western dominated colonial society" (Yates, 1984, p. 538)? Christian
missionaries settled on the idea of so-called "handyman industrial education" whereby converts would be given "simple skills that would bring
them an independent income within their own village." Having carpentry
skills would give the evangelist the "opportunity to meet people and spread
the religious message more widely" while simple industrial training "would
help to squelch the formation of a Europeanized intellectual elite" (Yates,
1984, p. 542; Talbot, 1969, p. 8).

After studying at Williams College, Armstrong joined the Army. After the
war ended, Armstrong took a job in the Freedman's Bureau with the
education department. He was responsible for overseeing 34 missionaries, 7
officers, and all matters relating to freedmen in 9 Virginia counties. During
this period, the U.S. government embarked on the project of founding
schools for newly emancipated slaves. The first task of these segregated
institutions was to bring about "racial order, political stability, and material
prosperity to the American South" (Anderson, 1978, p. 61). In 1868, with
the help of the American Board Mission, Armstrong founded Hampton
Institute. According to Armstrong's biographer, "as he meditated upon
the development of the plan, the Hilo Manual Labor School for Native
Hawaiians, which he had observed in his boyhood, often occurred to his
mind as an example of successful industrial education for an undeveloped
race" (Talbot, 1969, p. 155). Armstrong himself was quoted as saying that:
"It meant something to the Hampton School, and perhaps to the ex-slaves

of America, that, from 1820–1860, the distinct missionary period, there was worked out in the Hawaiian Islands, the problem of the emancipation, enfranchisement and Christian civilization of a dark-skinned Polynesian people in many respects like the Negro race" (Lindsey, 1995, p. 1). Armstrong went on to explain:

> The thing to be done was clear: to train selected Negro youths who should go out and teach and lead their people, first by example ... to give them not a dollar that they could earn for themselves; to teach respect for labor ... and to those ends to build up an industrial system for the sake not only of self-support and intelligent labor, but also for the sake of character (Talbot, 1969, p. 157).

Armstrong's experiences with "race management" in Hawaii gave him increased legitimacy in the United States, where similar experiments with providing industrial education to Whites had been dismal failures. In a letter to his mother, Armstrong lamented that, "I have to face the fact that a manual-labor school *never yet* succeeded in the North" (Talbot, 1969, p. 165). Knowing "the judgment that had been passed on [industrial education] by public opinion" Armstrong was careful to stress the success of the model abroad (Talbot, 1969, p. 158). As his biographer continues, "the Southerners could respect, if they could not love, an official with semi-foreign antecedents" (Talbot, 1969, p. 151). Thus, as a national institution, Hampton strongly bore the imprint of its colonial predecessors. Indeed, Hampton was partially supported by charitable donations grouped "with contributions to foreign missions" (Talbot, 1969, p. 224).

In 1880 Armstrong recommended that Booker T. Washington, a graduate of Hampton who eventually taught there, be named the leader of Tuskegee Institute, another industrial school for Blacks which was to be modeled on Hampton. Armstrong and Washington were very close (Washington, 1901/1996, p. 26). Armstrong put Washington in charge of the Native American students at Hampton. He also put him in charge of Hampton's night school. Washington described these experiences as having "helped to prepare me for my work at Tuskegee later" (Washington, 1901/1996, p. 49). Tuskegee opened on July 4, 1881.

In an 1895 speech at the Atlanta Exposition, Washington dealt explicitly with the problem of how to reconcile economic integration, social segregation, and political subordination. He was well aware that as Blacks were increasingly integrated into the economic life of the United States, their consciousness of racial oppression and their desires for political representation and redress were also increasing. Thus he took care to stress that economic cooperation would not lead to social or political integration.

> Our greatest danger is that in the leap from slavery to freedom we may overlook the fact that the masses of us are to live by the production of our hands, and fail to keep in mind that we shall prosper in proportion as we learn to dignify and glorify common labor and put brains and skill into the common occupations of life; shall prosper in proportion as we learn to draw the line between the superficial and the substantial, the ornamental gewgaws of life and the useful. No race can prosper till it learns that there is as much dignity in tilling a field as in writing a poem. It is at the bottom of life we must begin, not at the top.... Cast down your bucket where you are (Washington, 1901/1996, p. 107).

Robert Park shared Booker T. Washington and E. D. Morel's opinion that the world Hampton and Tuskegee made could and should be recreated in colonial Africa. Therefore, in addition to being Washington's publicist, Park worked closely with him to develop a strategy for taking the principles Washington outlined in his 1895 Atlanta Exposition address and making them the basis for British colonial rule in Africa.

Sociological Theory, Liberal Imperialism, and the "Negro Question"

When Park and other sociologists discussed the nature of the American race problem and its solution prior to the end of WWI, they didn't question the validity of placing America's race problem within a worldwide colonial dynamic. "Whenever the black man has met the white, whether in America or in Africa, a race problem has arisen" Park (1916, p. 304) explained. Sociologists felt that the race problem in the American South mirrored the race problems found in other colonies – particularly in Africa – where Whites were outnumbered and economies based on the export of agricultural commodities demanded new systems of labor compulsion. Park attributed the fact that "the little village of Tuskegee has become, within a comparatively few years, world renowned" to its being "situated in a part of the state where the Negroes outnumber the whites five to one" and having dealt "at first hand with a problem that touches the profoundest interests of life, moral, political and religious" (1906, p. 349). Thus a major task of sociological research was not only to "gather up the information yielded by the colonizing powers' encounter with the colonized world" (Connell, 1997, p. 1519) but also to apply that knowledge to the task of solving the "Negro Problem" or "Native Question" – "the most grave, the most complicated, and from certain points of view, the most fascinating problem the world has ever known" (Park, 1906, p. 349).

The "Negro Problem" gave sociologists like Park a research agenda. Thirty years after leaving Tuskegee Park reflected back on how his "seven winters at Tuskegee" functioned as "a sort of internship during which I gained a clinical and first-hand knowledge of a first class social problem" (1941, p. 41–42). Park drew from a wide range of data sources "on the processes that were slowly but inevitably changing Negro life and the South," including letters about which he "learned much about the race problem" (1941, p. 42). But he also sought to know the Negro "though their faces, their customs, and their cultures" (1941, p. 42). As such he observed the methods of teaching at Tuskegee which he described as "not only the most original but the most elemental and fundamental" he had encountered anywhere (1941, p. 42). For example, he eagerly attended the annual "Negro Farmer's Conference" sponsored by Booker T. Washington, which he later said provided the "most moving and informing" knowledge; and "more intimate, more suggestive and, at the same time, more actual than any formal investigation or report could possibly have been" (Park, 1941, p. 43).

Park always said he found Negro–White relations in the South to be a "laboratory" for assessing the processes and forms of interaction characteristic of races and social groups thrown into contact. "Among no other people is it possible to find so many stages of culture existing contemporaneously" he wrote (Park, 1919, p. 115). Because Tuskegee was "simply one point in the larger circle of Negro life which it connects" Park was able to travel to places like the Sea Islands, off the coast of South Carolina (Park, 1912a, p. 376). He described the people he saw there as "densely ignorant" with "quaint and curious customs" (1913a, p. 149). He also visited "remote parts of the black belt where the Negroes still lived very much as they did in slavery times" (1913a, p. 150).

Meeting Tuskegee students and residents in the neighboring towns provided ample opportunities to get know "the Negro's real character" (1906, p. 353). Park would go into private homes, observing what types of books, pictures, and artifacts they contained. He would look in cupboards to see what kind of food his informants ate. He asked them detailed questions about their budgets – how much they made and how much they spent. He would consult census records to ascertain the number of land owners. Park felt that "pure poetry, even gossip, so far as it reflects the dominant attitude of the races and parties involved, may furnish material for the student of race relations" (1924, p. 154). Therefore, he would ask residents about the history of their families and their plans for their children and through that learn about the history of the area. Park described meeting a "withered old man who proved to be the patriarch of the community" whose "memory went back to the time when the region was a wilderness." By questioning him Park was able to ascertain "the whole story of the pioneers in the region, the manner in which the land was cleared and settled and the history of every family in the settlement" (Park, 1913a, p. 149). A decade later Park published an essay in the *Journal of Applied Sociology* on the "Race Relations Survey" wherein he described this kind of life history which was an "anecdotal record of first-hand experience" as "the sort of material which throws most light upon race relations and the fundamental traits of human nature" (1923a, p. 164).

Another benefit of being at Tuskegee was that one could not only get "first hand and accurate information in regard to the Negro" but, more importantly, knowledge of "the best methods of dealing with him" (Park, 1906, p. 353). Park firmly believed that "sociologists cannot solve their problems by dialectics merely, nor by making programs for other people to carry out. Sociology must be empirical and experimental. It must, to use Booker T. Washington's expression, 'learn by doing'; it must explore, invent, discover, and try things out" (Park, 1941, p. 45). Park referred to Tuskegee as a "great experiment station" because it was possible to apply sociological theories to real world situations (Park, 1906, p. 352). The University of Chicago sociologist, W. I. Thomas, agreed:

> A backward race always tends to imitate the weaker side of what we are pleased to call civilization – its luxury, leisure, vices, and classical learning – and in Tuskegee we have an opportunity to see the Negro developed under a leadership which selects and presents sane copies. When the habits of a race are suddenly changed, when a backward race in particular is thrown on its own resources, there is some disorganization of habit. We saw this in the freedmen after emancipation. We have a striking example in Liberia and Hayti. The old habits are not adequate to meet the crisis, the new ones are not formed. We see here a backward race being put in possession of a technique adequate to meet the crisis (Thomas, 1912, p. 885).

Tuskegee was the ideal venue for assessing the real world implications of adapted education; a theory which held that the content and purpose of education should be determined by sociological analyses of society and the individual. Proponents of adapted education gave prominence to the "findings of sociology" which acted as a "guide for the development of citizenship" (Lybarger, 1981, p. 179). In 1896 Albion Woodbury Small, the first chairman of the first sociology department at the University of Chicago, argued that the primary purpose of education was to ensure the "adaptation of the individual to such cooperation with the society in which his lot is cast." The task of the educator, therefore, was to "promote the adjustment of individuals to their appropriate functions within the whole" (Small, 1897, p. 843). Franklin Giddings, the first occupant of the chair of sociology at Columbia University, shared this view (Giddings, 1901, p. 95; 1914, p. vii). Many years later Park reflected back on how intertwined the theoretical and applied facets of adapted education were. "The education which any state, territory, or citizen gives its citizens should be based upon an intimate acquantaince with, and upon systematic investigation of, local conditions. In this way education will not only be related to the life of the local community, but the experiment and research involved in the effort to adapt education to local conditions will be itself a contribution to our knowledge of education in general" (1932, p. 698).

Giddings, Park, and Small agreed that the purpose of sociological research was to identify the "defects" in the consciousness of subaltern populations. These defects determined the "needs" that education was designed to correct. It was thus that the theories of Small and Giddings about the development of the social mind had relevance for "Negro Colleges." "The argument that the social mind developed through progressively more complex stages, culminating in the Anglo-Saxon mode of consciousness [provided] a sociological warrant for viewing one end of public education as placing school children...in contact with Anglo-Saxon ideals in order that they might value and respect those ideals even if their people as a group had not reached the Anglo-Saxon level of civilization" (Lybarger, 1981, p. 175). According to Small, education enabled individuals to "enjoy a maximum share of the development which his state in social evolution is empowered to accomplish" (1897, p. 842). Giddings made virtually the same point in *The Principles of Sociology*:

> [T]he same amount of educational effort does not yield equal results when applied to different stocks. There is no evidence that the now extinct Tasmanians had the ability to rise. They were exterminated so easily that they evidently had neither power of resistance nor any adaptability. Another race with little capacity for improvement is the surviving North American Indian. Though intellectually superior to the negro, the Indian has shown less ability than the negro to adapt himself to new conditions. The negro is plastic. He yields easily to environing influences. Deprived of the support of stronger races, he still relapses into savagery, but kept in contact with the whites, he readily takes the external impress of civilization, and there is reason to hope that he will acquire a measure of its spirit (Giddings, 1914, p. 328).

Park agreed with Giddings and Small that "the main purpose of all real education was the same" and that "the final aim of education was not mere knowledge but intelligent action – conduct" (1906, p. 351). In other words, the goal of education was to make "good citizens" and "good citizens" were to be educated so that "the greater needs of society as determined by those in social and political power were always accorded preference" (Correia, 1993,

p. 137). His belief that schools existed to educate people to assume specific, predetermined patterns of social interaction led Park to write:

> In the first place, in a school that is supported by the state or the general public, it is expected that not merely the individual but the general public will benefit. If it were not so, if education were a mere luxury or refinement, like a taste for literature or olives, there would be no excuse for asking the state or the general public to support it (1912a, p. 371).

The assumption that guided the development of Hampton and Tuskegee's curriculum was that the purpose of education was to "adapt" Blacks to their "natural" environment – the rural South. As Park explained:

> One of the characteristic features of an industrial school, such as we find here and at Hampton, is that what is ordinarily called the school is based on and connected with the work of an industrial community. Now, the purpose and importance of an industrial community as a basis for a school, consist in this, that it brings pupils and teachers together in relations that are not only healthy and normal but more intimate and personal than would be otherwise possible. In a school like this, teacher and pupil alike, each in their different and several ways, are engaged in a common work with a common purpose: cultivating the soil, raising their own food supply, erecting their own buildings, students and teachers working and learning, side by side. To a very large extent the students and teachers have produced the materials – the lumber and bricks – and from these have constructed the buildings of the school. In the same way they produce and prepare the food stuffs which they consume. As a result of this common life and labor in this little industrial community each student is led to realize all the varied connections, economic, moral and social, which bind him to every other member of the community. It is an education in social life (1912a, pp. 374–375).

Park maintained that Tuskegee not only taught Blacks "the value of common and ordinary labor" but also compelled them to "look inward to consider his own fitness for the occupation he purposes to take up" and "look outward to consider the place and the practical importance of the kind of work he purposes to do." Park was emphatic that Blacks not view education as a quest for "social distinction" but rather "a means by which to make himself more useful to the community" (1912a, p. 371).

Park had not been gone from Tuskegee for half a decade when he published "Sociology and the Social Sciences" in *The American Journal of Sociology* wherein he explained what made sociology distinct from history, philosophy, economics, etc. In the paper Park asserts that "it is the very essence of the sociological method to be comparative" (1921, p. 423). Although Park did not set foot on African soil until after he retired (Matthews, p. 1973) simply being at Tuskegee gave him access to a wealth of comparative data to support his belief that "the problem of the American

Negro was merely an aspect of a phase of the native problem in Africa" (Park, 1941, p. 41).

Bourdieu and Wacquant have argued that the "social particularity of American society and its universities have been imposed, in apparently de-historicized form, upon the whole planet" as evidence of the "cunning" of American imperialist reason (1999, p. 41). Theories of race relations have been "tacitly (and sometimes explicitly) raised to the status of universal standard whereby every situation of ethnic domination must be analyzed and measured." This, they conclude is one of the "most striking proofs" of America's symbolic domination. The career of Robert Park provides important clues as to how this state of affairs came to be. George Steinmetz makes the point that "U.S. sociologists are typically critics of power rather than consultants to it" (2005, p. 340). This has not always been the case, however. Park not only routinely wrote about the analytical continuities between domestic and colonial racial projects but also acted as a "consultant" to empire, using his position at Tuskegee to shape educational policies for colonized peoples around the globe. Indeed, White sociologists like Park who were employed by "Negro colleges" were instrumental in helping to diffuse "practices and identities from the imperial core to the dominated peripheries" (Steinmetz, 2005, p. 340). Robert Park played a central role in making Tuskegee and Hampton international hubs where colonial elites could gather to discuss, debate, and exchange sociological knowledge – particularly around education and its role in "race management." "In teaching the world to deal helpfully with the Negro, Tuskegee has aided the United States in dealing profitably with the people in Porto Rico [sic], in the Philippines and has helped to soften the intercourse of the Western world not merely with the people of Africa but with every race of people in the world" Park wrote (1906, p. 353). He firmly believed that "Tuskegee, Hampton, and some of the other industrial schools in the South offer, perhaps, some suggestions as to the solution of the Negro problem in Africa" (1912a, p. 377).

Park was able to get even more comparative data as a result of the 1912 conference that he and Washington organized. "The International Conference on the Negro at Tuskegee" drew colonial officials and missionaries from throughout the British Empire. This was an idea that Park had been working on since 1905 when he wrote to Washington asking if he would "be willing to write an article recommending that the Powers in Africa, the missionaries and educators, come together in an international conference to devise means for the systematic and harmonious extension of industrial training in Africa" (Harlan, 1983, p. 275). In his letter announcing the conference Booker T. Washington said: "The object of calling this conference at Tuskegee Institute is to afford an opportunity for studying the methods employed in helping the Negro people of the United States, with a view of deciding to what extent Tuskegee and Hampton methods may be applied to conditions in other countries" (Frissell, 1912, p. 196). The Tuskegee conference could not have come at a more propitious time. The British colonial office and a number of missionary societies were starting to review their traditional education policies. Two years prior to the launch of the conference, in 1910, the first World Missionary Conference was held. Representatives of the major missionary societies met to discuss and begin to determine the form of education that best suited the evangelization of the colonies.

Park described the conference as "international in fact as well as in name." The delegates came from the "sections of the world where the Negro is most thickly settled and where the race question is more or less acute." The delegates were "experts and specialists, who by training and sympathy are giving themselves without reservation to unraveling the Negro question." Park was able to engage with and learn from "one hundred and twenty persons representing twenty one foreign countries and colonies, and nearly every mission board in this country, educational and otherwise, doing work among the Negroes" (Park, 1912b, p. 347). He heard from such luminaries as D. D. Martin of the Stewart Foundation for Africa, Dr. Cornelius H. Patton, Home Secretary for the American Board of Commissioners for Foreign Missions, and the Reverend Martin Westling of the Swedish Missionary Society who was based in the French speaking West African colonies and the director of education in Jamaica.[1]

The 1912 Tuskegee conference ultimately changed the trajectory of Park's career. Park met W. I. Thomas, a professor of Sociology at the University of Chicago, at this meeting. Thomas, who introduced himself as "probably the only man present whose father had been a slaveholder" presented a paper on "Education and Racial Traits" in which he argued: "The real problem is to adjust educational policy not to mental traits in the biological sense but to the grades of culture existing among the different races" (Thomas, 1912, p. 378). Thomas called Tuskegee "the most considerable educational invention of modern times" and urged that "this idea of Negro cultural centers be developed further" (Thomas, 1912, p. 385). Park and Thomas agreed on the importance of spreading the gospel of industrial education. At the urging of W.I Thomas, Albion Small invited Park to a position as a part time lecturer, giving a course on race relations (Breslau, 1990). Park left Tuskegee for the University of Chicago in 1913 but remained on the Tuskegee payroll for his entire first year there (Zimmerman, 2010).

Park's move coincided with the outbreak of WWI. The war changed both the nature of racial domination and Black resistance. Called upon to analyze a rapidly changing world, the object of Park's sociological research remained the same (Blacks in the United States) as did his methods of analysis. What changed, however, was the theoretical lens with which he viewed race conflict and resistance. Before coming to Chicago, Park's experiences at Tuskegee and the CRA supported his view that "the colonization of black people in America had important ramifications for the colonization of people of color elsewhere" (Carnoy, 1974, p. 299). However, confronted with the flip side of the idea that "solutions of the negro problem in Africa" could be found in "Tuskegee, Hampton, and some of the other industrial schools in the South" or, in other words, that Black resistance to oppression in the United States might *also* be articulated in transnational and global terms, Park abruptly shifted his theoretical focus (Park, 1912a, p. 377). Indeed, the work that Park produced at Chicago is as notable for what it *didn't say* as for what it did.

While Park's post-Tuskegee work continued to draw on his experience in the South for examples, he focused primarily on plantation life (1913b, 1914, 1918, 1919). Even in papers like "Education in Its Relation to the Conflict and Fusion of Cultures: With Special Reference to the Problems of the Immigrant, the Negro, and Missions" (1918) he drew only minimally on events at Tuskegee and never delved into Tuskegee's international dimensions. Despite his claim that Tuskegee gave him "clinical and first-hand knowledge of a first class social problem" he didn't refer to his experiences there in "Experience and Race Relations" or "A Race Relations Survey," articles that appeared in the *Journal of Applied Sociology* in 1923 and 1924.

Likewise, Park made no mention of African or African American newspapers in "The Natural History of the Newspaper," an article he published in *The American Journal of Sociology* in 1923. Park certainly knew about the existence of these newspapers because, in a relatively minor essay in a non-sociological journal, he referred to them (Park, 1923a, p. 297). According to Boahen, during this time there was a "mushrooming of newspapers in the [African] coastal urban centers" which were "full of

attacks on the colonial system" (Boahen, 1987, p. 68). And Marcus
Garvey's *Negro World* enjoyed a lot of popularity (King, 1971, p. 71). And
Park didn't mention or investigate the reciprocal relationship between the
spread of African-American papers to East Africa and the growing
popularity of Tuskegee amongst East Africans (King, 1971, p. 71).

In an essay on "The City," Park described the political machine and the
relationship between the boss and the ward captain as calling out "old tribal
virtues" which "approached the conditions of primitive society" (1915,
p. 603). He used the term "racial colonies" to describe areas where "individuals of the same race or of the same vocation" lived. He believed that
"every great city has its racial colonies" and noted that "135th Street in the
Bronx [is] where the Negro population is probably more concentrated than in
any other single spot in the world" (1915, pp. 581–582). But he didn't discuss
how the "racial colonies" of Harlem, the Bronx, and the South Side of
Chicago

> expanded with theaters, cabarets, restaurants, and a budding literary scene. Caribbean
> immigrants poured in, bringing new forms of music and poetry and espousing fresh
> political theories. Jazz sunk roots in Chicago's South Side, the black capital of the
> Midwest. Black theaters became popular. A black film industry developed. Black
> communities, including many in southern towns, launched publications modeled after
> the established and profitable *Chicago Defender*. The NAACP's *The Crisis* gained tens of
> thousands of readers. Black clubs and Masonic lodges attracted members. Black themed
> books drew healthy sales. The year saw the first manufacture of black dolls for children
> (McWhirter, 2011, p. 15).

Of all these events, Park gave the last one McWhirter mentions, the
manufacture of Black dolls, the most sustained theoretical attention. "The
new Negro doll was a mulatto with regular features slightly modified in
favor of the conventional Negro type. It was a neat, prim, well-dressed,
well-behaved, self-respecting doll. Later on, as I understand, there were
other dolls, equally tidy and respectable in appearance, but in darker
shades with Negro features a little more pronounced." Park concluded
that, "nothing exhibits more clearly the extent to which the Negro has
become assimilated in slavery or the extent to which he has broken with
the past in recent years than this episode of the Negro doll" (1914, p. 618).
Given his interest in immigrant communities and newspapers (his
dissertation was on *Crowd and Public*) and given the explosive impact
that papers were having in Africa and across the diaspora, why would
Park gave more space and attention to Black dolls than he did to Black
newspapers?

THE "CUNNING" OF PARK'S IMPERIAL REASON, 1914–1935

Postcolonial literary scholarship has shown that literature uses "coded language and purposeful restriction to deal with the racial disingenuousness and moral frailty at its heart" (Morrison, 1992, p. 6). This insight is equally useful for nonfiction texts. The scholarship of Robert Park, no less than the novels of Herman Melville or Joseph Conrad, can be mined for its lapses, evasions, and coded racial language. Toni Morrison argues that much of American literature is a coded response to or has emerged in conversation with "a dark, abiding, signing Africanist presence" (1992, p. 5). Park's post-Tuskegee work on race, nation, citizenship, and culture can be viewed in a similar light. Indeed, Park's scholarship exhibits a similar attitude with respect to the impact of Africans and African-Americans on American culture that Toni Morrison has identified in White American literary critics' assessment of African-Americans contribution to canonical literature.

> This knowledge holds that traditional, canonical American literature is free of, uniformed, and shaped by the four-hundred-year old presence of, first, Africans and then African-Americans in the United States. It assumes that this presence ... has had no significant place or consequence in the origin and development of that culture's literature. Moreover, such knowledge assumes that the characteristics of our national literature emanate from a particular "Americanness" that is separate from and unaccountable to this presence (Morrison, 1990, p. 5)

Stow Persons argues that the broader field of assimilation studies at Chicago was marked by its evasiveness. When it came to the problem of assimilation, "the need for precise definition and analysis incumbent upon a sociology with scientific pretensions presented difficulties which the Chicago school could never satisfactorily surmount. ...Park in particular used a number of synonyms for assimilation which only obscured his meaning" while Thomas' "theories of disorganization and reorganization skirted the problems of assimilation without coming to grips with them" (Persons, 1987, pp. 77–78). I would go a step further than Persons and argue that Park, in order to avoid acknowledging or discussing both Pan-Africanism and the "Africanist presence" in American life, engaged in what Morrison calls "coded language and purposeful restriction...significant and under-scored omissions and startling contradictions" (1992, p. 6).

One set of those omissions had to do with the events surround World War I. The war changed life for Blacks and Whites in the United States.

As DuBois observed, World War I cut off the supply of cheap foreign labor and, in response to the needs of Northern manufacturers, "the migration of Negro workers out of the South increased steadily." This migration was "opposed by illegal and legal methods," not least "lynching, burning, and murder" (DuBois, 1920/1986, p. 738). World War I also had a dislocating effect on the global color line. The war enabled America's and Europe's racial prejudices to play out on a global stage. The American officer corps were disproportionately recruited from white southerners. The racial distinctions of civilian life carried over into the military as "white NCOs spat 'nigger' and 'coon' at every opportunity" (Lewis, 1993, p. 535). Likewise, after the war, "Europe sharpened the distinctions between empire and republic by drawing a firm racial line between the nations and the colonies" (Stephens, 2005, p. 36). Black colonial nations were excluded from the discussions at Versailles and the 1919 League of Nations. Yet, at the same time, since the war was "a war of empire that incorporated troops from around the world, including black subjects in the United States and the colonial dependencies" (2005, p. 26), it was "first opportunity for extended contact between Africans and American Negroes" (King, 1971, p. 58). Many East Africans active in the burgeoning anti-colonial movement, "learnt of the existence of the large, predominantly Negro colleges in the United States from the West Indian and West African troops" (King, 1971, p. 69).

One result was an intensification and spread of Black anti-colonial nationalism, the rise of Pan-Africanism, and communism. Black subjects the world over felt the sting of these injustices during and after the war and "North American Negroes [began] their determined agitation for the rights of Negroes throughout the world, and particularly in Africa" (DuBois, 1965, p. 8). DuBois and others began agitating for a pan African Congress to be held in Paris during the Versailles Peace Conference. In August of 1920 the nations that had been excluded from the discussions at Versailles and the League of Nations sent their delegates to the Universal Negro Improvement Association Convention (UNIA) held in Madison Square Garden. It was one of the largest gatherings of African descent people the world had seen up to that point. Garvey, like many others of his generation, had been profoundly influenced by the "new nationalist languages of freedom sweeping over the European empires in the context of World War I" (Stephens, 2005, p. 84). The 1917 Bolshevik revolution made a "deep and lasting" impact on Black intellectuals and "became a motivating force for shaping an alternative vision of racial revolution" (Stephens, 2005, p. 37).

Park produced a number of essays during and after the War that dealt with nationalism, assimilation, and race relations. In an era where fierce public debates were raging about the relationship between race, nation, and culture, all of his essays can also be seen as grappling with the following questions: What is "American" culture? What is the "American" nation? And what role does race play in mediating them both? In Park's work, he struggles with competing ideals. Should community be imagined as having come into existence through national homogeneity? Should race and nation be linked together symbolically – mediated through and by the color of a people's skin? Yet the essays that Park produced between 1914 and 1931 (the year he retired from Chicago) demonstrate that he was caught between a desire to downplay the potentially disruptive impact of anti-colonialism, Pan-Africanism, and communism on domestic race relations – which required stressing the "Americaness" and national belonging of African-Americans – while avoiding the unpleasant possibility that American culture bore the distinct imprint of the Black people who had been living there since the 1600s.

The Return of the Repressed: Park on the "Africanist Presence" in American Culture

Park had no choice but to admit the longevity of Africans in the American nation. "The first Negroes were imported into the United States in 1619. At the beginning of the nineteenth century there were 900,000 slaves in the United States. By 1860 that number had increased to nearly 4,000,000. At that time, it is safe to say, the great mass of the Negroes were no longer, in any true sense, an alien people" (Park, 1914, p. 613). "The Negro in America today," Park admitted, "is less a race than a nationality, that it, a people of different ethnic strains – Negro mingled with Scotch, Irish, and Indian" (1919, p. 306). If it was indeed true that "in America it has become proverbial that a Pole, Lithuanian, or Norwegian cannot be distinguished in the second generation from an American born of native parents" (Park, 1914, p. 607) was that also true for the "Negro" with his "different ethnic strains"? And if so, what were the implications for "Whiteness" as an identity?

It is this very issue that seems to haunt Park and no doubt played a part in his inability to acknowledge that American culture had also absorbed "Africanist" elements – biologically and socially. Park's unwillingness to concede that African-Americans were outside the U.S. nation (and therefore potentially sympathetic to Bolshevism and Pan-Africanism) or that they were Americans (and therefore that American culture also bore a distinct imprint of their heritage) were the reasons he embraced the "coded language and purposeful restriction" that Morrison identified as the favored mechanism by which American writers have dealt with the "racial disingenuousness and moral frailty" that lies in the nation's heart (Morrison, 1992, p. 6).

McKee points out that "for American sociologists, who were still concerned with the transition from agrarian to industrial, and also rural to urban, as well as with the integration of peasant immigrants from rural Europe, the typologies struck a sensitive nerve. They spoke to an American sociological concern – the development of the United States as a fully modern society – in a way that at the time had no counterpart in Europe" (1993, p. 104). Immediately upon leaving Tuskegee (but while still on Washington's payroll) Park began writing about this problem. He published the essay, "Racial Assimilation in Secondary Groups with Particular Reference to the Negro," in *The American Journal of Sociology* in 1914. Four years later "Education in Its Relation to the Conflict and Fusion of Cultures: With Special Reference to the Problems of the Immigrant, the Negro, and Missions," appeared in the *Publication of the American Sociological Society*. One year later (1919) he published "The Conflict and Fusion of Cultures with Special Reference to the Negro" in *The Journal of Negro History*.

Park was immediately confronted with the problem of what type of conceptual vocabulary he should use to describe cultural and racial mixture because it fed directly into the problem of to what extent American culture itself was a mixture of European and African elements. Park used Charles H. Cooley's definition of primary and secondary groups and his definition of assimilation emphasized that, due to slavery, alien peoples could be incorporated or "absorbed" into a community or state (1914, p. 611). Although he maintained that "slavery has been, historically, the usual method by which peoples have been incorporated into alien groups" Park cannot seem to decide whether Black–White relations are an instance of "individualistic groups where the characteristic relations are indirect and secondary" or "primary groups where relations are direct and personal" (1914, p. 612, 610). At times Park makes Black–White relations instances of primary relations – that is, akin to family – but introduced the caveat that the "intimacy" of the relations differed according to whether the Blacks in question were "field" or "house" Negroes. "The Negro in the southern states, particularly where he was adopted into the household as a family servant, learned in comparatively short time the manners and customs of his master's family" Park wrote (1914, p. 612). In a later essay he reiterated the point that "the plantation population, in spite of differences of race and status, constituted what I have described as a we-group. This was conspicuously the case of the members of the families and the house servants, between whom a lifelong intimacy existed" (1928, p. 235). He contrasted this state of affairs with that of "the assimilation of the Negro field hand, where the contact of the slave with his master and his master's family was less intimate [and whose] assimilation was naturally less complete" (Park, 1914, p. 612). He concluded, however, that "in the case of the Negro after his importation to America, assimilation followed rapidly and as a matter of course" (1914, p. 612). In Park's theoretical schema, Black–White relations on the plantations were, at the very least, a combination of primary and secondary relationships which became primarily secondary after the "intimacy" of the plantation was broken by the Civil War and Reconstruction. "When the Negro moved off the plantation upon which he was reared he severed the personal relations which bound him to his master's people. It was just at this point that the two races began to lose touch with each other. From this time on the relations of the black man and white, which in slavery had been direct and personal, became every year, as the old associations were broken, more and more indirect and secondary" (1919, p. 616).

By making the master-slave relationship (prior to Emancipation) one of "primary" relations with all the intimacy which that implies, Park also suggests that the American family – or at the very least the Southern family – is marked by its cultural and biological absorption of "Africanist" elements. As a result of these processes of "absorption" there were "a considerable number of Negro men and a larger number of Negro women in the Negro race who could easily and do occasionally pass for white" (Park, 1919, p. 305). The "mulatto slaves," Park acknowledged, "were sometimes the children of their master" (1931, p. 388). He described how children "respond to a black or yellow face as readily as they do to a white, depending upon the character and intimacy of the association" and how "in the South, it is a mark of distinction to have had a 'black mammy'" (Park, 1928, p. 237).

Park's extended contacts with African-Americans gave him some inkling of what fragments and memories of African culture still existed in slave communities. He described having spoken to "an old man living just outside of Mobile who was a member of what was known as the African colony. This African colony represented the cargo of one of the last slave ships that

was landed in this country just at the opening of the war. The old man
remembered Africa and gave me a very interesting account of the way
in which he was captured and brought to America" (1918, p. 269; 1919,
p. 118). He also discussed the "Sea Island Negroes" who spoke a "distinct
dialect" and retained "certain customs which [were] supposed to be of African
origin" (Park, 1919, p. 121).

Park was willing to admit biological amalgamation (but only saw it being
transmitted in one direction, that is, Whiteness being infused into Blackness).
His approach to culture was identical. In order to avoid grappling with the
unpleasant possibility that Blacks may have made a substantial contribution
to the making of America's national culture, Park proclaimed that "the
amount of African tradition which the Negro brought to the United States
was very small. In fact, there is every reason to believe, it seems to me, that
the Negro, when he landed in the United States, left behind him almost
everything but his dark complexion and his tropical temperament."
Admitting that the fact "seemed remarkable" he nevertheless maintained
that there were "but two African words that have been retained in the
English language" despite the fact that "slaves were still brought into the
United States clandestinely up to 1862" (1918, p. 267; 1919, p. 116). Park
concluded that, "the fact that the Negro brought with him from Africa so
little tradition which he was able to transmit and perpetuate on American soil
makes that race unique among all peoples of our cosmopolitan population"
(1918, p. 269; 1919, p. 118).

"With Special Reference to the Negro": Park on Assimilation and of Pan-Africanism

Park's discomfort with the idea that the amalgam that was American culture
had to contain "Africanist" elements, was matched by his discomfort with
the idea that the radical anti-colonial and Bolshevist elements that were
sweeping the globe would leave their imprint on African-Americans who, by
his own admission, were "gradually, imperceptibly, within the larger world
of the white man [forming] a smaller world, the world of the black man"
(Park, 1919, p. 617). Park agreed that African-American race consciousness
ran "parallel with the nationalist movement in Europe" and that "the
motives that have produced nationalities in Europe are making the Negro in
America, as Booker Washington says, 'a nation within a nation'" (Park,
1919, p. 621).

While Park seemed to take account of the fact that, particularly after World War I, the principle of national self-determination not only created several new nations in Europe but also had a profound impact on African descent peoples around the globe, he was especially hesitant to acknowledge the possibility that Blacks in America were cultivating loyalties to a worldwide black community that went above and beyond the American nation. Park consistently overlooked opportunities to engage with the varied internationalist forms that Black nationalism was taking, even though he had been aware of their existence since the 1912 Tuskegee conference. At the time Park observed that the Conference was having a salutary effect on African nationalism. "In W. Africa, the announcement of the Conference seems to have given a new impetus to the sentiment in favor of an African nationality, which is stirring in the back of the black man's head, in that part of the world. This is indicated by the numerous letters that were received from the leading natives. One of these was from Mr. Casely Hayford, a native barrister at law, at Sekondi on the Gold Coast, the author of *Ethiopia Unbound*, perhaps the first book written by a native to give expression to the sentiment of African nationality" (1912b, p. 117). The 1912 conference had also hosted representatives of "Negro churches in the South [who] are now sending missionaries to Africa" and Park received letters from the representatives of the Ethiopian Church in South Africa (Park, 1912a, p. 350). At this time Black Americans were beginning to try to realize their "long-frustrated desire" to "work on equal terms with whites for the improvement of the peoples of Africa" (King, 1971, p. 59).

Despite his prior knowledge of all of this and the events happening outside his door, Park's theoretical response was to try to dismiss any grounds for African-American engagement or connection to Africa, deemphasize any connection between racism at home and colonialism abroad, and insist on a model of national inclusion for the Black subject capable of maintaining the fiction that American culture did not bear any "Africanist" traces. It was thus that Park came up with the rather strange formulation that, when it came to Blacks in America, their "temperament is African but the tradition is American" (1919, p. 130).

In an essay on "The Conflict and Fusion of Cultures with Special Reference to the Negro" Park began with the rather disingenuous claim that the paper was "mainly concerned with the Negro, *not because the case of the Negro is more urgent than or essentially different from that of the immigrant,* but *because the materials for investigation are more accessible*" (1918, p. 263; 1919, p. 112, emphasis mine). Park then embarked on a series of intellectual maneuvers that would allow him to reverse the position he adopted in his 1914 essay, "Racial Assimilation in Secondary Groups with Particular Reference to the Negro" wherein he argued that the United States had been able to "swallow and digest every sort of normal human difference except the purely external ones, like color of skin" (p. 608) and that Blacks were "condemned to remain among us an abstraction, a symbol, and a symbol not merely of his own race but [of] that vague, ill-defined menace" (p. 611). Instead, Park insisted that Blacks were like other immigrants. The 1919 paper argued the exact opposite of what Park argued in an essay published only two years before which described African-Americans as "bound to live in the American community a more or less isolated life" and placed them "in a category different from that of the European immigrant"(1917, p. 229). Park went so far as to try to make the plantation a sort of "Ellis Island" where "each fresh arrival seems to have been much like that of the older immigrant towards the greenhorn. Everything that marked him as an alien was regarded as ridiculous and barbaric" (1919, p. 117).

Although the various Pan-Africanist movements stressed the common experiences of disenfranchisement and racism that linked African descent people around the globe, Park focused on the fact that Blacks had "lost under the disintegrating influence of the American environment much of their cultural heritage." He declared that Black Americans had been "utterly cut off and estranged from their ancestral land, traditions, and people" (Park, 1919, p. 118). Park went to considerable lengths to discount the possibility that, for Black Americans, ethnic nationalism and internationalism might not be mutually exclusive categories. "The Negro is, by natural disposition, neither an intellectual nor an idealist, like the Jew, nor a brooding introspective, like the East African," Park wrote. Park contrasted Jews who were "natural born idealists, inter-nationalists, doctrinaire, and revolutionist" with Blacks who "because of [their] natural attachment to known familiar objects, places, and person, [were] pre-adapted to conservatism and to local and personal loyalties" (1919, p. 130).

In "Race Prejudice and Japanese-American Relations," Park acknowl-edged the "barriers which formerly separated the races and nationalities of the world" had been broken down and replaced by "new intimacies" (1917, p. 225). He did not, however, mention African-Americans in that essay. In fact, he didn't discuss Pan-Africanism until 1923, in an essay on "Negro Race Consciousness as Reflected in Race Literature" that appeared in the *American Review*. "Emancipation has made the Negro free, but it had not made him in the full sense of the word, a citizen" Park wrote. "This has been and still is the enigma of thee Negro's existence" (Park, 1923b, p. 291). In this essay Park noted that "the American Negro no longer conceives his destiny has bounded by the limits of the United States. He is seeking alliances and creating loyalties that transcend the boundaries of our American commonwealth. The Negro in his racial relationship at least, is internationalist. He is becoming a citizen of the world" (1923b, p. 298). He also noted that "The unrest which is fermenting in every part of the world has gotten finally under the skin of the Negro. The Negro is not only becoming a radical, but he is becoming a Bolshevist, at least in spots." However, two years later Park still described the Negro as "just emerging and still a little afraid of the consequences of his newly acquired race consciousness" (1925, p. 677).

Park gave very little attention to the different forms that Black internationalism was taking. He never devoted an entire scholarly essay to the topic. Nor did he ever fully engage the issue in a mainstream sociological journal, preferring, instead, make oblique references. In a 1926 essay on "Our Racial Frontier in the Pacific" he slipped in a reference to the fact that the "continuous expansion of international communication and international politics [meant that] race relations have ceased to be a domestic problem. The rigid enforcement of racial distinctions at home leads 'oppressed' races to seek alliances abroad. The First Universal Races Congress, in London, in 1911, is an instance. The Pan-African Congress, which followed, is another. Race has in recent years come to be what religion has always been since the dawn of Christianity, an interest, which divides and unites people irrespective of national boundaries" (1926, p. 145–146). However, for the most part, Park held fast to his position "Negroes, in their struggle for equal opportunities, have the democratic sentiment of the country on their side" (1914, p. 622) and that "one of the greatest hardships the Negro suffered in this country was due to the fact that he was not permitted to be patriotic" (Park, 1919, p. 131).

Park always maintained that so-called "Mulattoes" were the "cultural advanced guard" and "center and focus of the intellectual life of the whole Negro race" (1931, p. 538). He insisted that these "natural leaders" had no allegiance or loyalty to Africa whatsoever. In an essay on "The Mentality of Racial Hybrids" he returned to the question of Pan-Africanism and concluded that "the Black man might dream of a return to Africa, to the land of his fathers, in order to set up there an independent state where he might work out his own salvation and that of his race. But such a future could not appeal with the same force to the mixed blood, particularly since his father was in most instances a white man" (1931, p. 548).

CONCLUSION

Sociology's analytic dependence on the "closure" provided by the nation state, coupled with the ubiquity and strength of the ideology of American exceptionalism, poses distinct challenges the sociology of race's postcolonial project. Racist and white supremacist appeals have been analyzed primarily as matters of "intra-national cultural projection about the boundaries of communal belonging" (Singh, 2005, p. 29). Likewise, for the most part, analyses of anti-racist resistance have also reinforced the idea that these struggles reside securely within the boundaries and history of U.S. political culture. The dominant theoretical paradigms in sociological race scholarship have been constructed so as to "write over" and "erase" not only the essential truth of the continuities in global and domestic racial projects but also sociology's active role in creating them.

If sociologists are to avoid repeating the mistakes of the past, they need to spend more time critiquing it. Over a decade ago, R. W. Connell correctly pointed to the fact that "sociologists take accounts of their origins seriously" (1997, p. 1512). We need to revisit our origins with an eye toward uncovering not only our discipline's role in the making of the colonial world but our discipline's active attempts to conceal that fact. In this essay I focused on the history of the education given to the colonized people of Africa and the diaspora because it is intimately bound up with both the history of American sociology, the history of domestic racism toward African Americans, and the history of British colonialism in West, South, and East Africa. In tracing the continuities between domestic and foreign racial projects I wanted to take Steinberg's (2007, p. 50) basic insight that sociology as a "racial ontology" even further and show that sociology evolved out a colonial racial ontology – thus putting a distinctly colonial gloss on Stanford Lyman's claim that "to trace the black man in American sociology is tantamount to tracing the history of American sociology itself" (1972, p. 15).

The first step along the journey of thinking through the ways in which colonialism operates as the "constitutive outside" of our discipline is to revisit and re-examine the histories of those scholars who have given our discipline "identity finding focus" in order to mine them for hidden histories and new insights (Connell, 1997, p. 1514). This essay has taken one of them, Robert Park, but there are many others who need similar kinds of treatment. Park was not the only sociologist who spent time at Tuskegee or crossed paths with Booker T. Washington. Max Weber, Friedrich Toennies, W. I. Thomas, and Thomas Jesse Jones all did as well. Historian Andrew

Zimmerman (2010, p. 186) has argued that Tuskegee Institute "played an important role in the development of sociology on both sides of the Atlantic." He is not the first to make such a claim. Two decades before him, historian John Stanfield (1985) declared that Booker T. Washington should be considered one of the founders of the Chicago school of race relations. More than a decade before that, historian Fred Matthews argued that "the sociology produced [at Tuskegee] became the scientific sociology of the 1920s and 1930s" (Matthews, 1973, p. 64). Thus far these studies have been done by historians, rather than historical sociologists. Therefore, they don't have an appreciation for (nor do they really engage with) the theoretical debates that had the most impact and influence on the field of sociology. Further work in this area is vital and important and will provide a much needed bridge between postcolonial studies and sociology.

Another important avenue of research which will further illuminate the colonial ontology of our discipline is to delve far more deeply into the colonial connections that that lay behind and went into the making of some of our discipline defining texts. One example that comes to mind is *The Protestant Ethic and the Spirit of Capitalism*. After Max Weber visited Tuskegee in 1904 he completed the second half of *The Protestant Ethic and the Spirit of Capitalism*. He had gone to Tuskegee to draw lessons from it for his own scholarly work. Historian Andrew Zimmerman suggests that *The Protestant Ethic* "treats a problem similar to that addressed by Tuskegee Institute, namely, what makes people work." He also points out that the text, which deals with the inner compulsion of European Protestants to work, "suggests the necessity of an external compulsion for all others" and proposes "an economic theory based on collective ethnic or cultural behavior rather than on the individual rationality of classical economics" (2010, p. 212).

Another example might be E. Franklin Frazier's *Black Bourgeoisie*. Frazier was a member of the Council on African Affairs, an organization which "insisted that 'our fight for Negro rights here [United States] is linked inseparably with the liberation movements of the people of the Caribbean and Africa and the colonial world in general'" (Von Eschen, 1997, p. 20). Frazier also directed the Division of Applied Social Sciences at UNESCO from 1951–1953. According to Platt, Franklin wrote *Black Bourgeoisie* "sitting in cafés in Paris" and the book was first published in France as part of a series called Recherches en sciences humaines (1991, p. 145). *La bourgeoisie noire* was discussed at the First Negro Congress of Writers and Artists in Paris in 1956. Fanon presented a paper "Racism and Culture" at the same meeting. Franklin could not attend the meeting but sent a message to the attendees. In his book *The Sexual Demon of Colonial Power: Pan-African Embodiment and Erotic Schemes of Empire*, Literary Critic Greg Thomas suggests that the "institutional screening of their most profound political insights [has] obscured the imperative of coupling Fanon and Frazier, thinking them together rather than apart, for purposes of both comparison and contrast" (2007, p. 51). Thomas concludes that the "domestication of [Franklin's] increasingly international consideration of class surely has contributed to this separation of intellectual kin" (2007, p. 71).

> A Conference of Negro Writers and Artists is of special importance at a time when a world revolution is in progress which will mark a new epoch in the history of mankind. This revolution is the culmination of changes which were set in motion by the…political expansion of Europe which resulted in the dominance of the Europeans over the other peoples of the earth (quoted in Thomas, 2007, p. 71).

Investigating the impact that Frazier's experience in France had, his pan-Africanist ties, and the reception of his work abroad are all topics that await the expertise of a postcolonial historical sociologist.

Finally, fascinating work is being done in the field of American studies about how "internationalist anticolonial discourse was critical in shaping black American politics and the meaning of racial identities and solidarities" in the immediate post WWI (Von Eschen, 1997, p. 2). Much more work can and should be done about how sociologists like E. Franklin Frazier, Charles S. Johnson, and Horace Cayton responded to this. This radical posture was subsequently eclipsed by "a dominant civil rights argument of the Cold War era, that discrimination at home must be fought because it undermined the legitimate U.S. leadership of the 'free world'" (Von Eschen, 1997, p. 3). Nikil Pal Singh suggests another interesting path of inquiry that could and should be taken up by postcolonial race scholars. Singh makes the provocative claim that "solving the 'Negro problem' at home" both affirmed the underlying theory of American nationhood and also proved that the United States was "the world's greatest democracy, whose ability to harmonize the needs of a heterogeneous population fitted it to be the broker of the world's security concerns and aspirations for social progress" (2005, p. 136). Making race relations an object of study can be and has been "offered as a vindication of the thesis that the United States, despite its failings, was equipped to mediate intra-national and supranational claims for social justice and civility" (Singh, 2005, p. 148). Sociologists clearly played a key role here and our discipline awaits further analysis of how the export, circulation, and subsequent universalization of America's sociological racial theories and practices played a role in the social processes Singh describes.

Kemple and Mawani (2009, p. 36) argue that, "we still need to write a 'history of the present' which would include a history of sociology itself." An important first step lies in acknowledging that sociology, no less than anthropology, literature, or history, shaped and was shaped by the colonial encounter. If there is any sub-field of Sociology where the "imperial unconscious" exists, it is in the sociology of race. It is there that we find not only sociology's "colonial gaze" but also the "epistemic reverberations" of our active attempts to elide and repress this aspect of our collective history.

NOTE

1. In addition to colonial officials, Tuskegee was also a popular destination for international students (Zimmerman, 2010, p. 182). Washington and Park expressed their hope that these students could give them "much valuable information as to the actual needs in the countries from which [they] come" (Park, 1912b, p. 349).

REFERENCES

Anderson, J. (1978). The Hampton model of normal school industrial education, 1868–1900. In V. Franklin & J. Anderson (Eds.), *New perspectives on black educational history* (pp. 61–96). Boston, MA: G.K Hall and Co.

Asad, T. (1991). From the history of colonial anthropology to the anthropology of colonial hegemony. In J. Clifford & G. Marcus (Eds.), *Writing culture*. Berkeley, CA: University of California Press.

Blauner, R. (1972). *Racial oppression in America*. New York, NY: Harper & Row.

Boahen., A. (1987). *African perspectives on colonialism*. Baltimore, MD: Johns Hopkins University Press.

Bourdieu, P., & Wacquant, L. (1999). On the cunning of imperialist reason. *Theory, Culture, and Society, 16*, 41–58.

Breslau, D. (1990). The scientific appropriation of social research: Robert Park's human ecology and American sociology. *Theory and Society, 19*, 417–446.

Carnoy, M. (1974). *Education as cultural imperialism*. London: Longman.

Connell, R. W. (1997). Why is classical theory classical? *American Journal of Sociology, 102*, 1511–1557.

Cooper, S., & Stoler, A. (1997). *Tensions of empire: Colonial cultures in a bourgeois world*. Berkeley, CA: University of California Press.

Correia, S. (1993). *For their own good: An historical analysis of the educational thought of Thomas Jesse Jones*. PhD Thesis. The Pennsylvania State University.

Dorbin, S. (1999). Race and the public intellectual: A conversation with Michael Eric Dyson. In G. Solson & L. Worsham (Eds.), *Race, rhetoric and the postcolonial* (pp. 81–126). Albany, NY: State University of New York Press.

DuBois, W. E. B. (1965). *The world and Africa*. New York, NY: International Publishers.

DuBois, W. E. B. (1920/1986). Science and empire. *W.E.B. DuBois: Writings*. New York, NY: The Library of America.

Frissell, H. (1912). Forty-fourth annual report of the principal. *The Southern Workman, 41*(May), 295–316.

Giddings, F. (1901). *Democracy and empire*. New York, NY: Macmillan.

Giddings, F. (1914). *The principles of sociology: An analysis of the phenomena of association and of social organization*. New York, NY: Macmillan.

Go, J. (2007). The provinciality of American empire: 'Liberal Exceptionalism' and U.S. colonial rule, 1898–1912. *Comparative Studies in Society and History, 49*, 74–108.

Harlan, L. R. (1983). *Booker T. Washington: The wizard of Tuskegee, 1901–1915*. New York, NY: Oxford University Press.

Henry, P. (1995). Sociology: After the linguistic and multicultural turns. *Sociological Forum, 10*(December), 633–652.

Hochschild., A. (1998). *King Leopold's ghost*. New York, NY: Houghton Mifflin.

Kemple, T. M., & Mawani, R. (2009). The sociological imagination and its imperial shadows. *Theory, Culture & Society, 26*, 228–249.

King, K. (1971). *Pan-Africanism and education: A study of race philanthropy and education in the southern states of America and East Africa*. London: Oxford University Press.

Lannoy, P. (2004). When Robert E. Park was (re)writing 'the city': Biography, the social survey and the science of sociology. *The American Sociologist, 35*(1), 34–62.

Lewis, D. L. (1993). W.E.B. DuBois: Biography of a race. In F. T. Struck (Ed.), *Foundation of industrial education*. New York, NY: Henry Holt and Company.

Lindsey, D. (1995). *Indians at Hampton Institute, 1877–1923*. Urbana, IL: University of Illinois Press.

Lybarger, M. (1981). *Origins of the social studies curriculum: 1865–1916*. PhD Thesis. University of Wisconsin, Madison, WI.

Lyman, S. (1972). *The black American in sociological thought*. New York: G.P. Putnam.

MaCLeod, C. (1997). Black American literature and the postcolonial debate. *The year book of English studies, 27*, 51–65.

Matthews, F. H. (1973). Robert Park, Congo reform, and tuskegee: The making of a race relations expert, 1905–1913. *Canadian Journal of History, 8*, 37–65.

McKee, J. B. (1993). *Sociology and the race problem: The failure of a perspective*. Urbana, IL: University of Illinois Press.

McWhirter, C. (2011). *Red summer: The summer of 1919 and the awakening of black America*. New York, NY: Henry Holt.

Morel, E. D. (1912). The future of tropical Africa. *The Southern Workman, 41*(June), 353–362.

Morrison, T. (1992). *Playing in the dark: Whiteness and the American literary imagination*. New York, NY: Viking.

Park, R. (1906). Tuskegee and its mission. *The Colored American Magazine, 14*, 347–354.

Park, R. (1912a). Education by cultural groups. *The Southern Workman, 41*, 369–377.

Park, R. (1912b). The international conference on the Negro. *The Southern Workman, 41*, 347–352.

Park, R. (1913a). Negro home life and standards of living. *Annals of the American Academy of Political and Social Science, 49*, 147–163.

Park, R. (1913b). Racial assimilation in secondary groups: With special reference to the Negro. *Publication of the American Sociological Society* VIII (p. 66–83). Reprinted in R. Ezra Park (Ed.), *Race and Culture: Essays in the Sociology of Contemporary Man* (pp. 204–220). New York: Free Press.

Park, R. (1914). Racial assimilation in secondary groups with particular reference to the Negro. *American Journal of Sociology, 19*, 606–623.

Park, R. (1915). The city: Suggestions for the investigation of human behavior in a city environment. *American Journal of Sociology, 20*, 577–612.

Park, R. (1916). A review of black and white in the southern states: A study of the race problem in the united states from a South African point of view by Maurice S. Evans. *The Journal of Political Economy, 24*, 304–306.

Park, R. (1917). Race prejudice and Japanese-American relations. Being 'Introduction' to J.F. Steiner, *The Japanese Invasion* (Chicago A.C. McClurg), p. vii–xvii. Reprinted in R. Ezra Park (Ed.), *Race and Culture: Essays in the Sociology of Contemporary Man* (pp. 223–229). New York: Free Press.

Park, R. (1918). Education in its relation to the conflict and fusion of cultures: With special reference to the problems of the immigrant, the Negro, and missions. *Publication of the American Sociological Society, 8*(3), 38–63. Reprinted in R. Ezra Park (Ed.), *Race and culture: Essays in the sociology of contemporary man* (pp. 261–283). New York, NY: Free Press.

Park, R. (1919). The conflict and fusion of cultures with special reference to the Negro. *The Journal of Negro History, 4*, 111–133.

Park, R. (1921). Sociology and the social sciences. *American Journal of Sociology, 26*, 401–424.

Park, R. (1923a). A race relations survey: Suggestions for a study of the oriental population of the pacific coast. *Journal of Applied Sociology, VIII*, 195–205. Reprinted in R. Ezra Park (Ed.), *Race and Culture: Essays in the Sociology of Contemporary Man* (pp. 158–165). New York, NY: Free Press.

Park, R. (1923b). Negro race consciousness as reflected in race literature. *American Review, 1*, 505–515. Reprinted in R. Ezra Park (Ed.), *Race and culture: Essays in the sociology of contemporary man* (pp. 284–300). New York, NY: Free Press.

Park, R. (1924). Experience and race relations: Opinions, attitudes, and experience as types of human behavior. *Journal of Applied Sociology, 9*, 18–24. Reprinted in R. Ezra Park (Ed.), *Race and culture: Essays in the sociology of contemporary man* (pp. 152–157). New York, NY: Free Press.

Park, R. (1925). Community organization and the romantic temper. *Social Forces, 3*, 673–677.

Park, R. (1926). Our racial frontier on the Pacific. *Survey Graphic, IX*, 192–196. Reprinted in R. Ezra Park (Ed.), *Race and culture: Essays in the sociology of contemporary man* (pp. 138–151). New York, NY: Free Press.

Park, R. (1928). The bases of race prejudice. *The Annals, CXXXX*, 11–20. Reprinted in R. Ezra Park (Ed.), *Race and culture: Essays in the sociology of contemporary man* (pp. 230–243). New York, NY: Free Press.

Park, R. (1931). Mentality of racial hybrids. *American Journal of Sociology, 36*, 534–551.

Park, R. (1932). The university and the community of races. *Pacific Affairs, 5*, 695–703.

Park, R. (1941). Methods of teaching: Impressions and a verdict. *Social Forces, 20*, 36–46.

Persons, S. (1987). *Ethnic studies at Chicago, 1905–1945.* Urbana, IL: University of Illinois Press.

Platt, A. M. (1991). *E. Franklin Frazier reconsidered.* New Brunswick: Rutgers University Press.

Raushenbush, W. (1979). *Robert E. Park: Biography of a sociologist.* Durham: Duke University Press.

Reilly, J. D. (1995). *Educating the other.* Unpublished doctoral dissertation, University of Connecticut, Storrs, CT.

Sassen, S. (2010). A new sociology of globalization. *Global Review, 1,* 3–4.

Shohat, E. (1992). Notes on the postcolonial. *Social Text, 31/32,* 99–113.

Singh, N. (2005). *Black is a country: Race and the unfinished struggle for democracy.* Cambridge: Harvard University Press.

Small, A. (1897). Some demands of sociology upon pedagogy. *American Journal of Sociology, 2,* 839–851.

Stanfield, J. H. (1985). *Philanthropy and Jim Crow in American social science.* London: Greenwood Press.

Steinberg, S. (2007). *Race relations: A critique.* Palo Alto, CA: Stanford University Press.

Steinmetz, G. (2005). Return to empire: The new U.S. imperialism in comparative historical perspective. *Sociological Theory, 23,* 339–367.

Stephens, M. (2005). *Black empire: The masculine global imaginary of Caribbean intellectuals in the United States, 1914–1962.* Durham: Duke University Press.

Stocking, G. (1991). *Colonial situations: Essays on the contextualization of ethnographic knowledge.* Madison, WI: University of Wisconsin Press.

Talbot, E. (1969). *Samuel Chapman Armstrong: A biographical study.* New York, NY: Negro Universities Press.

Thomas, W. I. (1912). Education and cultural traits. *The Southern Workman, 41*(June), 378–386.

Thomas, G. (2007). *The sexual demon of colonial power: Pan-African embodiment and erotic schemes of empire.* Bloomington, IN: Indiana University Press.

Vindex. (1900). *Cecil Rhodes: His political life and speeches.* London: Chapman and Hall.

Von Eschen., P. M. (1997). *Race against empire: Black Americans and Anticolonialism, 1937–1957.* Ithaca, NY: Cornell University Press.

Washington, B. T. (1901/1996). *Up from slavery.* New York, NY: Buccaneer Books.

Williamson, J. (1965). *After slavery: The Negro in South Carolina during reconstruction, 1861–1877.* Chapel Hill, NC: University of North Carolina Press.

Yates, B. (1984). Comparative education and the third world: The 19th century revisited. *Comparative Education Review, 28,* 533–549.

Zimmerman, A. (2010). *Alabama in Africa: Booker T. Washington, the German empire, and the globalization of the New South.* Princeton, NJ: Princeton University Press.

THE VIOLENCES OF KNOWLEDGE: EDWARD SAID, SOCIOLOGY, AND POST-ORIENTALIST REFLEXIVITY ☆

Jeffrey Guhin and Jonathan Wyrtzen

ABSTRACT

As a fountainhead of postcolonial scholarship, Edward Said has profoundly impacted multiple disciplines. This chapter makes a case for why sociologists should (re)read Edward Said, paying specific attention to his warning about the inevitably violent interactions between knowledge and power in historic and current imperial contexts. Drawing on Said and other postcolonial theorists, we propose a threefold typology of potential violence associated with the production of knowledge: (1) the violence of essentialization, (2) epistemic violence, and (3) the violence of apprehension. While postcolonial theory and sociological and anthropological writing on reflexivity have highlighted the former two dangers, we urge social scientists to also remain wary of the last. We examine the formation of structures of authoritative knowledge during the French Empire in North Africa, the British Empire in India, and the American interventions in Iraq and Afghanistan during the "Global War on Terror," paying close attention to how synchronic instances of

☆ Reprinted from *Postcolonial Sociology*, Political Power and Social Theory, Volume 24, 2013, pp. 231–262.

Postcolonial Sociology
Political Power and Social Theory, Volume 24, 113–144
ISSN: 0198-8719/doi:10.1108/S0198-8719(2013)0000024015

apprehension (more or less accurate perception or recognition of the "other") and essentialization interact in the production of diachronic essentialist and epistemic violence. We conclude by calling for a post-orientalist form of reflexivity, namely that sociologists, whether they engage as public intellectuals or not, remain sensitive to the fact that the production and consumption of sociological knowledge within a still palpable imperial framework makes all three violences possible, or even likely.

"Perhaps the most important task of all would be to undertake studies in contemporary alternatives to Orientalism, to ask how one can study other cultures and peoples from a libertarian, or a nonrepressive and nonmanipulative, perspective. But then one would have to rethink the whole complex problem of knowledge and power" (Said, 1994 [1979], p. 23).

WHY SOCIOLOGISTS SHOULD (RE)READ EDWARD SAID

Few books have impacted as many fields as dramatically as Edward Said's *Orientalism*, first published in 1978. Commenting on the book's effect on the secular study of Islam, Richard C. Martin wrote that "A single book changed the meta-discourse on what we were doing and what we should be doing" (2010, p. 903). Anthropologist Nicholas B. Dirks agreed, calling *Orientalism* "one of the most critical books for the reconceptualization of anthropology in the second half of the twentieth century" (2004, p. 23). The book also changed how scholars discuss an area no longer called "the Orient" (Martin, 2010, p. 903) helping scholars of other regions break out of a Eurocentric perspective and solidifying the postcolonial theory Said "is said to have created" (Brennan, 2000, p. 583; see also Gandhi, 1998, p. 25). Perhaps due to Said's own disciplinary location, much postcolonial theory has come from and dramatically affected the academic study of literature in the United States, though Said hoped an emphasis on theory would not overshadow a commitment to humanism, a theme to which he repeatedly returned in his later years (Said, 2000). Weathering prominent political criticism from Marxists (Ahmad, 1992; Nigam, 1999; O'Hanlon & Washbrook, 1992) and neoconservatives (Lockman, 2004) alongside rebuttals by anthropologists (Lewis, 1998; Richardson, 1990; Varisco, 2004) Middle East Studies scholars (Irwin, 2006; Lewis, 1982), and other area specialists (Rice, 2000), the book continues to have a significant impact across multiple disciplines.

But, its influence is barely felt in sociology departments. With some exceptions (Bhambra, 2007; McLennan, 2003; Salvatore, 1996; Steinmetz, 2007; Turner, 1974, 1978), sociologists have paid much less attention to *Orientalism* than fellow academics in humanities, areas studies, and anthropology. We see four primary reasons why sociology – both as a discipline and in its specific work with "foreign" cultures – could profit from a deeper interrogation of Edward Said's oeuvre. First, Said warns sociologists about the inevitably violent interactions between knowledge and power. Second, like many culturally sophisticated sociologists (e.g., Adams, 2005; Gorski, 2003; Steinmetz, 2007), Said recognizes the value of poststructuralist critiques without giving up hope for representational claims. Third, Said provides a powerful example of reflexive, public scholarship that draws from poststructuralist critiques; and fourth, we believe that, via Said, such a reflexive, public sociology could provide a valuable partner to post-colonial theory itself, which often makes use of sociological data, methods, and theory.

In the following discussion, we first revisit Said to develop a threefold typology of potential violences – essentialist, epistemic, and apprehensive – involved in the production of knowledge. We then turn to empirical cases of social scientific research conducted within the framework of French, British, and American empire to analyze the processes through which these violences of knowing interact over time to produce authoritative structures of knowledge such as the orientalist episteme targeted by Said. Having engaged and extended Said's warnings about the imbrication of knowledge and power, we conclude by proposing a post-orientalist reflexivity that is (1) acutely aware of the potential dangers of producing knowledge within a particular field of power and (2) strives to preserve a relative degree of autonomy while producing knowledge about "others" of great interest to policy makers.

THE VIOLENCES OF KNOWLEDGE

One of Said's primary contributions is his insistence on, and exegesis of, the fundamental relationship between knowledge and power, specifically the imbrication of knowledge with empire. Even "the estimable and admirable works of art and learning" Said analyzes in *Culture and Imperialism* are at the same time connected "with the imperial process of which they were manifestly and unconcealedly a part" (1993, p. xiv). If this is so for novelists like Dickens and Austen, then it is certainly even truer for those, including social scientists, who explicitly study "the Orient" or any other peoples who can be controlled. Said's *Orientalism* was intended as a direct rebuke to "the general liberal consensus that 'true' knowledge is fundamentally non-political (and conversely, that overt political knowledge is not 'true' knowledge) [which] obscures the highly if obscurely organized political circumstances obtaining when knowledge is produced" (Said, 1994 [1978], p. 10). Therefore, to be "a European or an American" who studies the Orient "means and meant being aware, however dimly, that one belongs to a power with definite interest in the Orient" (*ibid.*, p. 11).

Said's use of the word power draws, at different moments, from Gramsci's concept of cultural hegemony and Foucault's understanding of power as rooted within discourse. Both Gramsci and Foucault ably demonstrate how power is essentially about *violence*, particularly if violence is understood as the coercion of body and mind. Much of Said's and other postcolonial theorists' attention has focused on the latter, what Bourdieu refers to as "symbolic violence which is not aware of what it is" (1991 [1982], pp. 51–52). Said's work exposes the essentialist and epistemic levels of symbolic violence involved in the production of knowledge in an imperial relation between observer and observed. These are necessarily related to a civilizing project often carried out explicitly within educational settings that marked "the Englands, Frances, Germanys, Hollands as distant repositories of the Word" (Said, 1993, p. 223) which contained objective truth not only about the whole world but about the colonized's own selves. Said quotes Fanon: "for the native, objectivity is always directed against him." (*ibid.*, p. 258). This Nietzschean take on truth was even more fully developed in *Orientalism*, in which Said writes that "Orientalism was…a system of truths…in Nietzsche's sense of the word… My contention is that Orientalism is fundamentally a political doctrine willed over the Orient because the Orient was weaker than the West, which elided the Orient's difference with its weakness" (Said, 1994 [1978], p. 204).

Gayatri Spivak coined the term "epistemic violence" to refer to the power-knowledge configuration expressed in Orientalism, stating the "clearest possible example of [it] is the remotely orchestrated, far-flung, and heterogeneous project to constitute the colonial subject as Other. This project is also the asymmetrical obliteration of the trace of that Other in its precarious Subject-ivity" (Spivak, 1998, pp. 280–281). Her specific example of this is "a narrative of codification" via "the legitimation of the polymorphous structure of legal performance, 'internally' noncoherent and open at both ends, through a binary vision" (*ibid.*, p. 280). Spivak shows how "the British study of Indian history and languages led to the stabilization and codification of Hindu law" (*ibid.*, p. 282) which, alongside the British establishment of an intermediary class of English-educated natives, allowed "an explanation and narrative of reality [to be] established as the normative one" (*ibid.*, p. 281). Spivak then uses the concept to show how the subaltern – looking at the specific case of women who self-immolated on their husbands' funeral pyres – "cannot speak" (*ibid.*, p. 308). They cannot speak not because of their obvious absence from the academic elite writing about them (though that is certainly relevant) but because their means of speaking and understanding the world has been irrevocably changed by those in power. Even resistance to *suttee* (which Spivak points out does not actually mean bride-burning, though it has come to) is inescapably marked by colonialism and a desired return to a "tradition" which only came to exist as a result of colonial knowledge. "The case of *suttee* as exemplum of the woman-in-imperialism would challenge and deconstruct the opposition between subject (law) and object-of-knowledge (repression) and mark the place of 'disappearance' with something other than silence and nonexistence, a violent aporia between subject and object status" (*ibid.*, p. 306).

While a lot of the attention in the postcolonial canon has been focused on the essentialist and epistemic violences associated with the production of knowledge, it bears emphasizing that much of the violence involved in the colonial encounter was (and is) more than "symbolic"; colonial violence was by no means all in their heads. Said himself repeatedly insisted that knowledge produced about the "other" was then used to subjugate and control the material bodies and lands of colonized peoples. The use of knowledge to enact physical – and not just psychological – violence is a lacuna that can be too easily ignored by emphasizing the long-term processes of epistemic violence. Conceptualizing and categorizing the social reality of the "other" involves a complex nexus of symbolic and material realities.

We distill, from Said's and other postcolonial theorists' warnings, three overlapping forms of violence at risk in producing knowledge in an imperial field of power. It is important to note that each of these violences comes from forms of knowledge which might or might not be violent in and of themselves, but which *all* hold the potential for enabling acts of violence.

1. The first of these, which we are calling *the violence of essentalization*, involves a misrecognition in which essentialized, ahistorical categories and labels are used to classify the other and then to potentially enact physical and psychological violence upon them. Such essentialization is

central to Said's argument in *Orientalism*, which primarily focuses on the interrelated representational violence within the Western "cultural archive" that builds off and reinforces misrecognition, "seeing the essentialized orientality of the Orient" (Said, 1994 [1978], p. 255).

2. The second, and related, danger is what Spivak refers to as "*epistemic violence*" (1998, pp. 282–283) referring to a process in which Western forms of knowing, including social scientific concepts and categories, preclude or destroy local forms of knowledge. The "voice" of the subaltern is silenced a priori because its means of speaking has been replaced.

3. We would add a third type of violence, rarely focused on within postcolonial theory: *the violence of apprehension*. This applies to research that avoids the dangers of binarism or generalization intrinsic to essentializing and epistemic violences. We warn that even more or less accurate apprehension (or a laying hold of knowledge) of the "other" through careful and nuanced research retains a potential violence. It can still be used directly and indirectly to consolidate power and to enact physical and symbolic violence on the "other."

TIME AND THE VIOLENCES OF KNOWLEDGE

A critical distinction among the three violences of knowledge is their temporal dimension. The epistemic violence expressed in a structure of authoritative knowledge described by Fanon, Spivak, Said, Bourdieu, and others necessarily involves a diachronic process, with categories, classifications, and identities becoming naturalized and internalized over time. The violence of essentialization, in contrast, can happen synchronically at a single instance; it also works diachronically, where a series of repeated essentializations lead to persistent stereotypes. Apprehension also usually happens synchronically, with more or less accurate knowledge of the other gained in discreet increments. Once it is added to the authoritative knowledge structure, however, it inevitably contributes over the *long durée* to epistemic violence.

The essentialist violence described by Said necessarily relies on a diachronic evolution of forms of knowledge about the Oriental other, but can also entail synchronic instances of violence in which essentialized categories and typologies inform decision and policy-making in real ways leading to concrete acts of violence. Said's overarching structure of authoritative knowledge – what Foucault would call an episteme and what Said is calling Orientalism – is a force with causal power, and one of its results is a longstanding, diachronic pattern of epistemic violence, violence which is created by and creates synchronic moments of essentialization. This essentialization is necessarily violent because of the violent nature of mis-recognition itself (Fanon, 2004 [1963]) and contributes to a pattern of epistemic violence that is inseparable from longstanding structures of oppression. In conjunction, the violence of essentialization and epistemic violence affect both the observer and the observed, the dominator and the dominated, and in the still too real context of empire, the colonizer and the colonized (King, 1990; Nandy, 2010).

Said and other postcolonial scholars have been rightly concerned about what we are calling the structure of authoritative knowledge, but have less explicitly theorized the process by which the orientalist episteme is produced. By attending to the interaction of the three violences of knowledge over time, it is possible to more accurately account for the possibilities and dangers of knowledge about the "other." Where do the essentializations and binary categories that form Orientalism's building blocks come from? We contend postcolonial critiques of epistemic and essentializing violence have under-theorized the symbolic and very real physical risks of what we have labeled the violence of apprehension. While essentialist forms of knowledge might have been outright lies, it seems possible that some are based upon what were at least initially more or less accurate descriptions of at least *some* members of the community being represented. When we talk about the more or less accurate knowledge involved in the violence of apprehension, we do not mean a positivist, pre-interpretive perception of the "way things really are" so much as a careful, nuanced approximation of heterogeneous social life derived from rigorous field or archival work. More or less accurate does mean access to "truth"; it just means better than the sorts of false binaries one could make up from one's armchair.

This more optimistic epistemology is fundamental to the postcolonial critique: essentializations are problematic because they are *not true* (even if this assumption has often gone somewhat unacknowledged as it risks reeking of positivism). Spivak defends herself from such a charge in her article, arguing that her intention "is not to describe 'the way things really were'" (1998, p. 281) even though it seems she is doing exactly that, or, at the very least, describing how certain historical narratives were the way things *really weren't*, which might be the best a deconstructionist can do. Said is less apologetic about righting the historical record, and he devotes the latter two books of the "Orientalism trilogy" – *The Question of Palestine* (1979) and *Covering Islam* (1981) to showing how wildly wrong Western media and intellectuals have been about Palestine, the Middle East, and Islam.

In later writings, Said acknowledges that an Orientalist critique based on a straightforward power motive, for example, that Europe wants to dominate the Orient and produces whatever forms of knowledge necessary to achieve that goal, is simply too simple. He acknowledges that "Even the mammoth engagements in our own time over such essentializations as 'Islam,' the 'West,' the 'Orient,' 'Japan,' or 'Europe' admit to particular knowledge and structures of attitude and reference, and those require careful analysis and research" (Said, 1993, p. 52). Said does not deny that Orientalist research could produce "a fair amount of exact positive knowledge about the Orient" (Said, 1994 [1978], p. 52). The problem *was not that all of the knowledge was wrong*. The problem was what "accurate" knowledge was used to accomplish synchronically and what it fed into diachronically. In discreet moments, more or less accurate knowledge will be used by those in power as a tool to more effectively implement violent action. When fed into larger, diachronic structures, this violence of apprehension almost inevitably results in epistemic violence and the violence of essentialization. Our warning about the violence of apprehension does not presume a positivist representation of social life. Interpretation is obviously necessary. However, certain interpretations are clearly stronger than others, and that strength is adjudicated by gathering more or less accurate data to support interpretive claims (Reed, 2011).

We are particularly interested in how small synchronic moments of data gathering help empires to consolidate epistemic power and solidify certain interpretations. The perfect example of this sort of data gathering is what Foucault documents in his work, particularly *Discipline and Punish* (1995 [1977]) and *A History of Sexuality* ((1990 [1976]). The focus on small measurements of prisoners' and confessors' daily lives is exactly the sort of "accurate" knowledge that is then fed into larger epistemes, contributing to both the violence of essentialization and epistemic violence. In a similar way, social scientists might gather knowledge about Muslim women in an Egyptian religious movement (Mahmood, 2005), African-American students in an urban high school (Fordham, 1996), or the relationship between AIDS activists and medical research (Epstein, 2006): in each of these cases, there is a marshaling of evidence to make a certain interpretive argument, and both the synchronic moments in themselves and the larger arguments they compose can be used by the state or other large institutions to further consolidate power and even inflict physical violence. This risk of the violence of apprehension is not confined to the production of social scientific knowledge within historic empires; it remains a threat in today's implicit and explicit imperial power configurations.

SOCIOLOGICAL KNOWLEDGE AND EMPIRE

In his later book, *Culture and Imperialism* (1993), Said lays out a strategy for responding to the structure of authoritative knowledge and the essentializing and epistemic violences he identified in *Orientalism*. Using a metaphor from Western classical music, Said proposes a contrapuntal rereading of the Western cultural archive, a comparative approach displaying a "simultaneous awareness both of metropolitan history that is narrated and of those other histories against which (and together with which) the dominating discourse acts" (1993, p. 51). Rather than a purely deconstructive exercise or a "decolonization" of the cultural archive, Said's goal is to trace both imperial processes and resistances to arrive at a point that "alternative or new narratives emerge, and they become institutionalized or discursively stable entities" (*ibid.*). In this rereading of canonical texts, it is possible to explore identities, or, for our purposes "categories," not as "essentializations...but as contrapuntal ensembles" (*ibid.*, p. 52).

Though this type of post-orientalist project has made inroads in other disciplines, a contrapuntal rereading of the sociological and social scientific archive has only been attempted by a few scholars. One example, though not necessarily inspired by Said, is Connell's (1997) interrogation of how the mid-20th century construction of a metropolitan-centric canon of "classical theory" in American sociology invented a foundational narrative that concealed the much broader context of imperial expansion and colonization that informed the early development of the discipline in the 19th and early 20th centuries for both European and American sociology and reinforced a disciplinary specialization on the metropolitan problems of industrialization, secularization, democratization, and urbanization. In the past decade, other scholars have begun to put empire and colonialism back on the sociological radar (Adams, 2005; Barkey, 2008; Charrad, 2001; Go, 2008; Goh, 2007; Mawani, 2009; Steinmetz, 2007). However, as Kemple and Mawani (2009, p. 239) observe, "this literature has had limited influence on (re)shaping the discipline's boundaries and in revealing how its ontological moorings, categories, and modes of analysis have been fundamentally structured by imperial pursuits and formed within cultures of colonialism."

The nascent project, represented in this special journal issue, of exploring and revealing sociology's "imperial unconscious" (Go, 2011) and "imperial shadows" (Kemple & Mawani, 2009) is very much in-line with the Saidian contrapuntal method, reading the Western sociological canon with an ear for counter-themes, resistances, and silences connected to the rise of the discipline within the historical milieu of expanding empire. Within the framework of the three violences outlined above, this approach is concerned with exposing a process of diachronic epistemic violence in the construction and professionalization of a theoretical tradition whose employment of universalistic categories of knowledge is unaware of the historical factors, often connected to an imperial context, which gave rise to this structure of authoritative knowledge. These attempts at a critical postcolonial disciplinary reflection represent a much-delayed (when compared to sister disciplines such as anthropology and history) sociological response to the orientalist critique.

To "provincialize sociology" (Burawoy, 2005a, p. 20) by clearly exposing forms of epistemic violence embedded in the discipline, an important first step is to sociologically analyze how the three violences of knowledge interacted (and continue) to interact over time in the context of empire to produce a structure of authoritative knowledge. From the early 19th century, sociological approaches served as a "handmaiden" for European imperial powers engaged in the process of conquering and ruling alien indigenous populations. Beginning from the Scientific Expedition that accompanied Napoleon's campaign to Egypt (1798–1801), the evolution of the social sciences, in France and in other metropolitan centers, was imbricated with imperial expansion, and implicitly and explicitly complicit in the violences of apprehension, of essentialization, and, over time, epistemic violence (El Shakry, 2007; Mitchell, 1988; Said, 1994 [1978]). Though strategically and politically a failure, Napoleon's escapade in Egypt bore long-term fruit in the publication, begun in 1802, of the encyclopedic 23 volume *Déscription de l'Egypte*, which showcased the work of the 167 scholars, scientists, engineers, and artists attached to the French expeditionary corps who had completed an inventory of Egypt's antiquities, flora, fauna, agriculture, and irrigation systems and conducted ethnographic and geographical surveys. In addition to laying the foundation for Egyptology, the expedition set a precedent for a comprehensive scientific survey that was repeated in Algeria three decades later with the *Exploration scientifique de l'Algèrie* (1844–1867).

It was in Algeria that French colonial sociology (the distinction of anthropology as a separate discipline occurred much later) came into full-flower, as a cadre of military officers profoundly influenced by Saint-Simonian social theory at the *Ecole Polytechnique* were assigned to the country in the wake of the conquest which began in 1830. In 1844, Governor General Bugeaud, engaged in the brutal total pacification of Algerian territory and elimination of "'Abd al-Qader's" interior emirate, appointed Eugène Daumas as the head of the Direction of Arab Affairs. Under Daumas, an administrative system, the Arab Bureaus, was put in place in which elite native affairs officers had wide latitude, as Abi-Mershed has demonstrated, in implementing Saint-Simonian notions about social order which they clearly intended to eventually use back in the metropole: "From the very start of their colonial venture in the 1830s, the Saint-Simonians' alternative modernity in Algeria – with its particular modes for rationalizing and regulating colonial society, its specific understandings of evolution and change, of culture, race, and gender – was meant to reverse the flow of historical development and progress and to radiate from Algiers as a model for Paris to heed" (2010, p. 8).

In their efforts to know their subject populations in order to better rule them, many of the Arab Bureau officers and their institutional descendants in the French military later in Algeria and in Morocco, produced high-quality studies of local society, customs, and religion (Burke, 2008). Gellner describes French sociological and ethnographic work as "a kind of reconnaissance in depth, and it was the handmaiden of government" (1976, p. 139). The production of knowledge needed by the French to pacify and administer North Africa entailed the construction of a substantial institutional infrastructure dedicated to linguistic, ethnographic, socio-logical, and historical studies including the *Ecole d'Algiers* and the *Institut des Hautes Etudes Marocain* in Rabat (Burke, 2007). The colonial sociological gaze, first in Algeria and later in Morocco, was directed at rural Islam (particularly the Sufi networks that had mobilized such intense resistance against military conquest), tribal structure, Islam, Berber society, and the relationship between tribes and the central government (Burke, 2008; Montagne, 1930). These efforts produced a vast sociological and ethnographic archive accessed both in the empire and the metropole, including Durkheim's use of work done in Algeria's Kabyle region in the 1880s to support his theorization of mechanical solidarity.

The French case, in which a substantive sociological project of studying the "other" was carried out in North Africa over more than a century, provides valuable insight into how the types of violence outlined above interact and evolve in the process of imperial conquest and subsequent colonial administration. In his study of similar questions related to the

German Empire, Steinmetz (2007) emphasizes a causal arrow pointing from precolonial ethnographic (mis)representations (our violence of essentialization) about different indigenous populations toward variations in native policy implemented by different colonial states. However, the evidence from the French case (which came to the colonial game much earlier and, in Algeria, had a much less well-developed orientalist ethnographic archive *prior* to constructing the colonial state) reveals a much more complex interaction between the production of knowledge about indigenous groups and the exercise of power over them. Though undoubtedly French colonial officers and more professionally trained academics who engaged in sociological and ethnographic research in North Africa were influenced by some orientalized preconceptions, in many respects they remained remarkably open to new data, particularly because of the stakes in having more or less accurate knowledge in the midst of military campaigns. In fact, Burke makes an important observation that it seems the first generation of colonial sociology typically did the best work: "The further one gets from the blood and thunder of military conquest, so it seems, the less relevant and less reliable the ethnography" (2008, p. 160).

It seems the more important and common causal chain flows from what we have described as the violence of apprehension toward the violence of essentialization. This reading remains sensitive to synchronic instances of gathering more or less accurate data to their diachronic evolution, due to the influence of political considerations, toward essentialist and epistemic violence. The crystallization of what Burke (1973, 2008) calls the "Moroccan Vulgate" in the first decades of French rule in the sultanate illuminates this process. Though France had been on the ground in Algeria since 1830, Morocco, next-door to the west, remained uncolonized through the end of the 19th century due to a balance of diplomatic interests related to Britain's strategic concern with the Straits of Gibraltar and the route to India. It also remained relatively unknown to Europe (outside of coastal enclaves in which European merchants and diplomatic agents conducted business), and in 1900, France began to send in scientific missions to study Moroccan society, politics, and culture, laying the groundwork for a future intervention. Based out of Tangier, researchers carried out extensive surveys in the north and central Morocco, gathering information on tribal structure, the Moroccan government (*makhzan*), religious practice, agriculture, and economic information, "ready to renounce the convenient pieties of the colonial vulgate for a much more open, complex, and nuanced portrait of Moroccan society" (Burke, 2008, p. 167). Following the 1904 Entente Cordiale, however, in which France and Britain recognized their respective interests in Egypt and Morocco, France had a vested political interest in an eventual protectorate form of colonial association with the Moroccan government, which had the effect of incentivizing a particular reading of Moroccan society and politics, namely that the Moroccan state had historically been unable to effectively project power over a dissident interior and that the French therefore needed to "partner" in pacifying the country and developing its governing apparatus and economy.

Influenced by a particular set of imperial political considerations, this "vulgate" simplistically reduced the complexities of the Moroccan context (more or less accurately reflected in earlier research) into a set of interrelated binaries based upon a fundamental political division between the "land of government" and the "land of dissidence" – over which was laid ethnic (Arab vs. Berber), geographic (plains/coasts vs. mountains and cities vs. countryside), and religious (Muslim vs. more secular) divisions that grossly distorted the state's sociological vision. Thus, a sensitivity to hybridity and local knowledge expressed in earlier work was dumbed down into an essentializing shorthand which could be used by the colonial state to "see" North African society (Scott, 1998). In sum, the contingencies of imperial interests, dictated by a particular set of diplomatic considerations, impacted the subsequent construction of sociological knowledge about Morocco and crystallized a particular set of interpretations, embodying what we have labeled as the "violence of essentialization" and a type of "epistemic violence."

Dirks (2001) describes a similar interplay between the violences of apprehension and essentialization in his study of the rise of an "ethnographic state" in British India after the 1857 Sepoy Mutiny/Great Rebellion. In explaining the shift from a historiographical mode to an ethnographic mode, Dirks explains that the colonial state's fundamental concern after 1857 was determining who is loyal, which necessitated an increasingly comprehensive knowledge of Indian society in order to further British interests in order and the maintenance of rule. The logical end point of the positivist enterprise was the Ethnographic Survey carried out in conjunction with the census of 1901 under the direction of H. H. Risley. Dirks writes, "The last half of the nineteenth century witnessed the development of a new kind of curiosity about and knowledge of the Indian social world, exhibited first in the manuals and gazetteers that began to encode official local knowledge, then in the materials that developed around the census, which led to Risley's great ambition for an ethnographic survey of all of India" (Dirks, 2001, p. 41). This type of imperial empiricist sociology of India attempting to refine caste categories only succeeded in uncovering further layers of overlap and complexity, but, because the colonial state needed this type of knowledge to make Indian society "legible" (Scott, 1998), it simply encouraged more of an empiricist response that over time resulted in an increasingly codified and standardized ethnological knowledge. The epistemic violence that results from the colonial state's need to translate sociological knowledge into policy or law forms the context for Spivak's (1998) argument in "Can the Subaltern Speak?"

Another related dimension in which the synchronic process of a violence of apprehension is fused with the violence of essentialization occurs in the attempts by the colonial state to ascertain, encode, and reproduce an authentic native traditional sphere. The process of military conquest clearly necessitates the synchronic acquisition of reliably "accurate" knowledge about local conditions, but colonial states, in many instances, continued to expend tremendous efforts amassing data on local culture, religion, gender relations, handicrafts, law, customs, etc. after pacification has been completed. The overall purpose of this project is to maintain a separate native category, or multiple native categories defined according to criteria of cultural authenticity, perpetuating what Chatterjee (1993) calls the "fundamental rule of colonial difference." In this respect, it is likely the production of knowledge about local culture, society, or religion was often not totally inaccurate. The violence of apprehension occurs because this knowledge was then used to produce markers of native identity, the purpose of which was to reinforce a hierarchy between European colonizer and native colonized. And, over time, this violence of apprehension, which became translated into colonial policy to maintain static categories of native identity, led to the violence of essentialization and epistemic violence.

The complex interaction between the three violences of knowledge is applicable not only for historic cases of empire, but is also, as Said insists throughout his corpus, highly relevant to our contemporary context. By considering the synchronic and diachronic dimensions of the construction of knowledge about Islam, Muslim societies, and a geographical construction like the "Middle East" within the American academy over recent decades, it becomes clear that an imperial context continues to intertwine epistemic violence and the violences of apprehension and essentialization. Though it resonated across multiple disciplines, Said's direct criticism in *Orientalism* was aimed squarely at the field of Middle East Studies that developed in the United States during the Cold War. As with other area studies fields, Middle East Studies fused the humanities and social sciences in order to produce knowledge about a highly strategic non-Western region. Said's critique radically impacted the field, engendering both a hostile reaction from the old guard most clearly expressed in the long-standing feud between Said and Bernard Lewis and a hugely sympathetic introspection that led to a broad paradigm shift (Lockman, 2004). Three decades after *Orientalism*, Middle East studies remain polarized on multiple layers, perhaps most fundamentally by the Israel–Palestine conflict and most recently by the increasingly palpable neo-imperial context for the study of the Islamic world in the aftermath of the 9/11 attacks with the invasion and occupation of Afghanistan and Iraq and launching of the "Global War on Terrorism" by the United States government.

In the context of the terror threat and concrete imperial projections of American power in the so-called "Greater Middle East" (stretching from Morocco to Afghanistan), there has been an intensification of debates about the relationship between the funding and consumption of research about the region. To a large extent, most of the research carried out in U.S. universities about the Middle East, like other non-Western regions of the world, has been federally funded through Title VI of the National Defense Education Act (NDEA) of 1958, which along with the Fulbright-Hays program, were created to develop experts on the nonaligned bloc, expertise which was deemed essential for national security during the Cold War. In 1965, Title VI was incorporated in the Higher Education Act with a shift in emphasis from national security to the value of international studies in higher education (Department of Education, 2011). After the 9/11 attacks, Congress passed the first significant increases in funding for these programs since the 1960s. In June 2003, a congressional subcommittee held hearings on "International Programs in Higher Education and Questions of Bias" where Stanley Kurtz, a columnist for the *National Review*, criticized Title VI-funded area studies centers for being dominated by a postcolonial "ruling intellectual paradigm" founded by Edward Said, the core premise of which was "that it is immoral for a scholar to put his knowledge of foreign languages and cultures at the service of American power" (Kurtz, 2003). Along with fellow critics of university-based Middle East studies Daniel Pipes and Martin Kramer (2001), Kurtz questioned how much "bang for the buck" the U.S. government receives from its investment in the production of knowledge about the region. Soon thereafter, a bill, H.R. 3077, was passed by the House that would have created an "International Education Advisory Board" to advise Congress "on Title VI programs in relation to national needs with respect to homeland security, international education, international affairs, and foreign language training" (Govtrack, 2003). Though the bill did not reach the floor in the Senate, it represents an unresolved tension over federal funding of area studies research which oscillates between (1) the explicit goals of national security and direct feedback into the defense, intelligence, and homeland security components of the state and (2) the indirect benefits of fostering an increased knowledge and understanding of the world within the broader American public via the higher education system.

Beyond renewed Congressional interest in the outcomes of the funding it appropriates for area studies research (which is now threatened by budgetary spending cuts), there have also been direct efforts by the Department of Defense (DoD) to acquire social science research, with a specific interest in the Middle East and the broader Islamic World. In 2008, then Secretary of Defense, Robert Gates, announced a new program targeting $70 million of DoD money at the social sciences, "The Minerva Initiative," aptly named after the Greek goddess of wisdom and war. The Minerva Initiative's stated purpose is "By drawing upon the knowledge, ideas, and creativity of the nation's universities, the Department [of Defense] aims to foster a new generation of engaged scholarship in the social sciences that seeks to meet the challenges of the 21st century" (United States Department of Defense, 2011). In a speech to the Association of American Universities, Gates, a former President of Texas A&M University, outlined likely areas the initiative would support which included Chinese Military and Technology Studies, an Iraqi and Terrorist Perspectives Project (in which primary sources captured by the U.S. military would be made available to scholars), and Religious and Ideological Studies, which he explained could focus on "the conflict against jihadist extremism" and the "overall ideological climate within the world of Islam" that would develop "the intellectual foundation on which we base a national strategy in coming years and decades." A fourth area, the New Disciplines Project, is intended to engage additional disciplines including history, anthropology, sociology, and evolutionary psychology (United States Department of Defense, 2008). The goal here is clearly to construct what would amount to an even more explicit and streamlined military–academic complex.

The swing toward harnessing the social scientific production of knowledge more efficiently toward military and strategic purposes has, of course, not gone uncriticized, with vociferous opposition against the H.R. 3077 bill and the Minerva Initiative from academics concerned about intellectual freedom, selection bias, and a further militarization of the university system ("AAA Calls for Alternate Management of Minerva"; Beinin, 2004; Lockman, 2004). The American Anthropological Association and the independent Network for Concerned Anthropologists (NCA) added vociferous criticism about the U.S. Army's development of a Human Terrain System (HTS) in which anthropologists and other social scientists are embedded in combat units engaged in counter-insurgency operations in Iraq and Afghanistan to provide "empirical sociocultural research and analysis to fill a large operational decision-making support gap" (U.S. Army, 2011). In 2009, the Network for Concerned Anthropologists published a *Counter Counterinsurgency Manual* (Network of Concerned Anthropologists, 2009) exposing the ethical and intellectual conflicts surrounding the Pentagon's use of Human Terrain Teams, which would be directly involved in the violences of apprehension and essentialization we have described. They also, as the title indicates, took aim at the military's structure of authoritative knowledge signified by the 2006 U.S. Army Counterinsurgency Manual (Sewall, Nagl, Petraeus, & Amos, 2007), which was written by a team under General David Petraeus' direction to synthesize lessons learned since the 2003 Iraq invasion and lay out a new doctrine of COIN operations for the U.S. military. In tandem with pointing out the inaccuracies, plagiarisms, and misconceptions that riddle the manual, the fundamental concern of the authors of the *Counter Counterinsurgency Manual* is the concrete link between epistemic and physical violence that the military's desire to coopt anthropological, sociological, historical, economic, and political knowledge to improve the HUMINT, human intelligence, supposedly needed to successfully wage counterinsurgency operations. A similar organization, the Association of Concerned Africa Scholars (founded in the 1970s), has recently focused energies on resisting the renewed militarization and securitization of knowledge about the continent with the growth of the U.S. military's AFRICOM and the spread of the Global War on Terror.

Even for social scientists not directly tied to any of these official initiatives, the Departments of State, Education, Defense, and the intelligence agencies remain interested in all things Islamic. One's work, however free of the essentialist and epistemic violences described above, still retains a potential to feed into these diachronic processes or to synchronically inform decisions regarding the exercise and extension of imperial power. Perhaps the most poignant example concerns scholarship about the relationship between Islam and politics. Since 9/11, under both Bush and Obama, the U.S. government has been actively interested, obviously, in combating "bad Muslims" but also in encouraging "good Muslims" (Mamdani, 2004). Thus, as opposed to the violence of essentialization, which would treat the category of Islam and Muslim society simplistically, the U.S. government has an expressed interest in a careful discernment of a gradation from dangerous, "radical" streams to the safer, "moderate" groups. This policy imperative necessitates more or less accurate knowledge, an accurate apprehension of the heterogeneous nature of various Muslims societies and political contexts, which avoids claims to avoid simple binaries (e.g., Muslims are bad, non-Muslims are good) even as it inadvertently creates new ones (e.g., these Muslims are bad, but those Muslims are good). As result, even the most self-consciously nonessentialist work on Islamic social movements and parties (e.g., Schwedler, 2006; Wiktorowicz, 2001), the compatibility of Islam and democracy (e.g., Bayat, 2007; Esposito & Voll, 1996), or women and Islam (e.g., Abu-Lughod, 1998; Badran, 2009) are of interest in the formulation of U.S. policy. For example, Saba Mahmood laments the fact that United States power is linked to creating the "right" kind of Muslims (2006) yet, ironically, her landmark book *Politics of Piety* (2005), which deconstructs stereotypes about Muslim women's responses to the Islamic Revival in Egypt could easily be used by government authorities to simply recalibrate their checklist of what constitutes good and bad Muslims and further consolidate their power.

The post 9/11 engagement in the Global War on Terror and the construction of pseudo-colonial states in Iraq and Afghanistan thus bears a close resemblance to the 19th and 20th century French and British imperial examples described above in which the extension and operation of imperial power requires the production or acquisition of social scientific knowledge about populations that need to be controlled or managed. As with these earlier European cases, as Said emphasized, the American neo-empire is also largely focused on Muslim societies from North Africa to South Asia, and knowledge produced directly by the state or accessed from other sources, including academia, about the region is at a premium. In both the historical and contemporary cases we have presented, this knowledge can be produced synchronically – tribal mapping in Afghanistan by an embedded anthropologist – and diachronically – the crystallization of COIN doctrine in the U.S. military – to impose one or more of the three violences – apprehension, essentialization, and/or epistemic – in both nonphysical and physical ways. Given the inherent risk that even accurate apprehension of the other can be instrumentalized to enact physical violence or deformed into a type of essentialization in the process of being incorporated into an epistemic structure used to guide state policy, what then should we do as sociologists?

TOWARD A REFLEXIVE POST-ORIENTALIST SOCIOLOGY

One way out of this conundrum, a path advocated by Said, is to claim that culture has a "relative autonomy from the economic, social, and political realms" (1993, p. xii) and "is a concept that includes a refining and elevating element, each society's reservoir of the best that has been known and thought, as Matthew Arnold put it..." (1993, p. xiii). Culture here does not simply refer to "aesthetic forms" but to "all those practices, like the arts of description, communication, and representation" that "included... both the popular stock of lore about distant parts of the world and specialized knowledge available in such learned disciplines as ethnography, historiography, philology, sociology, and literary history" (1994, p. xii). It might appear a bit jarring to see Said advocating a position of cultural optimism in light of the at-times Nietszchean pessimism seen in *Orientalism*. Yet even in *Orientalism* – as is clear in this chapter's epigraph – Said was open to the possibility of relatively autonomous knowledge. Within the book one sees a constructive tension between Foucault, who argues that the authoritative power structure is unavoidable, and Gramsci, who is more optimistic about the possible uses of positive knowledge. Gramsci, and Said's reading of him, is not naive: there is no denying that hegemony exists or that power-structures control what is said and what is thought. Said acknowledges that the notions of culture he outlines are problematic because they can become linked to a xenophobic parochialism (itself sometimes linked to "religious and nationalist fundamentalism") and to "thinking of [culture] as somehow divorced from, because transcending, the everyday world" (1994, p. xiii). In Foucault's model, culture of any sort is fed into a sausage factory of power-knowledge, allowing an ever-deeper consolidation of power. In Said and Gramsci's model, the sausage factory still exists, and culture can contribute to it, but it doesn't have to. Relative autonomy is possible, but how can a social scientist try to achieve it?

The closest discipline to sociology to wrestle with this dilemma has been cultural anthropology, which, since the late 1950s, has struggled to reconcile itself with its past relationship to colonial power and the subsequent postcolonial and New Left critiques of the discipline, of which Said's was one of the most salient. James Clifford, argued that "recent trends" in anthropology – including the discussions generated by Said's *Orientalism* – "have cast radical doubt on the procedures by which alien human groups can be represented... These studies suggest that while ethnographic writing cannot entirely escape the reductionist use of dichotomies and essences, it can at least struggle self-consciously to avoid portraying abstract, a-historical 'others'" (1983, p. 119). He goes on that "neither the experience nor the interpretive activity of the scientific researcher can be considered innocent" (1983, p. 133) and that ethnography must be understood as "constructive negotiation involving at least two, and usually more, conscious, politically significant subjects" rather than one person writing about an "other" (1983, p. 133).

So what is to be done? Is positive knowledge still possible? Clifford writes that "paradigms of experience and interpretation are yielding to paradigms of discourse, of dialogue and polyphony" (1983, p. 133), paradigms which would be celebrated in the landmark book he co-edited with George E. Marcus, *Writing Cultures* (p. 133). Marcus would later ruminate that despite the body-blows anthropology had received, it had not given up entirely on "cultural translation, which is what ethnography is" (1998, p. 186). Even Talal Asad, the anthropologist who preceded Said in pointing out the imbrication of anthropology with empire and whose later work is famous for Foucault-inspired genealogies and a "conceptual, antihumanist, and antiprogressivist approach" (Scott, 2006, p. 139), is nonetheless amenable to histories which "track the movement forward from past to present of some idea or institution or practice" (Scott, 2006, p. 138) and to ethnography itself, which Asad believed could still be fixed:

> I believe that it is a mistake to view social anthropology in the colonial era as primarily an aid to colonial administration, or as the simple reflection of a colonial ideology. I say this not because I subscribe to the anthropological establishment's comfortable view of itself, but because bourgeois consciousness, of which social anthropology is merely one fragment, has always contained within itself profound contradictions and ambiguities – and therefore the potential for transcending itself. For these contradictions to be adequately apprehended it is essential to turn to the historical power relationship between the West and the Third World and to examine the ways in which it has been dialectically linked to the practical conditions, the working assumptions, and the intellectual product of all disciplines representing the European understanding of non-European humanity. (Asad, 1973, pp. 18–19)

Relative autonomy is possible for anthropologists. But they have to be careful, and that care is provided by reflexivity. While anthropologists have a somewhat different project than sociologists, we take seriously the need to be reflexive and the reminder that such reflexivity must (1) be aware of the location of the researcher and the complicated ways his or her knowledge might be used and (2) be humble regarding the importance of accuracy and representativeness in her knowledge and the possibility of it later being disproven.

What is interesting about these critiques of ethnographic method is that, despite their acknowledged debt to Edward Said's work in developing a reflexive anthropology, this reflexivity is generally about the dangers of enacting the violence of essentialization and contributing to epistemic violence. These are obviously valid concerns, but, again, we worry that such an exclusive focus ignores the possibility of what we are calling the violence of apprehension. Such a lacuna is perhaps the result of these critiques' historical position: written from the early 1970s to the mid to late 1990s, this disciplinary self-critique of ethnography occurred between two major moments of explicit United States' imperialism, which might explain why there was less concern about the ability of those in power to use more or less accurate academic knowledge to better consolidate power. More recently, anthropologists have become much more explicitly aware of the potential dangers of the violence of apprehension, as evidenced in the discussion above about AAA's, and other anthropologist networks, concern and criticism of attempts to harness anthropological methods and knowledge to aid in counterinsurgency and military-led state building. For the methodological mainstream, however, the violence of essentialization and epistemic violence remain the biggest worries for the discipline.

A similar blind spot affects the reflexive turn within sociology. Perhaps more than any other sociological theorist, Bourdieu, who began his career teaching at the University of Algiers in the late 1950s in the midst of the Franco-Algerian war and conducted field work in Kabylia, is aware of and provides sophisticated frameworks for the study of the relationship between knowledge and power which is such a concern for Edward Said and other postcolonial theorists. Said criticized Bourdieu for failing to explicitly address the relationship between empire and knowledge. In a noteworthy address to the American Anthropology Association, Said complains: "Is it farfetched to draw an analogy between Camus and Bourdieu in *Outline of a Theory of Practice*, perhaps the most influential theoretical text in anthropology today, which makes no mention of colonialism, Algeria, and so on, even though he writes about Algeria elsewhere? It is the exclusion of Algeria from Bourdieu's theorizing and ethnographic reflection that is noteworthy" (1989, p. 223). While Said was empirically wrong in this statement (*Outline* contains multiple passages and scores of footnotes referencing Algeria), it is true that Bourdieu's meta-theorization of the relationship between knowledge and power developed largely after he had returned to France – his taxonomy of forms of capital, analysis of symbolic violence, and later theorization of the state's "monopoly of legitimate symbolic violence" (Bourdieu, 1999; Bourdieu & Wacquant, 1992, p. 112) – remain bounded by a metropolitan horizon.

Within the typology of violences we have outlined, Bourdieu's call for a reflexive sociology is predominantly focused on the potential for essentialization and epistemic violence. But, this concern is less about the object of study and more about how these biases might corrupt the production of objective knowledge. The explicit goal of practicing a thorough "epistemic reflexivity" (Bourdieu & Wacquant, 1992) emphasized in his earlier work is a more rigorous scientization of the sociological project. As Marcus observes, "Self-reflexivity is for Bourdieu a renewed and more powerful form of the old project of the sociology of knowledge, but this time fully integrated as a dimension of sociological method" (1998, p. 195). Bourdieu is predominantly worried about getting sociological apprehension right.

To be fair to Bourdieu, though, it is important to recognize how he *indirectly* did incorporate the question of empire, particularly in his later, more transparently reflexive period. Writing about his early fieldwork in Algeria, Bourdieu explained that a guilty conscience about being a "participant observer in this appalling war" his response was to "do something as a scientist." Referring to the political context of the Algerian war in the late 1950s, he states: "In a historical situation in which at every moment, in every political statement, every discussion, every petition, the whole reality was at stake, it was absolutely necessary to be at the heart of events so as to form one's opinion, however dangerous it might have been – and dangerous it was" (Bourdieu & Wacquant, 1992, p. 33, quoted from Kocyba, Schwibs, & Honneth, 1986, p. 39). Bourdieu was acutely aware of the ethical dilemmas of his position in a brutal anti-colonial war as an academic sociologist funded by the French state. His response, much more fully developed in his later theorization of reflexivity, was to produce more accurate, more objective knowledge of Algerian society (and of French colonial society). He later mentions that his ethnographic work in Algeria had sensitized him to the "'epistemocentrism' associated with the scholarly viewpoint," but his resulting concern focused on "the presuppositions and prejudices associated with the local and localized point of view of someone who constructs the space of points of view" (Bourdieu & Wacquant, 1992, p. 254). Bourdieu's fixation with "epistemic reflexivity," the origins of which he traced back to his ethnographic field work in Kabylia, features the sort of accountability we are calling for, but it only partially covers the types of violence associated with the production of knowledge within an imperial topography of power. Bourdieu's reflexive sociology is highly sensitive to the violence of essentialization and deeper structures of epistemic violence but, for him, these are a concern predominantly as problems of knowledge. His reflexive approach is intended to ensure the production of more objective and accurate sociological knowledge, but, in doing so, still leaves the door open for the violence of apprehension.

Michael Burawoy's famous call for a reflexive sociology runs into similar problems, as it focuses primarily on the values, goals, and audiences of sociological work than the potential for violence which we raise in this chapter. In his many writings about public sociology, he repeatedly insists the central questions sociologists must ask themselves is for whom and for what are they doing sociology (Burawoy, 2005a, p. 12), determining which values drive their work "by engaging in what Weber called value discussion, leading to what I will refer to as reflexive knowledge" (2004, p. 1606). He does ask if sociologists should "be concerned explicitly with the goals for which our research may be mobilized" (2004, p. 1606) and, in some of his writing about policy sociology, refers to its tendency to "legitimate solutions that have already been reached" (2005a, p. 9). Yet the vast majority of Burawoy's writing about public sociology have focused on "sociology's affiliation with civil society, that is public sociology, represent[ing] the interests of humanity – interests in keeping at bay both state despotism and market tyranny" (2005a, p. 24). Burawoy's reflexivity, in other words, is about the need to do good, rather than the need to avoid violence. Burawoy does obliquely acknowledge the kinds of violence that concern us here with his insistence that sociologists "provincialize" United States sociology (2005a, p. 22), but this refers to epistemic violence and the violence of essentialization and still misses the violence of apprehension.

This is not to denigrate Burawoy's call, which is similar to the later work of Pierre Bourdieu and the reflective humanism of Edward Said. We find all three personally inspiring and an appropriate model for sociological work. We recognize, however, that not all sociologists find public sociology so attractive or intellectually tenable (Hadas, 2007; Holmwood, 2007). While Burawoy says his questions are "for whom and for what" sociological knowledge is produced, he actually appears to be asking for whom and *toward* what, for example, what are the values that drive the end-goals of our research? For the purposes of this chapter, we can afford to be relatively agnostic about this values-question, as our most pressing concerns are about the "for what" which Burawoy often elides, for example, the real possibility of our knowledge making any of the three forms of violence possible. In other words, whether or not sociologists choose to take a stand against the war in Iraq or Afghanistan as sociologists or even simply as citizens, whether or not they intend their work to end or justify the wars, their research on Iraq or Afghanistan will be used by those in power.

While we have been emphasizing the implications of scholarship on the Middle East and Islam, it is important to remember that a sensitivity to how sociological knowledge will be used is vital for all fields within the discipline. Work on inner-city populations, on crime and the justice system, on migrant labor, on religious minorities, on "right wing terrorism" – to name only a few – are just as likely to be used by those in power. As we have discussed regarding the French and American imperial contexts, states or major corporations want "operationalizable" knowledge that can be used to implement policy. The well-known dictum that "policy people only read one paragraph" might be an unfair characterization of officials' intellectual ambitions, but it demonstrates well the basic problem that subtle, nuanced, more or less accurate knowledge will inevitably be rendered blunt and essentialized to create government and corporate policies and strategies.

As the recent turn in anthropology has ably demonstrated, all representation is potentially violent: even the most careful ethnographer misses something in writing her field notes, and then misses even more when she turns those field notes into articles and books. While there can be certain strategies – among them various kinds of reflexivity – to acknowledge what is missing, these strategies are simply impossible to implement on a broad scale. Social scientists who study any marginalized groups within any society should be particularly sensitive to how the knowledge they produce – however sensitively collected and presented – is used by those in power, yet social scientists should also recognize that any data they produce – no matter how arcane the information gathered, no matter how protected the population studied – might well be used to consolidate power. We would propose that, in addition to worrying about whether or not our work as social scientists "makes a difference," we should worry about the sort of difference our work makes.

CONCLUSION: WHY EDWARD SAID MATTERS

There appear to be two strategies to deal with these worries about our knowledge's potential implications for violence: the first is to avoid the problem by not producing positive knowledge and the second is to ensure that our knowledge is used the way we want it to, that is, as nonviolently as possible. Said does not ignore the stakes involved here, warning that "reading and writing texts are never neutral activities: there are interests, power, passions, pleasures entailed no matter how aesthetic or entertaining the work" (1993, p. 318). These stakes are particularly dire when writing about others, as Said describes how anthropologists must resolve "the almost insuperable contradiction between a political actuality based on force, and a scientific and humane desire to understand the Other hermeneutically and sympathetically in modes not influenced by force" (1993, p. 56). The problem, as we have been insisting throughout this chapter, is not only one of force occluding "accurate" knowledge whether diachronically or synchronically but also force using sensitively acquired more or less accurate knowledge for its own ends.

In an address to American anthropologists, Said warns that United States foreign policy is "heavily dependent on cultural discourse, on the knowledge industry, on the production and dissemination of texts and textuality, in short, not on 'culture' as a general anthropological realm, which is routinely discussed and analyzed in studies of cultural poetics and textualization, but quite specifically on our culture" (1989, p. 215). More importantly, he asks anthropologists about "intellectual dissemination, the exfoliation of scholarly or monographic disciplinary work from the relatively private domain of the researcher and his or her guild circle to the domain of policy making, policy enactment, and – no less important – the recirculation of rigorous ethnographic representations as public media images that reinforce policy" (1989, p. 218). As we have mentioned above, such ethnographic representations run the risk of possible violence because they can lead to essentialized understandings of the "other" or can produce an "epistemic violence" which undercuts local categories and knowledge. Yet these representations also have the potential for violence even if they are more or less accurate; Said gives the example of James Scott's *Weapons of the Weak*, "a brilliant empirical as well as theoretical account of everyday resistances to hegemony [which] undercuts the very resistance [Scott] admires and respects by in a sense revealing the secrets of its strength" (1989, p. 220). The culture and knowledge social scientists create can and often will be used by those in power. What are we to do?

Said's answer to this question at the end of his address to anthropologists is a bit unsatisfying, providing a vague insistence on seeing "Others not as ontologically given but as historically constituted" (1989, p. 225) which does not really resolve the possibilities for the three forms of violence we have outlined here. In the same address, however, Said provides a caveat "that the imperial system that covers an immense network of patron and client states, as well as an intelligence and policy-making apparatus that is both wealthy and powerful beyond precedent, does not cover everything in American society" (1989, p. 215). It is this possibility for standing outside of power that provides hope for Said and those who follow him, a possibility made tenable by his ultimately aligning with the Gramscian rather than the Foucauldian side of *Orientalism*. In an interview, he said that while writing the book, he "was already aware of the problems of Foucault's determinism...where everything is always assimilated and acculturated...The notion of a kind of non-coercive knowledge, which I come to at the end of the book, was deliberately anti-Foucault" (Said & Viswanathan, 2001, p. 80). In a much-cited collection of essays, Said laments that "what one misses in Foucault is something resembling Gramsci's analyses of hegemony, historical blocks, ensembles of relationships done from the perspective of an engaged political worker for whom the fascinated description of exercised power is never a substitute for trying to change power relationships within society" (Said, 1983, p. 222).

This description of Gramsci could just as easily describe Said, and it is in Gramsci that Said finds a balance between Matthew Arnold's positive view of culture and Foucault's suspicion of culture's relationship to power:

> ...as Gramsci is everywhere careful to note, cultural activity is neither uniform nor mindlessly homogenous. The real depth in the strength of the modern Western State is the strength and depth of its culture, and culture's strength in its variety, its heterogeneous plurality... [Gramsci] loses sight neither of the great central facts of power, and how they flow through a whole network of agencies operating by rational consent, nor of the detail – diffuse, quotidian, unsystematic, thick – from which inevitably power draws its sustenance... Well before Foucault, Gramsci had grasped the idea that culture serves authority, and ultimately the national State, not because it represses and coerces but because it is affirmative, positive, and persuasive. (Said, 1983, p. 171)

It is because of Gramsci's inspiration that Said is able to urge his fellow critics "to see culture as a historical force possessing its own configurations, ones that intertwine with those in the socioeconomic sphere and that finally bear on the State as a State" (1983, p. 171). Said was concerned because such an engagement is not happening, however, at least not in Said's field of comparative literature. Instead, an "ethic of professionalism" (1983, p. 4) has emerged, obsessing over small technical problems and rendering impossible the "autonomously functioning intellectual" (1996 [1994], p. 67) who "ought to be an amateur" (1996 [1994], p. 82). Such an amateur that is, someone unafraid to engage "even the most technical and professionalized activity" despite a lack of proper specialization is necessary because these debates are important for all citizens and not only specialists (1996 [1994], p. 82). Like Buroway's comments on sociology, Said laments that his discipline – which was once at the forefront of debates about society – has now more or less excused itself, the better to make time and space for highly technical debates (Said, 1982). Unlike Burawoy, Said does not support a scholarly division of labor: he would like all scholars to be public scholars.

However, one of the problems we find with "amateur intellectuals" is that they are not able to provide the sort of correction and accountability that specialization provides. While we share Said's wariness about guilds of scholars wholly removed from the world, we would point to the reflexivity of Marcus, Bourdieu, and Burawoy as providing examples of scholarship which is publicly focused but also adept at the latest theoretical and methodological innovations within a field of study and amenable to correction of its empirical content and theoretical approach. This type of reflexivity would enhance Said's larger goals. For example, in *Orientalism* and elsewhere, Said makes distinctly *sociological* causal arguments about institutions, discourses, and culture and, throughout his oeuvre, he cites sociologists and anthropologists approvingly. Yet the relative weakness of Said's causal arguments was one of the major criticisms of *Orientalism*, and better sociology would have made for a better book. Steinmetz's *The Devil's Handwriting* (2007), is, among other things, just such a correction and addition to the sociological arguments implicit in *Orientalism*. If postcolonial theorists are going to make causal arguments about culture and institutions, they might as well learn from sociologists how to make sociological claims. As McLennan argues, a major "overlap" between postcolonial theory and sociology is "the continuing necessity of 'sociology' in the generic, if not necessarily disciplinary, sense: an elementary and plausible sociology of current trends and developments, and some kind of articulation of 'the logic of the social'" (2003, p. 83).

In the other direction, sociologists ought to learn from postcolonial theorists how to be more careful and reflective about the relationship between the knowledge they create and the powers they (often unwittingly) support or repress. While openness to correction and an awareness of how our location affects what we produce are both vital forms of reflexivity of which Said was well aware, we have been stressing another kind that Said also insisted upon. Scholars must be aware of what their knowledge does, and they must find a place from which to produce and then observe that knowledge in relative autonomy from those in power. If, as Said claims, there is such a thing as a relative autonomy of culture, and if culture can stand up against the State and not only add to its power, then there is some possibility for more or less accurate knowledge that does not immediately contribute to the three violences we describe here.

We do not want to equivocate: the odds are that knowledge produced about high-interest groups will be used by government powers. Yet there is also the possibility that our knowledge might change minds and improve policy in a way that does not consolidate state power but rather works within civil society to lessen suffering, increase freedom, and makes lives more meaningful. To do so requires no small amount of Gramscian hope in the face of overwhelming odds, but it also requires a commitment by intellectuals – and for our purposes, sociologists – to pay attention to what their knowledge does and where their knowledge goes. In his address to anthropologists, Said says that, while writing *Orientalism*, "I did not feel that I could give myself over to the view that an Archimedean point existed outside the contexts I was describing, or that it might be possible to devise and deploy an inclusive interpretive methodology that could hang free of the precisely concrete historical circumstances out of which Orientalism derived and from which it drew sustenance" (1989, p. 211). Relative autonomy is not total autonomy, and we sociologists are responsible for what we create.

REFERENCES

Abi-Mershed, O (2010). *Apostles of modernity: Saint-Simonians and the civilizing mission in Algeria*. Stanford, CA: Stanford University Press.

Abu-Lughod, L. (Ed.). (1998). *Remaking women: Feminism and modernity in the Middle East*. Princeton, NJ: Princeton University Press.

Ahmad, A (1992). Orientalism and after: Ambivalence and cosmopolitan location in the work of Edward said. *Economic and Political Weekly, 27*, 98–116.

Adams, J (2005). *The familial state*. Ithaca, NY: Cornell University Press.

Asad, T. (1973). Introduction. In T. Asad (Ed.), *Anthropology and the colonial encounter* (pp. 9–24). London, SE1: Ithaca Press.

Badran, M. (2009). *Feminism in Islam: Secular and religious convergences*. Oxford: Oneworld.

Barkey, K (2008). *Empire of difference: The Ottomans in comparative perspective*. New York, NY: Cambridge University Press.

Bayat, A (2007). *Making Islam democratic: Social movements and the post-Islamist turn*. Stanford, CA: Stanford University Press.

Bhambra, G. K. (2007). Sociology and postcolonialism: Another 'missing' revolution? *Sociology, 41*, 871–884.

Bourdieu, P. (1999). Rethinking the state: Genesis and structure of the bureaucratic field. In G. Steinmetz (Ed.), *State/culture: State-formation after the cultural turn*. Ithaca, NY: Cornell University Press.

Bourdieu, P. 1991 [1982]. *Language and symbolic power* (J. B Thompson, Trans.). Boston, MA: Harvard University Press.

Bourdieu, P., & Wacquant, L. J. D. (1992). *An invitation to reflexive sociology*. Chicago, IL: University of Chicago Press.

Brennan, T (2000). The illusion of a future: 'Orientalism' as traveling theory. *Critical Inquiry*, *26*, 558–583.

Burawoy, M. (2004). Public sociologies: Contradictions, dilemmas, and possibilities. *Social Forces*, *82*, 1603–1618.

Burawoy, M. (2005a). 2004 ASA presidential address: For public sociology. *American Sociological Review*, *70*, 4–28.

Burke, E. (1973). The image of Morocco in French Colonial scholarship. In E. Gellner & C. Micaud (Eds.), *Arabs and Berbers: From the tribe to nation in North Africa* (pp. 175–199). Lexington, MA: Lexington Books, 1972.

Burke, E. (2007). The creation of the Moroccan Colonial archive, 1880–1830. *History and Anthropology*, *18*, 1–9.

Burke, E. (2008). The sociology of Islam: The French tradition. In E. B. Burke & D. Prochaska (Eds.), *Genealogies of orientalism: History, theory, politics* (pp. 154–173). Lincoln, NE: University of Nebraska Press.

Charrad, M. (2001). *States and women's rights: The making of postcolonial Tunisia, Algeria, and Morocco*. Berkeley, CA: University of California Press.

Chatterjee, P (1993). *The nation and its fragments: Colonial and postcolonial histories*. Princeton, NJ: Princeton University Press.

Clifford, J. (1983). On ethnographic authority. *Representations*, *12*, 118–146.

Connell, R. W. (1997). Why is classical theory classical? *American Journal of Sociology*, *102*(5), 1511–1557.

Department of Education. Office of Postsecondary Education. 2011. *The history of Title VI and Fulbright-Hays*. Retrieved from http://www2.ed.gov/about/offices/list/ope/iegps/history. html. Accessed on August 2, 2011.

Dirks, N. B. (2001). *Castes of mind: Colonialism and the making of modern India*. Princeton, NJ: Princeton University Press.

Dirks, N. B. (2004). Edward said and anthropology. *Journal of Palestine Studies*, *33*, 38–54.

El Shakry, O. S. (2007). *The great social laboratory: Subjects of knowledge in colonial and postcolonial Egypt*. Stanford, CA: Stanford University Press.

Epstein, S. (2006). *Impure science: AIDS, activism, and the politics of knowledge*. Berkeley, CA: University of California Press.

Esposito, J. L, & Voll, J. (1996). *Islam and democracy*. New York, NY: Oxford University Press.

Fanon, F. 2004 [1963]. *The wretched of the earth* (R. Philcox, Trans.). New York, NY: Grove Press.

Fordham, S. (1996). *Blacked out: Dilemmas of race, identity, and success at capital high*. Chicago, IL: University of Chicago Press.

Foucault, M. 1990 [1976]. *The history of sexuality, Volume I: An introduction* (R. Hurley, Trans.). New York, NY: Vintage.

Foucault, M. 1995 [1977]. *Discipline and punish* (2nd ed., A. Sheridan, Trans.). New York, NY: Vintage.

Gandhi, L. (1998). *Postcolonial theory*. New York, NY: Columbia University Press.

Gellner, E. (1976). The sociology of Robert Montagne (1893–1954). *Daedalus*, *105*(1), 137–150.

Go, J. (2008). *American empire and the politics of meaning: Elite political cultures in the Philippines and Puerto Rico during U.S. colonialism*. Durham, NC: Duke University Press.

Go, J. (2011). Sociology's imperial unconscious: Early American sociology in a global context. In G. Steinmetz (Ed.), *Sociology and empire*. Durham, NC: Duke University Press.

Goh, D. P. S. (2007). States of ethnography: Colonialism, resistance, and cultural transcription in Malaya and the Philippines, 1890–1930s. *Comparative Studies in Society and History*, *49*, 109–142.

Gorski, P. S. (2003). *The disciplinary revolution: Calvinism and the rise of the state in early modern Europe*. Chicago, IL: University of Chicago Press.

Govtrack. 2003. *H.R. 3077: International studies in Higher Education Act of 2003*. Retrieved from http://www.govtrack.us/congress/bill.xpd?bill=h108-3077&tab=summary. Accessed on August 4, 2011.

Hadas, M. (2007). Much ado about nothing? Remarks on Michael Burawoy's presidential address. *The American Sociologist*, *38*, 309–322. Accessed on July 13, 2011.

Holmwood, J. (2007). Sociology as public discourse and professional practice: A critique of michael burawoy. *Sociological Theory*, *25*, 46–66.

Irwin, R. (2006). *Dangerous knowledge: Orientalism and its discontents*. Woodstock, NY: Overlook Press.

King, M. L. (1990). *A testament of hope: The essential writings and speeches of Martin Luther King, Jr*. New York, NY: HarperOne.

Kocyba, H., Schwibs, B., & Honneth, A. (1986). The struggle for symbolic order an interview with Pierre Bourdieu. *Theory, Culture & Society*, *3*, 35–51.

Kramer, M. S. (2001). *Ivory towers on sand: The failure of Middle Eastern studies in America*. Washington, DC: Washington Institute for Near East Policy.

Kurtz, S. 2003. Studying Title VI: Criticisms of Middle East studies get a congressional hearing. *National Review Online*. Retrieved from http://www.nationalreview.com/articles/207236/studying-title-vi/stanley-kurtz. Accessed on July 13, 2011.

Lewis, B. 1982. The question of orientalism. *The New York Review of Books*, June 24. Retrieved from http://www.nybooks.com/articles/archives/1982/jun/24/the-question-of-orientalism/. Accessed on July 14, 2011.

Lewis, H. S. (1998). The misrepresentation of anthropology and its consequences. *American Anthropologist*, *100*, 716–731.

Lockman, Z. (2004). *Contending visions of the Middle East: the history and politics of orientalism*. Cambridge: Cambridge University Press.

Mahmood, S. (2005). *Politics of piety: The Islamic revival and the feminist subject*. Princeton, NJ: Princeton University Press.

Mahmood, S. (2006). Secularism, hermeneutics, and empire: The politics of Islamic reformation. *Public Culture*, *18*, 323–347.

Mamdani, M. (2004). *Good Muslim, bad Muslim: America, the cold war, and the roots of terror*. New York, NY: Pantheon Books.

Marcus, G. E. (1998). *Ethnography through thick and thin*. Princeton, NJ: Princeton University Press.

Martin, R. C. (2010). Islamic studies in the American Academy: A personal reflection. *Journal of the American Academy of Religion*, *78*, 896–920.

Mawani, R. (2009). *Colonial proximities crossracial encounters and juridical truths in British Columbia, 1871–1921*. Vancouver: UBC Press.

McLennan, G. (2003). Sociology, eurocentrism and postcolonial theory. *European Journal of Social Theory*, *6*, 69–86.

Mitchell, T. (1988). *Colonising Egypt*. Cambridge: Cambridge University Press.

Montagne, R. (1930). *Les Berbères et le Makhzen dans le Sud du Maroc*. Paris: F. Alcan.

Nandy, A. (2010). *The intimate enemy: Loss and recovery of self under colonialism*. New York, NY: Oxford University Press.

Network of Concerned Anthropologists. (2009). *The counter counterinsurgency manual*. Chicago, IL: Prickly Paradigm Press.

Nigam, A. (1999). Marxism and the postcolonial world: Footnotes to a long march. *Economic and Political Weekly, 34*, 33–43.

O'Hanlon, R., & Washbrook, D. (1992). After orientalism: Culture, criticism, and politics in the third world. *Comparative Studies in Society and History, 34*, 141–167.

Reed, I. A. (2011). *Interpretation and social knowledge: On the use of theory in the human sciences*. Chicago, IL: Chicago University Press.

Rice, J. P. (2000). In the wake of orientalism. *Comparative Literature Studies, 37*, 223–238.

Richardson, M. (1990). Enough said: Reflections on orientalism. *Anthropology Today, 6*, 16–19. Accessed on July 16, 2011.

Said, E. W. (1994 [1978]). *Orientalism*. New York, NY: Vintage.

Said, E. W. (1979). *The question of Palestine*. New York, NY: Times Books.

Said, E. W. (1981). *Covering Islam: How the media and the experts determine how we see the rest of the world*. London: Routledge & Kegan Paul.

Said, E. W. (1982). Opponents, audiences, constituencies, and community. *Critical Inquiry, 9*, 1–26.

Said, E. W. (1983). *The world, the text, and the critic*. Boston, MA: Harvard University Press.

Said, E. W. (1989). Representing the colonized: Anthropology's interlocutors. *Critical inquiry, 15*, 205–225.

Said, E. W. (1993). *Culture and imperialism*. New York, NY: Knopf.

Said, E. W. (1996 [1994]). *Representations of the intellectual: The 1993 Reith lectures*. New York, NY: Vintage Books.

Said, E. W. (2000). Presidential address 1999: Humanism and heroism. *Publications of the Modern Language Association of America, 115*(3), 285–291.

Said, E. W., & Viswanathan, G. (2001). *Power, politics, and culture: Interviews with Edward W. Said*. New York, NY: Pantheon Books.

Salvatore, A. (1996). Beyond orientalism? Max Weber and the displacements of 'essentialism' in the study of Islam. *Arabica, 43*, 457–485.

Schwedler, J. (2006). *Faith in moderation: Islamist parties in Jordan and Yemen*. Cambridge: Cambridge University Press.

Scott, J. C. (1998). *Seeing like a state: How certain schemes to improve the human condition have failed*. New Haven, CT: Yale University Press.

Scott, D. (2006). The tragic sensibility of Talal Asad. In D. Scott & C. Hirschkind (Eds.), *Powers of the secular modern: Talal Asad and his interlocutors* (pp. 134–153). Palo Alto, CA: Stanford University Press.

Sewall, S., Nagl, J. A., Petraeus, D. H., & Amos, J. F. (2007). *The U.S. Army/Marine corps counterinsurgency field manual*. Chicago, IL: University of Chicago Press.

Spivak, G. (1998). Can the subaltern speak? In C. Nelson & L. Grossberg (Eds.), *Marxism and the interpretation of culture* (pp. 271–316). Urbana, IL: University of Illinois Press.

Steinmetz, G. (2007). *The devil's handwriting: Precoloniality and the German colonial state in Qingdao, Samoa, and Southwest Africa*. Chicago, IL: University of Chicago Press.

Toussaint, S. (1999). Honoring our predecessors: A response to Herbert Lewis's essay on 'The misrepresentation of anthropology and its consequences'. *American Anthropologist, 101*, 605–609.

Turner, B. S. (1974). *Weber and Islam: A critical study*. London: Routledge & Kegan Paul.

Turner, B. S. (1978). *Marx and the end of orientalism*. London: Allen & Unwin.

United States Army. 2011. *Welcome to the HTS Home Page. The human terrain system*. Retrieved from http://humanterrainsystem.army.mil/. Accessed on August 4, 2011.

United States. Department of Defense. 2011. *The Minerva initiative*. Retrieved from http://minerva.dtic.mil/. Accessed on August 4, 2011.

United States. Department of Defense. 2008. *Association of American Universities (Washington, DC): As delivered by Secretary of Defense Robert M. Gates, Washington, DC*. Retrieved from http://www.defense.gov/speeches/speech.aspx?speechid=1228. Accessed on August 4, 2011.

Varisco, D. M. (2004). Reading against culture in Edward Said's culture and imperialism. *Culture, Theory & Critique, 45*, 93–112.

Wiktorowicz, Q. (Ed.). (2001). *The management of Islamic activism: Salafis, the Muslim Brotherhood, and state power in Jordan*. Albany, NY: State University of New York Press.

NEO-BOURDIEUSIAN THEORY AND THE QUESTION OF SCIENTIFIC AUTONOMY: GERMAN SOCIOLOGISTS AND EMPIRE, 1890s–1940s [☆]

George Steinmetz

What were the specific properties of the field in which the colonial science of people like Maunier produced its discourse on the colonial world [?] ... We need to analyze the relationship this relatively autonomous scientific field had with, on the one hand, the colonial power, and, on the other, the central intellectual power, that is to say, the metropolitan science of the day.

"Les conditions sociales de la production sociologique: sociologie coloniale et decolonisation de la sociologie," contribution to a conference on Ethnology and Politics of the Maghreb, June 5, 1975. (Bourdieu, 1993a, p. 51)

This paper explores the connections between the discipline of sociology and imperial politics. More specifically, I ask why some of the sociologists who study empires are able to keep a certain degree of analytic distance from their object of analysis, while others are drawn into direct or indirect dependence on the empires they study. Bourdieusian sociology of science defines this as a problem of *scientific autonomy* and scientific heteronomy

[☆] Reprinted from Political Power and Social Theory, Volume 20, 2009, pp. 71–131.

Political Power and Social Theory, Volume 20, 145–206
Copyright © 2009 by Emerald Group Publishing Limited
All rights of reproduction in any form reserved
ISSN: 0198-8719/doi:10.1108/S0198-8719(2009)0000020009

(Bourdieu, 1988, 2004). Colonialism and imperialism are certainly not the only objects of study that often undermine scientific objectivity. Almost all research in the social sciences deals with topics and objects whose very existence is seen as oppressive or objectionable. Empires are an interesting example of a contentious object of analysis because of their enormous prestige in certain times and places and their ignominious reputation in much of the world since the 1960s. For over a century, colonial and noncolonial empires and their allied research organizations have offered employment, professional awards, and economic resources to sociologists and other scientists in exchange for practical, applicable results.

The loss of scientific independence is not simply a function of professional rewards and financial resources, however. The question of autonomy in scientific work is shadowed by the psychic issue of ego autonomy. Since Freud, the problem of ego autonomy has usually been focused on difficulties in gaining independence from parental figures. In his classic psychobiography of Max Weber, Mitzman (1985) focuses almost entirely on the impulses and impediments to Weber's intellectual work and intimate life that resulted from this original triangle. More recently however psychoanalytic theory has begun applying concepts such as transference, symbolic and imaginary identification, and ego ideals and ideal egos to the entire sweep of social existence. If we return to Mitzman's case study, this broadened perspective would suggest analyzing Weber's relations with a whole array of personages, while retaining a focus on the originary genesis of the subject in the parental triangle. Scientists are surrounded by figures who have mentored, influenced, and praised them and also by others who have personally dominated, challenged, debated, ridiculed, and disdained them and their work. Positive identifications and negative cathexes both compound the problem of scientific autonomy, as Mitzman (1985) shows. The work of scientists, like that of poets, writers, and artists (Bloom, 1997), is shaped by powerful identifications with idealized role models, by positive and negative transferences, and most broadly by the unconscious and its fantasies, wishes, needs, and drives.

Connecting social and psychic mechanisms in the study of scientific autonomy and other social practices is part of a larger project of constructing a *neo-Bourdieusian social theory*. A reconstructed (neo- or post-) Bourdieusian approach needs to integrate social and psychic mechanisms and to accentuate the historicizing tendencies in Bourdieu's work – tendencies that led him toward a conjunctural mode of accounting for ruptural historical events[1] and a historicist understanding of his own key categories such as symbolic capital and field as being linked to a specific world-historical time and place (Steinmetz, 2010a). I refer to the theoretical approach that results from historicizing Bourdieusian theory and specifying its psychoanalytic microfoundations as historical socioanalysis.

The "historical" part of this formula suggests that any and all social science needs to remain aware of the cultural, geographical, and epochal situatedness of all causal mechanisms or structures.[2] The psychoanalytic aspect is reflected in the shift from "sociology" to "socioanalysis" (a move made by Bourdieu himself) and in reinterpretation of Bourdieu's concepts of habitus and symbolic capital as involving, respectively, imaginary and symbolic identifications (Steinmetz, 2006a). The psychoanalytic and historical emphases in this approach reinforce each other, since it is at the level of the individual and the individual unconscious that we can most clearly perceive the basic historical principles of overdetermination, accident, conjuncture, and unpredictability, principles that need to be applied in the analysis of any social event or process (Steinmetz, 2008a). In this chapter, I will try to show how Bourdieu's account of scientific autonomy and heteronomy is enriched through an account of autonomy's psychofoundations.

I will focus here on two German sociological analysts of empire, Max Weber and Richard Thurnwald, both of whom faced threats to the autonomy of their scientific work on empires – threats that emanated specifically from the German empire(s) in which they lived and from the empires they took as their analytic objects. The cases of Weber and Thurnwald stake out two extremes on a spectrum of postures concerning scientific autonomy. I will ask how we might account for their differing ability to main scientific independence.

SOCIOLOGY AND EMPIRE

Anthropologists have long discussed the ways in which their discipline has been entangled, consciously and unconsciously, with the colonized populations they study. A foundational text in this regard was Michel Leiris' *Phantom Africa* (L'Afrique fantôme; Leiris, 1934), which described an African ethnographic expedition led by Marcel Griaule as a form of colonial plunder. Leiris criticized anthropologists' focus on the most isolated, rural, and traditional cultures, which could more easily be described as untouched by European influences, and he saw this as a way of disavowing the very existence of colonialism. In 1950, Leiris challenged Europeans' ability even to understand the colonized, writing that "ethnography is closely linked to the colonial fact, whether ethnographers like it or not. In general they work in the colonial or semi-colonial territories dependent on their country of origin, and even if they receive no direct support from the local representatives of their government, they are tolerated by them and more or less identified, by the people they study, as agents of the administration" (Leiris, 1950, p. 358). Similar ideas were discussed by French social scientists throughout the 1950s. Maxime Rodinson argued in the Année sociologique that "colonial conditions make even the most technically sophisticated sociological research singularly unsatisfying, from the standpoint of the desiderata of a scientific sociology" (Rodinson, 1955, p. 373). In a rejoinder to Leiris, Pierre Bourdieu acknowledged in Work and Workers in Algeria (Travail et travailleurs en Algérie) that "no behavior, attitude or ideology can be explained objectively without reference to the existential situation of the colonized as it is determined by the action of economic and social forces characteristic of the colonial system," but he insisted that the "problems of science" needed to be separated from "the anxieties of conscience" (2003, pp. 13–14). Since Bourdieu had been involved in a study of an incredibly violent redistribution of Algerians by the French colonial army at the height of the anticolonial revolutionary war, he had good reason to be sensitive to Leiris' criticisms (Bourdieu & Sayad, 1964). Rodinson called Bourdieu's critique of Leiris' thesis "excellent" (1965, p. 360), but Bourdieu later revised his views, noting that the works that had been available to him at the time of his research in Algeria tended "to justify the colonial order" (1990, p. 3). At the 1974 colloquium that gave rise to a book on the connections between anthropology and colonialism, Le mal de voir, Bourdieu called for an analysis of the relatively autonomous field of colonial science (1993a, p. 51). A parallel discussion took place in American anthropology somewhat later, during the 1960s. At the 1965 meetings of the American Anthropological Association, Marshall Sahlins criticized the "enlistment of scholars" in "cold war projects such as Camelot" as "servants of power in a gendarmerie relationship to the Third World." This constituted a "sycophantic relation to the state unbefitting science or citizenship" (Sahlins, 1967, pp. 72, 76). Sahlins underscored the connections between "scientific functionalism and the natural interest of a leading world power in the status quo" and called attention to the language of contagion and disease in the documents of "Project Camelot," adding that "waiting on call is the doctor, the US Army, fully prepared for its self-appointed 'important mission in the positive and constructive aspects of nation-building'" a mission accompanied by "insurgency prophylaxis" (1967, pp. 77–78). At the end of the decade, Current Anthropology published a series of articles on anthropologists' "social responsibilities," and Human Organization published a symposium entitled "Decolonizing Applied Social Sciences." British anthropologists followed suit, as evidenced by Asad's (1973) collection Anthropology and the Colonial Encounter. During the 1980s, authors such as Gothsch (1983) began to address the question of German anthropology's involvement in colonialism. The most recent revival of this discussion was in response to the Pentagon's deployment of "embedded anthropologists" in Afghanistan and elsewhere in the Middle East. The "Network of Concerned Anthropologists" in the AAA asked "researchers to sign an online pledge not to work with the military," arguing that they "are not all necessarily opposed to other forms of anthropological consulting for the state, or for the military, especially when such cooperation contributes to generally accepted humanitarian objectives ... However, work that is covert, work that breaches relations of openness and trust with studied populations, and work that enables the occupation of one country by another violates professional standards" ("Embedded Anthropologists", 2007).[3] Other disciplines, notably geography, economics, area studies, and political science, have also started to examine the involvement of their fields with empire.[4]

With very few exceptions, however, historians of sociology have not been interested in this set of issues (but see Connell, 1997, 2007; Steinmetz, 2010b). Sociologists have, however, been deeply involved in studying, counseling, and criticizing empires from the discipline's intellectual beginnings in the 19th century through to the present. Each phase of sociology's disciplinary development has been embedded within, or shadowed by, new developments in imperial politics. Auguste Comte, who first popularized the word "sociology," discussed early modern colonialism in his Cours de philosophie positive, asking "whether the colonial system on the whole accelerated or retarded the overall development of modern society," and concluding that colonialism actually "retarded social development" by promoting "retrograde thought and social immobility" (Comte, 1830–1842, Vol. 6, pp. 128–129, 133–134).[5] Many of sociology's 19th-century predisciplinary founders were directly concerned with colonialism, including John Stuart Mill, who worked on native policy for the British East Indies Company in India (Zastoupil, 1994), de Tocqueville (2001), who developed policies for colonial Algeria and India, and Albert Schaffle, who wrote a book-length essay on "colonial political studies" (Schäffle, 1886–1888). Sociology emerged as a university academic discipline in precisely the same decade as the European scramble for Africa (the second wave of global colonialism), United States colonial expansion in the aftermath of the

Spanish-American war, and the development of imperialist spheres of influence, treaty ports, and coastal colonies in China. Few attentive contemporaries, one might think, could fail to speculate about the reasons for this imperial upsurge, the looming dissolution of the Ottoman Empire, the crumbling of the Qing dynasty in China, or the rivalries pushing European states toward war with one another.

Many of the founders of sociology as an academic discipline in the decades leading up to the World War I focused on traditional land empires or modern colonialism. The leading figure in the first generation of academic sociology in Germany, Max Weber, analyzed land empires throughout his entire academic career. His brother Alfred Weber published on European colonialism (Weber, 1918, 1935, 2000) and the Chinese empire (Weber, 1943). Alfred Vierkandt published a treatise on Naturvölker and Kulturvölker (natural and cultural peoples), developing a distinction that under-girded German colonial discourse and policy (von Vierkandt, 1896).[6] Oppenheimer's (1929) System of Sociology included a volume on ancient Rome. Grünfeld (1913) published a study of European treaty port colonies in China.[7] Leopold von Wiese, a leading figure in Weimar and post-1945 German sociology, wrote extensively on his travels in India, Hong Kong, and the German colony in Qingdao, China (von Wiese, 1914a, 1914b, 1922), and published a semi-pornographic colonial novel set in British colonial Ceylon (von Wiese, 1923).

Sociologists in other countries were equally focused on empire during sociology's foundational period. The first international "Congress of colonial sociology," attended by a number of French university professors, was held in Paris in 1900.[8] A large number of French sociologists were connected to colonialism as their analytic object, research setting, or source of analytic raw material, and these numbers increased during the interwar period and the two decades after World War II. Several of the founders of US sociology were involved in the Anti-Imperialist League, an organization described by Albion Small as a precursor of the American Sociological Society (Small, 1916, p. 775). Franklin Giddings became a supporter of American imperialism (Giddings, 1900). W. E. B. Du Bois wrote about colonialism continuously from World War II (Du Bois, 1915) until his death in Ghana in 1963. Dutch sociologist Steinmetz (1903) analyzed indigenous or "customary law" in European colonies. Most of the early founders of British sociology were involved in Britain's imperial ventures in one way or another, including Benjamin Kidd, whose Control of the Tropics (Kidd, 1898) compared different approaches to colonial rule, and Geddes (1917, 1947), who was both a critic of imperialism and a direct contributor to British rule in India. When the World War I shattered Europe's long-lasting peace, social scientists began to speculate about the "atavistic" elements allegedly lying behind Germany's imperialist aggressiveness (Schumpeter, 1951; Veblen, 1915). W. E. B. Du Bois argued that German bellicosity was driven by British and French efforts at "relegating Germany to a second place in colonial imperialism," and that support for Nazism was strengthened by Germany's loss of colonies after 1919 (Du Bois, 1986 [1940], p. 724, 1975 [1945], p. 108).

In Weimar Germany, which had lost its colonial empire in World War I, sociologists became more, not less interested in colonialism (e.g. Brinkmann, 1921).[9] Arthur Salz, a political economist and sociologist who was close to the Weber's (Lassman, Velody, & Martins, 1988, p. 206), published an important study of political imperialism (Salz, 1931). Norbert Elias, a student of Alfred Weber's, discussed the application of his Freudian thesis of the "civilizing process" to colonial situations ([1939] 1994, pp. 463–363). Sociological interest in colonialism also expanded in France under the influence of Marcel Mauss, Durkheim s nephew, who inherited his status as the leader of a group of sociologists between the wars, and who combined generalizing theory with ethnographic data from primitive (i.e. colonized) peoples. Mauss was a member of the Committee for the Defence and Protection of Indigenous Peoples, a group that protested colonial abuses but without challenging the existence of colonialism per se (Sibeud, 2002, p. 23, n. 10), but he called in 1913 for the creation of a bureau of ethnography that would "activate ethnographic studies in France, and particularly in the French colonies" (quoted in Conklin, 2002, p. 267). Most importantly, Mauss helped to create the Institut d'Ethnologie (Ethnological Institute), dedicated to the memory of Durkheim, in 1925 (Karady, 1982). The Institute's mandate was to study the French colonies (Lévy-Bruhl, 1925 [1910]). It overlapped to some extent with the national École coloniale (Amselle, 1993) and received its principal funding from the colonies, but sought to approach colonial problems more scientifically and autonomously and did not seek to place its students in colonial service (Conklin, 2002, p. 287; De L'Estoile, 2002, pp. 294–295). Nonetheless, Mauss and the Institute's other founders insisted that the Institute "was at the disposal of colonial governments and protectorates for any information concerning expeditions (French or foreign), the study of indigenous races, the conservation and study of monuments and collections, or the study of social facts" (Mauss quoted in Fournier, 2006, p. 237). Several generations of Mauss' students (and their students) conducted pioneering research in and on colonized societies.

After 1933, Nazism reawakened German dreams of continental imperialism and colonial empire and gave rise to new theories of German continental imperialism (Arendt, 1951; Neumann, 1942), some in the guise of Zwischeneuropa ("intermediate Europe"; Wirsing, 1932), others as an eastern-oriented Grossraum or "greater space" (Kaiser, 1968; Schmitt, [1941] 1991). Many of the sociologists who stayed in Germany after the Nazis seized power in 1933 turned their attention to applied policy research, contributing to ethnic policymaking in occupied Eastern Europe and helping with plans for a renewed German colonial empire in Africa (Gutberger, 1996; Klingemann, 1996, 2002, 2009; Linne, 2002; Schmokel, 1964; Weinberg, 1963). Ethnosociologist Richard Thurnwald and his student and editorial assistant Wilhelm Mühlmann (Michel, 1992, 1995) were particularly involved in the study of empire before, during, and after the Nazi era.

After 1945, Soviet expansionism focused social scientists' attention on the causes and results of continental imperialism. The ongoing process of decolonization was embedded within discussions of the passage from European colonialism to informal US hegemony and postcolonial "underdevelopment" (e.g., Balandier, 1956; Bourdieu, 1959). French sociologists' focus on questions of colonialism reached a kind of apotheosis after 1945, lasting for several decades, as the pages of the Cahiers internationaux de sociologie and the revived Année sociologique were filled with analyses of colonized and decolonizing societies. Ethnosociologists like Jacques Soustelle, Germaine Tillion, Paul Mus, Paul Mercier, Georges Balandier, and Pierre Bourdieu were directly or indirectly involved in late colonial administration.[10] US policies of informal empire were analyzed and organized by modernization theories, which were subsequently criticized starting in the late 1960s (Mazrui, 1968). Sociological research on colonialism first reemerged in the United States at the end of the 1950s with Wallerstein's Ph.D. dissertation on Ghana and the Ivory Coast and his edited volume on "the colonial situation" (Wallerstein, 1959, 1966). Historical sociological research on European colonialism was conducted in the early 1970s (Hermassi, 1972; Magubane, 1971) and then subsided, emerging once again in the 1990s (Go, 1999; Steinmetz, 1995, 1997). Since the beginning of the 21st century, the new American imperialism has captured the attention of a growing number of sociologists (e.g. Calhoun, Cooper, & Moore, 2006; Go, 2008; Mann, 2003; Steinmetz, 2003), while also inspiring sociological research on a number of other empires. A few contemporary sociologists in Germany and France have also worked on ancient empires (Breuer,

1987) and modern colonial empires (Bertrand, 2005, 2008; Dezalay & Bryant, 2008; Lardinois, 2008; Saada, 2007).

TOWARD A THEORY OF SCIENTIFIC AUTONOMY

This brief overview of the analytic and practical contributions of academic sociologists to the study and practice of empire raises a number of questions. What explains the rise and fall of sociological interest in empire over time and the variation of interest across national settings? When and why do sociologists tend to focus on their "own" empires and when do they become interested in earlier empires or in other nation's colonies? How do theoretical and methodological approaches to the study of empire vary across disciplines? And what are some of the most promising theories of empires, regardless of their conditions of origin?

Pierre Bourdieu's analysis of the field is a very helpful first step in understanding science, as he shows in Homo Academicus (1988) and elsewhere. To understand why some scientists tend to adjust their research to the field of power (business, the state, religious institutions) while others resist the pull of such forces, Bourdieu suggests that we need to look at scientists' holdings of inherited and field-specific scientific capital, and to analyze their scientific strategies in relation to their location in a space of positions and possibilities. Bourdieu understands the field as an arena of specialized practice that is partially independent of external forces, partly autonomous from the field of power.[11]

Field theory avoids the dual error of construing science either as a function of extra-scientific forces (capitalism, empire, scientists' personal background and current social situation) or as remaining entirely independent of such external factors.[12] Against the first set of theories we need to acknowledge that scientific research is often driven by discussions and conflicts located entirely within scientific fields rather that by discourses originating in non-academic realms. At the very least, scientific fields provide a sort of buffer, a prism of refraction, through which external discourses have to pass in order to be taken up by scientists. Nor can holdings of economic or symbolic capital be immediately or automatically deployed to advantage in new fields of endeavor. All forms of capital have to undergo a process of conversion or adaption to the peculiarities of the field in which a subject is currently active.

Field theory also rejects the second approach, which understands pure science completely on its own terms, as oblivious to and unaffected by the extra-scientific world. Science's autonomy can only ever be relative or partial. The limits on scientific autonomy are revealed within the (partially autonomous) scientific field itself. A field's relative autonomy is often combined with its configuration as a chiastic structure. Every social field is a battlefield, a terrain of symbolic conflict. There is an overall polarization in the field between heteronymous and autonomous poles, each correlated with unequally distributed field-specific symbolic capital. Actors located closer to the heteronymous pole will tend to orient their practices to external forces in the overarching field of power such as economic markets or the state.

Analyzing science as a field helps explain why European scholars, even those located in the same country and historical period, may not share the same views of colonialism, empire, or anything else (Steinmetz, 2008b, 2008c). Some views are shared by all of the participants in a field – the field's illusio or common commitment to the arbitrary stakes and history of the game. This common culture coexists, however, with intense disagreements about substantive matters and stark differences at the level of individual habitus, resources, and holdings of symbolic capital. It should be possible to identify a shared illusio and sense of the rules and stakes of the game in any field, as well as autonomous and heteronymous poles and a hierarchy of unevenly distributed field specific symbolic capital.

It is an empirical question whether any particular type of practice takes on the properties or a field at all. The researcher also needs to establish in every case whether certain representations and practices come to be recognized by all participants in a field as more or less distinguished, or whether instead a field remains unsettled with respect to internal ranking. Once a field is settled, it becomes possible to argue that certain actors systematically gain symbolic profits from their habituses and practices at the expense of others. Settled fields are in this respect structures of symbolic violence in which the arbitrariness of their definitions of excellence is hidden by the tacit consensus of the dominant and the dominated. Dominant positions are frequently, though not always, located at a field's autonomous pole.

The contending and dominating positions within a given scientific field vary over time and across disciplines. For example, German colonial ethnology was dominated by biological racism in the late 19th century but this began to shift around World War I, and during the Weimar Republic cultural diffusionist and "cultural circles" (kulturkreis) positions became dominant. Adolf Bastian, a founder of German academic anthropology, the Royal Ethnographic Museum in Berlin, and the Berlin Ethnological Society, argued that human "races" were "different species" and that black Africans were less intelligent than other races and should be compelled to manual labor (Bastian, 1884, p. 31, 1860, Vol. 3, p. 396). Felix von Luschan, who succeeded Bastian as head of the Berlin Ethnological Museum and held the first Anthropology Chair at Berlin University, initially focused on body measurements and designed a chromatic scale for classifying skin color, but argued later in his career that "the concept of 'race' as a whole [was] imprecise" (Laukötter, 2007, p. 159) and that "the only savages in Africa are whites suffering from 'Tropenkoller' (colonial madness)" (von Luschan, 1915, p. 11). Ethnologist Leo Frobenius defended forced labor at the first German Colonial Congress in 1902, and he argued during his second African expedition that "you have to treat the Negro harshly" and defending flogging as punishment. But Frobenius later became highly critical of colonial racism. His argument that the "idea of the barbaric Negro is a European invention" made him into an icon for some early pan-Africanists like Aimé Césaire (Gothsch, 1983, pp. 117ff., 120, 131; Césaire, 2000, p. 53). In French colonial social science, ethnology continued to defend a view of African culture as timeless and unchanging even after 1945, while sociologists like Georges Balandier and Paul Mercier insisted on a historical approach to African cultures as fully caught up in modernity and change (Balandier, 1953, 1955a, 1955b; Balandier & Mercier, 1952; Mercier, 1951, 1954).

Autonomy from empire also varied by research topic, discipline, and historical period. Before 1918 a great deal of the research on colonized societies was carried out by colonial officials. Pre-1914 institutions like the École coloniale in Paris, the Berlin Seminar for Oriental Languages, the Hamburg Colonial Institute, and the Dutch Royal Academy in Delft (later Leiden) were largely staffed by officials, military men, and missionaries with colonial experience. There was a great deal of back-and-forth between colonial activities and academic social science. For example, the missionary Carl Gotthilf Büttner was dispatched to Otjimbingwe in German Southwest Africa by the Rhenish Missionary Society in 1872. In addition to becoming an outspoken advocate of German colonialism (Büttner, 1885, p. 39; Menzel, 1992), Büttner helped the new German "imperial commissary" (Kaiserlicher Kommissar) Heinrich Goering convince Herero chief Kama-herero to sign a "protection treaty" with the German government in 1885. In 1887 Büttner was appointed to teach Swahili at the newly founded Seminar for Oriental Languages, where he trained administrators and soldiers bound for the colonies and edited the Zeitschrift für afrikanische

Sprachen from 1887 to 1890. The College de France created a chair in Muslim Sociology and Sociography in 1902 "with funds from the Governor General of Algeria and the protectorates of Tunisia and Morocco," and the first appointment to the chair was "a former military man, Alfred le Chatlier" (Clark, 1973, p. 55). Berber specialist Robert Montagne was assigned to direct the Sociological Section of the Native Affairs Bureau (Direction des Affaires Indigènes) in the French colonial state in Morocco in 1917 (Seddon, 1973). After 1918, the study of colonialism and colonized societies gained some autonomy from colonial governance. Hamburg's Colonial Institute became the core of Hamburg University and the Berlin Seminar for Oriental Languages and Halle Colonial Academy turned themselves into schools of foreign studies.

Of course, there are certain historical moments and political systems in which the autonomy of science is severely eroded, and Nazi Germany is an extreme example of an assault on academic autonomy. Jewish and other non- "Aryan" and liberal or left-wing academics were purged from the universities and prevented from publishing. The state had the power to decide who would be hired, fired, and permitted to attend scientific conferences, which institutes, universities, and disciplines would even exist and how much money they would get, and whether books or dissertations could be published. Alfred Rosenberg's organization, which included from 1941 a "Hauptamt Soziologie," enforced conformity with Nazi doctrine – albeit with less effectiveness than other parts of the Nazi state, and even if it was internally riven by differences. The party also propagated the use of official linguistic formulae (LTI – Lingua Tertii Imperii; Klemperer, 2006), which infiltrated the work of social scientists, for example in the use of the term Umvolkung rather than Assimilation in work on the Germanization of Eastern European populations. Scientific autonomy was further undermined by the state-mandated creation of interdisciplinary fields like "colonial science" and Ostforschung.[13] Entire disciplines, including sociology, were largely folded into these interdisciplinary, applied research fields. Publishing opportunities disappeared in many areas (Derks, 1999) even as research budgets skyrocketed for the Kaiser Wilhelm Society and other institutions (Szöllösi-Janze, 2001, p. 14).

The Nazi concept of Gleichschaltung (coordination) points to a severe reduction of cultural and scientific independence from the state. Gleichschaltung means something like a coordination of spheres, or in Bourdieusian terms a synchronziation of fields (Bourdieu, 1988, pp. 173–180). But even in Nazi Germany scientific work continued to operate partially according to its own internal rules and dynamics. This was true of disciplines that were not related to immediate policymaking and also of some domains from which the state demanded concrete, applied results. Programs such as the phantasmagorical "Welteislehre" (doctrine of cosmic ice; see Nagel, 1991) or Nazi "German physics" never achieved "discursive monopoly or predominance" (Ash, 1999, p. 346) within their respective scientific arenas. Research on tropical medicine sponsored by the Colonial Department of the Reichsforschungsrat may never have been put into practice, but it was supposed to be medically sound (Reichsforschungsrat, 1942). In this respect, Bourdieusian field theory converges with arguments that the Nazi regime was "in no way simply hostile to science" (Szöllösi-Janze, 2001, p. 11). Just as the Nazi state was a "polycratic" field of permanent internal power struggles (Broszat, 1981) rather than monolithic and internally coherent, so too many scientific fields in Nazi Germany continued to display a wide array of individual strategies of accommodation and independence, and retained a chiastic structure with more autonomous and more dependent poles. According to Walker (1989, p. 85), "Instead of viewing the interaction between National Socialism and science in terms of black and white, in terms of 'nazis' and 'enemies/victims of the nazis', the grey areas must be investigated, where scientists both opposed and supported certain aspects of National Socialist policy." Langewiesche (1997) has detailed the divergent forms of "self-Gleichschaltung" among a group of Tubingen professors from different disciplines shortly after the Machtergreifung; Klingemann (2009) has done the same with respect to sociologists in Nazi Germany. A similar diversity of stances characterized scientists and intellectuals who went into the so-called inner emigration, like Alfred Weber.

In order to make sense of the different types of accommodation and distancing from the state we need to understand the official political position on the object of analysis. This is more difficult than it sounds, because official policy discussions of land and sea empires were often internally divided. It is usually possible to discern a dominant government position on imperial issues during the Nazi period, but not in Wilhelmine Germany and even less during the Weimar Republic. Before 1933, a social scientist who wanted to coordinate his interpretation of empire with the views of extra-scientific elites was forced to make a selection from an array of options. After 1933, and especially with the creation of the Kolonialpolitisches Amt (KPA) of the NSDAP, an official approach to colonialism emerged. The curriculum for KPA training courses for colonial administrators was "based on instructions approved by [KPA head Franz Ritter von] Epp and by Alfred Rosenberg" (Schmokel, 1964, p. 155). Government officials like Rudolf Asmis, Oskar Karstedt, and Rudolf

Karlowa detailed the official approach in books, decrees, and periodicals like Deutscher Kolonial-Dienst. Asmis' 1940 "German Colonial Catechism" represented "a kind of constitutional document for the future" colonial empire (ibid., p. 162). Karstedt, a KPA official, covered the same ground in his book on "problems of native policy in Africa" (Karstedt, 1942) as Thurnwald did in his 1939 book Koloniale Gestaltung (Colonial Organization). The lines between academic and government colonial specialists were extremely blurred. Counsel-General Karlowa of the Ribbentrop Bureau discussed colonialism in a volume edited by the academic ethnologist Diedrich Westermann, in which the latter presented his ideas on native policy (Westermann, 1937). Writers like Westermann and Thurnwald were able to align their writing with the official party line, supporting territorial segregation between blacks and whites and a ban on mixed marriage in the colonies, along with other mainstays of the "Colonial Catechism" (Thurnwald, 1937, 1938a).

Social science was able to maintain pockets of partial autonomy in Nazi Germany, especially before 1938.[14] Views of Max Weber were highly diverse but far from uniformly negative (Klingemann, 1996, Chap. 9). The Festschrift for Ferdinand Toennies, who lost his job in 1933 and stepped down as head of the German Sociological Society, was published in 1936 in Leipzig, with essays by the anti-Nazis Franz Boas and Gerhard Colm and refugee Karl Löwith, a Social Democratic economist who had been active against Nazi organizations in Germany and had emigrated in 1933 to teach at the University in Exile of the New School for Social Research. Werner Landecker, a member of the German-Jewish Kulturbund, earned a law degree in Berlin in 1936 with a dissertation on international law (Landecker, 1999).[15] Anthropologist Leonhard Adam lost his position in 1933 but continued to edit Zeitschrift für vergleichende Rechtswissenschaft (Journal of Comparative Jurisprudence) in Germany until 1938. Adam was the original editor of the 1937 Lehrbuch für Völkerkunde, to which Thurnwald and his student Mühlmann contributed. When controversy arose around Adam's role Theodor Preuss took over as editor, but Adam still contributed a chapter. Even this was too much for the Nazi Americanist Walter Krickeberg, whose attack on Thurnwald and Mühlmann for collaborating with Adam triggered an infamous "debate" in Krickeberg and Thurnwald both tried to prove that the other was more "Jewish" (Fischer, 1990; Krickeberg, 1938; Thurnwald, 1938b; Timm, 1977, pp. 63–67). At the same time, this dispute demonstrated that Nazism had not produced scientific homogeneity; Krickeberg's Kulturkreis (cultural areas) approach and Thurnwald's own "functionalism" continued to coexist, and the polarization between the two frameworks inside Ethnology was one of the underlying reasons for the fight (Mühlmann, 1937).[16]

EGO AUTONOMY

Bourdieu's analysis of the field is a helpful first step in understanding science, as shown by Homo Academicus (Bourdieu, 1988) and other studies. At the same time, Bourdieu was reluctant or unable to develop the psychic underpinnings of his categories of habitus, symbolic capital, and field (Steinmetz, 2006a). He recognized the importance of such a project increasingly over time, arguing that sociology and psychoanalysis were equally valuable ways of "constructing the same object" (Bourdieu, 1999a, 1999b, p. 512). Bourdieu interwove psychoanalytic arguments with his own theory, for example in The Rules of Art, where he argues that the ambivalence of the central figure in Flaubert's Sentimental Education, Frédéric, with respect to his own inheritance "may find its principle in his ambivalence towards his mother, a double personage, obviously feminine, but also masculine in that she substitutes for the disappeared father" (Bourdieu, 1996, p. 10). In Pascalian Meditations, Bourdieu uses a psychoanalytic logic in explaining the genesis of subjects suited with "the durable disposition to invest in the social game" and to compete in social fields. This requires the transition from self-love to a "quite other object of investment" (Bourdieu, 2000, p. 166). Socioanalysis (his new word for sociology)[17] and psychoanalysis, he argued, "should combine their efforts" to explain "the transition, described by Freud ... from a narcissistic organization of the libido, in which the child takes himself (or his own body) as an object of desire, to another state in which he orients himself towards another person, thus entering the world of 'object relations,' in the forms of the original social microcosm and protagonists of the drama that is played out there" (2000, p. 116). Bourdieu was as much concerned with "heirs who refuse to inherit" as with those who follow their prescribed path. This openness to non-reproductive logics refutes those critics of Bourdieu who see him as uniquely focused on social reproduction (Steinmetz, 2010). In Pascalian Meditations, Bourdieu discussed individual differences in the ability even to form an integrated habitus. An overaccommodating personality, he suggested, may be connected to a "rigid, self-enclosed, overintegrated habitus," while an opportunist or adaptive personality type might allow the habitus to dissolve "into a kind of mens momentanea, incapable of ... having an integrated sense of self" (Bourdieu, 2000, p. 161).

A psychoanalytic approach is centrally important to our current concern. Scientific autonomy cannot be separated from other forms of autonomy, including the psychic autonomy of the individual scientists. But integrating the psychoanalytic and the socioanalytic levels forces us in each case to ask: autonomy from what? To answer this question we need to turn to the basic analytic unit or starting point in the sociology of sociology, which is the individual sociologist. Even if "society intervenes at the very centre of the creative project," the immediate place where this creative project is generated is the individual artist, writer, scientist, sociologist, etc. (Bourdieu, 1971 [1966], p. 166). Like other cultural fields, sociology is structured around the unequal distribution of a species of symbolic capital specific to the field (sociological, or social-scientific capital). The main way in which scientific recognition is generated is through individual achievements such as publications and discoveries (Merton, 1973). Bourdieu is interested in the variable levels of autonomy that individuals and groups of scientists maintain vis-à-vis the external field of power and other fields. But he does not consider other axes of individual autonomy.

Any individual faces a range of different objects upon which he may become dependent or from which he may seek autonomy. Analytically these objects can be seen as ranging from the most proximate to the most distant from the individual.[18] The most distant objects include other galaxies, solar systems, and planets, but these are unlikely to shape sociologists' scientific practices. Slightly less distant from the individual sociologist are the great political empires and foreign states and transnational economic and cultural systems. Here too we have to be cautious, even when dealing with social scientists focused on empires as their objects of analysis, in drawing any rapid conclusions about causality. On the one hand, the reemergence of assertive foreign military interventions by the United States after 2001 went hand in hand with a sharp increase in specialists in US empire. But the unevenness of this interest cross-nationally, across different fields of the human sciences, and even within a specific American discipline like sociology suggests that many other factors are at work in translating a real world event or process into an object of scientific investment. As Max Weber wrote, social life is a "vast chaotic stream of events, which flows away through time," meaning that something other than its mere existence must be present to make a given event the object of scientific scrutiny (Weber, 1949, p. 111). Moving down to a slight more proximate level we arrive at the national-level extra-scientific powers with which Bourdieu was most concerned: business and the state. National-level fields that lie outside science will also influence scientists' choices and strategies mainly in indirect or mediated ways, as they are translated into the terms of a specific field. But some scientists will be exposed or expose themselves more directly to influences outside science, usually because they are relatively poor in their own field's specific symbolic capital, as discussed above.

Continuing our movement toward the individual scientist we arrive finally at this immediate field of activity. But for Bourdieu, fields are not only agonistic battlefields, sites of competition and conflict. They are also the primary domains in which individuals seek recognition for the value of their work from other participants in the same field. Even in his earliest analysis of fields Bourdieu emphasized their dual character as arenas of struggle and mutual recognition (Bourdieu, 1971 [1966], p. 170). All fields, especially loosely structured ones like sociology, depend for their very existence on a constantly renewed web of acts of mutual recognition and non-recognition (i.e. non-membership in the field) and ongoing assessments of the relative value in the field's specific hierarchy of each actor and action. Bourdieu quotes Sartre: "there are some qualities that come to us solely from the judgment of others" (Sartre, 1988, p. 77). But Bourdieu does not use the words autonomy and heteronomy to discuss the ways in which people define themselves in relation to other participants in the same field. For Bourdieu, autonomy is assessed by examining the relationship between an actor in a field (or a field in its entirety)[19] and forces lying outside the field. But if we construct the individual as a kind of Nomos, we can immediately see that interpersonal or I-Thou relations pose problems of autonomy and heteronomy for the individual. The "entry into the world of 'object relations" and the "orientation toward others," mentioned by Bourdieu, lead individuals not only to differentiate themselves from others but also to unconsciously identify, emulate, introject, and imitate others (or imagos of others).[20] Such dynamics are of central importance for the analysis of any field.

The relevance of individual unconscious identifications with others for understanding science can be clearly seen if we move to the final intra-individual level and ask about psychic autonomy. Of course Freud uses the term autonomy only a few times in his work and "only as in everyday language" (Gullestad, 1993, p. 22). In Freudian Ego Psychology, autonomy refers to the independence of the ego from the id (Rapaport, 1967), and in the work of Erik Erikson, autonomy means "deciding for oneself when faced with a significant other" (Gullestad, 1993, p. 28), that is, being "an individual who dares to march out of step." Theories of ego autonomy thus differentiate between "the ego's autonomy from the drives on the one hand, and from the environment on the other" (Hurvich, 2005, p. 474).

Imitation and conformity are partly rooted in a universal feature of human psychic existence, namely, the adoption of ego ideals and ideal egos in the process of forming unconscious identifications.[21] It is not possible to escape from this dependence by abandoning ego ideals, since, as Cornell (2003, p. 144) notes, the very suspicion of ego ideas is itself another kind of ideal, an "ego ideal of how we should be." Nonetheless it should be possible to gain some conscious control over unconscious identifications and from the "drives" more generally (Rapaport, 1951), that is, to gain some control over unconscious sources of scientific action.

Ego autonomy in both of the main senses — autonomy from unconscious drives and wishes and autonomy from significant others and the environment — is of central importance for understanding scientific activity, since scientists are caught up in complex relations of mentorship and emulation on the one hand and differentiation and competition on the other. In order to understand why some scientists become conformists, adjusting their research to the field of power, while others resist the pull of such forces, we need to combine socioanalytic and psychoanalytic approaches. Psychoanalysis is better suited to understanding why some individuals form a "rigid, self-enclosed, overintegrated habitus" while others are opportunist or adaptive and incapable of "having an integrated sense of self" (2000, p. 161).[22]

We can now revisit the question: What makes some individual scientists better able or more predisposed to maintain their scientific autonomy than others? In part this is a function of inherited economic capital, which may allow someone like Flaubert in the French literary field or Max Weber in the German social science field to pursue activities that flout or even do the opposite of the demands of powerful state and economic actors. However, some individuals are predisposed to heteronomy despite their economic independence, while others doggedly pursue an autonomous path despite economic hardship. To understand such variations we might distinguish between the opportunist personality type and the subject who is predisposed to obey an internal superego and to resist external demands. In fields that are already poorly autonomized, like sociology, the first type will tend to gravitate toward dominant powers outside the field. Sociology has periodically seen waves of identification with biology, economics, physics, and other external sciences. The willing adjustment of many German social scientists to the demands of the Nazi state suggests a different sort of external identification. As for the second, "integrated" personality type, it is important to note that this can strengthen both autonomous and heteronymous scientific stances, depending on the contents of the identifications.

Alfred Weber's identification with his older brother led him to develop his own version of "value neutrality" under the guise of the "free floating intelligentsia," even as he came to reject the doctrine of value freedom as presented by Max Weber (Demm, 2000a, pp. 37, 264). A figure like Hamburg sociology professor Andreas Walther, however, illustrates that a highly independent, even rigid personality could arrive at scientific stances that were heteronymous. Walther adopted views that were unpopular, even suspect, in the sociological field during the Weimar period, defending quantitative, presentist, American-style sociology, which he believed was disdained by most of his German sociological colleagues for its "crass positivism" (Walther, 1927). Walther greeted the Nazi takeover and became a party member in March 1933, and become more prominent in the sociology discipline, supervising 33 dissertations in Hamburg after 1933 (Wassner, 1985, p. 51). The heteronymization of his sociological research in the Nazi period thus seems to have stemmed not from an opportunist "mens momentanea" but from a rigid, self-controlled, and self-righteous personality structure rather than a labile, opportunist one.

These considerations might help us understand the scientific choices of the two sociologists examined in this paper. Of course (pace Mitzman, 1985), we cannot really hope to psychoanalyze people who did not leave records of a self-analysis or psychoanalysis. What we can do is analyze their texts, letters, and other records, asking how they dealt with issues of scientific and personal autonomy in these records. Fortunately these sociologists left ample direct and indirect records of their views of scientific and ego autonomy.

EMBATTLED AUTONOMY, 1880–1945

Max Weber and Richard Thurnwald present two very different patterns of scientific autonomy and dependence. Weber (1964, 1920), was recognized as the leading German sociologist during his lifetime.[23] The Max Weber "myth" in Heidelberg in the decade before World War I rivaled that of his acquaintance, the poet Stefan George (Honigsheim, 1926; Norton, 2002, pp. 475–480; Radkau, 2009, pp. 293–297). At the meetings of the German Sociological Association between 1910 and 1933, no name was mentioned more frequently than Max Weber's (Kaesler, 1984, p. 41). He was called the most important "maker of sociology" by the other German sociologists interviewed by Earle Edward Eubank in 1934 (Kaesler, 1991).

Sociologically, Weber exemplified the 19th century model of the German university professor, in which Besitz (economic capital) formed the precondition for Bildung or academic culture, and also allowed for considerable scientific autonomy. This was true for Weber at least after he married Marianne Schnitger (Roth, 2001, p. 549) and obtained his first professorship at Freiburg in 1894 (Weber, 1988, pp. 199–201). Before that time Weber was financially dependent on his father. Shortly after Weber received the status of Ordinarius (full professor) at Heidelberg in 1897 his father died in a series of events that triggered his nervous breakdown. His teaching and research came to a halt and he resigned his professorship in 1903, again becoming financially dependent, this time on his mother (Mitzman, 1985, pp. 148–153; Radkau, 2009, p. 282). In 1908, Marianne inherited a great deal of money (Radkau, 2009, pp. 280–283), easing the Webers' financial condition. Weber had already started to reemerge with the publication of The Protestant Ethic and the Spirit of Capitalism in 1904–905, and he began to play a central role in the nascent German discipline of sociology and in academia and politics more generally, finally accepting a chair in economics at Vienna in 1919 and Lujo Brentano's chair at Munich in 1920, where he moved just before he died.

Weber attached central importance to autonomy. Much of his writing during the 1890s can be interpreted at least in part in the context of his obsession with his own and his mother's autonomy from his overbearing, patriarchal father, Max Weber, Sr., and his desire to escape from "abject dependence" (Mitzman, 1985, pp. 124, 133; Radkau, 2009, p. 110). An example is Weber's argument that the Prussian rural laborers' exodus from the eastern estates was rooted in a desire for liberation from patriarchal feudal authoritarianism, as opposed to a strictly economic calculus. Weber associated the Prussian Junkers with his father, whom he saw as a conformist, "comfortable" petty bureaucrat who "enabled himself 'to keep pace with this living standard' only by pirating his wife's inheritance" (Mitzman, 1985, pp. 48, 123). Many of his research projects, including his research on the Prussian rural laborers in the 1890s and his study of the "psychophysics" of industrial labor (Weber, 1984a, 1984b), were financed by the Verein für Sozialpolitik (Radkau, 2009, pp. 79, 267), and Weber's attack on the Verein's old guard for mixing politics and science may have been partly driven by his overflowing rage at authority figures who placed him in a situation of dependence.[24] Weber intervened directly in several different arenas bearing directly on the question of scientific autonomy, above all in his doctrine of "value-free science" (Nau, 1996; Weber, 1949, [1919] 1958), even if he did not seem to apply the doctrine systematically and continued to allow himself to mix science and politics even as he anathe-mized it in others (Mommsen, 1984).[25] Weber thus presents a case of heightened economic autonomy, living much of the time on family money rather than his own earnings. In psychic and scientific terms, however, his relationship to autonomy was more complicated.

Richard Thurnwald was the son of an Austrian factory manager (Melk-Koch, 1989, p. 31) who had studied law, sociology, and Orientalism and published two of his earliest articles on the bildungsbürgerliche topics of ancient Egypt and Babylonia (Thurnwald, 1901, 1903–1904). At the outset, then, he seemed to combine Besitz and Bildung much like Weber and so many other 19th century German professors. However, Thurnwald's shift from ancient history to the ethnology of Melanesians and Africans corre-spond to mounting personal economic difficulties. Born in the 1860s like Max Weber, Thurnwald was sociologically younger than him, an eternal "newcomer" to the German social scientific field who was closer to the younger German academics during the Weimar Republic than to the estab-lished mandarins.[26] Thurnwald converted from Catholicism to Protestantism when he moved to Germany after his university studies and never returned to Austria. He spent fourteen years outside Germany, begin-ning with two long research trips to New Guinea (1906–1909 and 1912–1914). During this period he became known among his academic sponsors as "bedurfnislos" (frugal).[27] Thurnwald began his teaching career as a Private Docent at Halle (1919–1923) and became an "extraordinary" professor (that is, without full health and pension benefits) for Sociology and Ethnology at Berlin University in 1923 at the age of 56 (Asen, 1955, p. 200). According to his biographer, Thurnwald probably lost a great deal of money in the postwar inflation and struggled financially after a messy divorce, leading him to request emergency funds from his employer repeat-edly (Melk-Koch, 1989, pp. 253, 262). Thurnwald eagerly accepted offers as visiting professor at Yale in 1931–1932 and 1935–1936 and was willing to take a permanent job at any American college or university in this per-iod, but was ultimately unsuccessful.[28] Only at the age of 77 did Thurnwald finally obtain a position as full professor (Ordinarius) at Berlin University, which was now located in the Soviet occupied zone. Thurnwald gave up this position in 1949 and moved to the newly founded Free University in West Berlin, where he was bumped back down to the rank of Honorarprofessor (Melk-Koch, 1989, pp. 281–282). Thurnwald's research and publications consistently received outside funding: his first three year trip to German New Guinea (1906–1909) was financed by the Berlin Ethnological Museum and the Baessler Stiftung; his second trip to

New Guinea in 1912 was paid for by the deutsche Kolonialgesellschaft and German Colonial Office. During the Weimar Republic his research was sponsored by the International Institute of African Languages and Cultures (IIALC) and the Australian National Research Council; his journal Zeitschrift für Völkerpsychologie und Soziologie (renamed Sociologus in 1931) was subsidized by the Notgemeinschaft der deutschen Wissenschaft.

Given these differing levels of inherited economic capital one might expect Weber's writings on empire to show more autonomy from their objects of analysis than Thurnwald's. At first glance, however, this does not seem to be the case. Weber was, if anything, more vehemently imperialist in his political views than Thurnwald, starting in the 1890s and culminating in World War I, when he and his brother Alfred actively campaigned for a system of informal German hegemony over "Mitteleuropa" (Central Europe; Mommsen, 1984, pp. 205–206, 211–227). Weber was much more involved in party politics than Thurnwald throughout his entire lifetime. Thurnwald's best known work appears at first glance to respond mainly to ideas and movements within sociology and ethnology, the two university disciplines in which he held professorial chairs. He founded the journal Sociologus in the mid-1920s and was the leading German representative of functionalist ethnography. If we remained at the level of the text and failed to place Thurnwald's evolving views in the shifting context of their production, we might reach the mistaken conclusion that he actually had a greater distance from imperialist ideas and politics than Weber. Weber's pattern of source selection in The Religion of China seems at first glance to reflect his bourgeois social class background, since the most negative views of China were found among the European merchant classes at the time.[29] In fact, Weber's selection of evidence was guided by a different logic, a strategy adjusted to the autonomous logic of the sociological field (see later). And if we examine Thurnwald's entire oeuvre, following the peregrinations of his thinking over the course of more than half a century, it becomes clear that he constantly adjusted his analysis to leading ideas and dominant figures in domains quite distant from his own academic disciplines. In the decade before 1914 Thurnwald's writing on colonialism was framed as if he were participating in the colonial state field (Steinmetz, 2008b) rather than the metropolitian academic field. Between 1918 and 1923 Thurnwald echoed the clamorous public discourse of the revanchist movement that was trying to reclaim Germany's lost colonies. In the United States, between 1930 and 1936 Thurnwald echoed the views of American anthropologists and sociologists like Boas, Lowie, Herskovits, Sapir, and Wirth, all of whom were more critical of racism and colonialism than the majority of German professors at the time. One he returned to Germany, however, Thurnwald's research quickly became closely aligned with Nazi imperial goals and racist ideals (between 1937 and 1945).

This contrast between Thurnwald and Weber seems at first glance to be partly explained by their respective holdings of economic capital and differing amounts of field-specific symbolic capital. Economically more vulnerable and scientifically less established than Weber, Thurnwald gravitated toward the heteronomous pole of the German social science field.

Above and beyond this, Thurnwald's entire personality seems to have been highly adaptive, even opportunist, while Weber's personality was stubbornly, even "heroically" individualistic. Weber was willing to challenge the united opinion of the German historians and historical economists on value- free science and to attack the most established academic Mandarins such as Karl Knies and Rudolf Stammler (Weber, 1975, 1977a, 1977b), and he personally confronted Erich Ludendorff in 1918 on German military strategy (Mommsen, 1984, p. 325). Weber's insistence that science had to keep a great distance from the state was powerfully motivated by his personal quest for autonomy from his father, mother, and other figures of authority in his personal life. By contrast, Thurnwald seems to have been driven to conform to the demands of every field he entered, however temporarily. The reasons for this difference are impossible to determine without further biographic evidence. But we can examine the two sociologists' writing in more detail, trying to discern their practical stance toward autonomy.

Weber as a Modernist Mandarin: The Example of The Religion of China

Weber was concerned with empires, including the German empire(s), throughout his adult life. In addition to his Habilitation thesis on Rome (Weber, 1891) he wrote several long essays on ancient civilizations (Weber, 1976). His 1895 Freiburg University inaugural lecture was a full-throated defense of German imperialism (Mitzman, 1985, p. 143; Mommsen, 1984, pp. 37–40; Weber, 1989). During World War I, Weber focused on extending German hegemony over Eastern Europe "largely by indirect means," using a "concept of German imperialism" that was "scarcely modest" (Mommsen, 1984, p. 206). In Economy and Society Weber returned to ancient land-based empires and brought them into the same analytic framework as modern imperialism. Here Weber found "features that have since recurred in basic outline again and again and which still recur today," including the reciprocal impact of economic and political impulses and the centrality of "honor" and the importance of the "prestige of power" (Weber, 1978, Vol. 2, pp. 910–921).

It is in his magnum opus (Tenbruck, 1999), the three-volume Sociology of Religion (Gesammelte Aufsätze zur Religionssoziologie), that the question of autonomy from the imperial object of analysis is posed most acutely for Weber. Weber devoted a large section of the first volume, which he completed just before his death, to the Chinese empire (Weber, 1964). China was the key comparative case for Weber since it had the "strongest predisposition for capitalism," including "a world lead in technological innovation until early modern times, a hard-working mentality geared to practical solutions, a layer of moneyed merchants and a rational state administration" (Honigsheim, 1923, p. 276; Radkau, 2009, p. 277). At the moment when Weber began his research and writing, China was still subject to German imperial manipulations and Qingdao was a formal German colony. Prussia had concluded a separate treaty with China after the Second Opium War, opening China to Prussian traders and missionaries and allowing Prussia to open a legation in Beijing. In 1897 Germany seized Qingdao and triggered a chain reaction of European annexations of Chinese coastal colonies. Germany headed the allied military campaign against the Boxer Rebellion in 1901 and German troops massacred alleged Boxer sympathizers in a series of notorious expeditions. After the rebellion the Chinese Crown Prince was compelled to travel to Berlin in order to formally apologize and kowtow before the Kaiser. In Shandong province German marines tried to extend Germany's power beyond the official borders of the Qingdao colony in a separate set of aggressive moves (Steinmetz, 2007, Chap. 7). During the decade before World War I, however, certain forces inside the German government started backing away from the idea of continuing to occupy a conquered colony inside China, advocating instead a peaceful cultural penetration of the country and cultivation of the Chinese state as a potential military ally in East Asia.

The Religion of China is a text in which Weber's stance of scientific neutrality seems to be severely at risk of breaking down. Weber's central question was why China had failed to develop a modern form of rational capitalism despite the existence of many preconditions. His answer focused on the economic ethic of Confucianism, which was oriented toward "adjustment to the world" rather than the "rational transformation of the world."[30] Confucianism prevented the rationalization not only of the capitalist economy but also of the state, law, education, and even poetry and the basic Chinese personality structure.[31] Weber completely avoided discussing the possible effects of imperialism on China's development. His description of China as timeless and unchanging and his explanation for its alleged stasis seemed to replicate the classic European and German discourse known as Sinophobia, which had flourished since the middle of the 18th century. Weber seemed to reject the alternative, equally well-wrought European vision of China's Mandarin elite as a meritocratic aristocracy of talent who provided a check on the willful dictatorship of the Emperor (Steinmetz, 2007, Chap. 6).

Weber's arguments about China were simply incorrect, as was already pointed out by a contributor to the Max Weber festschrift in 1923, the Sinologist and former Austrian envoy to China Arthur von Rostorn (von Rosthorn, 1923; Walravens, 2005, pp. 101–102). Weber himself pointed to the "provisional" nature of his findings (Weber, 1920, p. 13). Rather than assuming from the start some kind of scientific bias on Weber's part, however, we should begin by focusing on the process by which he assembled the raw materials for his text. Although he spoke at length with the German traveler and mystic Count Hermann von Keyserling, who saw China as possessing an ideal form of government and advanced aesthetic sensibilities, Weber's views of India as an "orgiastic" culture was were closer to Keyserling than his views of China (von Keyserling, 1925, Vol. 2, pp. 106–107; Radkau, 2009, pp. 466–468). Indeed, there is no evidence that Weber had any single privileged informant on China. He heard von Rostorn lecture on ancient Chinese religions to the "Eranos Circle" in Heidelberg in 1906 and again in Vienna in 1918 (Schmidt-Glintzer, 1989, pp. 15, 41). Weber made patterned selections from the expertise and literature available to him.[32] The fact that Weber began his three-volume sociology of religion with China — after first presenting Protestantism — was not an arbitrary decision. It emphasized Weber's' debt to Hegel, including Hegel's uncompromising Sinophobia, which had itself been a philosophical translation of the discourse of the European merchants in East Asia.[33] The overall design of Weber's comparative religion project, organized around a discourse of lack, echoed the well-established thesis of Chinese stagnation, which Hegel described as the arrested development of Oriental freedom ("The Oriental World knows only that One is Free").

But from the very beginning of the Sinophobic discourse in the 18th century it had met with challenges and reputations. Even in German universities, among the best-known Sinologists, there was an opposing view that painted a more nuanced picture of Confucianism and Chinese history. Yet Weber ignored or dismissed these various forms of "Sinophilia."

One possible explanation for Weber's choice of evidence is simply that he wanted to prove that ascetic Protestantism alone was capable of generating capitalism — that he "cherry-picked" his evidence. Although this is entirely plausible it is difficult to reconcile with his "ascetic" scientific program and his expressed wish, in the introduction to the Collected Essays on the Sociology of Religion, that the Sinologist would "find nothing essential that he would have to judge as simply false" (Weber, 1920, p. 13). A second possible explanation for his source selection is that Weber was, as he himself sometimes said only half in jest, a "class-conscious bourgeois" (Mommsen, 1984, p. 109). His work could then be read as a direct transcription of merchant capitalist interests.[34] There are several problems with this account. First, the typical merchant class discourse on China was drenched in straightforward racism, but Weber's texts, while perhaps exemplifying a form of cultural racism, never strayed into socio-biological explanations of Chinese backwardness. Weber insisted that it was "obviously not a question of deeming the Chinese 'naturally ungifted' for the demands of capitalism" (Weber, 1964, p. 248). Most importantly, Weber is best characterized neither as bourgeois nor as a Bildungsburger (member of the educated middle class), but rather as having had a foot in both classes and a mixed or cleft habitus (Bourdieu, 2007). Furthermore, Weber's social background and class position was not expressed directly in the academic social science field but was translated into terms and postures appropriate to that field — as is always the case with semi-autonomous fields.

Indeed, Weber invented a whole new position in the German academic field. The overarching field of the social and human sciences in Germany was divided broadly at the end of the 19th century between two poles: on the one hand the various historicisms codified as Geisteswissenschaften and on the other hand the array of positivisms and naturalisms that denied any difference between the natural and human sciences. The first grouping was associated with Ringer's (1969) German "Mandarins." Weber himself is responsible for Ringer's concept, having compared the old-style German professoriate, with their "humanist, exclusive and bookish literary education," which stamped them as "belonging socially to the cultured status group," to the Chinese Mandarins (Weber, 1964, p. 121). The second group were the academic "Modernists," in Ringer's terms, who challenged the long-lasting hegemony of the German Mandarins and their classical, philological, humanistic approach.

Despite Weber's frequent jibes at the German Mandarins, however ("nothing is more horrible to me than the arrogance of the 'intellectual' and learned professions," he wrote to Marianne before their marriage

[Weber, 1988, pp. 187–188]), he was not as unambiguously allied with the Modernists in the academic field as Ringer suggests. In Ringer's (2004) view, Weber was a modernist, not a mandarin, since he supported the modernization of 19th-century German higher education. Nonetheless, Weber was definitely, or also, part of the social science field's dominant, consecrated elite and a Mandarin through and through. He participated in the Eranos circle in Heidelberg, whose members were all male full professors. He was both attracted to and repelled by Stefan Georg and his elitist cult. An art collector, Weber was able to live "basically on the proceeds of a successful sale of [his] Klinger collection" before Marianne's inheritance in 1908 (quoted in Radkau, 2009, p. 282). Weber was a music connoisseur and his study of the "rational and sociological foundations of music" (Weber, 1921) was one of his first investigations of the concept of rationalization.

Still, Ringer is partly correct in arguing that Weber was not an academic Mandarin. Instead there a rather consistent pattern in Weber's work of seeking a middle-ground position between the modernist and mandarin poles. His strategy of creating a new position in a nascent social science field is reminiscent of Flaubert's strategy in the French literary field, as described by Bourdieu (1996). Weber wrote his Habilitation thesis in a classic "German Mandarin" field – Roman history – and he addressed a classic German Mandarin problem – Rome's decline. But he attempted "to grasp classical antiquity with the plainest and most modern instrument, an analysis of agrarian measurement techniques" (Radkau, 2009, p. 72). In an extremely non-historicist move Weber compared Roman land policy to contemporary Prussian policy rather than emphasizing ancient Rome's uniqueness (Weber, 1891, 1976). Indeed, the Verein für Sozialpolitik understood Weber's Habilitation thesis as qualifying him for a study of Polish laborers in the German present (Konno, 2004, p. 45). Along similar lines, Weber sought in his epistemological writings to overcome the split between historicism and positivism, interpretive description and causal explanation. His concept of the ideal type represented a compromise between the internal logical consistency of an ideal (as in the abstract economic theory of the Austrian school of marginal utility), and the concrete historical reality that was preferred by the German historical school of economics (Radkau, 2009, p. 260). In Economy and Society Weber even spoke of Marktgemeinschaft (market community), merging the two mutually exclusive antithetical poles of Toennies' famous Gemeinschaft und Gesellschaft model (Radkau, 2009, p. 414). His argument in favor of specialized sciences rather than the traditional generalism of the German Mandarins was coupled with a vigorous campaign to exclude applied policy research from sociology (Rammstedt, 1988). Weber's pursuit of this median strategy inside the academic field was not a direct effect or reflection of his social class background, but was an effort to occupy a position that was homologous to his position in the overarching field of power. The midpoint in the field of power between bourgeois and Bildungsbürger, economic and cultural capital, was roughly homologous to the midpoint between the Mandarin and modernist positions inside the university social sciences field.

Weber's sociology of religion project has the same intermediate quality. On the one hand, he concerned himself in the midst of the Great War with the seemingly esoteric topics of Confucianism, Daoism, Buddhism, and Hinduism. He studied British censuses of India rather than fighting against Britain on the battlefield – the only one of Helene Weber's sons who did not fight (Radkau, 2009, p. 464). On the other hand – and this is the "modernist" side – Weber refused to accept the traditional German Mandarin Sinologists as his guides to Chinese history. Weber ignored the literature of the German Jesuits in China, from Johann Adam Schall von Bell to Athanasius Kircher, who had praised Confucianism, and he ignored 19th century university Sinophiles like Johann Heinrich Plath, Wilhelm Schott, Georg von der Gabelentz, Wilhelm Grube, and Gustav Klemm, director of the Royal Library in Dresden and author of the ten-volume Cultural History of Mankind, who defended China's "wonderful form of government, wise laws, advanced moral institutions, in sum, its unique culture" and observed that the Chinese were justified in viewing Europeans as barbarians in the wake of Opium Wars (Klemm, 1847, pp. ii, 510; Leutner, 1987). Weber's central question was also a "modernist" one: Rather than asking why China had declined – a question linked to ancient and premodern visions of history as a cycle of empires – he asked why China had supposedly always been stagnant – an assumption closer to modern race-theoretical thinking and evolutionary social theories.

In making these arguments, Weber aligned himself with De Groot and von Richthofen. Both of these China specialists occupied the most prestigious category of academic position in Germany: Professor Ordinarius at Berlin University. But von Richthofen was located in a modern discipline, geography, and had a highly practical background, having worked as geographer in California gold mining camps and traveled through China for four years in the pay of a European Chamber of Commerce, scouting out locations for a German invasion and penetration of China in the 1860s and 1870s (von Richthofen, 1897, 1898, 1907). Weber recommended

Richthofen's China diaries to his readers (Weber, 1964, p. 252, n. 1). De Groot's social trajectory also differed from the classical German Mandarin Sinologists. His background was not in the European universities and libraries but in the Dutch East Indies, where he had worked for years as a missionary and colonizer. Both men held views of China that were closer to the typical colonial merchant than to a classic 19th century German Sinologist. The Orientalists Schott and Grube, who had also been at Berlin University, did not have this practical side but were armchair philologists.

Weber distanced himself from China specialists who were located outside the university field or in structurally inferior academic positions. He ignored the writing of Ku Hung-Ming, a neo-Confucian intellectual and anti-imperialist who had studied and published in Germany, and he ignored the writing of Alfons Paquet, who published essays praising Ku Hung-Ming and traditional China (Paquet, 1911, 1912, 1914). Weber downplayed the work of the liberal Protestant missionary and Sinologist Richard Wilhelm, who had founded a Confucius Society in colonial Qingdao that was aimed at strengthening the Confucian tradition. Contrary to Weber, Wilhelm traced China's problems to "alienation and despiritualization" resulting from western interventions, not to Confucianism. But Wilhelm was associated with the Protestant Weimar mission society at the time of Weber's research.[35] Weber also distanced himself from Sinologist Otto Franke, who also had a practical background as a diplomatic interpreter. Franke was critical of German imperialism in China and was associated at the time with the less prestigious Hamburg Colonial Institute.[36] Both Sinologists were loosely associated with a growing, cosmopolitan, anti-imperialist group of intellectuals that started to emerge in Europe and the colonies before 1914, gaining strength during the interwar period. But few of these emerging anti-imperialists were located in prestigious universities or positions. The faculty members at the Berlin Seminar for Oriental Languages were separated from the regular faculty at Berlin University by a powerful social barrier. The Seminar for Oriental Languages was involved in the more practical work of training interpreters and officials for overseas and colonial postings, and also had "native" teachers. Weber did refer to one publication in the seminar's journal in The Religion of China (1964, p. 258, n. 49), but he ignored an article that directly challenged his thesis in that journal in 1913. The article was written by one of the Seminar's Chinese language instructors, Wang (1913).[37]

Sinologists who directly opposed Western imperialism were even more untouchable for Weber than traditional German Mandarins. First, the academic anti-imperialist position, unlike Weber's own supposedly strictly "personal" imperialist views, posed a threat to academic freedom. Weber supported the hiring of socialists and Marxists in German universities and enthusiastically welcomed Jewish, Russian, and socialist students into his circle in Heidelberg, but he insisted that they avoid politics in their teaching and scientific research.

In sum, Weber sought out authorities in the Chinese studies field whose positions were structurally homologous to his own – modernist elite university mandarins. Weber's strategizing in the semi-autonomous academic field led him to select the very Sinophobic tropes which his basic thesis on the uniqueness of the Protestant ethic required, and for which he should have had a natural predilection according to reductionist sociologies of knowledge. My hypothesis is that these simpler explanations are nonetheless incorrect, even if they would predict (or retrodict) the same "outcomes" in his text. According to my explanation, Weber would have become more open to the work of modernist Sinophiles like Richard Wilhelm and Otto Franke if they had moved into prestigious university chairs during his lifetime. Since no modernist Sinophilic Sinologists held the position of Ordinarius in a German university before 1920, it is impossible to test this hypothesis directly.

Richard Thurnwald as a Case of Scientific Adaptability

Unlike Weber, who had an omnivorous appetite for new objects of study, Thurnwald worked on the same themes throughout his adult life, and his views on theoretical and methodological matters remained fairly constant. But his analysis of imperialism shifted rather dramatically, tracking prevailing trends either in German imperial politics or abroad. Thurnwald and Weber may have had equally imperialist political opinions before 1920, but Thurnwald was less scientifically autonomous than Weber. This can be shown by reconstructing his views on race theory, colonial native policy, and European and German colonialism more generally. Thurnwald's autonomy from extra-scientific imperial politics and discourses seemed to be greatest during the Weimar Republic and the first half of the 1930s, when he held an "extraordinary" professorship at Berlin University, taught at Yale, and conducted research in Tanganyika and New Guinea. In this period, Thurnwald's views of colonialism evolved slowly from dependence on the field of power to a sort of dependence on prevailing views within academic circles. After 1936, his views of colonialism came to be tightly synchronized with official Nazi colonial ideology.

Whereas Max Weber expressed sketicism about the relevance of eugenic theory and racial biology for sociology at the first meeting of the German Sociological Society in 1910, Thurnwald allied himself with race theory in the decade before World War I, publishing dozens of his earliest articles starting in 1904 in the Archiv für Rassen- und Gesellschafts-Biologie, a journal he also co-edited. At the beginning of the 1920s he was still seen as the relevant social scientist to write the entries on "race," "racial hygiene," and "racial struggle" for a new Dictionary of Politics (Herre, 1923). In 1924, however, Thurnwald published an article critical of reductive socio-biological approaches. For the next decade Thurnwald largely avoided race-sociological discussions altogether (Amidon, 1998). In his theory of "leadership and social sifting" (Thurnwald, 1926a), biological selection was treated as a result of social processes rather than as an independent variable; "natural selection" was explicitly dismissed as explaining human societies (1935a, p. 94). Only after Thurnwald resettled in Nazi Germany in 1936 did he begin to publish in journals like Zeitschrift für Rassenkunde. Still, he remained less enthusiastic about the Nazi discourses of race than his student Mühlmann, who published a major treatise on "The Science of Race and Ethnos" in 1936 (Mühlmann, 1936).

Thurnwald's writing on colonialism and native policy falls into five main periods: pre-1914, 1914–1922, 1922–1930, 1930–1936, and 1936–1945. Before 1914, his views even in scientific publications are framed as if he were participating in the colonial state field as much as the metropolitian acdemic field (Steinmetz, 2008b). His first article on the topic, entitled "Colonial Native Policy" (Thurnwald, 1905), was a detailed review of a lecture by Hans Zache, a colonial official in German East Africa. Here for the first time Thurnwald presented a simple argument that he would repeat throughout his life: control of native labor is the "actual problem of native policy" in tropical colonies, since Europeans and North Americans are physically unsuited for physical labor in the tropics and since colonialism's raison d'être is economic exploitation (1905, p. 632). Thurnwald seemed to approve of Zache's argument that "as colonizers, we are the tools of a principle of evolution or development which is that the lower cultures are replaced by the higher ones." He agreed that "it is therefore is a question of which qualities [the white man] finds already present in the Negro that can be used to contribute to the cultural development that is being directed by the whites." Most native tribes, Thurnwald continued, were "work-shy." The Negro's passivity "predestines him to be a Knecht of the Herrenvölker, the prototype of the slave" (1905, p. 632). Thurnwald did not disagree with Zache's assertion that the African never advanced beyond the stage of sensuality and daydreaming and was an instinctive liar, incapable of creating state-like institutions. Even the classic 19th century colonial trope of the inexorable extinction of the Naturvölker confronted with superior western culture surfaced here.

European ethnographic discourse was imported into the colonial state, which operated like a political field in Bourdieu's sense, one in which the dominant form of field-specific symbolic capital was ethnographic capital – a claim to a superior understanding of native culture (Steinmetz, 2008b). Colonizers' social positions in the colonial state field were related to the positions they took in the ongoing battle of claims to ethnographic superiority. German colonial ethnographic representations of black Africans were not entirely homogenous at this time (Steinmetz, 2007). Zache was staking out a racist extreme in the battle of ethnographic representations. The fact that Thurnwald repeated Zache's views with little dissent was surprising both because Zache was anything but a scientist and because even within the colonial state field, university educated officials tended to base their claims to authority on displays of hermeneutic insight and linguistic ability (Steinmetz, 2007). Thurnwald did not seem to realize or to care that he was embracing a view of the African that was typically associated with military figures. This social haplessness, this failure to understand the rules of the game or even which game was being played, pointed to a trait that reappears again and again over Thurnwald's career.

In 1905, Thurnwald was still a metropolitan social scientist with no experience in overseas colonies. Five years later, having returned to Germany from his first Oceanic expedition, Thurnwald repeated his earlier idea that the white man "is the brain, which sets the arms and legs of the native in motion" (1910a, p. 192, also 1910b, p. 608). He now added a claim to a kind of practical usefulness on the part of the ethnographer: "if the white man wants to use his superior intellect to influence and steer the laborer, who is better adapted to the climate, he needs to know how the native feels and thinks, what he views as right and wrong" (1910a, p. 192). Having lived for three years in the colonies Thurnwald had internalized the rules of the colonial field. As an academic schooled in several foreign languages and disciplines, Thurnwald gravitated toward a position in the colonial state field that made his own qualities seem essential to the colony's operations. In another article published the same year in a colonial journal (Koloniale Rundschau), Thurnwald offered to "sketch the various social types used as labor power in the South Seas," since the correct evaluation of the native workforce leads to the use of each racial type according to its abilities ... Out of the chaos of mere contiguity [Nebeneinander] emerges the orderliness of stratification (Uebereinander) organized according to individual endowments and abilities. (1910b, p. 609, 632)

A "correct evaluation" of the problem would be a scientific one, not one based on applying military or capitalist categories to the highly esoteric and impenetrable native cultures. In a subsequent essay called "Applied Ethnology in Colonial Policy" (1912a), Thurnwald argued that "native policy ... circles around [the] problem" of controlling native workers "through our cultural power" ("durch geistige Machtmittel"), since we can no longer "hunt, catch and chain natives like animals." Of course, German colonizers in Southwest Africa and East Africa had just finished doing just that — treating natives like hunted animals — in a series of military campaigns between 1904 and 1908. Thurnwald's position was thus directed not against colonial ideas from some distant past but against contending German social forces in the immediate colonial present. Thurnwald's consistent emphasis on the need for a psychological ethnology of the colonized suggests an effort to privilege another arena where colonizers led by crass military and economic visions of native culture could not compete with academics. Thurnwald was also already beginning to embrace a mild relativism, writing that "there is no absolute measure of the worth of a given culture." He aligned himself with the native policies of regulated preservation of indigenous culture that were associated with some of the more liberal German colonial governors in the Pacific such as Wilhelm Solf and Erich Schultz in German Samoa.[38] Thurnwald now wrote that "it is meaningless to try to assimilate the natives" to "our Nordic conditions": the colonizer should "intervene only to regulate, not to destroy." In the larger publication based on his first expedition to New Guinea Thurnwald argued for seeking "an appropriate symbiosis" between European and local culture (1912b, p. 19). Colonial racists at the time vehemently opposed any such "synthesis," and were in the midst of passing laws to ban racial intermarriage in the German colonies. Thurnwald's views had become sociologically "appropriate" for his position in the colonial field.

Thurnwald spent six years in overseas colonies between 1906 and 1914, so it is perhaps understandable that his statements during this period seem directed toward other colonial actors rather than fellow social scientists. And yet the publications referred to in the preceding paragraph were all published while Thurnwald was in Germany between his overseas research trips. There is no evidence that he hoped to find employment in the colonies, even though he received research support from the Colonial Office. The fact that Thurnwald engaged in battle mainly with contenders in the colonies reveals a pattern of intellectual heteronomy that cannot be explained by financial difficulties or problems in gaining a professorship in Germany.

Thurnwald did initiate a polemic against the dominant school in the German ethnological field in the same 1912 lecture on "Applied Ethnology in Colonial Policy." In addition to his "protest" against the "poor understanding" of native subjectivity by colonial officials, he attacked "the way in which scientific ethnographic studies of natives sometimes see it as an honor to deal with the most unpractical things, with bows and arrows and drums and so on." Ethnography, Thurnwald argued, "is not exhausted by illuminating historical influences." Here he was throwing down the gauntlet to the dominant grouping in the German ethnological field, the cultural-historical or Kulturkreis school. Thurnwald's alternative was to open ethnology to other disciplines, especially sociology, law, psychology, and biology. In a period of poorly established disciplinary boundaries, Thurnwald's move represented an embrace of academic heteronomy – heteronomy vis-à-vis other disciplines. Without arguing that all forms of interdisciplinary stem from a position of field-specific weakness, this is a recognizable pattern (Bourdieu, 1991b).

The second phase in Thurnwald's colonial analysis begins in the last two years of World War I, after he returned to Germany from New Guinea via California, and ends with his move from Halle to Berlin. Thurnwald (1917a, 1918a) wrote a series of articles that echoed the colonial movement's arguments for Germany's retention of its colonies as a guarantee of peace. In an article, on "Holland and its Colonial Policies" he repeated his prewar argument in favor of a "humane" native policy. He now found an example of human colonialism in the Dutch framework of "ethical politics." Here colonial "rule is founded in a superiority of the spirit, unlike the English method of economic force or other nation's use of direct violence" (1917b, p. 40). In 1918, Thurnwald jumped into the same broad debate in which the Weber brothers were pushing for German hegemony over Central and Eastern Europe and wrote that "the war must bring us an expansion of our Lebensraum," including "adequate colonial possessions" (1918b, p. 43). Responding to British claims that Germany had been an immature and especially brutal colonizer (Union of South Africa, 1918), Thurnwald insisted that "native policy before war was much more humane in the German than in the English colonies" (1918b, pp. 53–54). Thurnwald joined the Halle Colonial Academy just as Germany was losing its colonies in 1918, and he participated in discussions about transforming it into a school of foreign studies (along the lines followed by the Hamburg Colonial Institute and the Berlin Seminar for Oriental Languages).[39] In 1922, he lectured at Halle on the possibility of a non-bellicose (unkriegerische) colonialism.[40] This seems to have been motivated by ongoing discussions of the League of Nations mandate colonies.

Rather than becoming an embittered German colonial revanchist like so many former colonial governors and officers, Thurnwald moved away from colonialism altogether in the third phase, following the 1922 lecture. It was at this time that he became an "extraordinary" professor (Extraordinarius) at Berlin University. Although he had participated in all three German "colonial congresses" before the war (1901, 1902, 1905, 1910a, 1910b, 1910), Thurnwald did not participate in the fourth colonial congress in 1924.[41] He now seemed to accept Germany's loss of colonies (Thurnwald, 1929a, p. 8). During the 1920s, he worked on his five-volume, 1,618-page Human Society (Die Menschliche Gesellschaft), considered to be his lasting achievement alongside his ethnographic discoveries in Oceania.[42] In the introduction to volume one of Die Menschliche Gesellschaft Thurnwald addressed the "crisis" in native life that had been precipitated by sustained contact with the colonizer's culture and superior technology (Thurnwald, 1931–1935, Vol. 1, pp. 21–22). The rest of Die Menschliche Gesellschaft dealt exclusively with non-European "traditional" societies, however, and did not analyze the impact of Europe or European imperialism at all.

In the fourth phase of Thurnwald's work on colonialism, starting at the end of the 1920s, he began paying more attention to ongoing transformations – mainly negative ones – in colonized societies. The theme of change in colonized societies was the main focus of a series of publications based on a research trip to Tanganyika in 1930–1931, including the book Black and White in East Africa (1935a) and a series of articles (Thurnwald, 1929a, 1929b, 1931a, 1931b, 1931c, 1932a, 1932b, 1932c, 1935b). Thurnwald claimed that his new emphasis on problems of "acculturation" was a response to the shock of seeing a "Negro at the typewriter" (the title of Thurnwald, 1932c) in Tanganyika and revisiting New Guinea in 1934 and seeing the "transition of a savage society from almost complete integrity to a growing disintegration of the old order" (Thurnwald, 1936a, p. 347). European colonialism had brought peace and economic development to previously warlike societies, but in doing so had mainly made things worse. Chiefly authority and traditional culture had been broken, and the "spice had been taken out of native life with the loss of

independence and of the excitement they had derived from fighting"
(1936a, p. 353). Thurnwald analyzed cultural mixing by distinguishing
between "culture" and "civilization" (echoing Alfred Weber's, 1920–1921
treatment of that distinction). The civilizational level, defined as technology
and technical knowledge, could still be seen as progressing, but cultures
could not be arrayed along any progressive, linear scale (Thurnwald,
1935a, p. 4, 1939a, pp. 422–423).[43] This writing on colonial acculturation
was accompanied by a growing skepticism about European cultural
superiority. Cultural hybridity and "primitive thinking" were both found
among Europeans as well the colonized, pace Lévy-Bruhl (1925 [1910]).
Thurnwald also began analyzing the emergence of anticolonialism in an
"awakening Africa" (1935a, p. 80). Attending a conference at Howard
University's sociology department in 1936, he discussed the "crisis of
imperialism"with representatives from Africa, China, and India, and with
"colored Americans." Here he argued that "inherent in imperialism is the
'hybris,' the overbearing insolence of the dominant stratum," which "inescapably leads to its nemesis," in the guise of "a new generation of natives
has grown up which has been educated in schools by Europeans, in ways of
thought that are European, and in using devices introduced by Europeans"
(1936b, p. 84).

Thurnwald's work in this fourth phase, during which he lived mainly in
the United States, underscores the fact that he was highly responsive not
just to political power but to his more immediate academic environment.
His thinking in this period seems to have been more responsive to developments inside American anthropology and sociology than to events in the
colonized world or discussions in the German disciplinary fields. Or rather:
the impact of colonial changes on Thurnwald's work is filtered through the
discourse of his non-German academic colleagues. After all, the colonized
world had been in "crisis" since the beginning of modern colonialism;
European rule had always been characterized by the production of cultural
hybridity and a technological advantage over the colonized. Also revealing
is that Thurnwald did not mention meeting with representatives of anti-
colonial movements while in Africa but only at an African-American
university. He carried on a lively correspondence with American anthropologists and sociologists who were more advanced on race questions than
most of the professors Thurnwald associated with in Germany. Thurnwald
struck an explicitly anti-Nazi stance in this period in correspondence with
Boas and other Jewish professors, writing to Boas in 1933 that "we learn
with disgust and consternation of the occurrences provoked by the new
government in Germany. We Auslandsdeutsche should also all dissociate

ourselves from this government."[44] During this period Thurnwald's funding came mainly from non-German sources, although Berlin University continued to hold his position open for him. His East Africa research was sponsored by the International African Institute in London, whose funding came from the Rockefeller Foundation (Adedze, 2003, p. 338).

In the fifth phase, Thurnwald's work was aligned with the Nazi state and Nazi imperial ideologies. His first major article after returning to Germany from the United States, entitled "Die Kolonialfrage," represented a sharp departure from his work in the years immediately preceding it. In "The Crisis of Imperialism" (1936b) he had condemned colonialism. Now Thurnwald argued that Germany should regain its African colonies to obtain Lebensraum and tropical raw materials (1937, pp. 66–69). Thurnwald set out to refute the "colonial lie," that is, the argument codified in the Versailles Treaty that disqualified Germany as a competent colonial power. In a 500-page book called Koloniale Gestaltung (Colonial Development, 1939b) and a 120-page article (Thurnwald, 1940) he compared German colonial practices with those of Britain, France, and other European powers. Here and in a secret report for the Colonial Law Committee of the Akademie für Deutsches Recht Thurnwald elaborated a specifically Nazi form of colonial administration and a plan for "the organization of native labor in East Africa and its organization on a National Socialist basis" (Thurnwald, 2001 [1938]). Nazi terminology and concepts like race, space (Raum), and Lebensraum now structured his discussion of colonialism. German colonialism was to be governed by the "Führer principle" (Timm, 1977, p. 634). The "white's claim to lead the native" was grounded in fact that the colonizer brings progress to the colonized, and expropriation of the natives' land was defended as making it more productive and allowing the native to increase his "Lebensraum" (1939b, p. 433). The possibility of anticolonialism was now traced to "Bolshevist" propaganda coming from American blacks (1939b, p. 378). In addition to polemicizing against Weimar-era and especially "Frankfurt" sociology as having been corrupted by the "poisoning" influence of Jews (Timm, 1977, p. 622), Thurnwald argued that "the numerous South African Jews" joined the British in opposing the Boers' exemplary segregation policies (2001 [1938], p. 625). African colonies should be divided into three zones: one for whites only, a mixed zone, and native reservations. Natives would need a "work card" in order to work in the white space. The colonized would govern themselves inside their reservations under the oversight of a resident German "native caretaker." Rather than lumping all natives together under a single rubric, Thurnwald specified that there would be a plurality of

distinct "black spaces" for each tribe. In addition to reservations
Thurnwald also allowed for "worker colonies next to larger plantations,
mines, or other large firms." For Thurnwald it was important that Africans
"mainly pursue their traditional agrarian activities" and "be allowed to put
on their old festivals and dances." In this and other respects Thurnwald's
Nazi-era analysis continued to develop themes from the fourth phase.
Native legal proceedings were to be carried out by the native chief, under
the Caretaker's supervision.[45] The goal of German colonialism, Thurnwald
insisted, was to prevent "the rise of a black proletariat," which would have
"nasty consequences" (Thurnwald, 2001 [1938], p. 627).

The culmination of Thurnwald's self-Gleichschaltung was his proposal
for an institute for ethnological research that would encompass "ethnographic research at home" (Volksforschung in der Heimat) alongside
research on overseas and colonized societies (Timm, 1977, p. 622).
Thurnwald had long insisted that sociology should not respect the distinction between primitive and modern, European and non-European societies
(Zwiedeneck-Südenhorst, 1936). But by calling on Berlin University to
bridge this gap at this precise moment, Thurnwald was essentially giving
his approval to projects of harnessing Ostforschung to Ostpolitik, that is,
putting ethnosociology to work in the service of the Nazi colonization of
Eastern Europe. Ethnological research on Eastern Europe was by this time
focusing on the project of sorting out the populations that could be
successfully Germanized from the others, and Thurnwald's protege
Mühlmann was one of the most active participants in this reorientation of
ethnological science toward applied research on the European east. The
official justification for conquering the east was to create Lebensraum
and to mobilize a pliant work force, although genocidal annihilation
soon emerged as the leading state goal. In 1942, Thurnwald asked for a
reduction in his course load because he was working on "a series of
reports on the deployment of foreign workers" for the Reichsministerium
für Bewaffnung und Munition.[46] Thurnwald was thus at least implicitly
accepting the removal or massacre of populations that would not be contributing to German projects. Combined with the fact that Thurnwald
had noticed (and at the time, criticized) attacks on Jews in Germany
since 1933, it seems impossible that he could not have imagined what
would happen to those who were not useful for slave labor or ethnic
assimilation. By the end of the 1930s, the distance between Thurnwald's
scientific work and official Nazi imperial policy had narrowed to the
vanishing point.

CONCLUSION: EGO AUTONOMY AND SCIENTIFIC AUTONOMY REVISITED

If Max Weber was scientifically autonomous and Thurnwald a seeming mirror of the dominant forces in his immediate environment at any given time, what about the two scholars who initially stood in their shadows, Alfred Weber and Wilhelm Mühlmann? Questions of scientific ego autonomy would seem to be particularly acute in cases like these.[47]

Alfred Weber was born in 1868 and was economically autonomous like his brother, although he never married. Like Max he wrote a Habilitation thesis with a famous professor historical national economics (Gustav Schmoller). After teaching at Prague from 1902 to 1907 Alfred obtained a professorship at Heidelberg, where he remained for the rest of his life (he died in 1958). If anything he struck an even more autonomous stance in the academic sphere, even if he became skeptical of Max's value free doctrine fairly early. During the 1920s he presided over an exciting interdisciplinary social science research center, the Heidelberg Institute for State and Social Sciences (Blomert, 1999; Blomert, Esslinger, & Giovannini, 1997). Most of the rising stars in sociology and the other social sciences passed through Heidelberg in the Weimar period, more specifically through the Institute for State and Social Sciences, and many studied with Alfred Weber.[48] Weber was the one of the only Heidelberg University professors not driven into exile in the Nazi period who did not compromise with the Nazis (Demm, 2000a, pp. 267–308; Remy, 2002). After 1945 Weber was part of a "Committee of Thirteen" untainted faculty members charged with helping the occupying American military powers to denazify the university. Weber favored more extensive purges than any other Heidelberg faculty member (Remy, 2002, pp. 138, 160) and was adamant about restoring the university's autonomy from the state and the professors' autonomy from administrators. In short, his position on scientific autonomy was similar to that of his brother's, except that he accepted a necessary normative dimension in scientific work. This position, already articulated before 1914, became even more pronounced after the Nazi era (Weber, 1955, pp. 37–43).

Alfred Weber also followed his own path in his research. Before 1907 he was known for his studies of home work, cartels, and imperialism (Demm, 2000a, p. 83). While in Prague he supervised the doctoral thesis of none other than Franz Kafka, the world's greatest analyst of psychic abasement vis-à-vis both bureaucratic authority and father figures (Demm, 2000a, p. 43).[49] Alfred's contribution to industrial location theory (Weber, 1929

[1909]) pursued a strategy similar to Max's by combining the two great contending economic schools at the time, Austrian marginal utility theory and German historical economics (Demm, 2000a, p. 67). Between 1910 and 1935, Alfred became known as the main voice of historical and cultural sociology in Germany and internationally (Weber, 1935, 1997). His 1935 magnum opus, Kulturgeschichte als Kultursoziologie (Cultural History as Cultural Sociology) could not find a publisher in Nazi Germany and came out in the Netherlands. Weber continued to write, and in 1943 he published Das tragische und die Geschichte (The Tragic and History), which revisited the same Oriental civilizations as Max Weber's sociology of religion but with a completely different question: what explains the variable presence of a "tragic" worldview in various cultures? That this was an oblique criticism of the ongoing German politics of the present hardly needs stating, especially after Marianne Weber explained the way in which participants in her discussion circle even during the Nazi period could say "something to us which seemed exceptionally close to our present-day experiences" even while appearing to be remote (Weber, 1977a, p. 235).

Alfred Weber dealt with imperialism on three different occasions. In 1904 he published "Germany and economic imperialism," which analyzed the new "protectionist imperialism" that was seeking to turn the "undeveloped parts of the world into permanent economic dependencies of the present-day developed parts" by throwing up "imperialism barbed wire" around their borders (Weber, 2000, pp. 394, 396). Weber calmly assembled statistics to show that Germany had nonetheless been able to increase its exports to protected colonial markets. His conclusion was that Germany "can't accomplish much at all with imperial policy" (ibid., p. 387). This data-backed conclusion not only flew in the face of the liberal imperialist circles that the Weber brothers frequented but was also at odds with the power-political imperialism that Max Weber continued to defend. During World War I, Alfred joined Max in projects to strengthen German hegemony over Mitteleuropa (Demm, 1990, p. 207; Weber, 1999, pp. 178–229). Alfred argued at this time that the smaller eastern nations would become dependent on the German "leading nation" (Demm, 1990, p. 209). Alfred described this informal imperialism as a "great organizational federation of equal, self-governing parties" that would "eliminate the imperial form" altogether (1999, p. 203). After 1918 Alfred became a vocal critic of both European colonialism and German imperialism (Weber, 1924). His treatise on world history summarized modernity under the conceptual heading of western imperial expansion ("das expansive Abendland seit 1500") and discussed the creation of a "global Occident" (Welt-Abendland) with its colonial empires, and the rise of a "uprising of the masses" in the global peripheries, societies that "had arrived at the threshold of history when they create a new synthesis" from their own traditions and western modernity (1935, p. 405, 408).

So far the only moment of loss of autonomy seems to be World War I, when Alfred became a fervent social Darwinistic militarist and a liberal imperialist. The obvious place to look, however, is the psychic level. Alfred looked up to his older brother even as a child. He shared a lover with him, Else Jaffe-Richthofen, and probably knew "that Else loved Max more than himself" (Radkau, 2008, p. 21). Alfred came eventually to be known as "Minimax" and W.e.b.e.r. or "will eigenen Bruder endlich revidieren" ("wants to finally revise his own brother"; Demm, 2000a, p. 61). After the war he suffered the humiliation of hearing Talcott Parsons, his erstwhile student and now the leading sociologist in the world, declare that Alfred Weber was not a sociologist at all (von Beyme in Demm, 2000b, p. 220). Rene Konig, the rising star of West German sociology, derided Alfred as a philospher of history and not a sociologist. In a widely-read text, Konig assimilated Alfred Weber to "historical and social philosophers" like Spengler (König, 1958, p. 151) – an enormous insult for the anti-Nazi who was now a Social Democrat. The hopelessly antiquated German historian Hans-Ulrich Wehler argued that the "republication" of Alfred Weber's work was "a mistake," since Weber's work was "hopelessly antiquated." German sociologist Walter L. Bühl said that Alfred Weber's work was "a complete failure," a form of "cultural criticism loaded with ressentiment" (Molt, 2002, p. 89). Interestingly, most of these critics of Alfred Weber are themselves strongly identified with the work of Max Weber. Despite this extremely difficult situation Alfred Weber seems to have navigated questions of ego autonomy effectively.

The same cannot be said for Wilhelm Mühlmann. Mühlmann had defended a doctoral dissertation on the secret Arioi society in precolonial Tahiti in 1932 (Mühlmann, 1932) but faced an even more difficult academic job market than Thurnwald had. In 1932, when Thurnwald was in the United States and complaining about the Nazis in his letters, Mühlmann was already dropping hints about his sympathies for Hitler. In a letter to Thurnwald Mühlmann observed that "many of the students of my age are running into the arms of the Nazis."[50] In October 1932 Mühlmann published an article comparing "cornerstones and horns" in Tahitian and Jewish culture.[51] In March 1933, after the Nazi seizure of power, Mühlmann wrote to Thurnwald saying that some people, and not only Jews, were thinking of leaving Germany, and that "I too thought about emigrating but came to the conclusion that I would stay."[52] Mühlmann flourished professionally during the Nazi period, often at the expense of Jewish and other professional competitors whom he badmouthed politically. He defended the Nazi ban on marriage between Christians and Jews (Mühlmann, 1936, pp. 536—537), and wrote a memo arguing that ethnologists who did not follow modern (Nazi) sociobiological views should be fired from ethnographic museums – at a time when he was searching for just such a position (Michel, 1995, p. 150). He went on the attack against the rival Kulturkreis ethnological school as a "degeneration of science" (Mühlmann, 1942, p. 292) pursued by "Catholic Jews" (Michel, 1995, p. 151) like Wilhelm Schmidt, founder of the Vienna school (Petermann, 2004, p. 599), who denied the importance of race as opposed to culture (Mühlmann, 1937). Mühlmann's career benefited from close connections to several key figures inside the notorious Rosenberg Office, and Alfred Rosenberg directly funded Mühlmann's research (Michel, 1992, p. 91). Mühlmann described the Jews as a Scheinvolk or "sham people" (Mühlmann, 1942) and, along with Gypsies, as "rootless or uprooted ... sifting itself again and again out of all ethnic communities of vagabonds, vagrants, bums, and so on, whose sociological connections with Jews and Gypsies has been amply demonstrated" (Mühlmann, 1942, p. 294).

The culmination of Mühlmann's transformation into a Nazi social scientist involved a change in his main object of research from Polynesians to Eastern Europeans. This responded to the Nazi regime's privileging of eastern conquest and its fervent anti-Semitism. Other ethnologists such as Otto Reche turned toward Ostforschung (Eastern European studies). Mühlmann was one among many who challenged the boundaries between Völkerkunde and Völkskunde (Blome, 1941). This shift was already indicated by his growing interest in Jewish customs in 1932. Between 1942 and 1944 he published a string of publications on the problem of "trans-folking" (Umvolkung) – a Nazi neologism for the Germanization of certain ethnic groups in the occupied zones or the absorption of smaller ethnic groups into larger, more powerful ones. The corollary of trans-folking in actual policy was the extermination of the Jews and other inhabitants of the occupied zones who were not seen as viable candidates for assimilation. Mühlmann explained this in a scientific essay written during the early part of the Holocaust:

> trans-folking as a process obeys geopolitical-strategic laws. Just as the aim of war is the annihilation of the enemy, so the goal of trans-folking is ethnic extermination. Subjective ethnic conversion under the superior weight of the foreign ethnic gradient

corresponds to surrendering to the enemy in war ... The suffering ethnos constitutes small and tiny ethnic islands that become ever more tightly surrounded and finally give way before the flood of the stronger ethnic group. (Mühlmann, 1942, p. 296)

Mühlmann went on to publish a book-length study of trans-folking (Mühlmann, 1944) and to write on the ethnic composition of Eastern and Southeast Europe (Mühlmann, 1943). He appeared frequently as a speaker at the Nazi Institute for Border and Foreign Studies, which was responsible for applied research on ethnic issues in the occupied zones. Even if the defenders of trans-folking ultimately lost out to the stronger and more brutal "race faction" (Klingemann, 1989, p. 21) inside this Institute and the Nazi state more generally, this does not gainsay Mühlmann's complete loss of scientific autonomy.

It would be easy to explain the increasingly Nazified, applied orientation of Mühlmann's work in terms of economic hardship and the lack of a permanent university position. But there seems to be more involved. Mühlmann had worked very hard for Thurnwald in the early 1930s, doing most of the editorial work for the journal Sociologus. But Thurnwald got most of the international credit, especially in the United States and especially after the journal went bilingual in 1932. Thurnwald was institutionally too weak to be able to help Mühlmann economically. The fact that he "escaped" to the United States in the first half of the 1930s may have aroused some resentment in his student as well. But Mühlmann owed most of his central research ideas to Thurnwald, being strongly identified with the "functionalist" approach that Thurnwald had introduced into German anthropology. Mühlmann's attacks on the Kulturkreis school echoed Thurnwald's more measured, scientific criticisms. Even the racial, sociobiological turn in Mühlmann's work was indebted to Thurnwald, whose earlier work on "social sifting" as a kind of social evolutionary mechanism was re-biologized by Mühlmann. In sum, Mühlmann seems to have been pushed toward Nazi protectors by his relative poverty and also by a desire for scientific ego autonomy from his former mentor and weak patron.

My assumption in this paper is that scientific autonomy is worth defending. This does not necessarily entail erecting a tall wall between science and politics or the outside world. More than anyone else, Pierre Bourdieu has convincingly shown why "there is no opposition between autonomy and engagement" (Bourdieu & Wacquant, 1992, pp. 187–188). Even an engaged, militant sociology needs to start from a position of relative scientific autonomy.

NOTES

1. Bourdieu's account of the crisis of May 1968 in *Homo Academicus* (Bourdieu, 1988, pp. 159–193) follows an explanatory strategy that is very similar to Althusser's in "Contradiction and Overdetermination" (Althusser, 1990). Bourdieu breaks here with any residual notion in his work of a singular universal trajectory from tradition to modernity (a tendency seen in his studies of Algeria, rural Béarn, and French state formation, for example). The events of May 1968 are explained instead by the "synchronization of crises latent in different fields," the transformation of a "regional crisis" into "a general crisis, a historical event" (Bourdieu, 1988, p. 173). This occurs when the acceleration produced by a regional crisis is able to bring about a coincidence of events which, given the different tempo which each field adopts in its relative autonomy, should normally start or finish in dispersed order or, in other words, succeed each other without necessarily organizing themselves into a unified causal series."

2. As I argue in Steinmetz (2008a), the causal mechanisms of the social sciences are best described as social structures, to avoid possibly misleadingly *mechanical* connotations of the word mechanism (Steinmetz, 1998). Psychic structures are the "mechanisms" of psychoanalytic theory and science. But if social and psychological structures are analytically distinguishable, they are often not only combined but condensed with one another (along with various natural mechanisms ranging from biological to meteorological ones) in the genesis of human practices (Bhaskar, 1986, pp. 109–112).

3. See also Mulrine, 2007. On anthropology and colonialism, see Leclerc (1972), Asad (1973), Gothsch (1983), Stocking (1991), Zimmerman (2001), Penny (2002), and Steinmetz (2004).

4. On area studies and comparative political science, see Morrissey (1976), Wallerstein (1997), Robin (2001), and Vitalis (2005); for geography, see Godlewska and Smith (1994) and Smith (2003); and for economics, see Mirowski (2005).

5. The word "sociologie" was actually used as early as the 1780s by the Abbé: Sièyes but was made famous by Comte (Guilhaumou, 2006).

6. Treatments of Vierkandt by historians of sociology tended to ignore his "anthropological" work (Hochstim, 1966, p. 27), due to a retrospective narrowing of the sociological field and the resulting belief that "primitive" societies had always been the sole property of anthropology.

7. See Papcke (1993, ch. 5) on Grünfeld, a forgotten figure who committed suicide in Germany in 1938 after completing Die Peripheren (1939).

8. *Congrès international de sociologie colonial (Paris: A. Rousseau, 1901),* 2 Vols.

9. Of course, the Weimar Republic was still referred to as Das deutsches Reich; the word Reich had different connotations in German than the English and French words "empire" (Bosbach & Hiery, 1999). Despite the political pressures of nominalism, however, the Kaiserreich was an Imperium insofar as it annexed and ruled over outlying foreign areas (Alsace, parts of Poland, Austria, and Denmark) whose subjects did not have entirely equal rights; moreover the head of state was called Kaiser, or Caesar, and Roman images abounded (Steinmetz, 2006b). Like traditional land empires, Imperial Germany was regionally multinational or

cosmopolitan, a magnetic center exerting hegemonic cultural attraction over smaller nations and peripheral elites.

10. Jacques Soustelle, a student of Marcel Mauss and specialist in the Native American cultures of Mexico, was Governor General of French Algeria in 1955. He recruited Germain Tillion, a specialist in Algeria, to take charge of education, and she implemented a network of social centers (Centres Sociaux) which provided practical education, job training, medical care, and other forms of welfare to Algerian peasants (Forget, 1992). Paul Mus was a specialist in Buddhist and Sanskritist cosmology who became a critic of French colonialism and the American war in Vietnam and coined the term Union fraçaise, which he imagined as a "postimperial entity" (Bayly, 2009, p.196) that would be a "free and equal 'association' between the former colonial state and its ex-colony" (Larcher-Goscha, 2009, pp. 214–215). Mercier and Balandier were sociologists working in French west Africa in the late 1940s and early 1950s who ran a number of social science research centers and became highly critical of colonialism. Pierre Bourdieu, finally, was sent to Algeria in 1955 at the age of 25 for his military service and took a position as assistant professor at the University of Algiers and published his first book, Sociologie de l'Algérie, in 1958. He went on to conduct field research on the impact of capitalism on Algerian workers (Darbel, Rivet, Seibel, & Bourdieu, 1963) and the uprooting and resettlement of Algerian villagers (Bourdieu & Sayad, 1964). Both of these studies were commissioned by the French government and sponsored by the Association of Demographic, Economic, and Social Research., which was trying to reform French colonialism. But Bourdieu became a strong supporter of an "Algerian Algeria" (Nouschi, 2003; Silverstein & Goodman, 2009; Yacine, 2004).

11. On field theory, see Bourdieu (1991a, 1993b, 1996, 1999a).

12. To see how this approach can illuminate the empire-knowledge relationship we need to briefly recall the prevailing approaches in the literature on imperial knowledge. The first approach, associated with Said (1978), sees metropolitan science as a determinant that shapes the third world, including the colonies. The second approach inverts this account and explains science as a product of social conditions, as a function of social class or of some other social properties of intellectuals, or of capitalism, colonialism, or another social system. The third approach, which is positivistic or commonsensical, sees science as entirely independent of external influences. According to this third approach any writing that is clearly subordinated to outside powers is simply unscientific. I will not consider other approaches to the sociology of science in this paper except where needed and noted. I have shown elsewhere that precolonial ethnographic descriptions of non-European cultures did shape later German colonial native policies but only insofar as these discourses were adopted by colonial officials and wielded as cultural weapons in their struggles for power and status inside the colonial state (Steinmetz, 2007).

13. See Aufgaben der deutschen Kolonialforschung, edited by Kolonialwissenschaftliche Abteilung des Reichsforschungsrates (1942), which was published only for internal government use (nur für den Dienstgebrauch). On the entire field of colonial sciences in Nazi Germany, see Schmokel (1964).

14. For example, faculty at Cologne were able to prevent the head of the western section of the Nazi "University Lecturers' League" Willy Gierlichs from obtaining

a regular professorship due to his lack of a "major scientific publication" (Klingemann, 1996, p. 63).

15. Landecker went into exile the following year, earning a Ph.D. in sociology at the University of Michigan and eventually becoming a tenured sociology professor there (Lüschen, 2002).

16. Other examples: Nazi sociologist Karl Valentin Muller had "no objections to a possible race-mixing" in a German-dominated Czechoslovakia, even if this violated Himmler's views on race; in 1942 the Nazi Rektor of Königsberg University recognized three distinct schools in German economics (Klingemann, 2002, p. 191; idem, 1996, p. 187).

17. Bourdieu probably introduced the neologism socioanalysis because it resonated with psychoanalysis.

18. Each of these objects can also be considered from the standpoint of their own problems of autonomy and independence; each of them can be constructed as a Nomos, that is, a system seeking some sort of internal order. The idea of the Nomos is different from Luhmann's autopoetic system because it is not necessarily defined by a binary linguistic code.

19. Bourdieu is also interested in the overall autonomy of entire fields. Compared to other fields, social science (including sociology) "is particularly exposed to heteronomy, because external pressure is particularly strong there and because the internal conditions for autonomy (in particular the requirement of a 'ticket of entry') are very difficult to set up" (Bourdieu, 2004, p. 87).

20. Alexander (1995, pp. 144–145) makes almost the opposite critique of Bourdieu, arguing that his theory of habitus differs from psychoanalysis in failing to understand the social self as empirically autonomous and differentiated from others. In the work of the 1990s, however, Bourdieu increasing focused on the ego-analytic tradition discussed by Alexander, which "emphasized the body, the breast and the body ego [as] reference points from which the self must differentiate, not as mirror- images with which the self is identified" (ibid.). I am arguing instead that Bourdieu theorizes differentiation but does not theorize relations of similitude, mirror-images, ego ideals and ideal egos, and other identifications. For Bourdieu, similarities among different individuals' representations and practices stem from similarities at the level of habitus, and not from psychic identifications and mirroring. It is precisely this level of identifications, which involves direct relations between individuals and ego ideals (or ideal egos), which needs to be integrated into Bourdieu's theory. Admittedly, however, Bourdieu is vague about the means by which habituses are "orchestrated," so that Alexander's critique has some merit.

21. Identification in psychoanalysis is an unconscious mental process "by which someone makes part of their personality conform to the personality of another, who serves as a model" (de Mijolla, 2005, p. 787). On the difference between ego ideals and ideal egos, see Freud (1914, 1921), Laplanche and Pontalis (1973), de Mijolla-Mellor (2005), and Lagache (1961).

22. The difference between a controlling superego and a labile, opportunist psychic structure also helps us understand the original choice of a profession. The extreme forms of autonomy and heteronomy can be associated in the first case with the "heir who, so to speak, refuses to inherit, that is, to be inherited by his

inheritance" (Bourdieu, 1996, p. 11) and in the second with heirs located on the "main diagonal" of the social mobility table.

23. Of course there has always been disagreement on Weber's influence on German sociology during the 1920s (see for example Schroeter, 1980). Weber's place in the field between 1909 and 1933 (and even through the Nazi period; see Klingemann, 1996) was central insofar as he had the greatest amount of field-specific symbolic capital; this is a different criterion than Weber's "influence." The postwar West German discussion of Weber began in earnest with the 1964 convention of the Deutsche Gesellschaft für Soziologie (Kaesler, 2002).

24. In the "rural laborer study" (Landarbeiter-Enquête) Weber analyzed the supposed threat to the eastern German border zones posed by Polish immigration and the factors motivating Prussian-German rural laborers to emigrate. The study thus combined "sociological analysis with 'volkstumspolitischer Agitation'" (Klingemann, 2002, p. 177). His contribution to the study of the psychophysics of labor was driven "above all by the question of [enhancing] the profitability of the [workers' contribution] to the capitalist process of production" ([63]Demm, 2000a, p. 72), a thoroughly "bourgeois" orientation that went against the more social political orientation of the older members of the Verein für Sozialpolitik.

25. Weber's later campaign to separate academic sociology from politics was directed partly against the Verein für Sozialpolitik and also against the politicization of the university lecture-hall by the German Mandarin professors (Josephson, 2004).

26. Thurnwald moved to Berlin from Austria in 1900 and converted from Catholicism to Protestantism in 1904 (Melk-Koch, 1989).

27. Melk-Koch (1989, p. 162), quoting the head of the commission in charge of staffing and preparing the Kaiserin-August-Fluß-Expedition in which Thurnwald participated.

28. The reasons for his failure to get a job in the United States were explained to Thurnwald in a letter from sociologist L. L. Bernard (June 26, 1936, Yale University Library [hereafter YUL], Thurnwald papers).

29. See Steinmetz (2007) on European merchant class Sinophobia and Kaiser Wilhelm's hyper-Sinophobia.

30. Weber (1964, pp. 235–242, 249).

31. Confucianism itself had actually undergone a certain rationalization, according to Weber, but in a form that was antithetical to the socioeconomic on rationalization.

32. In Schmidt-Glintzer's reconstruction of the writing and publication of volume one of the Religionssoziologie there is no information on the libraries and other sources Weber used, other than a letter to von Rosthorn (Schmidt-Glintzer, 1989, pp. 42–43).

33. Steinmetz (2007, p. 402). Schmidt-Glintzer (1989, p. 6) emphasizes the "tradition of beginning with China," and surely has Hegel's philosophy of history in mind.

34. This seems to be the argument of Allen (2004), for example.

35. Wilhelm worked as a missionary and teacher in Qingdao from 1899 to 1919, and received an honorary doctorate from Frankfurt University in 1922 and was given an Honorarprofessur in 1924. He taught at Beijing University between 1922

and 1924, and from 1924 until his death in 1930 at Frankfurt am Main, where he founded the Sinological Institute (Hirsch, 2003).

36. Franke was appointed to the first German chair in Sinology at the Hamburg Colonial Institute in 1909. After the war, Franke held De Groot's Chair at Berlin University (1923–1931).

37. According to historian Jonathan R. Herman (personal communication), Wang Ching Dao did the initial translations from Chinese for Martin Buber's publication of two Chinese texts, although Wang was only credited for unspecified q assistance in the prologue.

38. Thurnwald met Schultz in the Pacific in 1909 and later recruited him as a contributing editor for his journal Sociologus. As State Secretary of the Colonial Office, Solf helped finance Thurnwald's research in New Guinea in 1914 (Melk-Koch, 1989, p. 129, 189).

39. See "Gründung einer Kolonialakademie in Halle/Saale am 6.11.1908," in Bundesarchiv Berlin, R 8023 (Deutsche Kolonialgesellschaft); Richard Thurnwald to Geheimrat, February 23, 1921, Halle, on connecting colonial studies to the Auslandsstudiendienst; "Eine neue Aktionsprogramm der Kolonialakademie," Halle, February 25, 1921 (the last two in YUL Thurnwald papers).

40. "Wie weit ist unkriegerische Kolonisation möglich?" Notes for lecture, Halle Colonial Academy, July 17, 1922, in YUL Thurnwald papers.

41. See Grosse (1993, p. 77) and Verhandlungen des deutschen Kolonialkongresses 1924 zu Berlin am 17. und 18. September 1924 (Berlin: Verlag Kolonialkriegerdank, 1924).

42. Volume 6 of Die Menschliche Gesellschaft was published posthumously (Adam, 1955, p. 152).

43. Thurnwald specified that the separation between civilization and culture was a heuristic device. These were two different ways of looking at the same process: civilizational technologies are stamped by the culture that uses them while culture also has a technical side (Thurnwald, 1939a, p. 426).

44. Thurnwald to Boas, March 26, 1933. See Thurnwald to Chefredakteur Dr. Klein, Deutsche Allgeimeine Zeitung, March 26, 1933, in which he criticizes the "serious and unjustifiable outrages against Jews" and recalls that many German-American Jews "stepped in to defend Germany" during and after World War I, including Boas, who was a founder of the Notgemeinschaft. Both letters in Thurnwald papers, YUL.

45. Thurnwald's proposal was in some respects actually more "liberal" than German policies directed in Namibia before 1914 which had attempted to reduce the Herero to a propertyless proletariat. In other respects his organizational model reproduced elements of the Germans' earlier colonial policies. Reservations and worker colonies (werfts) had existed in German South West Africa before 1914. The Native Caretaker was reminiscent of the German "native commissioners" who had been assigned to werfts and tribes. The native commissioners in German Southwest Africa were supposed to organize and spy on the colonized and encourage them to work and "lose their warlike attributes," but they were also intended as advocates for native interests against illegal abuses by employers and settlers (Zimmerer, 2001, p. 123).

46. According to Timm (1977, p. 623), quoting from Thurnwald's personnel file at the Humboldt University. It is unclear whether, and how much, Thurnwald was paid for these reports. On the Ministry for Ammunition and forced labor, see Naasner (1994).

47. I can only sketch the beginnings of an answer here but plan to return to these two cases in a future essay.

48. See the transcript of Weber's (1929) seminar with Karl Mannheim on Lukács' History and Class Consciousness (in Demm, 1999, pp. 443–462).

49. According to Lange-Kirchheim (1977), Kafka's "In the Penal Colony" is "ideologically and in many sections even stylistically dependent" on Alfred Weber's article "the civil servant" (Weber, 1927); see also Harrington (2007).

50. Mühlmann to Thurnwald, October 10, 1932, in YUL, Thurnwald papers, Box 2, folder 27.

51. Mühlmann to Thurnwald, October 18, 1932, in YUL, Thurnwald papers, Box 2, folder 28.

52. Mühlmann to Thurnwald, March 21, 1933, in YUL, Thurnwald papers, Box 2, folder 39.

REFERENCES

Adam, L. (1955). In memoriam: Richard Thurnwald. *Oceania, 25*(3), 145–155.

Adedze, A. (2003). In the pursuit of knowledge and power: French scientific research in West Africa, 1938–65. *Comparative Studies of South Asia. Africa and the Middle East, 23*(1–2), 335–344.

Alexander, J. C. (1995). *Fin de siècle social theory: Relativism, reduction, and the problem of reason.* New York, NY: Verso.

Allen, K. (2004). *Max Weber: A critical introduction.* London: Pluto Press.

Althusser, L. (1990). Contradiction and overdetermination. In *For Marx* (pp. 87–128). London: NLB.

Amidon, K. S. (1998). "Diesmal fehlt die Biologie!" Max Horkheimer, Richard Thurnwald, and the Biological Prehistory of German Sozialforschung. *New German Critique, 35*(2), 103–137.

Amselle, J.-L. (1993). Anthropology and historicity. *History and Theory, 32*(4), 12–31.

Arendt, H. (1951). *The origins of totalitarianism.* New York, NY: Harcourt Brace Jovanovich.

Asad, T. (1973). *Anthropology and the colonial encounter.* New York, NY: Humanity Books.

Asen, J. (1955). *Gesamtverzeichnis des Lehrkörpers der Universität Berlin.* Leipzig: O. Harrassowitz.

Ash, M. G. (1999). Scientific changes in Germany 1933, 1945, 1990: Towards a comparison. *Minerva, 37*, 329–354.

Balandier, G. (1953). Messianismes et nationalismes en Afrique Noire. *Cahiers internationaux de sociologie, 14*, 41–65.

Balandier, G. (1955a). *Sociologie actuelle de l'Afrique noire; dynamique des changements sociaux en Afrique centrale.* Paris: Presses universitaires de France.

Balandier, G. (1955b). *Sociologie des Brazzavilles noires.* Paris: A.Colin.

Balandier, G. (Ed.). (1956). *Le Tiers-Monde, sous-développement et développement*. Travaux et documents No. 27.PUF. Paris: Institut national d'études démographiques.

Balandier, G., & Mercier, P. (1952). *Particularisme et evolution. Les pêcheurs Lebou du Sénégal*. Études Sénégalaises, no. 3. Saint-Louis, Sénégal: Centre IFAN-Sénégal.

Bastian, A. (1860). *Der Mensch in der Geschichte. zur Begründung einer psychologischen Weltanschuung* (Vols. 3). Leipzig: O. Wigand.

Bastian, A. (1884). *Allgemeine Grundzüge der Ethnologic*. Berlin: D. Reimer.

Bayly, S. (2009). Conceptualizing resistance and revolution in Vietnam: Paul Mus' understanding of colonialism in crisis. *Journal of Vietnamese Studies, 4*(1), 192–205.

Bertrand, R. (2005). *Etat colonial, noblesse et nationalisme à Java: la tradition parfait*. Paris: Karthala.

Bertrand, R. (2008). Des gens inconvenants. Javanais et Néerlandais à l'aube de la rencontre imperial. *Actes de la recherche en sciences sociales, 171–172*, 104–121.

Bhaskar, R. (1986). *Scientific realism and human emancipation*. London: Verso.

Blome, H. (1941). *Bericht über die Arbeitszusammenkunft deutscher Völkerkundler in Göttingen am 22. und 23. November 1940*. Göttingen: n.p.

Blomert, R. (1999). *Intellektuelle im Aufbruch: Karl Mannheim, Alfred Weber, Norbert Elias und die Heidelberger Sozialwissenschaften der Zwischenkriegszeit*. München: Hanser.

Blomert, R., Esslinger, H.-U., & Giovannini, N. (Eds.). (1997). *Heidelberger Sozial- und Staatswissenschaften: das Institut für Sozial- und Staatswissenschaften zwischen 1918 und 1958*. Marburg: Metropolis.

Bloom, H. (1997). *The anxiety of influence: A theory of poetry* (2nd ed.). New York, NY: Oxford University Press.

Bosbach, F., & Hiery, H. (Eds.). (1999). *Imperium/Empire/Reich: ein Konzept politischer Herrschaft im deutsch-britischen Vergleich (An Anglo-German comparison of a concept of rule)*. München: K.G. Saur.

Bourdieu, P. (1959). La logique interne de la civilisation algérienne traditionnelle. In Secrétariat social d'Alger (Ed.), *Le sous-développement en Algérie* (pp. 40–51). Alger: Éditions du Secrétariat social d'Alger.

Bourdieu, P. (1971 [1966]). Intellectual field and creative project. In M. D. Young (Ed.), *Knowledge and control: New directions for the sociology of education* (pp. 161–188). London: Collier-Macmillan.

Bourdieu, P. (1988). *Homo academicus*. Cambridge, UK: Polity Press.

Bourdieu, P. (1990). *The logic of practice*. Stanford, CA: Stanford University Press.

Bourdieu, P. (1991a). Political representation: Elements for a theory of the political field. In *Language and symbolic power* (pp. 171–202). Cambridge, MA: Harvard University Press.

Bourdieu, P. (1991b). On the possibility of a field of world sociology. In P. Bourdieu & J. S. Coleman (Eds.), *Social theory for a changing society* (pp. 373–387). Boulder, CO: Westview Press.

Bourdieu, P. (1993a). For a sociology of sociologists. In *Sociology in question* (pp. 49–53). London: Sage.

Bourdieu, P. (1993b). Some properties of fields. In *Sociology in question* (pp. 72–77). London: Sage.

Bourdieu, P. (1996). *The rules of art*. Cambridge, UK: Polity Press.

Bourdieu, P. (1999a). Rethinking the state: Genesis and structure of the bureaucratic field. In G. Steinmetz (Ed.), *State/culture* (pp. 53–75). Ithaca, NY: Cornell University Press.

Bourdieu, P. (1999b). *The weight of the world: Social suffering in contemporary society.* Cambridge: Polity Press.

Bourdieu, P. (2000). *Pascalian meditations.* Cambridge, UK: Polity Press.

Bourdieu, P. (2003). Colonialism and ethnography. Foreword to Pierre Bourdieu's Travail et travailleurs en Algérie. *Anthropoiogy Today,* 19(2), 13–18.

Bourdieu, P. (2004). *Science of science and reflexivity.* Chicago, IL: University of Chicago Press.

Bourdieu, P. (2007). *Sketch for a self-analysis.* Cambridge: Polity.

Bourdieu, P., & Sayad, A. (1964). Paysans déracinés, bouleversements morphologiques et changements culturels en Algérie. *Études rurales, 12,* 56–94.

Bourdieu, P., & Wacquant, L. (1992). *An invitation to reflexive sociology.* Chicago, IL: University of Chicago Press.

Breuer, S. (1987). *Imperien der alten Welt.* Stuttgart: Kohlhammer.

Brinkmann, C. (1921). *Weltpolitik und Weltwirtschaft im 19. Jahrhundert.* Bielefeld: Velhagen & Klasing.

Broszat, M. (1981). *The Hitler state: The foundation and development of the internal structure of the Third Reich.* New York, NY: Longman.

Büttner, C. G. (1885). Die Missionsstation Otjimbingue in Damaraland. *Zeitschrift der Gesellschaft für Erdkunde zu Berlin, 20,* 39–56.

Calhoun, C., Cooper, F., & Moore, K. (Eds.). (2006). *Lessons of empire. Imperial histories and American power.* New York, NY: The New Press.

Césaire, A. (2000). *Discourse on colonialism.* New York, NY: Monthly Review Press.

Clark, T. N. (1973). *Prophets and patrons: The French university and the emergence of the social sciences.* Cambridge, MA: Harvard University Press.

Comte, A. (1830–1842). *Cours de philosophie positive.* Paris: Bachelier.

Conklin, A. (2002). Civil society, science, and empire in late Republican France: The foundation of Paris's museum of man. *Osiris,* 2nd series, *17,* 255–290.

Connell, R. (2007). *Southern theory.* Cambridge: Polity.

Connell, R. W. (1997). Why is classical theory classical? *American Journal of Sociology,* 102(6), 1511–1557.

Cornell, D. (2003). Autonomy re-imagined. *Journal for the Psychoanalysis of Culture,* 8(1), 144–149.

Darbel, A., Rivet, J.-P., Seibel, C., & Bourdieu, P. (1963). *Travail et travailleurs en Algérie.* Paris: Mouton.

De L'Estoile, B. (2002). Science de l'homme et "domination rationnelle". Savoir ethnologique et politique indigène en Afrique coloniale française. *Revue de synthèse,* 4th series, *3–4,* 291–323.

de Mijolla, A. (2005). Identification. In A. de Mijolla (Ed.), *International dictionary of psychoanalysis* (pp. 787–792). Detroit, MI: Macmillan Reference.

de Mijolla-Mellor, S. (2005). Ego ideal, ego ideal/ideal ego. In A. de Mijolla (Ed.), *International dictionary of psychoanalysis* (pp. 479–481). Detroit, MI: Macmillan Reference.

de Tocqueville, A. (2001). In J. Pitts (Ed.), *Writings on empire and slavery.* Baltimore, MD: Johns Hopkins University Press.

Demm, E. (1990). *Ein Liberaler in Kaiserreich und Republik: der politische Weg Alfred Webers bis 1920.* Boppard am Rhein: H. Boldt.

Demm, E. (1999). *Von der Weimarer Republik zur Bundesrepublik: der politische Weg Alfred Webers 1920–1958.* Düsseldorf: Droste.

Demm, E. (2000a). *Geist und Politik im 20. Jahrhundert: gesammelte Aufsätze zu Alfred Weber.* Frankfurt: Lang.

Demm, E. (2000b). *Alfred Weber zum Gedächtnis. Selbstzeugnisse und Erinnerungen von Zeitgenossen.* Frankfurt am Main: Peter Lang.

Derks, H. (1999). Social sciences in Germany, 1933–1945. *German History, 17*(2), 177–219.

Dezalay, Y., & Bryant, G. (2008). L'impérialisme moral. Les juristes et l'impérialisme Américain (Philippines, Indonésie). *Actes de la recherche en sciences sociales, 171–172,* 40–55.

Du Bois, W. E. B. (1915). The African roots of war. *Atlantic Monthly, 115,* 707–714.

Du Bois, W. E. B. (1975 [1945]). *Color and democracy: Colonies and peace.* Millwood, NY: Kraus-Thomson Organization.

Du Bois, W. E. B. (1986 [1940]). Dusk of dawn. In W. E. B. Du Bois (Ed.), *Writings* (pp. 549–802). New York, NY: Library of America.

Elias, N. ([1939] 1994). *The civilizing process.* Oxford: Blackwell.

Fischer, H. (1990). *Völkerkunde im Nationalsozialismus. Aspekte der Anpassung, Affinität und Behauptung einer wissenschaftlichen Disziplin.* Berlin: D. Reimer Verlag.

Forget, N. (1992). Le Service des Centres Sociaux en Algérie. *Matériaux pour l'histoire de notre temps, 26,* 37–47.

Fournier, M. (2006). *Marcel Mauss: A biography.* Princeton, NJ: Princeton University Press.

Freud, S. (1914). On narcissism: An introduction. *Standard Edition, 14,* 65–143.

Freud, S. (1921). Group psychology and the analysis of ego. *Standard Edition, 18,* 67–143.

Geddes, P. (1917). *Ideas at war.* London: Williams and Norgate.

Geddes, P. (1947). In. J. Tyrwhitt (Ed.), *Patrick Geddes in India.* London: L. Humphries.

Giddings, F. H. (1900). *Democracy and empire, with studies of their psychological, economic, and moral foundations.* New York, NY: The Macmillan Company.

Go, J. (1999). Colonial reception and cultural reproduction: Filipino elite response to U.S. Colonialism. *Journal of Historical Sociology, 12*(4), 337–368.

Go, J. (2008). *American empire and the politics of meaning: Elite political cultures in the Philippines and Puerto Rico during U.S. colonialism.* Durham: Duke University Press.

Godlewska, A., & Smith, N. (Eds.). (1994). *Geography and empire.* Cambridge, MA: Blackwell.

Gothsch, M. (1983). *Die deutsche Völkerkunde und ihr Verhältnis zum Kolonialismus: ein Beitrag zur kolonialideologischen und kolonialpraktischen Bedeutung der deutsche Völkerkunde in der Zeit von 1870 bis 1975.* Baden-Baden: Nomos.

Grosse, P. (1993). *Kolonialismus und Öffentlichkeit im späten Kaiserreich: Die Deutschen Kolonialkongresse 1902, 1905 und 1910.* Magisterarbeit, Freie Universität Berlin.

Grünfeld, E. (1913). *Hafenkolonien und Kolonieähnliche Verhältnisse in China, Japan und Korea; eine kolonialpolitische Studie.* Jena: G. Fischer.

Guilhaumou, J. (2006). Sieyès et le non-dit de la sociologie: du mot à la chose. *Revue d'histoire des sciences humaines, 15,* 117–134.

Gullestad, S. E. (1993). A contribution to the psychoanalytic concept of autonomy. *Scandanavian Psychoanalytic Review, 16,* 22–34.

Gutberger, J. (1996). *Volk, Raum und Sozialstruktur. Sozialstruktur- und Sozialraumforschung im "Dritten Reich".* Münster: Lit.

Harrington, A. (2007). Alfred Weber's essay "the civil servant" and Kafka's "in the penal colony": The evidence of an influence. *History of the Human Sciences, 20*(2), 41–63.

Hermassi, E. (1972). *Leadership and national development in North Africa: A comparative study.* Berkeley, CA: University of California Press.

Herre, P. (Ed.). (1923). *Politisches Handwörterbuch.* Leipzig: K.F. Koehler.

Hirsch, K. (2003). *Richard Wilhelm, Botschafter zweier Welten.* Frankfurt am Main: IKO-Verlag für Interkulturelle Kommunikation.

Hochstim, P. (1966). *Alfred Vierkandt. A sociological critique.* New York, NY: Exposition Press.

Honigsheim, P. (1926). Der Max Weber Kreis in Heidelberg. *Kolner Vierteljahrshefte für Soziologie, 5*(3), 270–287.

Hurvich, M. S. (2005). Ego autonomy. In A. de Mijolla (Ed.), *International dictionary of psychoanalysis* (pp. 473–474). Detroit, MI: Macmillan Reference.

Josephson, P. (2004). Lehrfreiheit, Lernfreiheit, Wertfreiheit: Max Weber and the University teachers congress in Jena 1908. *Max Weber Studies, 4*(2), 201–219.

Kaesler, D. (1984). *Die frühe deutsche Soziologie 1900 bis 1934 und ihre Entstehungs-Milieus.* Opladen: Westdeutscher Verlag.

Kaesler, D. (1991). *Sociological adventures: Earle Edward Eubank's visits with European sociologists.* New Brunswick: Transaction Publishers.

Kaesler, D. (2002). Max Weber: Vom akademischen Außenseiter zum soziologischen Klassiker. Einleitung des Herausgebers. In D. Kaesler (Ed.), *Max Weber: Schriften 1894* (pp. vii–xxxvi). Stuttgart: Alfred Kroner.

Kaiser, J. H. (1968). Europäisches Großraumdenken. Die Steigerung geschichtlicher Größen als Rechtsproblem. In H. Barion, E.-W. Böckenförde, E. Forsthoff, & W. Weber (Eds.), *Epirrhosis. Festgabe für Carl Schmitt* (pp. 529–548). Berlin: Duncker & Humblot.

Karady, V. (1982). Le problème de la légitimité dans l'organisation historique de l'ethnologie française. *Revue française de sociologie, 23*, 17–35.

Karstedt, O. (1942). *Probleme afrikanischer Eingeborenenpolitik.* Berlin: E. S. Mittler & Sohn.

Kidd, B. (1898). *The control of the tropics.* New York, NY: The Macmillan Company.

Klemm, G. (1847). *China, das Reich der Mitte.* Leipzig: B. G. Teubner.

Klemperer, V. (2006). *The language of the Third Reich: LTI – Lingua Tertii Imperii: A Philologist's Notebook.* London: Continuum.

Klingemann, C. (1989). Angewandte Soziologie im Nationalsozialismus. 1999. *Zeitschrift für Sozialgeschichte des 20. und 21. Jahrhunderts, 4*(1), 10–34.

Klingemann, C. (1996). *Soziologie im Dritten Reich.* Baden-Baden: Nomos Verlagsgesellschaft.

Klingemann, C. (2002). Ostforschung und Soziologie wahrend des Nationalsozialismus. In J. M. Piskorski, J. Hackmann, & R. Jaworski (Eds.), *Deutsche Ostforschung undpolnische Westforschung im Spannungsfeld von Wissenschaft und Politik* (pp. 161–203). Osnabrück-Poznan: Poznanskie Towarzystwo Przyjaciol Nauk.

Klingemann, C. (2009). *Soziologie und Politik: Sozialwissenschaftliches Expertenwissen im Dritten Reich und in der frühen westdeutschen Nachkriegszeit.* Wiesbaden: VS Verlag für Sozialwissenschaften.

König, R. (1958). *Soziologie.* Frankfurt am Main: Fischer.

Konno, H. (2004). *Max Weber und die polnische Frage (1892–1920): eine Betrachtung zum liberalen Nationalismus im wilhelminischen Deutschland.* Baden-Baden: Nomos.

Krickeberg, W. (1938). Review of Lehrbuch der Völkerkunde. *Zeitschrift für Ethnologie*, 69, 464–466.

Lagache, D. (1961). La psychanalyse et la structure de la personnalité. *La psychanalyse*, 6, 5–58.

Landecker, W. S. (1999). *Die Geltung des Völkerrechts als gesellschaftliches Phänomen: eine rechts- und sozialwissenschaftliche Analyse aus dem Jahr 1936*. Münster: Lit.

Lange-Kirchheim, A. (1977). Franz Kafka: "In der Strafkolonie" und Alfred Weber: "Der Beamte". *Germanisch-Romanische Monatsschrift*, N.F. 27, 202–221.

Langewiesche, D. (1997). Die Universität Tübingen in der Zeit des Nationalsozialismus: Formen der Selbstgleichschaltung und Selbstbehauptung. *Geschichte und Gesellschaft*, 23, 618–646.

Laplanche, J., & Pontalis, J.-B. (1973). *The language of psychoanalysis*. New York, NY: W.W. Norton & Company.

Larcher-Goscha, A. (2009). Ambushed by history: Paul Mus and Colonial France's 'Forced Reentry' into Vietnam (1945–1954). *Journal of Vietnamese Studies*, 4(1), 206–239.

Lardinois, R. (2008). Entre monopole, marché et religion. L'émergence de l'Etat colonial en Inde, années 1760–1810. *Actes de la recherche en sciences sociales*, 171–172, 90–103.

Lassman, P., Velody, I., & Martins, H. (Eds.). (1988). *Max Weber's 'Science as a Vocation'*. London: Unwin Hyman.

Laukötter, A. (2007). The time after Adolf Bastian: Felix von Luschan and Berlin's Royal Museum of Ethnology. In M. Fischer, P. Bolz, & S. Kamel (Eds.), *Adolf Bastian and his universal archive of humanity: The origins of German anthropology* (pp. 153–165). New York, NY: G. Olms.

Leclerc, G. (1972). *Anthropologie et colonialisme*. Paris: Fayard.

Leiris, M. (1934). *L'Afrique fantôme*. Paris: Gallimard.

Leiris, M. (1950). L'ethnographie devant le colonialisme. *Les temps modernes*, 58, 357–373.

Leutner, M. (1987). Sinologie in Berlin: Die Durchsetzung einer wissenschaftliche Disziplin zur Erschließung und zum Verstandnis Chinas. In H.-Y. Kuo (Ed.), *Berlin und China* (pp. 31–56). Berlin: Colloquium Verlag.

Lévy-Bruhl, L. (1925 [1910]). *How natives think*. New York, NY: A.A. Knopf.

Linne, K. (2002). *'Weisse Arbeitsführer' im 'kolonialen Ergänzungsraum'. Afrika als Ziel sozial- und wirtschaftlicher Planungen in der NS-Zeit*. Münster: Monsenstein & Vannerdat.

Lüschen, G. (2002). In memoriam Werner S. Landecker 30.04.1911–19.05.2002. *Kölner Zeitschrift für Soziologie und Sozialvsychologie*, 54, 617.

Magubane, B. (1971). A critical look at indices used in the study of social change in colonial africa. *Current Anthropology*, 12(4–5), 419–445.

Mann, M. (2003). *Incoherent empire*. London: Verso.

Mazrui, A. A. (1968). From social Darwinism to current theories of modernization: A tradition of analysis. *World Politics*, 21, 69–83.

Melk-Koch, M. (1989). *Auf der Suche nach der menschlichen Gesellschaft: Richard Thurnwald*. Berlin: Reimer.

Menzel, G. (1992). *C. G. Büttner*. Wuppertal: Verlag der Vereinigten Evangelischen Mission.

Mercier, P. (1951). *Les tâches de la sociologie*. Dakar: Institut français d'Afrique noire.

Mercier, P. (1954). Aspects des problèmes de stratification sociale dans l'Ouest Africain. *Cahiers internationaux de sociologie*, 17, 47–65.

Merton, R. K. (1973). The ambivalence of scientists. In *The sociology of science* (pp. 383–412). Chicago, IL: University of Chicago Press.

Michel, U. (1992). Wilhelm Emil Mühlmann (1904–1988) – ein deutscher Professor. Amnesie und Amnestie: Zum Verhältnis von Ethnologie und Politik im Nationalsozialismus. *Jahrbuch für Soziologiegeschichte, 1991*, 69–117.

Michel, U. (1995). Neue ethnologisches Forschungsansätze im Nationalsozialismus? Aus der Biographie Wilhelm Emil Mühlmann (1904–1988). In T. Hauschild (Ed.), *Lebenslust und Fremdenfurcht* (pp. 141–167). Frankfurt am Main: Suhrkamp.

Mirowski, P. (2005). How positivism made a pact with the postwar social sciences in America. In G. Steinmetz (Ed.), *The politics of method in the human sciences: Positivism and its epistemological others* (pp. 142–172). Durham, NC: Duke University Press.

Mitzman, A. (1985). *The iron cage. An historical interpretation of Max Weber* (Rev. ed.). New Brunswick: Transaction.

Molt, P. (2002). Alfred Weber heute. *Die politische Meinung, 387*(February), 89–95.

Mommsen, W. J. (1984). *Max Weber and German politics, 1890–1920*. Chicago, IL: University of Chicago Press.

Morrissey, M. (1976). Imperial designs: A sociology of knowledge study of British and American dominance in the development of Caribbean social science. *Latin American Perspectives, 3*(4), 97–116.

Mühlmann, W. E. (1932). *Die geheime Gesellschaft der Arioi: Eine Studie über polynesische Geheimbünde, mit besonderer Berücksichtigung der Siebungs- und Auslesevorgänge in Alt-Tahiti.* Berlin University, doctoral dissertation.

Mühlmann, W. E. (1936). *Rassen- und Völkerkunde: Lebensprobleme der Rassen, Gesellschaften und Völker.* Braunschweig: Friedr. Vieweg & Sohn.

Mühlmann, W. E. (1937). Politisch-katholische Rassenforschung? *Volk und Rasse, 12*, 35–38.

Mühlmann, W. E. (1942). Umvolkung und Volkwerdung. *Deutsche Arbeit, 42*(1), 287–297.

Mühlmann, W. E. (1943). Das rassische Bild. In K. C. von Loesche & W. Mühlmann (Eds.), *Die Völker und Rassen Südosteuropas* (pp. 38–56). Vienna: Volk und Reich Verlag.

Mühlmann, W. E. (1944). *Assimilation, Umvolkung, Volkwerdung: Ein globaler Überblick und ein Programm.* Stuttgart: Kohlhammer.

Mulrine, A. (2007). The culture warriors. *U.S. News and World Report*, December 10, 34–37.

Naasner, W. (1994). *Neue Machtzentren in der deutschen Kriegswirtschaft 1942–1945: die Wirtschaftsorganisation der SS, das Amt des Generalbevollmächtigten für den Arbeitsansatz und das Reichsministerium für Bewaffnung und Munition, Reichsministerium für Rüstung und Kriegsproduktion im nationalsozialistischen Herrschaftssystem.* Boppard am Rhein: H. Boldt.

Nagel, B. (1991). *Die Welteislehre: ihre Geschichte undihre Rolle im "Dritten Reich".* Stuttgart: Verlag für Geschichte der Naturwissenschaften und der Technik.

Nau, H. H. (1996). *Der Werturteilsstreit: die Äußerungen zur Werturteilsdiskussion im Ausschuss des Vereins für Sozialpolitik (1913).* Marburg: Metropolis-Verlag.

Neumann, F. L. (1942). *Behemoth: The structure and practice of national socialism.* London: V. Gollanez Ltd.

Norton, R. E. (2002). *Secret Germany: Stefan George and his circle.* Ithaca, NY: Cornell University Press.

Nouschi, A. (2003). Autour de Sociologie de l'Algérie. *Awal. Cahiers d'etudes Berbères, 27–28*, 26–29.

Oppenheimer, F. (1929). *System der Soziologie, Vol. 4, part 1, Rom und die Germanen.* Jena: Gustav Fischer.

Papcke, S. (1993). *Deutsche Soziologie im Exil.* Frankfurt: Campus.

Paquet, A. (1911). Vorwort. In H.-M. Ku (Ed.), *Chinas Verteidigung gegen europäische Ideen* (pp. i–xiv). Jena: E. Diederichs.

Paquet, A. (1912). *Li, oder Im neuen Osten.* Frankfurt am Main: Rutten & Loening.

Paquet, A. (1914). Der Kaisergedanke. *Der neue Merkur, 1,* 45–62.

Penny, H. G. (2002). *Objects of culture.* Chapel Hill, NC: University of North Carolina Press.

Petermann, W. (2004). *Die Geschichte der Ethnologie.* Wuppertal: Peter-Hammer-Verlag.

Radkau, J. (2008). Max Weber between "eruptive creativity" and "disciplined transdisciplinarity". In F. Adloff & M. Borutta (Eds.), *Max Weber in the 21st century* (pp. 13–30). Florence: EUI working papers.

Radkau, J. (2009). *Max Weber: A biography.* Cambridge, UK: Polity.

Rammstedt, O. (1988). Wertfreiheit und die Konstitution der Soziologie in Deutschland. *Zeitschrift für Soziologie, 17*(4), 264–271.

Rapaport, D. (1951). The autonomy of the ego. *Bulletin of the Menninger Clinic, 15,* 113–123.

Rapaport, D. (1967). The autonomy of ego. In M. Gill (Ed.), *The collected papers of David Rapaport* (pp. 357–367). New York, NY: Basic Books.

Reichsforschungsrat. (1942). *Aufgaben der deutschen Kolonialforschung.* Stuttgart: W. Kohlhammer.

Remy, S. P. (2002). *The Heidelberg Myth: The nazification and denazification of a German University.* Cambridge, MA: Harvard University Press.

Ringer, F. K. (1969). *The decline of the German mandarins: The German academic community, 1890–1933.* Hanover, NH: Wesleyan University Press.

Ringer, F. K. (2004). *Max Weber – An intellectual biography.* Chicago, IL: University of Chicago Press.

Robin, R. (2001). *The making of the cold war enemy: Culture and politics in the military intellectual complex.* Princeton, NJ: Princeton University Press.

Rodinson, M. (1955). Review of Naissance du proletariat marocain. *Année sociologique 1952,* 3rd series, *6,* 371–373.

Rodinson, M. (1965). Sociologie de l'Islam. *Année sociologique 1964,* 3rd series, *15,* 360–364.

Roth, G. (2001). *Max Webers deutsch-englische Familiengeschichte 1800–1950: mit Briefen und Dokumenten.* Tübingen: Mohr Siebeck.

Saada, E. (2007). *Les enfants de la colonie: les métis de l'empire franç-ais entre sujétion et citoyenneté.* Paris: Découverte.

Sahlins, M. (1967). In). The established order: Do not fold, spindle, or mutilate. In I. L. Horowitz (Ed.), *The rise and fall of project Camelot: Studies in the relationship between social science and practical politics.* Cambridge, MA: MIT Press.

Said, E. W. (1978). *Orientalism.* New York, NY: Vintage.

Salz, A. (1931). *Das Wesen des Imperialismus.* Leipzig: B.G. Teubner.

Sartre, J.-P. (1988). *"What is literature?" and other essays.* Cambridge: Harvard University Press.

Schäffle, A. (1886–1888). Kolonialpolitische Studien. *Zeitschrift für die gesammte Staatswissenschaft, 42,* 625–665. 43, 123–217, 343–416; 44, 59–96, 263–306.

Schmidt-Glintzer, H. (1989). Einleitung, Editorischer Bericht. In Max Weber, Die Wirtschaftsethik der Weltreligionen. Konfuzianismus und Taoismus. H. Schmidt-Glintzer (Ed.), *Max Weber Gesamtausgabe* (Vol. 2, Part 19, 1–25, 31–73). Tübingen: Mohr.

Schmitt, C. ([1941] 1991). *Volkerrechtliche Grossraumordnung mit Interventionsverbot für raumfremde Machte* (4th ed.). Berlin: Duncker & Humblot.

Schmokel, W. W. (1964). *Dream of empire: German colonialism, 1919–1945.* New Haven, CT: Yale University Press.

Schroeter, G. (1980). Max Weber as outsider: His nominal influence on German sociology in the twenties. *Journal of the History of the Behavioral Sciences, 16,* 317–332.

Schumpeter, J. A. (1951). *Imperialism and social classes.* New York, NY: A. M. Kelley.

Seddon, D. (1973). Introduction. In R. Montagne (Ed.), *The Berbers: Their social and political organisation* (pp. xiii–xl). London: Cass.

Sibeud, E. (2002). Ethnographie africaniste et 'inauthenticite' coloniale. French politics. *Culture and Society, 20*(2), 11–28.

Silverstein, P. A., & Goodman, J. A. (2009). Introduction. Bourdieu in Algeria. In J. E. Goodman & P. A. Silverstein (Eds.), *Bourdieu in Algeria* (pp. 1–62). Lincoln: University of Nebraska Press.

Small, A. (1916). Fifty years of sociology in the United States (1865–1915). *American Journal of Sociology, 21*(6), 721–864.

Smith, N. (2003). *American Empire: Roosevelt's geographer and the prelude to globalization.* Berkeley, CA: University of California Press.

Steinmetz, G. (1995). Distorting mirrors: Exoticism, assimilation, and aesthetic reflexivity in German colonialism. Paper given at the inaugural conference for the German Studies program at the University of Texas, Austin.

Steinmetz, G. (1997). Theorizing the colonial state: The German overseas empire, 1880–1914. Paper presented to the annual meetings of the American Sociological Association, Toronto.

Steinmetz, G. (1998). Critical realism and historical sociology. *Comparative Studies in Society and History, 40*(1), 170–186.

Steinmetz, G. (2003). The "Devil's handwriting": Precolonial discourse, ethnographic acuity and cross-identification in German colonialism. *Comparative Studies in Society and History, 45*(1), 41–95.

Steinmetz, G. (2004). The uncontrollable afterlives of ethnography: Lessons from German 'salvage colonialism' for a new age of empire. *Ethnography, 5*(3), 251–288.

Steinmetz, G. (2006a). Bourdieu's disavowal of Lacan: Psychoanalytic theory and the concepts of "habitus" and "symbolic capital". *Constellations, 13*(4), 445–464.

Steinmetz, G. (2006b). Imperialism or colonialism? From Windhoek to Washington, by way of Basra. In C. Calhoun, F. Cooper, & K. Moore (Eds.), *Lessons of empire: Imperial histories and American power* (pp. 135–156). New York, NY: The New Press.

Steinmetz, G. (2007). *The Devil's handwriting: Precoloniality and the German colonial state in Oingdao, Samoa, and Southwest Africa.* Chicago, IL: University of Chicago Press.

Steinmetz, G. (2008a). Logics of history as a framework for an integrated social science. *Social Science History, 32*(4), 535–554.

Steinmetz, G. (2008b). The colonial state as a social field. *American Sociological Review, 73*(4), 589–612.

Steinmetz, G. (2008c). La sociologie historique en Allemagne et aux Etats-Unis: un transfert manqué (1930–1970). *Genèses, 71,* 123–147.

Steinmetz, G. (2010a). Bourdieu, historicity, and historical sociology. *Cultural Sociology, 10*(1).

Steinmetz, G. (2010b). Sociology and its imperial entanglements. Introduction. In G. Steinmetz (Ed.), *Sociology and empire.* Durham, NC: Duke University Press.

202 GEORGE STEINMETZ

Steinmetz, S. R. (Ed.) (1903). *Rechtsverhältnisse von eingeborenen Völkern in Afrika und Ozeanien.* Berlin: Julius Springer.

Stocking, G. W., Jr. (Ed.) (1991). *Colonial situations: Essays on the contextualization of ethnographic knowledge.* Madison, WI: University of Wisconsin Press.

Szöllösi-Janze, M. (2001). National Socialism and the sciences: Reflections, conclusions, and historical perspectives. In M. Szöllösi-Janze (Ed.), *Science in the Third Reich* (pp. 1–36). Oxford: Berg.

Tenbruck, F. H. (1999). *Das Werk Max Webers: gesammelte Aufsätze zu Max Weber.* Tübingen: Mohr Siebeck.

Thurnwald, R. (1901). Staat und Wirtschaft im alten Ägypten. *Zeitschrift für Sozialwissenschaft, 11*(697–714), 769–788.

Thurnwald, R. (1903–1904). Staat und Wirtschaft in Babylon zu Hammurabis Zeit. *Jahrbücher für Nationalökonomie und Statistik, 26*(4), 644–675. 27(2), 64–88, 190–202.

Thurnwald, R. (1905). Koloniale Eingeborenenpolitik. *Archiv für Rassen- und Gesellschafts-Biologie, 2,* 632–636.

Thurnwald, R. (1910a). Das Rechtsleben der Eingeborenen der deutschen Südseeinseln, seine geistigen und wirtschaftlichen Grundlagen. *Blätter für vergleichende Rechtswissenschaft und Volkswirtschaftslehre, 6*(5–6), 178–191.

Thurnwald, R. (1910b). Die eingeborenen Arbeitskrafte im Sudseeschutzgebiet. *Koloniale Rundschau, 10,* 607–632.

Thurnwald, R. (1912a). Angewandte Ethnologie in der Kolonialpolitik. In Internationale Vereinigung für vergleichende Rechtswissenschaft und Volkswirtschaftslehre in Berlin (Ed.), *Verhandlungen der ersten Hauptversammlung für vergleichende Rechtswissenschaft und Volkswirtschaftslehre in Berlin zu Heidelberg vom 3. bis 9* September 1911 (pp. 59–69). Berlin: Franz Vahlen.

Thurnwald, R. (1912b). *Forschungen auf den Salomo-Inseln und dem Bismarck-Archipel, Vol. I: Lieder und Sagen aus Buin.* Berlin: D. Reimer (E. Vohsen).

Thurnwald, R. (1917a). Kolonien oder Weltwirtschaft? *Koloniale Rundschau, 9/10,* 385–395.

Thurnwald, R. (1917b). Holland und seine Kolonialpolitik. *Das neue Deutschland, 6*(2), 39–40.

Thurnwald, R. (1918a). Die Kolonien als Friedensburgschaft. Vortrag vom 26.1.18. *Blatter für vergleichende Rechtswissenschaft und Volkswirtschaftslehre, 14*(4–6), 170–185.

Thurnwald, R. (1918b). Der Wert von Neu-Guinea als deutsche Kolonie. *Koloniale Rundschau, 1/2,* 43–56.

Thurnwald, R. (1926a). Führerschaft and Siebung. *Zeitschrift für Völkerpsychologie und Soziologie, 2*(1), 1–18.

Thurnwald, R. (1929a). Deutschlands Anteil an den kolonialen Problemen von heute. *Der Kolonialfreund, 7,* 7–9.

Thurnwald, R. (1929b). The social problems of Africa. *Africa: Journal of the International African Institute, 2*(2), 130–137.

Thurnwald, R. (1931a). Soziologische Forschungen über die Veränderungen im Leben des Afrikaners unter den Einwirkungen der europäischen Zivilisation. *Forschungen und Fortschritte, 7*(2), 17–18.

Thurnwald, R. (1931b). Soziale Wandlungen in Ostafrika. *Zeitschrift für Völkerpsychologie und Soziologie, 7*(2), 148–168.

Thurnwald, R. (1931c). Die neue afrikanische Welt. *Koloniale Rundschau, 9–10,* 193–199.

Thurnwald, R. (1931–1935). *Die menschliche Gesellschaft in ihren ethno-soziologischen Grundlagen.* Berlin: W. de Gruyter.

Thurnwald, R. (1932a). Social transformations in East Africa. *The American Journal of Sociology, 38*(2), 175–184.

Thurnwald, R. (1932b). The psychology of acculturation. *American Anthropologist, 34*(4), 557–569.

Thurnwald, R. (1932c). Die Neger an der Schreibmachine. Soziale Wandlungen in Afrika. (Mit Bildern von der Schomburgh-Afrika-Expedition). *Die Koralle, 8*(4), 154–157.

Thurnwald, R. (1935a). *Black and White in East Africa. The fabric of a new civilization.* London: Routledge.

Thurnwald, R. (1935b). Wirtschaftliche Wandlungen bei ostafrikanischen Völkern. *Jahrbücher für Nationalökonomie und Statistik, 142,* 541–561.

Thurnwald, R. (1936a). The price of the white man's peace. *Pacific Affairs, 9*(3), 347–357.

Thurnwald, R. (1936b). The crisis of imperialism in East Africa and elsewhere. *Social Forces, 15*(1), 84–91.

Thurnwald, R. (1937). Die Kolonialfrage. *Jahrbücher für Nationalökonomie und Statistik, 145,* 66–86.

Thurnwald, R. (1938a). Kolonialwirtschaftliche Betriebe. *Jahrbücher für Nationalökonomie und Statistik, 148,* 48–62.

Thurnwald, R. (1938b). Zur persönlichen Abwehr. *Archiv für Anthropologie, 24*(3/4), 300–302.

Thurnwald, R. (1939a). Methoden in der Völkerkunde. In O. Reche (Ed.), *Kultur und Rasse, Otto Reche zum 60. Geburtstag gewidmet von Schülern und Freunden* (pp. 420–428). München: J.F. Lehmanns Verlag.

Thurnwald, R. (1939b). *Koloniale Gestaltung. Methoden und Probleme überseeischer Ausdehnung.* Hamburg: Hoffmann und Campe Verlag.

Thurnwald, R. (1940). Die fremden Eingriffe in das Leben der Afrikaner und ihre Folgen. In H. Baumann, R. Thurnwald, & D. Westermann (Eds.), *Völkerkunde von Afrika* (pp. 455–573). Essen: Essener Verlagsanstalt.

Thurnwald, R. (2001 [1938]). Bericht zu der Sitzung der Arbeitsgemeinschaft Eingeborenenarbeit und – sozialrecht vom 11.7.38 über die Organisierung der Eingeborenenarbeit in Ostafrika und ihre Gestaltungsmöglichkeit auf nationalsozialistischer Grundlage. In W. Schubert (Ed.), *Akademie für Deutsches Recht 1933–1945, Protokolle der Ausschüsse, Ausschuß für Rechtsfragen der Bevölkerungspolitik (1934–1940) und Ausschuß für Kolonialrecht zusammen mit den Entwürfen des Kolonialpolitischen Amts (1937–1941); Sachverständigenbeirat für Bevölkerungs- und Rassenpolitik im Reichsministerium des Inneren (1933/1939)* (Vol. 12, 617–627). Berlin: De Gruyter.

Timm, K. (1977). Richard Thurnwald: 'Koloniale Gestaltung' – ein 'Apartheids-Projekt' für die koloniale Expansion des deutschen Faschismus in Afrika. *Ethnographisch-Archäologische Zeitschrift, 18,* 617–649.

Union of South Africa (1918). *Report on the natives of South-West Africa and their treatment by Germany.* London: HMSO.

Veblen, T. (1915). *Imperial Germany and the industrial revolution.* New York, NY: The Macmillan Company.

Vitalis, R. (2005). Birth of a discipline. In D. Long & B. C. Schmidt (Eds.), *Imperialism and internationalism in the discipline of international relations* (pp. 159–182). Albany, NY: State University of New York Press.

von Keyserling, H. G. (1925). *The travel diary of a philosopher.* London: J. Cape.

von Luschan, F. (1915). *Anthropological view of race*. New York, NY: Hamburg-Amerika Linie.

von Richthofen, F. F. (1897). *Kiautschou, seine Weltstellung und voraussichtliche Bedeutung*. Berlin: Verlag von Georg Stilke.

von Richthofen, F. F. (1898). *Schantung und seine Eingangspforte Kiautschou*. Berlin: Dietrich Reimer.

von Richthofen, F. F. (1907). *Ferdinand von Richthofen's Tagebücher aus China*. Berlin: Dietrich Reimer.

von Rosthorn, A. (1923). Religion und Wirtschaft in China. In M. Palyi (Ed.), *Hauptprobleme der Soziologie. Erinnerungsgabe für Max Weber* (pp. 221–238). München and Leipzig: Duncker & Humblot.

von Vierkandt, A. (1896). *Naturvölker und Kulturvölker*. Leipzig: Duncker & Humblot.

von Wiese, L. (1914a). Die gegenwärtige Stellung Ceylons in der Weltwirtschaft im Vergleich mit Vorder- und Hinterasien. *Weltwirtschaftliches Archiv, 3*(1), 139–162.

von Wiese, L. (1914b). Die Rodias auf Ceylon. *Archiv für Rassen- und Gesellschaftsbiologie, 11*(1), 33–45.

von Wiese, L. (1922). *Briefe aus Asien*. Köln: Rheinland-Verlag.

von Wiese, L. (1923). *Nava. Eine Erzählung aus Ceylon*. Jena: Diederichs.

Walker, M. (1989). National socialism and German physics. *Journal of Contemporary History, 24*(1), 63–89.

Wallerstein, I. (1959). *The emergence of two West African nations, Ghana and the Ivory Coast*. PhD dissertation, Columbia University.

Wallerstein, I. (Ed.). (1966). *Social change: The colonial situation*. New York, NY: Wiley.

Wallerstein, I. (1997). The unintended consequences of area studies. In N. Chomsky, I. Katznelson, R. C. Lewontin, D. Montgomery, L. Nader, R. Ohmann, R. Siever, I. Wallerstein, & H. Zinn (Eds.), *The Cold War and the university: Toward an intellectual history of the postwar years* (pp. 195–231). New York, NY: New Press.

Walravens, H. (2005). Rosthorn, Arthur von. In *Neue Deutsche Biographie* (Vol. 22, 101–102). Berlin: Duncker & Humblot.

Walther, A. (1927). *Soziologie und Sozialwissenschaften in Amerika*. Karlsruhe: Verlag G. Braun.

Wang, C. D. (1913). Die Staatsidee des Konfuzius und ihre Beziehung zur konstitutionelle Verfassung. *Mitteilungen des Seminars für Orientalische Sprachen zu Berlin, 16*(1), 1–49.

Wassner, R. (1985). *Andreas Walther und die Soziologie in Hamburg. Dokumente, Materialien, Reflexionen*. Hamburg: Institut für Soziologie der Universität Hamburg.

Weber, A. (1918). Das Selbstbestimmungsrecht der Völker und der Friede. *Preussische Jahrbucher, 171*, 60–71.

Weber, A. (1920–1921). Prinzipielles zur Kultursoziologie. (Gesellschaftprozeß, Zivilisationsprozeß und Kulturbewegung). *Archiv für Sozialwissenschaft und Sozialpolitik, 47*, 1–49.

Weber, A. (1924). Deutschland und die europäische Kulturkrise. *Die neue Rundschau, 35*, 308–321.

Weber, A. (1927). Der Beamte. In, *Ideen zur Staats- und Kultursoziologie* (pp. 81–101). Karlsruhe: Braun.

Weber, A. (1929 [1909]). *Alfred Weber's theory of the location of industries*. Chicago: The University of Chicago Press.

Weber, A. (1935). *Kulturgeschichte als Kultursoziologie (uitgeversmaatschappij, n.v)*. Leiden: A. W. Sijthoffs.

Weber, A. (1943). *Das Tragische und die Geschichte*. Hamburg: H. Govert.

Weber, A. (1955). *Einführung in die Soziologie*. Munich: R. Pieper & Co.

Weber, A. (1997). *Schriften zur Kultur- und Geschichtssoziologie (1906–1958)*. Alfred-Weber-Gesamtausgabe (Vol. 8). Marburg: Metropolis.

Weber, A. (1999). *Politische Theorie und Tagespolitik (1903–1933)*. Alfred-Weber-Gesamtausgabe (Vol. 7), Marburg: Metropolis.

Weber, A. (2000). *Schriften zur Wirtschafts- und Sozialpolitik (1897–1932)*. Alfred-Weber-Gesamtausgabe (Vol. 5), Marburg: Metropolis.

Weber, m. (1891). *Die römische Agrargeschichte in ihrer Bedeutung für das Staats- und Privatrecht*. Stuttgart: F. Enke.

Weber, M. (1920). *Gesammelte Aufsätze zur Religionssoziologie* (Vol. 1). Tübingen: Mohr.

Weber, M. (1921). *Die rationalen und soziologischen Grundlagen der Musik*. München: Drei Masken Verlag.

Weber, M. (1949). "Objectivity" in social science and social policy. In E. A. Shils & H. Finch (Eds.), *The methodology of the social sciences* (pp. 50–112). Glencoe, IL: Free Press.

Weber, M. (1964). *The religion of China: Confucianism and Taoism (Hans H. Gerth, trans.)*. New York, NY: Free Press.

Weber, M. (1975). *Roscher and Knies: The logical problems of historical economics*. New York, NY: Free Press.

Weber, M. (1976). *The agrarian sociology of ancient civilizations*. London: NLB.

Weber, M. (1977a). Academic conviviality. *Minerva, 15*(2), 214–246.

Weber, M. (1977b). *Critique of Stammler*. New York, NY: Free Press.

Weber, M. (1978). *Economy and society* (Vols. 2), Berkeley, CA: University of California Press.

Weber, M. (Ed.). (1984a). *Zur Psychophysik der industriellen Arbeit 1908–1912. Gesamtausgabe*. Part one, (Vol. 11). Tübingen: Mohr.

Weber, M. (Ed.) (1984b). Die Lage der Landbarbeiter im ostelbischen Deutschland, 1892. *Gesamtausgabe*, Part one, (Vol. 3), Tübingen: Mohr.

Weber, M. (1988). *Max Weber: A biography*. New Brunswick: Transaction.

Weber, M. (1989). The national state and economic policy. In K. Tribe (Ed.), *Reading Weber* (pp. 188–209). London: Routledge.

Weber, M. ([1919] 1958). Science as a vocation. In E. A. Shils & H. A. Finch (Eds.), *The methodology of the social sciences* (pp. 77–128). Glencoe, IL: Free Press.

Weinberg, G. L. (1963). German colonial plans and policies 1936–1942. In W. Besson & F. F. H. v. Gaer (Eds.), *Geschichte und Gegenwartsbewusstsein* (pp. 462–491). Göttingen: Vandenhoeck and Ruprecht.

Westermann, D. (Ed.). (1937). *Beiträge zur deutschen Kolonialfrage*. Essen: Essener Verlagsanstalt.

Wirsing, G. (1932). *Zwischeneuropa und die deutsche Zukunft*. Jena: Diederichs Verlag.

Yacine, T. (2004). Pierre Bourdieu in Algeria at War. *Ethnography, 5*(4), 487–509.

Zastoupil, L. (1994). *John Stuart Mill and India*. Stanford: Stanford University Press.

Zimmerer, J. (2001). *Deutsche Herrschaft über Afrikaner: Staatlicher Machtanspruch und Wirklichkeit im kolonialen Namibia* (2nd ed.). Münster: Lit.

Zimmerman, A. (2001). *Anthropology and antihumanism in imperial Germany*. Chicago, IL: University of Chicago Press.

Zwiedeneck-Südenhorst, O. v. (1936). Ethnosoziologie? Grundsätzliches und Antikritisches zu
Thurnwalds Werk 'Die Menschliche Gesellschaft'. *Jahrbücher für Nationalökonomie und
Statistik, 144,* 528–555.

This Article has been Cited by

Go, J. *Introduction: Entangling Postcoloniality and Sociological Thought,* 3–31. [Abstract] [Full
Text] [PDF] [PDF].
Goswami, M. Provincializing. *Sociology: The Case of a Premature Postcolonial Sociologist,*
145–175. [Abstract] [Full Text] [PDF] [PDF].
Steinmetz, G. (2010). Charles Tilly, German historicism, and the critical realist. *Philosophy of
Science. The American Sociologist, 41,* 312–336. [CrossRef].
Steinmetzm, G. (2014). The sociology of empires, colonies, and postcolonialism. *Annual
Review of Sociology, 40,* 77–103. [CrossRef].

"PROVINCIALIZING" SOCIOLOGY: THE CASE OF A PREMATURE POSTCOLONIAL SOCIOLOGIST ☆

Manu Goswami

ABSTRACT

This essay seeks to extend the original gambit of this forum, of thinking possible modes of postcolonial sociology, unto a more relational terrain. It takes as its point of departure the vexed status of history in sociology and the hermeneutic suspicion of comparison in postcolonial theory. Any potential rapprochement between postcolonial theory and sociology must engage with the deeply incongruent status of history and comparison across these fields. I attempt to bridge this divide historically by revisiting an anti-imperial internationalist sociology forged in interwar colonial India. I seek thereby to show what Pierre Bourdieu called a "particular case of the possible" and to participate in ongoing efforts to "provincialize" sociology.

This forum invites us to think possible modes of a postcolonial sociology. If we follow the cartographic logic of many cross-disciplinary reflections,

☆ Reprinted from *Postcolonial Sociology*, Political Power and Social Theory, Volume 24, 2013, pp. 145–175.

Postcolonial Sociology
Political Power and Social Theory, Volume 24, 207–237
ISSN: 0198-8719/doi:10.1108/S0198-8719(2013)0000024012

of surveying a particular field for the evidence of another, then one line of response might appear relatively straightforward. This might entail mapping postcolonial theories or concepts at work in different sectors of sociology. We might track such concepts as "hybridity" (Bhabha, 1994), the "rule of colonial difference" (Chatterjee, 1993), or "epistemic violence" (Spivak, 1988) in "third-wave" historical sociologies of empire (Adams, 1996, pp. 12–28; Go, 2008; Magubane, 2003; Steinmetz, 2007). Or we might situate programmatic debates within sociology in relation to different strands of postcolonial theory exploring how they variously side-step, intersect, or take them up. Examples in this vein might encompass the older problematic of "multiple modernities" (Eisenstadt, 2002, 1998), Michael Burroway's recent call for a "subaltern global sociology" (Burroway, 2005a, 2005b), Ulrich Beck's program for a post-national and multi-centric "methodological cosmopolitanism" (Beck & Grande, 2010), or synthetic engagements with postcolonial theory (Seidman, 1996; McLennan, 2003; Ray & Radhakrisnan, 2010). Such efforts might well serve to consolidate or advance existent or emergent thematic overlaps. Yet all such mappings presume a broad alignment, a basic congruence, between the organizing terms and tasks of the distinct fields in consideration. They run the risk of ignoring why the envisioning of a postcolonial sociology might strain credulity or must rely on a certain suspension of disbelief.

The dissonance derives not only from the overt disjunction between disciplinary sociology and postcolonial theory as abstract singulars. That is the way postcolonial theory is a cross-disciplinary project that is broadly poststructuralist in its epistemological mooring whereas disciplinary sociology, especially in the United States, has been strongly positivist. Nor does it only stem from the entrenched regionalism of sociology expressed in the ways Europe and North America have been the ground and gauge for explanatory models about modernity and capitalism, revolutions and political subjectivity, nationalism and development, urbanization, and secularization. But from the way, it is arguably as difficult to envisage a sociological postcolonialism, the implied corollary, of a postcolonial sociology. For in their Anglo-American development, postcolonial studies appear as among sociology's more non-sociological, even stridently post-sociological, "others." What role could or should heterodox sociologies play in postcolonial studies, were things to be as they might? Can we think of a postcolonial sociology and a sociological postcolonialism in tandem? And how ought postcolonial theory to be sociological today? These questions are as much about postcolonial theory as they are about sociology. Beginning with this symmetric difficulty opens out the original gambit of the forum, of possible modes of postcolonial sociology, unto a more relational terrain – the vexed status of history in sociology and the hermeneutic suspicion of comparison in postcolonial theory. Any potential rapprochement between postcolonial theory and sociology must engage with the deeply incongruent status of history and comparison across these fields. This does not imply that there is no intelligible ordering possible across these disjunctions. But it does enjoin us to recognize that bridging ventures are as much a matter of political and ethical choice as a problem of pure speculative or theoretical construction.

It is in this spirit that I take up the prospective gamble of this forum. As a historian of South Asia who has sought to negotiate the distance between postcolonial theory and social theory, my engagement is at once more specific and more general than the convention of an inter-field mapping. It is more general insofar as I am concerned less with the reception of particular sociologists or classical social theorists within postcolonial studies than the vexed status of sociological discourse in postcolonial theory. It is more specific insofar as I seek insights into this broad problematic historically, by excavating an anti-imperial sociology forged in colonial India.

My argument proceeds in two steps. I open by briefly outlining how the postcolonial suspicion of sociology combines both a reproach against conceptual abstraction and a critique of developmental historicism. This orientation derives not just from a poststructuralist dispensation. It is conditioned by the long shadow cast by modernization theoretical models, and their associated logics of comparison, in what were once called "area studies," long regarded as the object not the instigator of social science theories. There is no simple alignment between the epistemological concerns of postcolonial theory and the generalizing, explanatory "habitus" of post-positivist or anti-positivist sociology (Brubaker, 1993; Sewell, 2005). Given this estrangement one mode of thinking a reflexive sociology and a sociological postcolonialism together resides in exploring the differentiated global history of sociology. By this I mean less the institutional con-solidation of sociology as a formal discipline across regional fields in the twentieth century than its contingent crystallization as an anti-systemic political and conceptual vocation (Calhoun, 2007; Uberoi, Sundar, & Deshpande, 2007; Steinmetz, 2009). The second part of my essay focuses on the work of Benoy Kumar Sarkar (1887–1949), the most prominent social scientist in interwar colonial India, and a fierce critic of dominant nationalism. He alchemized into emergent sociology the expansive aspira-tion toward a non-imperial future that coursed through interwar colonial worlds. Deeply committed to sociology as a political vocation yet an unrelenting critic of its imperial common sense, he prefigured a line of critique commonly associated with late-twentieth century postcolonial theory. From the perspective of histories of social science, this analytic was remarkable for its reflexivity about the predicament of universalistic paradigms in an imperial age. In a 1917 lecture at Clark University, he named this collective burden as a joint overcoming of "colonialism in politics and ... *Orientalisme* in science" (Sarkar, 1922, preface, iv). This project sought to combine a "critique of Occidental reason" (Sarkar, 1922, p. 1) with a demonstration of the political claim that contemporary anti-imperial movements were the embodiment and emblem of the future in the present.

Focusing on the meaning and use of sociology by a dissident colonial intellectual serves two interlinked purposes. First, it provides a critical illustration of what Pierre Bourdieu, in his oft-repeated citation of Gaston Bachelard, called "a particular case of the possible" (Bourdieu, 1994, p. 16). Sarkar's effort to establish commensurability across world deemed separate and bounded exemplified the ways comparison works simultaneously as an epistemological practice and a vernacular politics. Second, revisiting such projects participates in ongoing efforts to "provincialize" sociology by expanding the conventional historical and geographical coordinate of received sociological cannons (Burroway, 2005a, 2005b; Chakrabarty, 2000). Histories of sociology beyond a "classical" terrain might usefully instruct and reorient alike a post-Eurocentric sociology and a sociologically inflected postcolonialism (Connell, 1997). This effort is broadly akin to the practice of many second-wave historical sociologists who mobilized classical social theory as a critical resource (Adams, Clemens, & Orloff, 2005, pp. 1–74; Calhoun, 1996). Yet it rejects the "past-as-background-to-present" rendering of historical time that imparted a presumptive objectivism to second-wave historical sociologies and re-enforced a wider "methodological nationalism" (Goswami, 2002, 2004). A post-positivist (and post-Eurocentric) historical sociology implies moving beyond not only conceptions of historical temporality as a quantitative metric, a lineal temporal sequence, or a temporal container of discrete processes. It entails attending to the multiple logics of historicity (Chakrabarty, 2000; Sewell, 2005), including how "struggles to create a future," to borrow Phillip Abrams's phrase, saturate everyday practices (Abrams, 1982, p. 8).

POSTCOLONIALISM AND SOCIOLOGY

Postcolonial theory is a diverse ensemble of cross-disciplinary projects. Here I focus on what a recent anthology names the "Indian Postcolonial," specifying the dominant, if not exclusive, historiographic and regional provenance of postcolonial theory (Boehmer & Chaudhary, 2010). Postcolonial theory in this sense signals not only a widely influential critique of Eurocentric frameworks. It is associated with a hermeneutic suspicion of the explanatory remit and comparative impetus of dominant social science. The signature feature of the quarrel with social science is a joint reproach against conceptual abstraction and developmental historicism. Dipesh Chakrabarty's *Provincializing Europe* is arguably the single-most influential and innovative articulation of this critique, one that posits European thought and social science as virtually interchangeable (Chakrabarty, 2000).

Chakrabarty takes as his point of departure the place-dependence of all social and political thought. Locating himself within the historical and political forms of an Indian modernity, he argues that European thought as social science enforces commensurability by smudging the heterogeneity of concrete lifeworlds. "Europe," Chakrabarty observes, "remains the sovereign theoretical subject of all histories, including the ones we call 'Indian', "Chinese', 'Kenyan', etc" (Chakrabarty, 2000, p. 29). This "hyperreal Europe," that is, the imaginary Europe of the social sciences, is sustained by conceptual abstractions (civil society, citizenship, democracy, abstract labor, and such) that negate nonhistorical forms of temporality and non-secular modes of social being. The repression of difference by conceptual abstractions cannot be easily countered by another lexicon or conceptualization because the "European intellectual tradition is the only one alive" within and beyond "social science departments." Yet, at the same time, social-scientific concepts such as democracy, citizenship, and civil society refract a broader history of collective aspirations for political and social universality. As a consequence, the relationship between postcolonialism and of "Europe" as social science is necessarily paradoxical, even tragic. This predicament can be named but neither resolved nor overcome. European thought as social science is

> both indispensable and inadequate in helping us to think through the various life
> practices that constitute the political and the historical in India. Exploring – on both
> theoretical and factual registers – this simultaneous indispensability and inadequacy of
> social science thought is the task this book has set itself (Chakrabarty, 2000, p. 6).

The positioning of social science as simultaneously inadequate and indispensable bears a strong kinship, as the literary critic and novelist Amit Chaudhuri observes, with Derrida's declaration of the "necessity but impossibility" of Western Metaphysics (Chaudhuri, 2004). The postcolonial discontent with social science is not very far from the position of Paul Feyerabend, the postmodern philosopher of science, for whom the history of Western thought can be told as "A Tale of Abstraction versus the Richness of Being" (Feyerabend, 1999). The trouble with social science, from this vantage, is its conceptual abstraction. The Latin *abstrahere*, to abstract, means to "draw away or remove" (something from something else); it carries an intrinsic epistemological negativity. That the loss of sensuous particularity is internal to all concept formation, as a very condition of the possibility of knowledge, has elicited various responses from empiricism to a romanticism of origins. For the German social philosopher Georg Simmel it underlined the "tragedy of human concept formation" evinced in "the fact that the higher concept, which through its breadth embraces a growing number of details, must count upon increasing loss of content" (Simmel, 1990/1900, p. 221). For Simmel this tragedy was borne of a specific historical transformation, one tied to the contradictory double-coding of the money form as a site of both "infinite possibility" and deepening estrangement. The postcolonial critique of abstraction has centered less on the social locus of abstractions as such, than the ideological complicity between universalizing abstractions and imperial domination. These commitments place it adjacent to yet distinct from other epistemology centered critiques of dominant social science, whether the tradition of Western Marxism exemplified by Frankfurt school critical theory or more recent varieties of post-structuralism.

The vexed status of the sociological in postcolonial theory seems at first sight rooted within a generic poststructuralism. Yet it carries the traces of a more specific geopolitical condition – the encounter with sociological models of comparison grounded within American-style modernization theory and orthodox Marxism. From the vantage of Chakrabarty's "hyper-real Europe," mainline social science inherits the temporalized imperial logic that shunted non-European societies into a figurative "waiting room" before they could obtain a measure of collective political autonomy.

> Historicism – and even the modern, European idea of history – one might say, came to non-European peoples in the 19th century as somebody's way of saying "not yet" to somebody else (Chakrabarty, 2000, p. 8).

Chakrabarty's usage of historicism, a notoriously contested concept, as a stand-in for history has sparked debate (Chakrabarty, 2008, pp. 85–96; Dietze, 2008, 69–84). The emphasis on the geographical origins of concepts (abstract labor, nation, citizenship) as a key measure of conceptual adequacy and the posited equivalence between "European thought" and social science are also open to contest. The first tends toward a romanticism of origins that brackets complex historical-geographies of co-constitution as much as the latter sets up a hermeneutic circle that cannot easily be "squared," to invoke Judith Shklar's critique of Heideggerian hermeneutics (Shklar, 1986). It cannot be "squared" because the positing of a fixed, unitary, closed whole, "Europe," renders the analytical, as opposed to an affective or place-based, standpoint of the interpreter ambiguous. But these ambiguities have not tempered the wider appeal of Chakrabarty's melancholy reckoning with extant social science. Part of the remarkable resonance of *Provincializing Europe* as a cross-disciplinary project lies in its ethnographic fidelity to the lived experience of incommensurability of many scholars of non-Western worlds pressed into morphing heterogeneous social worlds into the straitened lexicon of mid-twentieth century modernization theory. Although modernization theoretical perspectives were not an exclusive derivation of disciplinary sociology, their broadly "sociological" imprint came to exercise a kind of trandisciplinary hegemony in the US academy. They hinged, as is well known, upon an ideal-typical and idealized notion (in a perverse fulfillment of Weber's "one-sided distillation") of the modern "West" as the convergent attractor of economic and political development *tout court*. For the mandarins of modernization theory – the Shilesian project of social science and classic works by W. W. Rustow, Daniel Thorner, Samuel Huntington, among others – the emergent terrain of "new nations" represented an opportunity to advance and entrench comparative methods. It was almost as if the import of the political revolution wrought by decolonization by the mid- twentieth and late-twentieth century – the transformation of an inter-state field from an initial 50 states to some 200 – was simply to increase the empire of comparison for social science. Even as modernization accounts lost substantive plausibility, the spatio-temporal ontology they presupposed – the notion of discrete and bounded societies and cultures across which a "homogeneous empty time" of uniform economic and political development flowed – underpinned a wider swath of comparative models across disciplinary fields (Anderson, 1998; Miyoshi & Harootunian, 2002. On the history of modernization theory see Ekbladh, 2011; Gilman, 2007). Their thralldom was especially acute within "area-studies," the terrain within which postcolonial studies, at least in the US academy, first took hold.

The reaction-formation against the inadequate empirical content and universalizing abstractions of reigning sociological schemas has been formative. It has spawned on the one hand, a renewal of epistemological considerations about the complex forms of equivalence and context-dependence of analytical concepts, practical categories, and social forms. Yet it has also led to a counter-valorization of the singular, the unique, even the non-representable. In a wide-ranging defense of non-positivist comparative studies, George Steinmetz, critically identifies postcolonialism and holocaust studies as principal arenas for the post-Kuhnian articulation of notions of incommensurability. Postcolonial theorists tend to conflate, he notes, the "very real 'violence of abstraction' in social practice with a less compelling argument that [social] scientific abstraction is necessarily violent" (Sayer, 1987; Steinmetz, 2004, p. 388). If formalistic models of comparison in mainline sociology erase the historicity of comparison as an epistemological practice (including the imperial genealogy of such fields as comparative philology, law, ethnology), the postcolonial suspicion of comparison tends to establish an a priori limit to its possibility. It does so by rendering singularity or difference less a dialectical product of a particular historical process, encounter, or formation – that is, something to be inferred from a sociohistorical analysis – than a pre-given basis for the inevitable failure of comparison as such. But incomparability only exists within a field of comparison. It is an intrinsically relational term that can mark the limits of the intelligibility or adequacy of a specific comparison. We cannot represent the radically singular or cognitively grasp the incomparable as such (Osborne, 2005). Or we cannot do so without insulating social and cultural phenomenon from the multiple and multiply-scaled processes that forge and transform them and keep their moving on the move (Goswami, 2005). This does not mean that all social practices or cultural concepts warrant comparison. The point is rather the limits of reckonings of comparison as either a formalistic heuristic or an a priori impossibility.

The methodological fetish of "comparativism," to borrow Rogers Brubaker's apt phrase, as a formal heuristic in historical sociology obscures the ways all theoretical concepts are inherently comparative (Brubaker, 2003. For broader debates in sociology see McMichael, 1990; Mongia, 2007; Skocpol & Somers 1980; Tilly, 1997). The alignment of macrohistorical and comparative approaches is rooted, Brubaker argues, in methodological convention not intellectual substance. Ironically, it underlines the relatively subaltern status of history within mainline sociology. The very "out-sourcing" of history to the subfield of historical sociology renders it a variable method rather than an ontological dimension of social life. The methodological privileging of "huge comparisons" (Tilly, 1984) in mainline historical sociology (and comparative politics) and counterclaims of incommensurability provide little purchase on the historical making of comparison as a simultaneously scholarly and vernacular practice. From this vantage, all theoretical concepts (democracy, nationalism, capitalism) entail a dialectic of the particular and universal – empirical specificity and conceptual determination – precisely because of their historicity. The critical task is to specify the dynamic and relational "grounds of comparison" across contexts, to reframe comparability as the endpoint of historical analysis rather than a pre-given point of departure (Chea, 1999). The rapidly proliferating historical literature on questions of comparison, part of wider debates about global histories, has proceeded with little reference to much less substantive engagement with the comparative methods deployed by second-wave historical sociology (Bayly, 2004; Harootunian & Ok Park, 2005; Kocka, 2003; Lorenz, 1999; Subrahmanyam, 2005; Werner & Zimmermann, 2006). This absence is a function not only of the estrangement of history and sociology as disciplinary forms but the manifest limits of second-wave historical sociology's unreflectively nation-centered, inter-state, and Eurocentric presumptions. These shifts, across and within history and sociology, underscore the urgency of reflexive, historically attuned comparative schemas.

The impetus of first-wave postcolonialism was, for the reasons suggested above, overtly driven by epistemological concerns. Postcolonial scholarship has tended to focus less on providing alternate theorizations of social and cultural formations than on marking the limits of received conceptual schemas or bearing witness to the concrete multiplicity that exceeds or escapes ordinary social science. It has, in other words, been an instance of a negative dialectics. There is consequently a strong incongruence, even incommensurability in the Kuhnian sense, between the terms and tasks that have oriented postcolonialism and mainline historical sociology (Kuhn, 2002). This breach poses serious challenges even as it is generative. For it enforces grappling anew with apparently settled questions. To what extent does the spatio-temporal genesis, including the theoretical prehistory, of social and cultural concepts and methods impinge upon their use in the present? Can categories such as "capitalism," "abstract labor," "democracy," "ecology" avoid the fate of becoming little more than intellectual markers, and symbolic enhancers, of processes of domination and hegemony, of shoring up "a hyper-real Europe"? Do the political and historical forms of postcolonial societies represent, as Partha Chatterjee asks, the untheorized exception of normative liberal analysis? (Chatterjee, 2011). Can and should there be general concepts – concepts of sufficient generality to anchor the range and scope of a genuinely global and reflexive historical social science – at all? Alternatively, can there be critical

cross-disciplinary projects or a reflexive social theory without such categories? Can we fashion a critical approach to problematics that are
manifestly global and universal in scale and scope – economic crisis,
ecological catastrophe, steep inequalities – without resorting to categories of
the universal? Addressing these questions is a collective and necessarily
open-ended endeavor. In what follows I explore the uncanny presaging of
some of these questions, often seen as belonging wholly to a post-positivist,
post-nationalist, postcolonial era, in the work of an interwar colonial
sociologist.

A PREMATURE POSTCOLONIAL SOCIOLOGIST

Benoy Sarkar's intellectual formation occurred amid a wider efflorescence of
radical politics in interwar colonial India (Bose, 2006; Sarkar, 1983; Sinha,
2006) that coalesced in the wake of the collapse of the *swadeshi* movement
(Bayly, 1986; Goswami, 2004; Sarkar, 1973), the first mass-mobilization
campaign of Indian nationalism. Its internationalism was literally manu-
factured across a global terrain amidst an eleven year political exile between
1914 and 1925 that encompassed Cairo, Dublin, London, Shanghai,
Japanese-occupied Manchuria, New York City, Berlin, Cologne, Paris, and
Rome. His prodigious *oeuvre* composed in multiple languages (Bengali,
English, German, French, Italian),[1] and published across regional public
spheres, spanned debates in emergent and established fields, especially
sociology, political economy, aesthetics, political theory, and demography.
His lectures at various US universities in the late-teens were facilitated by
the Columbia University economist Edwin Seligman[2] – who as a protégé of
Gustav Von Schmoller, the leading figure of the second-wave German
historical school, shared Sarkar's commitment to the German historical
school of political economy – and the philosopher John Dewey (Bender,
1997; Mukherjee, 1953, p. 14). A self-taught polyglot, Sarkar was an
advocate and example of the affinity between internationalism and
translation as a lived practice. This commitment was concretized in a rich
corpus of translations that included works by Friederich List, Freidrich
Engels, Paul Lafargue (a leading communard and Karl Marx's Cuban-born
son-in-law) and in essays composed and published in German, French and
Italian.[3] It also fueled the pedagogic ambition of such works as, *Political
Philosophies since 1905* (Sarkar, 1928a, 1928b), and the eight-volume
popular Bengali-language work, *Vartaman Jagat* (*Contemporary World*),
serialized in vernacular journals during Sarkar's exile, that combined

travelogue with meditations on such emergent theories and movements as Freudian psychoanalysis, feminism, welfare economics, and cubism (Sarkar, 1914a, 1914b). It is hard to think of a scholarly career in late-colonial India that realized more fully what Benedict Anderson, in a study of anti-imperial anarchism, calls the "true, hard internationalism of the polyglot" (Anderson, 2005, p. 5).

Upon his return from political exile in 1926, Sarkar was appointed as professor of economics at Calcutta University and established research institutes focused respectively on political economy, Asia, Germany, Italy, and the United States.[4] A commemorative article by Haridas Mukherjee (the first historian of the *swadeshi* movement), in the early 1950s, claimed that with the "solitary exception of Mahatma Gandhi" there is no "living leader of thought in India to whose name *ism* has ever been applied" (Mukherjee, 1950, p. 134). Mukherjee considerably inflated the popular reach of Sarkar's work. Yet it is hard to dispute its general currency during the 1920s and 1930s. Indeed, by the 1930s, Sarkarism had come to name sociology as such (Deshpande, 2007, p. 506. Also see Chatterji, 2007; Flora, 1993, 1994; Frykenberg, 2001). Sarkar not only inaugurated a comparative and historically oriented sociology in colonial India (Chaudhury, 1940; Dass, 1938, 1939; Mukhopadhyay, 1944). His sociological project was internationalist in a categorical sense. It was overlaid by three interlocking strands: an emphasis on the historical category of the possible; a dual rejection of imperialism and cultural nationalism; and an insistence that equality was the central problematic of political and epistemological struggles alike.

This new analytic was first elaborated in the 1912, *Science of History and Hope of Mankind* (*Itihas Bijnan O Manavjatir Asha*), that sought to advance a "philosophico-comparative method" attuned to temporal "uniformities in the sequence and co-existence" of social movements (Sarkar, 1912, preface, p. v) This framing directly echoed his intellectual mentor, the neo-Hegelian philosopher Brajendranth Seal, who had, a decade prior, urged a model of comparison where the "objects compared" were seen as "of coordinate rank" treated as belonging "more or less to the same stage in the development" of world culture (Seal, 1899, p. i). Seal had mounted a sharp critique of the lineal, evolutionary schema of Spencerian sociology for reducing social multiplicity to an untenable "uniform formula" and the "historico-genetic" method that informed the work of the German historical school for its conception of development as a lineal, punctual series (pp. iii, iv). These comparative methods relied upon an "abstract and arbitrary standard" derived from European history that could only configure societies outside it as either "monstrous forms of life" or "primitive ancestral forms, the earlier steps of the series" (p. iv). As a consequence "mere European side-views of Humanity" had long substituted for "the world's panorama" as such (p. v).

While Sarkar shared Seal's mandate of forging a new comparative method, it departed from Seal's deep pessimism about its realization. The central task was to secure, Sarkar argued, a rapprochement between the "science of History" and the "hopes and aspirations of man" (*manavjatir asha*)" (Sarkar, 1912, p. 11). The proper vocation of history was universal in the specific sense of encompassing "the whole of human life and its thousand and one manifestations" (p. 12). What bears emphasis here is the advocacy of a new measure of historical analysis, namely, its fidelity to collective hope, to conceptions of the possible. This urging was tied, as elaborated below, to a paradigmatically modernist assertion *and* expression of an actor-oriented sociological schema. It was one that Sarkar, would explicitly name in 1916 as "futurist" (Sarkar, 1916, pp. 87–89).

Sarkar's sociology sought to conceive the present in a manner that enabled the possibility of participating in history, one that opened up rather than foreclosed transformative practice. The signature categories of this project were *visvashakti* and Shakti/*Viriya*. The term *visvashakti* was a neologism: a literal welding of *visva* (world) and *shakti* (power) it was first used in 1914 and translated in subsequent English-language works as "world-forces" or "disposition of world-forces" (Sarkar, 1914a, 1914b, 1932, pp. 371–377). *Visvashakti* referred to the objective configuration of political and economic relations on a worldwide scale in a specific historical moment. Akin to emerging conceptions of world history, the concept provided a basis for reframing histories seen as discrete and separate as interdependent. The term refigured the well-known concept of *atma-shakti* (*atma* as self and *shakti* as power), advanced by Rabindranath Tagore, the Bengali philosopher-poet and 1913 Nobel laureate, in the early years of *swadeshi* promising the joint realization of an autonomous nation and self (Chakrabarty, 2000; Chatterjee, 2011; Sarkar, 1973) *Visvashakti* marked a scalar reorientation from the self to the world.

Sarkar skewered assertions of nationhood as the culmination of an inner dialectic insisting that "what an individual nation regards as the principal factor of its own progress, as the chief and indispensable elements of its own glory is only a by-product of the general process of the whole of human affairs (Sarkar, 1912, p. 21). The adoption of a comparative optic alone would illustrate that the supposed "individuality" of societies – their "peculiar social and literary life" and "structural characteristics" – were in actuality "joint-products" of a historical system of "world-forces" (p. 27). Following the epochal shift of the industrial revolution, there was scarce ground for disputing the "development of nations through international relations" (p. 48). What made possible the liberation of Greece was the inter-imperial competition of England, Russia and Turkey that remapped politics across Europe into a tripartite division of "foes, friends, and neutrals." The constitution of the German Empire and the unification of Italy, events that had galvanized late-19th century Indian nationalism, were similarly founded upon the refraction of local political struggles by a wider geopolitical arena (p. 43). The advocacy of an analytic attuned to "constant interactions and intercourses of life and thought" signaled a turn from the "what" to the "how" of sociopolitical change (p. 66).

A decade later, writing from the town of Bolzano, which Germany had lost to Italy in WWI, Sarkar revisited the question of nationalism in light of the spectacular reconstitution of political space wrought by the First World War. In *The Politics of Boundaries* he argued for an "emancipation" of theories of nationalism from "on the one hand, the mystical associations forced upon it by the ardour of patriots and idealists, and, on the other, from the clean-cut logicality or comprehensiveness injected into it by political philosophers" (Sarkar, 1926, p. 7). The nation was a contingent geopolitical formation, and as such, its *differentia specifica* was "not unity, but independence":

> Nationality is not the concrete expression of a cult or culture or race or language, or of the Hegelian "spirit" or "genius" of a people. It is the physical (territorial and human) embodiment of political freedom, maintained by military and economic strength. The problem of nation-making ... is establishing a sovereign will in territorial terms, i.e., giving sovereignty a local habitation and a name (p. 7).

Both here and in a later work (Sarkar, 1937), the comparative referent of Eastern Europe, particularly Czechoslovakia, haunted Sarkar's realist and anti-organicist critique of philosophical idealist renderings of nationhood. The fact that Czechoslovakia's accelerated path to political-economic sovereignty had hinged on the recognition extended by Britain, France and the United States exemplified the conjunctural making of nationhood. For Sarkar the dynamics of a geopolitical field that had mobilized, destroyed, and remade entire societies and states in the accelerated conjuncture of the Great War underscored the limits of historicist and idealist concepts of nationhood.

Sarkar's internationalist rendering of nationhood resonated with a contiguous effort by Marcel Mauss, the French sociologist and socialist.

Best known for his 1925 theorization of the gift and logics of reciprocity, Mauss's scattered essays on the nation and internationalism articulated a convergent critique of historicist claims of national particularity (Mauss, 1969). Both Sarkar and Mauss identified the fact that *all* nations claimed singularity as a central paradox of nationalism. Yet their acknowledgment of geopolitical inequality led them to affirm nationalist aspirations in colonial worlds even as they opposed idealist and historicist approaches to nationalism. Mauss observed that nationalist movements in colonial worlds were "modern facts which are noteworthy, laudable and relatively common. That a people wants to have its men of commerce, its jurists, its bankers, its teachers, its newspapers, its art, is a sign of the need for true independence, total national liberty, to which so many populations aspire, hitherto deprived as they are of these goods" (*ibid.*, p. 603). Yet dominant European nationalism, following the carnage of the Great War, was tied to a militant, even murderous, particularism. Writing in 1920, Mauss argued that the increase in "the number, the force and the grandeur of nations" had only deepened the loud "individuation of nations and nationalities" and sociological theories had tended to reproduce, not contest, such claims (*ibid.*, p. 628). Political, literary, and cultural shifts were "ordinarily described as the product of a national genius by virtue of a sort of sociological vitalism," when in actuality they were "the product of modifications due to the environment characterized by the proximity of other societies" (p. 628). Mauss advocated a relational analytic that in uncovering "contacts, superimpositions, amalgams, mixtures, compositions" between nations and societies would spur an internationalism grounded in an everyday logic of reciprocity not competition.

Sarkar's unusual intellectual history, *The Social Philosophy of Masaryk*, first delivered as a talk to the Bengal Institute of Sociology, followed such a relational analytic. It was, by any measure, a novel enterprise, unprecedented for its comparative focus on Eastern European intellectual traditions and notable for its historical embedding of ideas of nationhood in a shifting geopolitical terrain. It posited and sought to explain the break between Masaryk's cultural conception of the nation expressed in his 1895 *Cezka Otaska* (the Czech Question) and the realist geopolitical understanding of his 1925 historical memoir *Svetova Revoluce* (World Revolution). Masaryk's shifting vision of nationhood exemplified, for Sarkar, the intimacy between geopolitical conjunctures and conceptions of the possible. The organizing assumption of the early work that the "nation created the state" accorded with a broader nineteenth century tradition of German romanticism that spanned Herder to Adam Muller to Fichte (Sarkar, 1937, p. 8). This schema privileged the "folk or people as *inneres Vaterland* (inner or internal fatherland)" as normatively and logically prior to "the external fatherland, i.e., the state" (p. 8). Its concrete expression was a "cultural program," an internal shoring up of nationality, rather than a direct engagement with independent statehood. This vision was rooted within a "geopolitik" actuality where the reproduction of the Austo-Hungarian Empire was widely perceived as a necessary condition for the stability of South-eastern Europe. No "Czech nationalist," could therefore "dream" of an eventual end of empire (p. 8). A specific geopolitics delimited the horizon of the possible.

Underlining this interplay on a comparative terrain Sarkar turned to examples from colonial India. Rabindranath Tagore's notion of the nation advanced in his famous 1904 speech *Swadeshi Samaj* (indigenous/national society) was, he claimed, formally similar to the "German romantic notion of *volk*" echoed by the early Masaryk. But while Tagore had posited a fundamental antinomy between an alien state and an organically forged national *samaj* (society), no such dichotomy between state and nation was expressed in Masaryk's early work (p. 9). Yet despite this difference there was a broad affinity between Masaryk's and Tagore's concept of nationhood rooted in a shared imperial structure and philosophical idealism. In an astute commentary on European debates about nationalism, Sarkar claimed that Ernest Renan, the French rationalist philosopher, marked a critical departure from widely influential German idealist conceptions. Renan's 1892 lecture *"Qu'est-ce qu'une nation* or What is the Nation?"* was the first, Sarkar noted, to distinguish between the objective, external and the subjective, internal constituents of a nation. Against the familiar mantra of a common "race, language, religion, historical tradition, myths, geography," it decreed collective political will as the principal determinant of nation making (p. 10). The nation as the expression of collective political will represented the antithesis of cultural nationalism. The fact that Masaryk's embrace of political realism occurred in the aftermath of the Great War was, for Sarkar, methodologically conclusive. An altered geopolitical conjuncture had made it plausible to hope that the rival states determined to breakup the Austro-Hungarian Empire might aid, however unwittingly, the liberation of the "subject, oppressed and small nationalities" embedded within it (p. 11).

Sarkar's concept of *visvashakti* was not a precocious structuralist category linked to an account of the mechanical reproduction of geopolitical and socioeconomic inequalities. Quite the converse; it represented a modernist language and assertion of political agency. The dynamism of Sarkar's account of historical change rested on the actual and prospective capacities of strategic action in altering the web of "mutual alliances and enmities" and shifting the "center of [political-economic] gravity" (Sarkar, 1912, pp. 23, 48). The political modernism of this vision found expression in the claim that the "forces and conditions of the existing world" did not choke "human affairs and control the fortunes of movements" (p. 70). Existing social and geopolitical relations, the realm of the given, could be "modified, rearranged and regulated" by collective and individual action oriented toward the creation of "new circumstances and situations." Scholars need only recall, he observed, that revolutions were not just spawned by a "fortuitous conjuncture of circumstance." Their origins resided in the capacity of actors to seize and rework existing social and geopolitical forms thereby bringing about "new international arrangements" (p. 71).

In *The Politics of Boundaries*, Sarkar inveighed against theories that eternalized the state over and above political agency. There was, he claimed,

> (n)o mystical absoluteness or inalienability to the limits of a state .... [its] frontiers may advance or recede .... according to the dynamics of intersocial existence. The only architect of the world's historical geography from epoch to epoch is the *shakti-yoga* or energism of man (Sarkar, 1926, pp. 14–15).

While the efficacy of collective and individual agency varied across time, creative agency was deemed an anthropological invariant, one variously termed "*viriya*" (energism or energy), "*shakti*" (power), and "*shakti-yoga*" (unifying power). The concept of *Viriya/shakti*, was the correlative, in a subjective sense, of the objective configuration of "world-forces." *Shakti/viriya* in its specific signification as transformative political agency was an internal expression of *visvashakti*. Each constellation of world-forces represented the objectification of past aspirations and collective action.

Sarkar had concluded a pre-exile work with a militant, if diffuse, wager: "the interests of modern mankind are hanging on the activities of the 'barbarians' of the present-day world, who, by altering the disposition of the forces of the universe, are silently helping in the shifting of its centre of gravity to a new position." (Sarkar, 1912, p. 75). By the early 1920s, the conviction that the present was a transformative conjuncture came to correspond to the certitude with which he identified the bearers of a new historicity.

Published in Berlin in 1922, *The Futurism of Young Asia*, sought to meet the exorbitant burden of this mandate (Sarkar, 1922). It was at once a prospective alchemy of geopolitics, a trenchant skewering of dominant models of comparison, and a performative enactment of an egalitarian social science. The preface to the collection announced the "leitmotif of this volume" as "war against colonialism in politics and against *orientalisme* in science" (preface, p. iv). The challenge confronted by the work was therefore "twofold: political and cultural." It sought to outline the ontological complicity between imperial rule and social science (preface, p. iv). And to demonstrate the political futurism of contemporary anti-imperial struggles, for which "Asia" functioned as a political allegory rather than geographical concept. The opening essay was first delivered as a lecture at Clark University in November 1917 and published a year later in the *International Journal of Ethics* (the current journal *Ethics*) [Sarkar, 1918]. It captures the peculiar mix of generalizing philosophical sweep and starkly outlined political positions that marked the work a whole. Its first paragraph was a frontal assault:

> Towards the end of the 18th century, Kant wrote the *Critique of Pure Reason*, the *Critique of Applied Reason*, and the *Critique of Judgment*. The basic idea of this Critical Philosophy was to examine the methods and achievements of the human intellect between the great awakening of the Renaissance and the epoch of the French Revolution. Kant's criticism was "creative," it led to the transvaluation of values as deep and wide as the ideas of 1789 .... If it is possible to generalize the diverse intellectual currents among the Turks, Egyptians, Persians, Hindus, Chinese and Japanese of the twentieth century ... it should be called the "critique of Occidental Reason." (Sarkar, 1922, p. 1)

The critique of "Occidental Reason" stemmed from the actuality of political domination that had "engendered ... a vast body of idolas" [preface, p. iii]. These encompassed claims of racial superiority, the "jingo cult of difference" between the Orient and the Occident, and the reduction of world history to a mere "preamble to the grand domination of the Orient by the Occident" (pp. 1–2). Iterated daily "in schools lessons and university lectures and newspaper stories" these postulates saturated "life and thought in the West" (p. 1). They made up the lineaments of what he called, over sixty years before Edward Said's work, *Orientalism*. While terms such as "Occidental reason" prefigure the language of current postcolonial studies, Sarkar's project was animated by a commitment to effect commensurability rather than claim radical alterity (Goswami, 2005).

Orientalism was nowhere more apparent, he argued, than in the "comparative method" that underwrote dominant social science. Comparative study had long been a monopoly of administrative-scholars who "had studied the life and institutions of their dependencies, colonies, protectorates, spheres of influence, and 'mandated' regions" (p. 3). Given this overt inequality the "mirror that has been held up to a servile and semi-servile Asia by Eur-America" was more fabulous than actual. Sarkar proceeded to demonstrate an abbreviated "specimen" of Orientalism through a reading of scattered passages from the first volume of Homer's Iliad (p. 6). Re-reading the Iliad through the textualist and generalizing optic of Orientalism would result, he continued, in a range of claims that the West had never known how "to act in union," that the alternation between treason and war was rooted in various ignoble practices from "concubinage" to "polygamous marriage," and that the only suitable form of government was therefore "unalloyed despotism" (pp. 4, 5). The point was to produce a structure of experience within the reader that approximated that of political and conceptual subjugation. Surely the "injustice of this method," he queried, was more visible when applied to a foundational text of Western civilization? (p. 5).

"Eur-America" named not an ontological difference but a geopolitical category allied with a specific temporal and epistemological schema:

> (i)n the first place, they do not take the same class of facts. They compare the superstitions of the Orient with the rationalism of the Occident, while they ignore the rationalism of the Orient and suppress the superstitions of the Occident ... Secondly, Eur-American sociologists do not apply the same interpretation to the data ... If infanticide, superstition, and sexuality are explained in one group ... by historical criticism ... anthropological investigations ... studies in adolescence, Freudianism, psychoanalysis ... these must be treated in the same way in the other instances as well ... and ... in the third instance ... scholars are not sufficiently grounded in "comparative chronology ... they compare the old conditions of the Orient with the latest achievements of the Occident (pp. 14–15).

There was no disputing that the Euro-American historical present was the "age of Pullman cars, electric lifts, bachelor apartments, long distance phones, Zeppelins and the 'new woman'" (p. 15). But prevailing comparative schemas assumed "that these have been the inseparable features of the Western world all through the ages" (p. 15). As a consequence, the proximate ascendancy of Euro-America was rendered into a continuous long-term teleology. Such synchronic comparisons not only reified differences between societies on a diachronic, developmental scale. The evolutionary time of this comparative schema translated the historical predicate of modernity into a static hierarchy.

Against this analytic of temporal distancing Sarkar advocated "parallelism" as the strategy for a new comparative sociology. The stock-in-trade of imperial ideologies was, he argued, the denial of the contemporaneity of colonial and semi-colonial societies and the relations of equivalence, the "coincidences in social life," made possible by the expansion of capitalism. He advanced parallelism as capturing two kinds of regularities routinely ignored: the "migration of ideas or institutions" across geocultural divides and basic psychic uniformity (p. 108). While the exact itinerary of ideas and institutions could not always be shown the latter helped account for their "naturalization and assimilation to the conditions of the new habitat." Sarkar exploited both possibilities even though the historical specificity of the former line-of-inquiry conflicted with the transhistorical assertion of psychological unity. The simultaneous presence of two divergent rationales was less a conceptual synthesis than a gamble on a future social science.

It was a directly political presumption of equality that enabled a short-circuiting of Orientalism. While assertions of "identities and resemblances" were in themselves as empty as the "tendency to discover diversities and differences," the former opened up a transformative politics:

> When the whole academic world, vitiated by imperialism as it happens to be, is obsessed with the dogma of diversity and divergence the bomb-shell which is destined to crush it can only be pervaded with the spirit of identity and resemblance. And this new message of equality, revolutionary as it is, is an outstanding element of the futurism of Young Asia. (Sarkar, 1923a, p. 92)

In a recorded speech at Berlin University in 1922, Sarkar had refused the role of Eastern messenger: "I am not here to advise you that Germany should have to import the message of Nature from India or the East." Instead, he sought to lay bare the imperial unconscious of social science: "I am here to announce to the world that reform in social science will be possible only when equality ... is accepted as the first postulate of all [social] scientific investigations" (Ghoshal, 1939, pp. 19–20). The repudiation of an ontological distinction between a spiritual East and a material West cut against the grain of prevalent cultural nationalisms and imperial ideology alike. It was considered new and newsworthy enough to prompt an interview by the *New York Times* in 1917 featuring a youthful Sarkar astride the newsworthy tag-line "Difference between East and West has been exaggerated" (*New York Times*, March 11, 1917, pp. 7, 4). The interview, exceptional for its focus on a colonial intellectual, sketched Sarkar's critique of this entrenched common sense, noting its tension with the position elaborated by Rabindranath Tagore, who had become, following his own break from *swadeshi* nationalism, an icon of a humanist internationalism (Chakrabarty, 2000; Chatterjee, 2005, 2011; Guha, 2003).

During an extended global tour in 1916–1917, Tagore had elaborated an ethical critique of nationalism, affirming the subject-position of "We, of no nations of the world" (Tagore, 1917/1973, p. 60). Arguing against "national carnivals of materialism" (p. 53) to audiences in Tokyo, he queried the conflation of "modernizing" movements with modernism insisting that

"modernizing is a mere affection of modernism ... It is nothing bu
mimicry, only affectation is louder than the original and it is too literal
(pp. 93–94). In this reckoning, "true modernism" was "independence c
thought and action, not tutelage under European schoolmasters." Bor
within an exclusionary European "civilization of power" (p. 33), nationa
ism in Asia would only ensnare "personal humanity" into "iron hoops" (pp
16–17). A decade later, addressing Indian nationalists, Tagore reiterated th
posited chain of equivalence between modernizing dreams, nationalism, an
Europe (Tagore, 1966). He decried the "feverish political urge" that le
many "to imagine ourselves to be dream-made Mazzinis, Garibaldis an
Washingtons" and to entertain economic doctrines "caught in the labyrint
of imaginary Bolshevism, Syndicalism or Socialism." These "were not th
natural outgrowths of Indian history." He continued: "As the film of th
dream-cinema is being unrolled before our eyes, we see the trade-mar
"Made in Europe" flashed in the corners, betraying the address of th
factory where the film originated." Against this mirage, he urged a
internationalism rooted in the "inner truth" of a Pan-Asian "ethic c
sacrifice" that was spiritual rather than materialist. The measure of "tru
modernism" was not only autonomy from European thought forms, but th
indigeneity of institutions and concepts. Tagore's anti-nationalist inte
nationalism carried a strongly utopian impetus. Yet its encompassing eth
of indigeneity also construed nonorganic political concepts (though no
curiously, aesthetic) as counterfeit. It remained epistemologically bound t
a central tenet of *swadeshi* nationalism, namely, an incommensurab
difference between a spiritual East and a material West. Sarkar, in contras
valorized political and social movements devised from heterogeneou
worlds, taking such hybrid assemblages as creative agency.

The Peruvian socialist intellectual Jose Mariategui offered a formall
similar political futurism. Writing in the late-1920s, Mariategui acknow
edged the force of Tagore's ethical critique of industrial modernity, placir
it within a utopian tradition that extended from John Ruskin (Mariategu
1971, pp. 117, 245). But he rejected the accompanying ontology of differenc
for its nonrecognition of the materiality of unfreedom. Writing with specif
reference to the so-called "Indian question" in Peru, Mariategui inveighe
against its conventional liberal framing as a moral rather than a politic.
problem. The "tendency to consider the Indian problem as a moral or
embodies a liberal, humanitarian, enlightened nineteenth century attituc
that in the political sphere of the Western world inspires and motivates th
"league of human rights" (p. 25). Such "appeals to the conscience c
civilization" had long punctuated the course of European colonialism on
world stage from the days of anti-slavery societies, but "humanitaria

teachings have not halted or hampered European imperialism, nor have they reformed its methods" (p. 26). Mariategui invested his hopes in the "solidarity and strength of the liberation movement of the colonial masses" (p. 25). In a passage that might well have been composed by Sarkar, Maritegui proclaimed that the "hope of the Indian is absolutely revolutionary. That the same myth, the same ideas, are the decisive agents in the awakening of other ancient peoples or races in ruin; the Hindus, the Chinese, etc. Universal history today tends as never before to chart its course with a common quadrant" (p. 29). The "et cetera" glossed the conviction of a linked series of anti-imperial struggles, which however concretely distinct, were by virtue of their temporal "consanguinity" the vectors of a new practical universalism (p. 29).

For colonial internationalists, like Sarkar or Mariategui, the central political and epistemological struggle centered on equality not cultural or spiritual autonomy. By starting out from equality, Sarkar sought to refigure the problem of historical representation from a narrowly scholarly one to a political questioning of the social function of the representations at stake. Once those outside "Eur-America" achieved equality – defined not just as political sovereignty but "equality in discussions of learned societies, in school rooms, theatres, moving picture shows, daily journals, and monthly reviews" – these new social and political subjects would redefine the sites of the enunciation of the modern (Sarkar, 1922, p. 22). They would come to bear, or more precisely, they already bore the promise of new historicities.

On a global scale the future resided with anti-imperial struggles that sought to realize, on a practical terrain, the critique of "Occidental Reason." It was in and through "the fire-baptism of this new war or series of wars that Asia seeks liberation from the imperialistic and capitalistic domination by Europe and America" (24). The Great War had emerged "neither out of the nationality problems in Europe nor out of the class-struggle in the Western World"; its origins lay in the expanding circuit of inter-imperial political and economic rivalry. This logic had even enfolded Japan, the only sovereign power in Asia, illustrating a "compulsory Occidentalization" (p. 19). This reckoning with Japanese imperialism, based upon his time in Manchuria, departed from its more sanguine treatment in works by Taraknath Das and the later alliance pursued with Japan during World War II by the dissident nationalist Subash Chandra Bose and his Indian National Army. Empire, whether European or Japanese, was a symptom of a "current international pathology." The "only possible therapeutic" against the multiplication of semi-colonial and colonial societies was their transformation, as the embodiment of a universal humanity in a negative guise, into a positive form of universality. The formal condition of this shift was political sovereignty.

The Russian Revolution served as a galvanizing comparative referent for the future of anti-imperial struggles. Sarkar acknowledged that "Lenin's anti-property democracy" was far from an accomplished fact. But the attempt had thrown up an entirely "new democratic type," with ramifying consequences for countries deemed "economically and intellectually backward" (p. 31). The "spontaneous emergence of soviets" had morphed the "Mirs of the Slavic peasants," the conventional marker of Russian "backwardness," into the repository of a new collective future. By repudiating imperial treaties undertaken by the Czarist regime and declaring "the independence of subject races both Asian and European," the Soviets had articulated a novel "parallelism" between the proletariat and the colonized (p. 34). They were a concrete exemplar that a democratic republic could be had without repeating the sequence, namely, "the industrial revolution, capitalist regime, and centralized parliamentary system by which Western Europe and the US were transformed in the nineteenth century" (p. 31). The Russian revolution had upended an ambient necessitarian teleology that, expressed in evolutionist, orientalist, and racialist schemas, foreclosed a substantively other world for marginal races, classes and regions. It suggested that the future belonged to historical latecomers.

The emphasis on the intersection among movements spoke to a larger conception of revolutionary events as containing a temporal surplus. In an arresting formulation, he likened "revolutionary ideals" to "the steam-engine and the U-boat" that as "goods of the modern age" were intrinsically "universal or cosmopolitan." His comparative study of the republican movement in China, for instance, elaborated not only its "family likeness" to the "ideals of 1789" and the American "Bill of Rights" (p. 181). He argued that the quest for a democratic model of political sovereignty must be seen as "an event in the liberalization of mankind" (p. 208). The anti-imperial and democratic idioms of Chinese Republicanism resonated with those deployed during the Mexican revolution by the "partisans of Caranza" and the "pre-Bolshevik revolution in Russia" (p. 181). The specific entanglements of political idioms and aspirations across Mexico, Russia, and China would come to frame subsequent revolution in "any of the lesser republics in Latin America as among any of the peoples in Asia or Africa." For revolution in the twentieth century was not the

"patent" of the individuals or races in and through whom they were born. Probably it is well-nigh impossible for a people to be essentially original in the manufacture of a revolution. For this we should perhaps have to wait for the epoch of socialism triumphant. That is likely to usher in a radically new psychology with its ethics of the rights of "human personality" as distinct from the conventional "rights of man" and "rights of woman," (p. 182)

The refusal to territorialize history in an ethnological register was tied to an internationalist conception of historical time. In this view revolutionary events made certain subsequent transformations possible, through a process of which they were either the origin or a decisive element. The significance of anti-imperial struggles could not be grasped through a past-oriented topology, that is, "from the platform of the history that was, but pragmatically, i.e., with reference to the result that is to be" (p. 208). The *Futurism of Young Asia* was a performative enactment of a political will to realize an egalitarian future. It was written as if this future was assured precisely because it was not. The most speculative, and overreaching, of his works, it captures the representational difficulty of picturing a substantively other future.

Sarkar's commitments intellectual and political were heterodox. They were at the other pole of his contemporary, the celebrated historian Sir Jadunath Sarkar, who as Dipesh Chakrabarty argues, embodied a commitment to a Rankean "scientific history" and an attendant "bourgeois distinction of the private and the public" tied to a "utopian" investment in the British Empire (Chakrabarty, 2010, p. 75, 88). Drawing upon Dewey's pragmatic philosophy, Sarkar observed that "Not 'Truth' but truths constitute the objective verdict of philosophy" upholding a vision of sociology as a political vocation rather than a scientific enterprise (Sarkar, 1928a, p. 1). This project remained a conceptual dominant despite a deepening disillusionment with the post-Lenin trajectory of the Soviet Union, the catastrophic effects of the Great Depression, and the near-absolute dominance of the political field by the Indian National Congress (an organization he condemned for its "Brahminical" mix of democracy and despotism) (Sarkar, 1939a). In the late-1930s, he continued to urge that the "sphere of human possibilities" had to become an integral component of social science (Sarkar, 1938a, p. 127). Otherwise, it would remain hostage to what he named as "history-riddenness" or the "disease of over-historicism" that could not grasp history as other than constraint (p. 131). This "disease," had inflected various "sociological *isms*" of the "third quarter of the nineteenth century" from "raciological interpretations" to "geographical monisms." They shared a common conviction that "races or classes that have not achieved anything in the past" could never lay claim to a different political or social order. Yet a genuinely universalistic sociology had to embrace the notion that the "pariahs of mankind" – ignored alike by contemporary "eugenicists, economists, political philosophers, socio-logists" – had a capacity for "developing a future" (p. 129). Extant theories had sentenced "alleged inferior races or classes" to a doubled erasure (p. 130). Not only did their present actuality "escape the serious attention of political-philosophers and culture-historians," they were denied the prospect of overcoming present inequalities. The exhortation to attend to the "prospec-tive capacities" of marginal social classes and races sought to show up the analytical and ethical deficit of historicist schemas (p. 128).

The urging of a future-oriented sociology was positioned against a shifting array of analytics that reduced history to a fixed sequential series and which could only envision the future of those deemed historical latecomers as a simple continuation of the present. Against them, Sarkar sought to retain a conception of the objectivity of world forces without twisting the sheaf of historical process into a single tight line. In a critical essay on the growing reach of the colonial science of eugenics he argued that the social and political future of what he named, the "hydra-headed multitude" in colonial India – the term encompassed Muslims and depressed classes, schedule and depressed classes as well as "railway coolies, plantation laborers, mine-workers, factory laborers, peasants" – was vitally open (Sarkar, 1938b, p. 350). The claim of history as an open-ended process, as characterized by "creative disequilibrium," was the ground for a transfor-mative politics and sociology alike (Sarkar, 1939b, p. 13). The alignment of politics with a future-oriented temporal logic and of sociology with a notion of the possible carried a dual impress. It accorded equality, if in a prospective mode, to those denied a substantively coeval present. And it located itself within the temporal register of a future anterior or what in the 1920s he had more confidently claimed as a "futurist" internationalism.

CONCLUSION

There is a notable disjuncture between Sarkar's interwar prominence and his reduction in the postcolonial era to what a recent anthology on Indian sociology laments as a regional footnote (Chatterji, 2007, p. 106). This postcolonial forgetting requires some accounting. His project did not properly belong to a particular disciplinary formation or political community. It was forged in an era before the formal consolidation of sociology as a professional discipline in colonial India. For M. N. Srinivas, the doyenne of post-independence Indian sociology trained by Evans Pritchard and Radcliffe-Brown, the conflation of Sarkarism with sociology, was a sign of the lack of a professionally grounded discipline in the late-colonial era (Deshpande, 2007, pp. 506–507). The dominant trajectory of sociology in the Indian academy in the decades following independence cleaved, with few exceptions, to the main lines of British social anthropology even as it enshrined "village studies" as its central ethnographic locus and thematic. With the nationalization of sociology as a disciplinary formation Sarkarism was easily, and rapidly, dispatched.

Situated between empire and nation, Sarkar's sociology was part of a wider interwar prospering of non nation-centered internationalisms. These were less a cohesive, univocal entity than an ensemble of "family-resemblance" practices that converged in the crucible of a globally refracted conjuncture. The universality they affirmed – whether Sarkar's "pariahs of mankind" (Sarkar, 1938a, p. 129), Jose Mariategui's "common quandrant" (Mariategui, 1971, p. 29); W. E. B. DuBois' futurist novel, *Dark Princess* that conjured the end of Western imperialism through the miscegenation between a Hindu Princess and an African-American male (DuBois, 1928); or C. L. R James's internationalist refiguring of the French Revolution in the Black Jacobins (James, 1989/1938) – was multivocal, demotic, fragmentary. Their linking of political and intellectual currents conventionally considered separate attests to a learned practice of insurgent comparison in an imperial age overrun by coercive and hierarchical differentiations. It invokes what Walter Benjamin, writing in 1933, called the "gift" of a "mimetic faculty," the ability to see likeness in difference, of engendering "nonsensuous similarities" (Benjamin, 1979/1938, pp. 65–69).

The neglect of sociologies beyond a received cannon consolidated in the crucible of a Cold War US academy has impoverished our sense of the global articulation of sociology as a critical vocation. It has obscured not only the variegated mobilization of sociology in non-European locales but the affiliations of interwar movements with subsequent waves of sociological internationalism. The internationalist sociology conjured by Dubois, Sarkar, among others, in the interwar era provides a historical and comparative vantage on those forged, for instance, during the global event of decolonization. We might consider here C. Wright Mill's enunciation of Cuban revolutionary hopes in *Listen, Yankee* or the making of world-systems theory amid the Bandung era of decolonization and geopolitical Non-alignment. It is well known, for instance, that Immanuel Wallerstein secured the English-language publication of Franz Fanon's, *The Wretched of the Earth,* a foundational text for postcolonial theory. But it is less appreciated that the lexicon of world-systems framework was inextricably tied to the political vernacular of Pan-Africanism or that postcolonial

Tanzania's mass utopian project of instituting an indigenous socialism provided the experiential bases for early works by Giovanni Arrighi on imperialism and African development (Jewsiewicki, 1987). These projects were profoundly cojunctural and internally distinct. Yet, considered together, they suggest the virtue of renewed attention to the history of sociology as a critical vocation on a genuinely global scale. Resurrecting a particular sociology from a particular anti-imperial archive represents one way of traversing current intellectual polarities and thereby expanding the resources for thinking in tandem possible futures of critical sociology and postcolonialism.

Postcolonial scholarship in the Western academy has helped turn places like India and South Africa from pure objects of received theory into instigators of new social science projects. It has disabled, if not entirely dislodged, the Eurocentric and nation-centered terms and tasks of regnant models of comparison. It is tempting to consider the reterritorialization of social theory as a critical vocation, as Jean and John Comaroff speculate, from an US-centered or Atlantic-centered domain to the global south (J. Comaroff & Comaroff, 2011). Contemporary Indian sociological debates, as exemplified by recent works on critical ecology, Maoist insurgencies, caste politics, or urban middle-class media forms, are notably divested of the epistemological preoccupations that characterized first-wave postcolonial theory in the Western academy (Baviskar, 1999; Sundar, 2007; Sundaram, 2009). Markedly institutionalist, social-movement-oriented, and "worldly," they has variously sought to make sense of the tectonic social, ecological, and political-economic shifts in post-socialist neoliberal India. For these efforts categories such as post-socialist or post-developmental have been more useful and proximate than those derived from postcolonial theory (Verdery & Chari, 2009). This place-bound distinction underlines not only the continued critical valence of conjunctural and transversal comparisons. It reminds us that common ground is often found less in a simple convergence of problematics than in the distinctions that hold them part.

NOTES

1. My discussion of Sarkar draws on an article by Goswami (2012). Sarkar's multi-lingual works include, "La Theorie de la Constitution dans La Philosophie Indienne", *Revue de Synthese Historique* , *31*(August–December 1920), 47–52; *Die Lebensanschauung des Inders* (Leipzig: Markert & Petters, 1923); "Die Struktur des Volkes in der sozialwissenschaftlichen Lehre der Sukraniti", *Kölner Vierteljahrshefte*

für Soziologie, 11(1933), 42–58; "Societa ed economis nell 'India antica e moderna', *Annali di Economia, 6*(2) (1930), 303–347.

2. Seligman was along with Dewey a doctoral advisor of B. R. Ambedkar, a chief architect of the Indian constitution, the most prominent Dalit leader, and a fierce political modernist.

3. Benoy K. Sarkar, *Parivar, Goshthi O Rashtra* (Calcutta, 1924) for the tr. *The Origins of Family, Private Property, and State* by Engels; *Dhana-Daulater Rupantar* (Calcutta, 1924) for the tr. *The Evolution of Property from Slavery to Civilization* by Lafargue; and *Negro Jatir Karamvir* (Calcutta, 1920) for the tr. *Up From Slavery* by Booker T. Washington.

4. These included the *Bangiya Dhana Vijnan Parishat* (Bengali Institute of Economics, est. 1926), *Bangiya Samaj Vijnan Parishat* (Bengali Institute of Sociology, est. 1937), *Bangiya Asia Parishat* (Bengal Asia Institute, est. 1931), *Bangiya German Samsad* (Bengal German Institute, est. 1933), *Bangiya Dante Sabha* (Bengal Dante Society, est. 1933), *Antarjatik Banga Parishat* (International Bengal Institute, est. 1934).

REFERENCES

Abrams, P. (1982). *Historical sociology.* Ithaca, NY: Cornell University Press.

Adams, J. (1996). Principals and agents, colonialists and company men: The decay of colonial control. *American Sociological Review, 61*(1), 12–28.

Adams, J., Clemens, E. & Orloff, A. (2005). Introduction: Social theory, modernity, and the three waves of historical sociology. *Remaking modernity.* Durham, NC: Duke.

Anderson, B. (1998). *The spectre of comparisons.* London: Verso.

Anderson, B. (2005). *Under three flags anarchism and the anti-colonial imagination.* London: Verso.

Bayly, C. (1986). The origins of swadeshi (home industry) In A. Appadurai (Ed.), *The social life of things: Commodities in cultural perspective,* London: Cambridge University Press, Cambridge.

Baviskar, A. (1999). *In the belly of the river: Tribal conflicts over development in the Narmada Valley.* Delhi: OUP.

Bayly, C. (2004). *The birth of the modern world, 1780–1914: Global connections and comparisons.* London: Oxford University Press.

Beck, U., & Grande, E. (2010). Varieties of second modernity: The cosmopolitan turn in social and political theory and research. *British Journal of Sociology, 61*(3), 409–443.

Bender, T. (1997). *Intellectuals and public life: Essays on the social history of academic intellectuals in the US.* Baltimore, MD: John Hopkins.

Bhabha, H. (1994). *The location of culture.* London: Routledge.

Benjamin, W. (Spring 1979/1938). *Doctrine of the similar,* New German Critique, No. 17.

Boehmer, E., & Chaudhary, R. (2010). *The Indian postcolonial: A critical reader.* New York, NY: Routledge.

Bose, S. (2006). *A hundred horizons.* Cambridge, MA: Harvard University Press.

Bourdieu, P. (1994). *Raisons pratiques: Sur la theorie de l'action.* Paris, Le Seuile.

Brubaker, R. (1993). Social theory as habitus. In C. Calhoun, E. LiPuma & M. Postone (Eds.), *Bourdieu: Critical perspectives.* Chicago, IL: University of Chicago.

Brubaker, R. (2003). Beyond comparativism, *theory and research in comparative social analysis*, Department of Sociology, UCLA, 1.

Burroway, M. (2005a). Conclusion: Provincializing the social sciences. In G. Steinmetz (Ed.), *The politics of method: Positivism and its epistemological others*. Durham, NC: Duke University Press.

Burroway, M. (2005b). For public sociology. *American Sociological Review, 70*(1), 4–28.

Calhoun, C. (1996). The domestication of historical sociology. In T. Mcdonald (Ed.), *The historic turn in the human sciences*. Ann Arbor, MI.

Calhoun, C. (2007). *Sociology in America: A history*. Chicago, IL: University of Chicago Press.

Chakrabarty, D. (2000). *Provincializing Europe: Postcolonial thought and historical difference*. Princeton, NJ: Princeton University Press.

Chakrabarty, D. (2008). In defence of provincializing Europe: A response to Carola Dietze. *History and Theory, 47*(1), 85–96.

Chakrabarty, D. (2010). Bourgeois categories made global: The Utopian and actual lives of historical documents in India. In M. Gordin, H. Tilley & P. Prakash (Eds.), *Utopia/ Dystopia: Conditions of historical possibility* (pp. 73–93). Princeton, NJ: Princeton University Press.

Chatterjee, P. (1993). *The nation and its fragments: Colonial and postcolonial histories*. Princeton, NJ: Princeton University Press.

Chatterjee, P. (2011). *Lineages of political society: Studies in postcolonial society*. Columbia, NY: Columbia University Press.

Chatterji, R. (2007). The nationalist sociology of Benoy Kumar Sarkar. In P. Uberoi, N. Sundar, & S. Deshpande (Eds.), *Anthropology in the East*. Delhi, OUP.

Chaudhuri, A. (June 2004). In the waiting-room of history. *London Review of Books, 26*(12).

Chaudhury, N. N. (1940). *Pragmatism and pioneering in Benoy Sarkar's sociology and economics*. Calcutta: Chuckervertty, Chatterjee & Co.

Chea, P. (1999). Grounds of comparison. *Diacritics, 29*(4), 3–18.

Comaroff, J., & Comaroff, J. L. (2011). *Theory from the South: Or, how Euro-America is evolving toward Africa*. New York, NY: Paradigm.

Connell, R. W. (1997). Why is classical theory classical. *American Journal of Sociology, 102*, 6.

Dass, B. (1938). *The works of Benoy Sarkar, educational, culture-historical, economic and sociological: A chronological statement*. Calcutta: Chuckervertty, Chatterjee & Co.

Dass, B. (1939). *The social and economic ideas of Benoy Kumar Sarkar*. Calcutta: Chuckervertty, Chatterjee & Co.

Dietze, C. (2008). Toward a history on equal terms: A discussion of provincializing Europe. *History and Theory, 47*(1), 69–84.

Deshpande, S. (2007). Fashioning a postcolonial discipline. In P. Uberoi, N. Sundar & S. Deshpande (Eds.), *Anthropology in the East*. Delhi: OUP.

Dubois, W. E. B. (1928). *Dark princess*. Oxford, MS: University of Mississippi.

Ekbladh, D. (2011). *The great American mission: Modernization and the construction of an American World order*. Princeton, NJ: Princeton University Press.

Eisenstadt, S. N. (1998). Early modernities. *Daedalus, 127*(3), 1–18.

Eisenstadt, S. N. (2002). *Multiple modernities*. New Brunswick: Rutgers.

Feyerabend, P. (1999). *Conquest of abundance: A tale of abstraction versus the richness of being*. Chicago, IL: Chicago University Press.

Flora, G. (1993). *The evolution of positivism in Bengal*. Napoli: Instituto Universitario Orientale.

Flora, G. (1994). *Benoy Sarkar and Italy*. New Delhi: OUP.

Frykenberg, R. (2001). *Benoy Kumar Sarkar, 1887–1949: Political rishi of twentieth century bengal. Explorations in the history of South Asia: Essays in honour of Dietmar Rothermund*. Delhi: OUP.

Ghoshal, S. K. (1939). *Sarkarism*. Calcutta: Chuckervertty Chatterjee and Co.

Gilman, N. (2007). *Mandarins of the future: Modernization theory in Cold War America*. Baltimore, MD: Johns Hopkins.

Go, J. (2008). *American empire and the politics of meaning: US colonialism and political culture in Puerto Rico and the Philippines*. Durham, NC: Duke University Press.

Goswami, M. (2002). Rethinking the modular nation form: Towards a sociohistorical approach to nationalism. *Comparative Studies in Society and History, 44*(4), 770–799.

Goswami, M. (2004). *Producing India: From colonial economy to national space*. Chicago, IL: Chicago University Press.

Goswami, M. (2005). Autonomy and comparability: Notes on the anticolonial and the postcolonial. *Boundary 2, 32*(2), 201–225.

Goswami, M. (2012). Imaginary futures and Colonial internationalisms. *American Historical Review. 117*(5), 1461–1485.

Guha, R. (2003). *History at the limit of world history*. New York, NY: Columbia University Press.

James, C. L. R. (1989/1938). *The Black Jacobins*. New York, NY: Vintage.

Jewsiewicki, B. (1987). The African prism of Immanuel Wallerstein. *Radical History Review, 39*, 50–68.

Kocka, J. (2003). Comparison and beyond. *History and Theory, 42*(1), 39–44.

Kuhn, T. (2002). *The road since structure: Philosophical essays*. Chicago, IL: Chicago University Press.

Lorenz, C. (1999). Comparative historiography: Problems and perspectives. *History and Theory, 38*(1), 25–39.

Mauss, M. (1969). La Nation. *Oeuvres 3: Cohesion sociale et division de la sociologie* (pp. 573–639). Les Editions de Minuit: Paris.

Magubane, Z. (2003). *Bringing the empire home: Race, class, and gender in Britain and colonial South Africa*. Chicago, IL: Chicago University Press.

Mariategui, J. (1971). *Seven interpretative essays on Peruvian reality*. University of Texas.

McLennan, G. (2003). Sociology, eurocentrism and postcolonial theory. *European Journal of Social Theory, 6*(1), 69–86.

McMichael, P. (1990). Incorporating comparison within a world-historical perspective: An alternative comparative method. *American Sociological Review, 55*(3), 384–397.

Miyoshi, M., & Harootunian, H. (Eds.). (2002). *Learning places: The afterlives of area studies*. Durham, NC: Duke University Press Books.

Mongia, R. (2007). Historicizing state sovereignty: Inequality and the form of equivalence. *Comparative Studies in Society and History, 49*(2), 384–411.

Mukherjee, H. (1950, February). Benoy Sarkar as pioneer in neo-indology. *Modern Review, 87*, 133–138.

Mukherjee, H. (1953). *Benoy Kumar Sarkar: A Study*. Calcutta, Chuckervertty: Chatterjee and co.

Mukhopadhyay, H. (1944). *Benoy Sarkarer baithake: Bingsa satabdir banga samskriti*. Calcutta: Chuckervertty, Chatterjee and Co.

Osborne, P. (2005). On comparability: Kant and the possibility of comparative study. *Boundary, 32*(2), 3–22.

Ray, R., & Radhakrisnan, S. (2010). The subaltern, the postcolonial, and cultural sociology. In J. Hall, L. Grindstaff & M.-C. Lo (Eds.), *Handbook of cultural sociology*. London: Routledge.

Sarkar, B. K. (1912). *Science of history and hope of mankind*. London: Longmans, Green and Co.

Sarkar, B. K. (1914a). Visvasakti, *Grihastha Prakasani*, Calcutta.

Sarkar, B. K. (1914b). *Varttman jagat*. Calcutta: Grihastha Publishing House.

Sarkar, B. K. (1916). *Love in Hindu literature*. Tokyo: Maruzen.

Sarkar, B. K. (1918). Futurism of young Asia. *International Journal of Ethics, 28*(4), 521–541.

Sarkar, B. K. (1922). *The futurism of young Asia and other essays on the relations between the East and the West*. Berlin: Verlag.

Sarkar, B. K. (1923a). Social philosophy in aesthetics. *Rupam: An Illustrated Quarterly Journal of Oriental, Art*, Nos. 15–16.

Sarkar, B. K. (1923b). *Die lebensanschauung des Inders*. Leipzig: Markert & Petters.

Sarkar, B. K. (1926). *The politics of boundaries and tendencies in international relations* (Vol. 1). Calcutta: N.M. Ray Chowdhury & Co.

Sarkar, B. K. (1928a). *The pressure of labor upon Constitution and Law, 1776–1928: A chronology of ideals and achievements in societal reconstruction*. Benares: Jnanmandal Press.

Sarkar, B. K. (1928b). *The political philosophies since 1905* (Vol. 1). Madras: B.G. Paul & Co.

Sarkar, B. K. (1932). *Naya banglar gora pattan, part 1*. Calcutta: Cakravarrti, Cyattarji & Co.

Sarkar, B. K. (1937). *The social philosophy of Thomas Masaryk*. Calcutta: Oriental Book Agency.

Sarkar, B. K. (1938a, August). The acceptable and the unacceptable in Bankim's social philosophy. *Calcutta Review, 68*(127).

Sarkar, B. K. (1938b, March). The eugenic potentialities of the alleged inferior races and classes. *Calcutta Review, 66*, 350.

Sarkar, B. K. (1939a, January). Demo-despotacracy and freedom. *Calcutta Review*.

Sarkar, B. K. (1939b, February). A shortcoming of the Hegel-Marxian dialectic. *Calcutta Review*, .

Sarkar, S. (1973). *The Swadeshi movement in Bengal, 1903–1908*. Delhi: OUP.

Sarkar, S. (1983). *Modern India, 1885–1947*. New Delhi: Macmillan.

Sayer, D. (1987). *The violence of abstraction*. Oxford: Blackwell.

Seal, B. (1899). *Comparative studies in Vaishnavism and Christianity with an examination of the Mahabharata legend about Narada's pilgrimage to Svetadvipa*. Calcutta: Hare Press.

Seidman, S. (1996). Empire and knowledge: More troubles, new opportunities for sociology. *Contemporary Sociology, 25*(3).

Sewell, W. (2005). *Logics of history: Social theory and social transformation*. Chicago, IL: University of Chicago.

Shklar, J. (1986). Squaring the hermeneutic circle. *Social Research, 53*(3), 449–473.

Simmel, G. (1990/1900). *The philosophy of money* (T. Bottomore & D. Frisby, Trans.), New York, NY, Routledge.

Sinha, M. (2006). *Specters of mother India: The global restructuring of Empire*. Durham, NC: Duke University Press.

Skocpol, T., & Somers, M. (2006). The uses of comparative history in macrosocial inquiry. *Comparative Studies in Society and History, 22*(2), 174–197.

Spivak, G. (1988). Can the subaltern speak? In C. Nelson and L. Grossberg (Eds.), *Marxism and the interpretation of cultures*. University of Illinois Press: Urbana-Champaign.

Steinmetz, G. (2004). Odious comparisons: Incommensurability, the case study and "small N's" in sociology. *Sociological Theory, 22*(3), 371–400.

Steinmetz, G. (2007). *The Devil's Handwriting: Precoloniality and the German Colonial State*. Chicago, IL: Chicago University Press.

Steinmetz, G. (2009). Scientific autonomy and pyschological autonomy: Max Weber, Richard Thurnwald and empire. *Political Power and Social Theory, 20*(2).

Subrahmanyam, S. (2005). *Explorations in connected history: Mughals and Franks*. Delhi: Oxford University Press.

Sundar, N. (2007). *Subalterns and sovereigns: An anthropological history of Bastar: 1854–2006*. Oxford: Oxford University Press.

Sundaram, R. (2009). *Pirate modernity*. New York, NY: Routledge.

Tagore, R. (1917/1973). *Nationalism*. San Francisco: Greenwod Press Reprints.

Tagore, R. (1966). From greater India. In A. Chakravarty (Ed.), *A Tagore reader*. Boston, MA: Beacon Press.

Tilly, C. (1984). *Big structures, large processes, huge comparisons*. New York, NY: Russell Sage Foundation.

Tilly, C. (1997). Means and ends of comparison in macrosociology. *Comparative Social Research, 16*, 43–53.

Uberoi, P., Sundar, N., & Deshpande, S. (Eds.). (2007). *Anthropology in the East: Founders of Indian sociology and anthropology*. Delhi: OUP.

Verdery, K., & Chari, S. (2009). Thinking between the posts: Postcolonialism, postsocialism, and ethnography after the cold war. *Comparative Studies in Society and History, 51*(1), 6–34.

Werner, M., & Zimmermann, B. (February 2006). Beyond comparison: Histoire croisée and the challenge of reflexivity. *History and Theory, 45*(1), 30–50.

HYBRID HABITUS: TOWARD A POST-COLONIAL THEORY OF PRACTICE ☆

Claire Laurier Decoteau

ABSTRACT

Sociologists have tended to construct theories of identity based on unitary notions of social location which avoid conceptualizing disjunction and contradiction and which therefore fail to capture certain characteristics of the postcolonial condition. This paper engages in a postcolonial re-reading of sociological theories of practice (in particular, Pierre Bourdieu's notion of habitus*). It does so through an analysis of the historical development of the field of health and healing in South Africa. From the beginning of the colonial enterprise, biomedicine resisted amalgamation with other forms of healing and insisted on a monotherapeutic ideology and practice whereas indigenous healing accommodated not only biomedicine, but invited pluralism within and across cultural and ethnic differences. As such, a bifurcated and parallel system of healing emerged, whereby Black South Africans practiced pluralism and white South Africans utilized biomedicine in isolation. This disjuncture became acrimonious in the post-apartheid era as the state attempted to forge*

☆ Reprinted from *Postcolonial Sociology*, Political Power and Social Theory, Volume 24, 2013, pp. 263–293.

Postcolonial Sociology
Political Power and Social Theory, Volume 24, 239–269
ISSN: 0198-8719/doi:10.1108/S0198-8719(2013)0000024016

a united health system and battle the AIDS epidemic. Despite the historical and contemporary bifurcations within the field of health and healing, people living with AIDS continue to subscribe to a hybrid health ideology. There is, therefore, a structural disjuncture between the realities of consumption *within the field of health and healing and the logic of the field as it is articulated in the symbolic struggle raging in the field of power. The field of health and healing is characterized, therefore, by a simultaneous bifurcation and hybridity – which is reflected in HIV-infected South Africans' beliefs and practices. In order to make sense of this puzzling disjuncture and its impact on subjects' trajectories of action, this paper draws insight from Pierre Bourdieu's theory of habitus and Homi Bhabha's conceptualization of hybridity – transforming each of them through their synthesis and application to the postcolonial context.*

Osiah was HIV positive and in denial. He ... participated in all the early HIV awareness campaigns ... and yet he chose not to take antiretroviral medication, and instead went to a traditional healer ... When we now have a choice and can provide ARV [antiretroviral] treatment that can save lives ... why does someone like Osiah ... reject that choice and seek treatments from traditional healers? (Berman, 2008)[1]

For many activists, scholars, policy-makers, and health-care professionals, this is the primary puzzle associated with HIV/AIDS in post-apartheid South Africa: why do people who have access to antiretrovirals[2] refuse them and choose instead to use indigenous healing[3]? This behavior is baffling to the dominant health community because of two commonly held assumptions about health-care decision-making in South Africa: (1) that access is the only obstacle to the use of biomedical health care; and (2) that biomedical and indigenous approaches to healing are mutually exclusive. These assumptions are consistently reiterated in health research *and* health policy interventions.

In the earlier years of the AIDS pandemic in South Africa, former President Thabo Mbeki's "AIDS denialism" was often blamed for the so-called "confusion" people faced in choosing health care. Denialism is the label most commonly utilized to describe the belief held by the former President and several key members of his Department of Health that HIV does not cause AIDS and that antiretroviral treatment is toxic. Denialism was largely responsible for the delay in rolling out antiretrovirals in the public health sector and, it has recently been suggested, for the loss of 365,000 lives (Chigwedere, Seage, Gruskin, Lee, & Essex, 2008; Dugger,

2008).[4] In 2003, the landscape of AIDS health care was radically transformed when the Treatment Action Campaign won a national court case that secured voluntary licenses for base-line antiretroviral treatment from two major pharmaceutical companies (Heywood, 2008).[5] By drastically reducing the cost of antiretroviral treatment and thereby obliterating the last logical rationale the Department of Health had presented to providing the drugs through the public health system, a reluctant government was forced to finally adopt a National Treatment Plan that included a large-scale roll-out of antiretroviral medication (Department of Health, South Africa, 2003). As of 2004, antiretroviral medication (or ARVs as they are commonly referred to) became readily available in South Africa's public health clinics free of charge, and people joyfully sounded the death knoll of denialism. And yet, as the quote above indicates, HIV-infected South Africans continued to utilize indigenous healing.

The symbolic struggle between the AIDS denialists and the treatment activists, which consumed the South African public sphere from at least 2000 through 2009, contributed to the reification of what I have termed "the myth of incommensurability": the notion that biomedical and indigenous treatments are irreconcilable and thus cannot (ontologically) and should not (scientifically) be combined. This has been done, in part, by grafting the colonial tropes of "modernity" and "traditionalism" onto health care choices. The users/consumers of healing, then, are asked to *choose* one or the other disposition, and told that a failure to do so could lead to further illness or even death. This perception has been exacerbated by the public provision of antiretrovirals, as patients are told, in no uncertain terms, not to mix the two forms of treatment because of fears of adverse drug interactions and the development of drug resistance. Despite these admonitions, I have found that most HIV-infected, Black South Africans rarely use either form of healing in isolation and subscribe instead to some form of hybrid health behavior.

This hybridity is informed by historical patterns of health pluralism. In fact, indigenous forms of healing survived the racial capitalism of the apartheid era through processes of adaptation and hybridization. Therefore, the fact that people continue to subscribe to hybrid health practices to manage and survive the AIDS epidemic is hardly surprising. And yet, what is surprising is that people do not claim this hybridity. Again and again, when asked what kinds of healing they use, or what forms of treatment they prefer, the people in my study told me, often quite emphatically, that they *only* used either biomedical or indigenous forms of healing. And yet, through my ethnographies of their health trajectories, I came to discover that despite what they *claimed*, they still *practiced* hybridity. What accounts for this disjuncture between what people say and what they do?

Since the beginning of the colonial enterprise and throughout the apartheid era, while biomedical healers resisted amalgamation with other forms of healing and insisted on monotherapeutic practices and ideologies, indigenous healing accommodated not only biomedical healing, but invited pluralism within and across cultural and ethnic differences (Digby, 2006, p. 346). This asymmetrical system turned acrimonious in the post-apartheid era, especially in debates over how to manage HIV/AIDS. In this article, I show how the conjuncture of events which marked the transition to post-apartheid and especially the onset of AIDS served to radically unsettle and ultimately transform the South African field of health and healing, so that today it is marked by a disjuncture between the layout and structure of the field, and the actions of those who negotiate it. Drawing on extensive ethnographic research conducted in townships and informal settlements in contemporary Johannesburg,[6] I illustrate how this simultaneous bifurcation (in terms of health production) and hybridity (in terms of health consumption) explains peoples' healing beliefs and practices. I end the article by offering a theory of action which takes radical disjunction into account and assesses the relevance of Bourdieu's theory of habitus and Bhabha's concept of hybridity for making sense of this case.

THE SOUTH AFRICAN FIELD OF HEALTH AND HEALING

Anthropological and historical accounts of colonial and apartheid South Africa are rife with tales of religious and health syncretism – most of which highlight the contestation inherent in the colonial encounter. In South Africa, as in other parts of the world, biomedicine was often used by the colonizers as a "tool of empire" (Flint, 2008, p. 119).[7] From the beginning of the colonial enterprise, biomedicine set itself up in antagonistic opposition to indigenous healers. Early missionaries (with and without medical training) viewed both witchcraft and divination to be "incompatible with Christianity" (Digby, 2006, p. 308) – though there was some early interest in African botany (*ibid.*, p. 311, 346). Similarly, British imperial authorities recognized biomedicine as the only plausible and effective healing system, but did not begrudge Africans using herbal remedies "provided they do no indulge in malicious practices" (Witchcraft

Proclamation Act of 1927, quoted in Digby, 2006, p. 321). Missionaries held that religious conversion necessitated cultural transformation, so Christianity was bound up with expectations of the acceptance of western biomedicine (*ibid.*, p. 334). Digby (2006) explains how this elicited a bifurcated and parallel system of health care:

> [M]edical cultures were shaped by larger patterns of estrangement in a segregated society, so that among whites a sense of racial superiority tended to filter – sometimes obscure – indigenous practices. There were therefore strong macro influences producing cultural resistance to the assimilation of indigenous ideas and practices, and this contributed to parallelism rather than pluralism in medicine. (p. 346)

To the dismay of many a colonist, Christian conversion and the criminalization of African healing did little to delimit the power or prevalence of African cosmology (J. Comaroff & Comaroff, 1991; Flint, 2008). Although white, biomedical practitioners remained resistant (if not hostile) toward indigenous healing, indigenous healers and African patients were more syncretic in their beliefs and practices. For example, biomedical doctors risked losing their licenses from the South African Medical and Dental Council if they collaborated with or referred patients to indigenous healers, and yet indigenous healers regularly referred patients to biomedical clinics, especially for diseases perceived as "Western," like tuberculosis (Digby, 2006, p. 354).

According to Karen Flint, biomedical doctors were introduced to the African population (in the middle of the 19th century) for three reasons: first, to diminish the power of indigenous healers and thus chiefs; second, to combat the dependence on "superstition" and beliefs in witchcraft amongst the colonized; and third, to maintain African health in order to protect the white population – this latter motivation became particularly prominent with the growth of industry in the 20th century (2008). The need to provide adequate primary health care to the African labor force on the diamond and gold mines was the primary motivation for the establishment of biomedical clinics in urban townships.[8]

As a result of the expansion of biomedical services to the Black populations, indigenous healing transformed as healers incorporated influences from colonial medicine and from other ethnic traditions. This partially occurred because of the new opportunities that mining communities, for example, offered healers to learn from one another *and* to treat new "white men's diseases" (Digby, 2006, pp. 278–280). Herbs were mixed with biomedicines to increase their potency or to treat new emerging diseases.

Under apartheid, the Witchcraft Suppression Act 3 of 1957 and the Amended Act 50 of 1970, made it illegal for "any person to exercise supernatural powers" or "to impute the cause of certain occurrences to another person" (Xaba, 2002, p. 9).[9] According to Thokozani Xaba (2005), the apartheid state was more successful at restricting the use of indigenous practices and medicines than previous governments had been (p. 123). The ban was effectively on the practice of divination, but because the distinction between herbalists (*inyangas*) and diviners (*sangomas*) was not properly understood, both groups faced repression, especially in urban areas (p. 124). The legislation banned divination only within the confines of "white South Africa," meaning it was still legal in rural areas and Bantustans (p. 121). The imposition of influx controls further stifled the practice in urban regions and especially the abilities of healers to gather herbs and import them into the cities (*ibid.*).

As under colonialism, the criminalization of indigenous forms of healing under apartheid did not dissuade people from using it. In fact, Xaba (2005) notes that because of increasing violence and hardship (and the inability or unwillingness of the police to manage it), more people turned to indigenous healing to protect themselves from harmful powers or criminal intent or to make them attractive to employers (pp. 123, 164–183). Others saw indigenous healing as a means of protesting apartheid ideologies and practices.[10] But for many, it was simply normal health practice: "under apartheid ... people used traditional healers as part of going to the clinic ... people went first to the traditional healer and then to the clinic."[11] Healers explain that though they needed to be careful about how publicly they advertised their services, the legislation did not keep them from practicing.[12]

It is important to note that throughout its long history in South Africa, biomedical healing has itself been domesticated and rendered intelligible through localized interpretations and practices. Although biomedicine resists hybridization, in the cultural lexicons of Africans, its diagnostic codes, illness categories, and therapies have been re-interpreted to fit peoples' experiences of illness – often by translating them into more familiar, indigenous lenses. In fact, some African doctors and nurses helped to facilitate this process (Digby & Sweet, 2002; Vaughan, 1991).

Indigenous healing has managed to survive colonialism and apartheid through adaptation (Digby, 2006, p. 371). And it continues to adapt to present day constraints, not least of which is the AIDS pandemic itself. Contemporary indigenous beliefs and practices exhibit some etiological traces from previous historical periods (Delius & Glaser, 2005; Green, 1994;

1999; Setel, Lewis, & Lyons, 1999), and are simultaneously mediated by contemporary social circumstances. Like any paradigm of knowledge, indigenous forms of healing reflect structural (social, economic, and cultural) transformations and inequalities and are, therefore, socially constructed and historically contingent. However, there are certain enduring ontological premises, epistemologies, and customs which characterize indigenous healing and make it amenable to hybridity. As Janzen notes, "therapeutic pluralism" is facilitated by the dynamism of African healing "traditions" (1981).

Aspects of both "tradition" and "modernity" are incorporated and synthesized in indigenous conceptualizations of the body and health.

> [T]raditional healers see this as an opposition of categories that can be combined, but that must be "balanced" in order to achieve well-being for the African person. They seek to incorporate both sets of ideas and knowledge into a single system of healing, while maintaining the opposition of "modern" and "traditional" as separate potentials whose interaction yields power ... Achieving the proper balance between the "African" and the "Western" is essential. This makes it possible for healers to remain completely open to Western medical practice while at the same time placing equal value on African healing practices and treatment with herbs. (Thornton, 2002)

There are two primary reasons for this accommodation of dualism. First, because illness has many different causes and origins from multiple different domains, including the social, spiritual, and physical, treatments must also be multiple. Illness can enter the body from diverse entry points, or can arise from a variety of unhealthy interactions; thus, healing must be performed using equally multiplicitous methods (Viljoen, Panzer, Roos, & Bodemer, 2003, p. 332). HIV actually brings on *other* diseases. AIDS is a syndrome, which refers to a set of symptoms that only collectively signify disease. The danger of HIV is that it breaks down the immune system, so that the body is at risk from multiple infectious agents, or opportunistic infections. Therefore, AIDS is not really *one* disease at all. Many indigenous healers recognize that a hybrid approach to healing, one which combines *both* biomedical and indigenous methods may be the most effective means of treating a disease as complicated and complex as HIV/AIDS.

In addition, according to an indigenous ontology, the boundaries of the body (and of subjectivity) are permeable.

> Although modern personhood tends to posit an autonomous agent, free from external sources and individualized to an ever-increasing degree ... "traditional" notions of personhood understand the self as "permeable and partible." They believe their bodies impart substances to and incorporate substances from other bodies. (Niehaus, 2002, p. 189)

Because subjects' selves are contiguous with both the social and ancestral world, the body cannot be healed in isolation; it must be situated within its social, material, and communal context. The individual is deeply embedded in networks of not only living kin, but an entire system of ancestral relations. The individual body cannot be extracted from those bonds of kinship if it is to be properly healed. Healers are *mediums* between the natural and the social, between the living and the dead, between the individual and the community. As such, indigenous healers occupy multiple social roles (Gumede, 1990; Thornton, 2009).

African patients use various logics to determine when and how to mix indigenous and biomedical healing (both historically and in the contemporary era). For example, there is a certain functional division of labor some people heed. If a person breaks her leg, she may have the bones set by a biomedical doctor,[13] but will go to her *sangoma* to understand *why* she broke her leg. It is very likely that such a mishap is an ancestral message of some kind. "While biomedicine asks what caused the condition and how, indigenous healing asks 'who' and 'why'" (Abdool-Karim et al., 1994, p. 6). In addition, indigenous healers cannot "look inside" the body; therefore, they often ask their patients to go to biomedical facilities to get X-rays or blood work (including CD4 counts), to verify their diagnoses.[14] Africans have often seen biomedical practitioners for what are perceived as "Western diseases" and for surgeries, whereas chronic or psychological ailments are considered the domain of indigenous healers, because they require more individualized forms of care (Digby, 2006, p. 386).

During one interview I conducted in 2003, a nurse who worked at the Chris Hani Baragwanath Hospital told me that the use of indigenous healing was declining; she was convinced that once antiretrovirals became readily available to the public, indigenous healing would become obsolete.[15] However, community members find this prediction absurd. As one community activist explained, "People will never stop going to traditional healers. That would be like suddenly abandoning your name because you are taking a new medication."[16] In other words, indigenous healing is synonymous with the ideological make-up of Black South Africans' identities.

Therefore, despite the current admonitions of health-care providers *against* hybrid health behavior, people continue to utilize indigenous healing despite the availability of antiretrovirals for a number of reasons. In a study conducted between 1999 and 2000 in Kwa-Zulu Natal, patients' responses to indigenous versus biomedical care were surveyed (Colvin, Gumede,

Grimwade, & Wilkinson, 2001). Indigenous healers were incorporated into a Tuberculosis Directly Observed Treatment (DOT) control program. Fifty-three patients were attended by indigenous healers and 364 were supervised by either clinic workers or lay community members.

> Overall, 89% of those supervised by traditional healers completed treatment, compared with 67% of those supervised by others ... The mortality rate among those supervised by traditional healers was 6%, whereas it was 18% for those supervised by others ... Interestingly, none of the patients supervised by traditional healers transferred out of the district during treatment, while 5% of those supervised by others did. (Colvin et al., 2001)

The reasons provided for the success of supervision by indigenous healers included the following: patients and indigenous healers have established long relationships of trust, and indigenous healers spend more quality time with their patients and exhibit much greater care and nurturance than biomedical health workers. In addition, indigenous healers live locally and are familiar with the patients' social settings (Colvin et al., 2001). Biomedical health-care workers (in part due to human resource constraints) rarely spend time explaining patients' symptoms and treatment options. Indigenous healers not only explain the problem, but do so in a language and conceptual framework the patient can immediately grasp.

> [T]raditional healers have a closer relationship with the people. They talk to them more ... rather than waiting for two hours on a bench, then finally getting a very dehydrated, tired doctor or nurse, saying "What's wrong with you? Ok, we'll take your blood" ... and then asking a whole bunch of embarrassing questions instead of engaging. I think ... people want to be engaged ... and traditional healers *know* the person and provide counseling ... they listen ... Because one of the things that I think is happening is that medical professionals are under so much pressure, especially in Soweto and other urban areas because you have a hundred people waiting. You can't give specialized attention ... You end up not really giving enough time to the person because it's always hurry hurry hurry ... a traditional healer hasn't got a queue, and because you are going there for different things, no one will identify you as someone with HIV because you go there.[17]

Thornton (2002) and Gumede (1990) also note that indigenous healers' approach is far more comprehensive and holistic than biomedical care. For indigenous healers, treating the body means understanding its social and material embeddedness. Whereas the biomedical approach assumes an autonomous, independent, and mechanistic body, indigenous healing helps *situate* illnesses and recognizes them as composites of cultural, social, environmental, historical, economic *and* biological factors. The healer also *uses* his or her own body and spirit (as well as insight about the patient's social location and psychological state) in order to heal the patient; thus healing is an intuitive and empathetic process (Thornton, 2002). Overall, indigenous health care is holistic, communal, and takes patients' material and social conditions into account.

Indigenous healers have long incorporated biomedical explanations and treatments into their own health practices, and my research shows that this has continued in the era of AIDS.[18]

> Traditional healing is going to have to change. Because of HIV/AIDS for one thing. We have to change some of our beliefs and practices in order to help prevent its spread and to take better care of people who are infected.[19]

> Now, a traditional health practitioner needs to be informed and to be educated on what is going on in the twenty-first century and align ourselves with that, whilst not forgetting where we come from.[20]

This ongoing accommodation in the era of AIDS should not be surprising given the history I have just provided. However, the international politicization of HIV/AIDS and the subsequent increase in attention paid to bio-politics at the global scale makes healing a primary site for hegemonic struggle. In the case of South Africa, this has manifested itself in a prolonged symbolic struggle between treatment activists and state denialists over the signification of AIDS, which has served to (newly) reify a myth of incommensurability, driving an essentialist wedge between different methods of healing.

THE SYMBOLIC STRUGGLE OVER HIV/AIDS

With its election to power in 1994, the African National Congress (ANC) was forced to transform from a militant revolutionary movement into a reputable governing body practically overnight. In the 1990s, it was faced with a legacy of immense inequality, international pressure to abandon social democratic ideals in exchange for market competitiveness, and a disease that would become an epidemic of unparalleled proportions. This particular conjuncture of events – the transition from apartheid to democracy, the adoption of neoliberalism, and the AIDS pandemic – served to both undermine and define the post-apartheid state's capacity and legitimacy on the global stage. The political transition itself is marked by an ambiguous volleying, on the part of the state elite, between contradictory ideological positions. On the one hand, the ANC embraces a pan-Africanist renaissance which incorporates a biting critique of Western cultural imperialism. On the other, the adoption of economic liberalism has wrenched open South Africa's national borders to the onslaught of international capital and its accompanying ideologies.

The dilemma that all postcolonial states face of attempting to sustain a national identity in the face of the deterritorializing forces of globalization is heightened in South Africa for several reasons: its late transition from colonialism, its efforts to maintain its position as an economic leader on the African sub-continent, and its need to deal successfully with the mutual pandemics of AIDS and poverty. AIDS and debates over healing, then, become overdetermined sites for working through what I have elsewhere termed the "postcolonial paradox," which entails a simultaneous need to respect the demands of neoliberal capital in order to compete successfully on the world market *and* a responsibility to redress entrenched inequality, secure legitimacy from the poor, and forge a national imaginary. In other words, postcolonial states must contend with the contradictory demands of global capital and national reconciliation and redistribution.[21]

In South Africa's symbolic struggle over AIDS, the "myth of incommensurability" was consistently invoked which exacerbated the bifurcation of the field of health and healing in the post-apartheid era. This "myth" relies upon the reification of two idealized constructs: "tradition" and "modernity," which are then mapped onto colonial distinctions between the "West" and "Africa." These mythical tropes have been consistently utilized in public sphere debates over HIV/AIDS, and they played a particularly prominent role in the debates surrounding "AIDS denialism."

Denialism was inspired by a strong belief that the international AIDS response was inherently colonialist and racist. Former President Thabo Mbeki denounced the explanation that HIV causes AIDS as a theory that was informed by racist assumptions about the voracity of Africans' sexual appetites and that effectively blamed the high rates of HIV in South Africa on individual behavior. Instead, Mbeki sought a *structural* explanation for Africa's high prevalence rates: poverty. He also questioned the power of the pharmaceutical industry and the massive profits it stood to gain from the AIDS pandemic in Africa, should ARVs be purchased to stem its tide.[22]

In addition, Mbeki suggested that biomedicine is an imperialist paradigm that ignores the cultural and racial identity of Africans and consistently insisted that "[t]he Western way of fighting AIDS will not transfer to Africa."[23] Indigenous healing was introduced into public sphere discourses on HIV/AIDS (by Mbeki's Minister of Health, Manto Tshabalala-Msimang), as an *alternative* to antiretroviral medication (*Sunday Independent,* 2004).

In this way, the state pitted indigenous healing against biomedical science, thereby maintaining an ideology of incommensurability.

And in fact, denialism's staunchest enemies – members of the Treatment Action Campaign – also contributed to this bifurcation and buttressed the idea that biomedical and indigenous forms of healing are mutually exclusive. This quote is from an interview with a prominent AIDS activist:

> The philosophical division between Western biomedical medicine and traditional medicine is something that you can't overcome ... either you believe in science or you don't. It's like religion. How it's going to pan out will depend on to what extent ... the traditional health system is able to give in ... because it's for their benefit ... But you won't be able to get away from the fundamental conflict.[24]

The public provision of antiretrovirals has, in many ways, exacerbated the perception of incommensurability. One informal settlement resident told me in a recent interview that during her training on the proper usage of ARV treatment, she was told (by the biomedical staff) never to use indigenous health care because it would "erase the effects of the ARVs."[25] And this has become a common story. Because ARVs are a lifetime commitment, biomedical practitioners are essentially forbidding their patients from ever using indigenous forms of healing. I asked this respondent if she followed this advice, and she admitted that she often used indigenous herbs to supplement her biomedical treatment. But she would never admit this to her doctor.

The constant invocation of the myth of incommensurability in debates over AIDS has symbolically bifurcated the field of health and healing, and the unequal distribution of capital in the field adds material weight to this division. Biomedicine has strong political and economic backing from the international pharmaceutical industry, supra-governmental organizations like the United Nations and the World Health Organization, as well as Western governments deeply invested in funding and policy initiatives throughout Africa (such as the US government's PEPFAR[26] program). Biomedical healing also plays a dominant role in South Africa's public health-care system. In contradistinction, indigenous healing exists largely as an informal and peripheral health-care option for poor, Black South Africans.[27]

The ANC has always taken a more holistic approach to health, and has discussed incorporating indigenous healing into the public health system (ANC, 1994). And yet, under denialism, the state used indigenous healing as a symbolic tool in the battle over treatment. There have been recent efforts by the state to institutionalize indigenous healing, but most of these efforts do so by policing and regulating it, and in a certain way, attempting to *biomedicalize* it. The Traditional Health Practitioners Act (Department of Health, 2007)[28] provides guidelines for the definition of indigenous healing, and the registration and certification of practitioners. Most indigenous healers with whom I spoke[29] welcome the legislation because they believe it will salvage the reputation of the profession from being associated with charlatanry and witchcraft. However, the Act mostly subjects the profession to scrutiny, and does little to actually provide institutional support for indigenous healing or provide healers with remuneration for their public services – two moves that would be essential if the profession were ever to be considered a health-care option on equal footing with biomedical healing. In the end, the legislation further bifurcates the two approaches by providing them each with separate legislation. This means that the mixing of health approaches is literally outside of the law. There is no policy or legislation that contends with the relationship *between* the two approaches to healing.

Indigenous healers also object to the way in which biomedicine seems to wield the power to determine the legitimacy of their profession. For example, biomedical doctors, pharmacists, and administrators sit on the Traditional Health Practitioner's Council while no indigenous healer sits on the South African Medical Association Board or the Health Professions Council. And recently, the South African Medical Research Council (MRC) in collaboration with the Medical Control Council (MCC) has begun to test the medical safety and strength of indigenous herbal remedies, or *muthi*.[30] In general, the indigenous healers with whom I spoke saw this as further biomedical imposition on their trade.

> Why should Western doctors test our medicines? What do they know about traditional healing? Will we get a chance to test *their* medicines, according to *our* standards? We have known about these medicines for centuries and knowledge about them has been passed down over the generations. Who are they to question our ancestors and their knowledge?[31]

There is an assumed ontological and epistemological impossibility of hybridization that underlies both of the dominant approaches which vyed for legitimacy in the symbolic struggle over HIV/AIDS. It was in the *interest* of those in dominant positions (of the state, of biomedicine) to maintain segregation between the healing approaches, and they each used the myth as *political* capital. For biomedical science, the reward offered for accepting and embracing biomedical "distinction" was the continued accrual of "modern" forms of capital (both economic and cultural) (Bourdieu, 1984, 1986). State denialism, on the other hand, *utilized* the

cultural capital of "authenticity" in order to purchase legitimacy from the
population. Therefore, "traditionalism" became its own *symbolic* reward.
In this way, Mbeki's denialism operated as a form of symbolic capital
(Bourdieu, 1979, 1989).

The field of health and healing is today more bifurcated and hierarchically
uneven than ever before in its history. Biomedical healing is invested with
economic, social, and symbolic capital from national and international
sources, *and* it has secured hegemony in the public health-care system. In
fact, in an effort to distance himself from his predecessor, the newest
President, Jacob Zuma, has fully embraced biomedical orthodoxy. In 2009,
Zuma announced a massive expansion of both treatment and prevention
efforts in South Africa (Dugger, 2009) in which he vowed to cut new
infections in half and scale up treatment to 80% of those who need it by
2011 (Sidibé, 2009). With the death of denialism (and the rapid expansion of
the ARV roll-out), biomedical hegemony has finally been secured. Health
activists in South Africa and beyond have been buoyed by what they see as a
victory, and very little attention has been paid to the underlying cultural
imperialism at work. Indigenous healing continues to exist largely as an
informal and peripheral health-care option for poor Africans, though it is
estimated that 80% of all South Africans utilize it today (Campbell, 1998;
Department of Health, South Africa, 2003; van der Linde, 1997). There is,
therefore, a structural disjuncture between the realities of *consumption*
within the field of health and healing and the logic of the field as it is
articulated in the symbolic struggle raging in the field of power.
Articulations of hybridity expressed in the era of AIDS, therefore, while
informed by historic strategies for navigating colonial and apartheid
inequality, are newly configured in the post-apartheid era.

HYBRID HABITUS

Ellen[32] is a *sangoma* (or diviner), and she also owns and operates a *shebeen*
(tavern), from her home – making her both a business and community
leader in Alexandra, a township located in the heart of Johannesburg. Both
Ellen and her husband are HIV-positive. Ellen's husband has a full-time job
which provides him and his entire family with comprehensive private health
care (a rarity in South Africa's townships). Following the advice of his
doctor, Ellen's husband began antiretroviral treatment during the time that
I was initially conducting in-depth interviews with her in 2005. She was very

wary of the course of therapy he had chosen to follow – especially when he began refusing his wife's *muthi* because his doctor had told him they would interfere with his drug regimen. She informed me that she surreptitiously infused his tea with *muthi* despite his objections. Then, at the urging of her husband, she visited his doctor who recommended she begin antiretroviral treatment as well. She was very conflicted, but in the end, she did begin triple cocktail therapy which she took in conjunction with her own indigenous remedies. When I asked her what finally made her decide to mix the two kinds of methods, she said that she had spoken with her ancestors and that they had guided her toward this hybrid approach. "In an ideal world, everyone would take both kinds of treatment."[33]

A project manager, whom I will call Tebogho, works for a respected NGO where I conducted research for several years in Soweto.[34] Tebogho earns her living by trying to convince HIV-infected people in her township to follow the regimens prescribed by their doctors and health-care professionals, including promoting the use of antiretroviral medication. Because of the habitus required of her by the NGO job, Tebogho often parrots common Western ideologies about "traditionalism," equating indigenous healing with ruralism, backwardness, and lack of education. However, I realized after some time that she was engaging in what Homi Bhabha might refer to as performative mockery (1994). Because of *my* identity, Tebogho was performing her "Western-ness" and therefore proving her ability to do her job well; however, as time progressed and we got to know each other better, I came to find out that she not only refuses to take antiretrovirals herself, but she prefers to use more indigenous remedies. "Those drugs have so many side-effects and sometimes they don't even work. I don't need them. I'd rather stick with natural remedies and *muthi* than put all those toxins into my system."[35]

Pheello Limapo was diagnosed with HIV in 2003, but believes he has been HIV-positive since at least 1994. He has two children, neither of whom is HIV infected. But his wife, Elizabeth is also HIV-positive. From the time I first met Pheello, he was a strong advocate of antiretrovirals (ARVs) and rejected indigenous healing completely. "I believe that traditional healing is part of our culture. I do believe that. I'm just not convinced that traditional healers can deal with HIV/AIDS, especially at the present moment. They've got no knowledge of this disease ... it's a problem."[36] Pheello expended a great deal of his energy and resources trying to get onto the ARV program in the early years of the roll-out. It took six months and a near-death health emergency to get a referral to one of the ARV sites, in which he finally enrolled in October 2005. His wife was not eligible to receive the drugs because she was not a South African citizen. While I was conducting research in 2006, Elizabeth and their daughter both fell extremely ill and Elizabeth almost died. After a harrowing few months when Pheello's every bit of energy and money was spent visiting them both in the hospital every day, they all returned home. Elizabeth's CD4 count was 10.[37] When I next saw Pheello, he pulled me aside and whispered, "Claire, remember how I told you I don't trust traditional healers? Well, I'm using them now." When I asked him why, he said: "Because I need help, and I don't know what else to do." They were eventually able to get Elizabeth onto ARV therapy, and they are both doing quite well today. When I asked Pheello recently if he was still utilizing the services of indigenous healers, he said that he was not.

But despite what Pheello actually claims, he has always mixed methods – he just doesn't use indigenous healing. Rather, he uses the cleansing rituals of the Zion Christian Church (ZCC). He joined right after he first tested HIV-positive.[38] The ZCC utilize natural mediums like water, coffee, and tea to cleanse the body of pollutants and evil spirits. Therefore, even though Pheello only seeks out the services of a *sangoma* (or diviner) in times of crisis, his beliefs about health and healing incorporate spiritual healing and notions of the occult.

Eight years ago, Thulani Skhosana fell ill and told no one. He hid his sickness as long as he could, but his HIV status was disclosed to his community by a lengthy hospitalization. After two terrifying months in the hospital, he returned home to find he had lost his job and his wife. He has not worked in these past eight years. Thulani is a strong advocate of using *only* indigenous healing. As he proudly declared in a focus group discussion:

> If I'm told I have to go to the clinic, I don't want to go. I haven't liked the clinic since I was young. Even today, I'm HIV-positive, and don't attend the clinic ... There is so much speculation about the ARVs ... I don't want anyone to tell me that I have to live like this, and if I don't live like that, I'll die. I don't like discipline ... Every day, I can't swallow something at the same time. I'm not a machine. That's my feeling. I don't have to take ARVs for now. Because I'm not ill. I can't get ill because I know how to take care of myself – living a healthy, positive life, instead of being programmed into something that you might fail or that might fail you. You can't fail yourself. But I always encourage people to take ARVs whenever they are sick. But me, I don't take any medication – even a Panado.[39] I don't take it.[40]

And yet, Thulani's reaction when he actually faces an acute illness is much more hybrid than he admits. In the fall of 2005, a rash began to develop on Thulani's hands, feet, and face. He visited his local *sangoma* to determine the cause of the infection and was then prescribed an indigenous unguent which he rubbed into his skin every day. However, he also spent the money, time, and energy to travel to the closest clinic, wait in line all day, and visit the doctor. He walked away with antibiotics, aspirin, and vitamin supplements. When faced with a medical emergency, Thulani's first impulse was to combine biomedical and indigenous treatments. To this day, Thulani stores all of the numerous remedies he has received and taken over the last eight years in a box. In it, an entire cornucopia of treatments lay side by side: natural herbs and roots, bio-medical prescriptions, spiritual amulets and candles, aspirins, several miracle cures, immune boosters, and the government-endorsed vitamins. Thulani's medicine chest is a material incarnation of the hybrid nature of South Africans' healing regimens and ideologies.[41]

As these cases show, many HIV-infected South Africans *identify* with one or another healing paradigm – largely because of what they have come to represent in public sphere discourses about HIV/AIDS. When they claim to follow one or another paradigm, they are making a *political* statement about where they stand in a broader debate about healing. But their *practices* reveal a historical and pragmatic hybridity because bodies serve as structural "memory pads" (Bourdieu, 2000, p. 141). It is only by understanding this complicated history and the layout of the field of health and healing that we can begin to understand the conjunctural effect of these mechanisms at play on peoples' actions and beliefs. But the subjects of this study are not merely acted upon in this process – they have played a role in configuring the structure of the field, or insuring its unique configuration such that the disjuncture between health production and consumption is maintained.

TOWARD A POSTCOLONIAL THEORY OF PRACTICE

In this 'post-colonial' moment, these transverse, transnational, transcultural movements, which were always inscribed in the history of 'colonisation,' but carefully overwritten by more binary forms of narrativization have, of course, emerged in new forms to disrupt the settled relations of domination and resistance ... They reposition and dis-place 'difference' without, in the Hegelian sense, 'overcoming' it. (Hall, 1996a, p. 251)

Throughout this article, I have shown how the contemporary field of health and healing is characterized by a simultaneous bifurcation (in terms of the *production* of health care) and hybridity (in terms of the *consumption* of health care). Making sense of this disjuncture between field and practice requires a theory of action where the tension between binary differentiation and the expansion of multiplicity is kept in play. However, sociological theories of action are largely ill-equipped to handle such a task. In the rest of this article, I engage in a postcolonial refashioning of Bourdieu's notion of habitus in order to explore the effects of disjunction on subjects' trajectories of action and the changing nature of hybridity over the *longue durée*.

In the American academy, the concept of habitus is often interpreted as being overly structuralist, overdetermined, and tied explicitly to class positionality (at the expense of other embodied identities). As such, it is usually interpreted as a rather conservative and even functionalist theory of action.[42] Such an interpretation severely delimits the theoretical capacities of the concept as it was developed over the course of Bourdieu's long career. In fact, Bourdieu first developed the concept of habitus while conducting field research in colonial Algeria (Bourdieu, 1962, 1979, 1990) where it was meant to describe a situation of disjuncture – when subjects' dispositions were necessarily out of sort with the newly imposed structural conditions:

> It was not by chance that the relationship between structures and habitus was constituted as a theoretical problem in relation to a historical situation in which that problem was in a sense presented by reality itself, in the form of a permanent *discrepancy* between the agents' economic dispositions and the economic world in which they had to act. (Bourdieu, 1962, p. vii)

He wrote that part of the job of the habitus is to synthesize binaries and overcome ontological contradictions (Steinmetz, 2006, p. 582). But in conditions of sustained, systemic disjunction (as in the case of colonialism), Bourdieu suggests that the habitus is unable to synthesize – it remains internally contradictory. As such, the theory of habitus was developed out of reflection of the strange disjunctures inaugurated by the colonial era, and should thus be well suited for analyzing their ongoing effects.

In my usage of the concept, habitus should be understood as a "strategy-generating principle enabling agents to cope with unforeseen and ever-changing situations" (Bourdieu, 1977, p. 72). In other words, the habitus arms subjects with an innovative capacity to move within and across various fields with differential hierarchies and rules of engagement. I show that it is informed not only by class location, but similarly by gender, race, nationality, educational level, and place of residence. In fact, I argue that the hybrid habituses incorporated by the subjects of post-apartheid *enable* and *shape* their ability to traverse the many boundaries that circumscribe their daily lives.

And yet, Bourdieu's theories do require some refashioning, to make them useful to postcolonial sociology. I have shown that despite the bifurcated nature of the field of health and healing *and* the powerful bio-political strategies in circulation in the post-apartheid era, certain members of the African population exhibit a hybrid habitus. There are two concepts within Bourdieu's conceptual apparatus which might explain this disjuncture: dominated taste (a taste for necessity) or hysteresis.

According to Bourdieu, "[a]lthough all members of the settled field agree on what counts as symbolic capital, the dominated may still hold proudly to a dissonant set of 'values' and even developed a *taste for necessity*, a taste for their own cultural domination" (Steinmetz, 2007, p. 323, my emphasis). The dominated are rooted in their material social conditions, and as such, their "tastes" are oriented toward products and symbols that have a direct correlation to or use-value in the material world (Bourdieu, 1984). The "realism" of the working classes in some ways necessitates the development of certain "tastes" to survive, but their refinement also serves to reify their own subjugated class position. Resistance is only possible if the subjugated *recognize* their own domination and engage in a symbolic struggle for recognition and legitimacy. In post-apartheid South Africa, one could interpret Africans' insistent usage of indigenous healing as a form of "dominated taste." However, this form of healing is not without its own cultural capital. In addition, the concept of dominated taste would only explain why people might subscribe to an indigenous ontology as opposed to a biomedical one; it cannot account for the reasons why people would *mix* methods in a field bifurcated by the myth of incommensurability.

For Bourdieu, hysteresis represents a kind of "structural lag" (1977, p. 85) between the "exertion of a social force and the deployment of its effects" (Wacquant, 2004, p. 392). Hysteresis occurs when a habitus, which was once fitted to its field, lingers on into a field with a new logic and structure. In other words, there is a delay between the imposition or inculcation of particular structural dispositions and subjects' capacity or willingness to grasp and practice them.

> In situations of crisis or sudden change, especially those seen at the time of abrupt encounters between civilizations linked to the colonial situation or too-rapid movements in social space, agents often have difficulty in holding together the dispositions associated with different states or stages, and some of them, often those who are best adapted to the previous state of the game, have difficulty in adjusting to the new established order. Their dispositions become dysfunctional and the efforts they may make to perpetuate them help to plunge them deeper into failure. (Bourdieu, 2000, p. 161)

However, Bourdieu believed this to be a temporary condition. In fact, he claimed that colonialism could not be overcome until the contradictions it left behind in the habituses of its subjects were grasped and then surmounted (Bourdieu & Sayad, 2004, p. 470).

According to this theory, then, those whose habituses are informed by the dual logics of indigenous and biomedical healing represent a certain kind of hysteresis. Because hybridity was required of the subjects of apartheid to navigate their segregated social worlds (and segregated systems of healing), hybridity could be interpreted as simply a leftover from the colonial era – something which should be overcome under post-apartheid. Yet, I have also argued that the postcolonial period, in South Africa, has been marked by the entrenchment of new binaries and structural inequalities – thereby requiring the adjustment of peoples' trajectories of healing and strategies of action. Because hybrid health behavior cannot be explained by the layout and structure of the field of health and healing, a form of hysteresis is still in play. This could be a product of the contradictions inherent in the field itself, or it could augur the reconfiguration of a new field in emergence, but I will argue this hysteresis may be permanent, not transitory or developmental.

At the end of his life, Bourdieu described his own habitus as *clivé*, or split – which was an effect of his own contradictory background – embodying the habitus of someone from a poor, rural area in southern France and simultaneously the habitus of a highly distinguished academic (Bourdieu, 2007; Steinmetz, 2006, p. 457; Wacquant, 2004, p. 382). Therefore, despite the fact that he kept insisting on the habitus's capacity to *synthesize* contradiction, Bourdieu did often *recognize* the fact that habituses were often internally contradictory (Bourdieu et al., 1999), split fundamentally because the subject was coercively forced to straddle two different social systems (1962, 1979, 2007). There is, then, a tension within the very concept of habitus between integration and fragmentation.

Steinmetz (2006) suggests that Jacques Lacan's theory of imaginary identification can help to make sense of this theoretical contradiction. According to this theory, identity is based on an imaginary identification with a *gestalt* or whole image of oneself in the mirror, despite the fact that the body and self is experienced as fragmentary and lacking. The "repressed memory of a 'body in pieces'" (Steinmetz, 2006, p. 459) haunts the subject throughout his life, thereby fueling the need to constantly identify with the *gestalt* image again and again. As Stuart Hall notes, identification is more than anything a process of forced reiteration (1996b). Re-analyzing habitus within this analytic paradigm "explains why a 'cloven' habitus is just as likely as a unified one ... The Imaginary is forever overcoded by the

Symbolic, which pushes against integration and toward fragmentation and difference" (Steinmetz, 2006, p. 458).

When South Africans identify with either "tradition" or "science," and in so doing, attempt to fix the signification of HIV/AIDS, they are engaging in an imaginary identification. The ideal "traditional" or "biomedical" body is simply a fantasy of integration and completion. But AIDS, and its wild chain of signifiers and unruly materiality, disrupts and disallows facile imaginary identifications. As do the material conditions in which people are forced to forge survival tactics and navigate severe structural inequalities. There is a tension, therefore, within the very identities of those living on the edges of the body politic, between integration and disjunction. And this is where an intervention from postcolonial theory is helpful.

Postcolonial theories of hybridity (in part because of their reliance on post-structuralism) help make sense of this tension between difference and multiplicity, between integration and fragmentation. Although colonial discourses attempted to secure the colonized within a "unified" discourse of radical alterity, within a "constitutive outside," the colonized refused "to be fixed in place" and slip "back across the porous or invisible borders to disturb and subvert from the inside" (Hall, 1996a, p. 252). Relying on Derridian poststructuralism, Homi Bhabha suggests that it is the ambivalence inherent in colonial desire which is responsible for creating the hybrid subjects of colonialism. The colonizer wishes for the colonial subject to be both similar and radically different. When the colonized perform the hybridity inculcated within them through the colonial encounter, this ambivalence "terrorizes [colonial] authority with the *ruse* of recognition, its mimicry, its mockery" (p. 115). The hybrid performances of the colonized, thus, unveil the simultaneous partiality and doubleness of colonial signification.

> Both colonizer and colonized are in a process of misrecognition where each point of identification is always a partial and double repetition of the *otherness* of the self – democrat and despot, individual *and* servant, native and child. It is around the "and" – that conjunction of infinite repetition – that the ambivalence of civil authority circulates as a "colonial" signifier that is *less than one and double*. (p. 97)

Colonial desire is "less than one" because identification is always only partial (the colonized is "*almost* the same, but not quite"), but it is also "double" because it embodies the ambivalences of power – the subjects of colonization incorporate the contradictions inherent in the system – they are both citizen and subject, both "civilized" and "barbaric," both "modern" and "traditional."

As such, hybridity puts the signifiers of colonial authority on display, which ultimately undermines their success. And in fact, the colonized engage in resistance through the strategic manipulation (which may or may not be conscious) of this hybridity.

And yet, one must tread carefully with postcolonial theory. It has been critiqued for essentializing and reifying binary difference. In the words of Paul Gilroy, "cultural production is not like mixing cocktails" (1994, pp. 54–55). But it has also been critiqued for ignoring or eliding the ever-deepening schisms of inequality which have been exacerbated by neoliberal globalization. For Ella Shohat (1992) and Arif Dirlik (1996), the "post"-colonial obsession with "hybridity" and the concordant desire to super-impose a certain multiplicity and in-between-ness over the subaltern experience, enacts a misrecognition of the various forms of domination that continue to operate in a global capitalist system. Therefore, as Stuart Hall notes (1996a), we have to be able to theorize both the ways in which binaries and structural inequalities continue to be reified, while simulta-neously recognizing the proliferation of hybrids: "We have to keep these two ends of the chain in play at the same time – over-determination and difference, condensation and dissemination" (p. 249).

The myth of incommensurability shows that binaries do operate with force in the field of health and healing in post-apartheid South Africa, and yet even those discourses are fundamentally ambivalent and serve to reinvent mythical tropes that matter, but that are also vulnerable.

> In order to understand the productivity of colonial power it is crucial to construct its regime of truth, not to subject its representations to a normalizing judgment. Only then does it become possible to understand the *productive ambivalence* of the object of colonial discourse – that "otherness" which is at once an object of desire and derision, an articulation of difference contained within the fantasy of origin and identity. (Bhabha, 1994, p. 67; my emphasis)

And yet, it is because the new rearticulation of the myth of incommensur-ability is emerging out of the mouths of the formally colonized that it is so powerful today. The binary between colonized and colonizer is still relevant, but it is also being reconfigured, and these ambivalent "post"-colonial discourses are an important part of that reconfiguration.

In his re-reading of Lévi-Strauss's *bricoleur*, Jacques Derrida (1978) suggests that certain binary oppositions (nature/culture; presence/absence; past/present) can be put in "play" such that their opposition, teleology, and hierarchy are disrupted and undermined. It is this Derridan deconstruction-ism that inspired Bhabha's theory of hybridity – specifically its capacity to mock and thereby terrorize the colonial significations of difference. As such, rather than a sign of an inability to get with the colonial program (as Bourdieu's concept of hysteresis might imply), hybridity may be a radical form of epistemic *bricolage* – a sign of resistance and subversion as opposed to oppression.

In post-apartheid South Africa, the people whose lives have been hardest hit by the dual pandemics of poverty and HIV/AIDS, engage in practices which undermine and contradict the dominant discourses which name and contain the virus, the forms of capital invested in the AIDS industry, and the operations of bio-power practiced by international health agencies, health-care institutions and the post-apartheid state. I argue that this disjuncture between the field of health and healing and the habituses of people affected by HIV necessitates the bodily incorporation and preserva-tion of a fundamentally contradictory logic of practice. The combination of rigid structural inequalities and the reinvigoration of the mythical colonial tropes of "modernity" and "tradition" are incorporated, reconfigured, but also undermined in the daily practices and beliefs of those living with HIV/AIDS.

This health hybridity is informed, in a palimpsestual fashion, by apartheid history and the fluid notion of the self inherent in indigenous ontology, but is also distinctly postcolonial – largely because AIDS, neoliberalism and the cultural bricolage made possibly by globalization, have introduced new objective structures, signifying systems and cultural practices. As Bhabha's theory makes evident, hybridity also has subversive capacities to unveil and mock colonial and neocolonial inscriptions, which render binary difference (and the processes of exclusion they facilitate) insecure. This allows the subjects of postcolonialism to both manage and contest its paradoxes. It also leaves open the possibility for radical reconfiguration. By refusing to abandon their hybridity (sometimes despite themselves), practitioners of hybrid health behavior could serve to transform the field (either through a consciously revolutionary process or slowly, over the *long durée*) especially because of the ways in which hybridity threatens biomedical hegemony.

What effect does a permanently disjointed habitus have on subjects' actions and identities? I would like to suggest that it requires a constant refashioning and reworking of one's identity in the process of action. Practicing hybridity, in this way, is onto-formative – it constantly (re)constitutes social reality in a processural and additive fashion. And thus, it allows those most affected by HIV/AIDS to navigate the symbolic, spiritual, and material boundaries that circumscribe daily life in South Africa's shanty towns.

ACKNOWLEDGMENTS

I would like to begin by thanking all of the residents of Sol Plaatjie and Lawley who have worked with me over the years, as well as the numerous indigenous healers who shared details about the history of the South African indigenous knowledge system and the impact HIV/AIDS has had on their beliefs and practices. In particular, I would like to thank indigenous doctors Martha Mongoya and Robert Tshabalala, as well as my research assistant, Torong Ramela. I am also thankful for the insightful feedback offered by George Steinmetz, Isaac Reed, and Andy Clarno on earlier drafts of the article, and the guidance of Julian Go and an anonymous reviewer for PPST.

NOTES

1. This same question is the subject of two recent books by McGregor (2005) and Steinberg (2008).
2. Antiretrovirals are the biomedical treatment for HIV. In common parlance, they are referred to as ARVs or ART (antiretroviral therapy).
3. Although most indigenous healers refer to themselves as 'traditional healers,' I find the terminology of 'traditional' problematic for a variety of reasons which are made apparent in this article; therefore, I use the term 'indigenous healing' in my own analysis, but many of my informants prefer the term 'traditional healing' which will be reflected in their quotes.
4. This is the estimated number of lives that would have been saved if antiretrovirals had been rolled-out in the public health sector in 2000 instead of 2004.
5. From 2002 to 2004, the TAC pursued action against industry abuse of patents through the Competition Commission, essentially suing GlaxoSmithKline and Boehringher Ingelheim and eventually securing voluntary licenses issued to generic manufacturers (Heywood, 2008).
6. The data in this article draws from a larger project for which I conducted 30 months of ethnographic in one formal township (Soweto) and two informal settlements (Lawley and Sol Plaatjie). I conducted focus group discussions with 250 people, including community stakeholders in each community, people living with HIV/AIDS, indigenous healers, and home-based care workers. I conducted multiple in-depth interviews with 165 people in my different research sites, including: people living with HIV/AIDS, home-based caregivers, NGO staff, nurses, and doctors, indigenous healers, spiritual healers, activists, and government officials. Those subjects whose names are used in this study have consented to the use of their names. All other participants' identities remain confidential.
7. This is a vast topic. See, for example, Anderson (2006), Arnold (1993), Gordon (2001), Olumwullah (2002), Prakash (1999), and Vaughan (1991).

8. For information on disease and health-care management in mining communities in South Africa, see Packard (1989), Marks and Andersson (1992), and Jochelson (2001).

9. Following previous patterns of criminalization, the Witchcraft Supression Act distinguished between divination and witchcraft on the one hand (which were deemed illegal), and the practice in herbal pharmacology on the other (which remained legal). See Xaba (2005) and Asforth (2005) for a discussion of the effects of these distinctions and bans.

10. Interview with Torong Ramela held on June 10, 2005 in Johannesburg.

11. Interview with Nurse Hilda Pheto held on July 14, 2009 in Johannesburg.

12. Interview with Dr. Robert Tshabalala held on July 22, 2005 in Orlando East, Soweto; interview with Dr. Sheila Khama held on July 14, 2009 in Johannesburg.

13. There are "traditional" bonesetters, so not all people heed such a structured division of labor.

14. Many of the healers I interviewed and spoke with in FGDs relied on biomedical technology in this way. This evidence is further supported by Mills (2005, pp. 141–143).

15. Interview with female nurse held in January 2003 at the Chris Hani Baragwanath Hospital, Soweto.

16. Interview with female community activist held in February 2003 in White City, Soweto.

17. Interview with Nurse Hilda Pheto held on July 14, 2009 in Johannesburg.

18. This was obvious from the FGDs I held with 131 indigenous healers in 2005 and 2006. These conclusions are further supported by a number of scholars who work closely with indigenous healers in the contemporary era: Green (1999), Thornton (2002), and Mills (2005).

19. Interview with Dr. Martha Mongoya held on September 3, 2005 in Orlando East, Soweto.

20. Interview with Dr. Sheila Khama held on July 14, 2009 in Johannesburg.

21. See Decoteau (forthcoming) for a more detailed analysis.

22. This analysis of Mbeki's denialism is supported by other scholars: see Mbali (2004); Fassin (2007).

23. This was a fairly consistent mantra that undergirded Mbeki's denialism. This exact phrase is found in the article entitled, "Castro Hlongwane, Caravans, Cats, Geese, Foot, & Mouth And Statistics: HIV/AIDS and the Struggle for the Humanisation of the African" (ANC, 2002) which was posted to the ANC website anonymously, but is widely believed to have been penned by Mbeki himself. For further information, see also Thornton (2008), Nattrass (2007), and Johnson (2005).

24. Interview with anonymous AIDS Law Project (ALP) activist held on November 24, 2005 in Johannesburg.

25. Interview with female HIV-infected community member held on June 26, 2009 in Sol Plaatjie.

26. The United States President's Emergency Plan for AIDS Relief. Retrieved from http://www.pepfar.gov/

27. In this article, I delimit my discussion of medical pluralism within the African population. For historical information on pluralism within other populations of color in South Africa, see Flint (2001, 2006) and Digby (2005, 2006).

28. The constitutionality of the Traditional Health Practitioners Act of 2004 (Department of Health, 2005) was recently challenged by Doctors for Life International on the basis of limited public consultation. In August 2006, the Constitutional Court ruled in favor of the Doctors for Life. In 2007, parliament re-enacted the Act, which was assented to by President Mbeki in January 2008 (Department of Health, 2007; Doctors for Life, 2006; Singh, 2008).

29. I participated in a task team, initiated by the Gauteng Department of Health to interface between healers and government officials for a full year; I conducted FGDs with 131 indigenous healers, and in-depth interviews with 44 of them – most of whom were leaders or members of indigenous healing organizations in the Johannesburg area.

30. "In 1997, a traditional medicines (TRAMED) research project was established by the Universities of Cape Town and the Western Cape with support of the MRC to create a data base of traditional medicines, conduct lab tests, and to develop systems for understanding essential traditional medicines used in the prevention and treatment of diseases" (Asforth, 2005, p. 152). The Medical Research Council established an Indigenous Knowledge Systems unit and has begun testing herbal remedies (MRC, 2011); and the National Adverse Drug Monitoring Centre (NADEMC), a special unit of the Medical Control Council, housed at the University of Cape Town also attempts to monitor the safety of medicine and test possible adverse effects of combining different kinds of drugs (MCC, 2011). For further information, see Decoteau (forthcoming).

31. Interview with Dr. Koka held on September 7, 2005 in Noord Wyk, Johannesburg.

32. This is a pseudonym.

33. Interview held on August 8, 2005 in Alexandra, Johannesburg.

34. I conducted exploratory research with this organization (which must remain anonymous to protect the participants' identities) in 2002–2003 and volunteered for them from December 1, 2004 – September 30, 2005. During this time, I worked extensively with support groups in Zola, Dobsonville and Orlando East, Soweto. "Tebogho" (a pseudonym) was my guide and closest contact during this field work.

35. I conducted interviews with "Tebogho" on April 6 and October 19, 2005; however, she would never talk about herself during an official interview. She told me this in the car, during one of our many trips to and from support groups in the Soweto area. Field notes, February 2, 2005, Soweto.

36. Interview with Pheello Limapo held on October 5, 2005 in Lawley. Pheello was my primary informant in Lawley. Over the course of the years, I conducted multiple in-depth interviews with him and have accompanied him to both the doctor and the hospital on a number of occasions.

37. A CD4 count (or T-cell count) measures the number of white blood cells per ml of blood. A healthy person has between 800 and 1,600 T-cells. Someone infected with HIV receives an AIDS diagnosis when her CD4 count has dropped to 200 (or if she is suffering from an opportunistic infection).

38. Interview held with Pheello Limapo on December 8, 2005 in Lawley.

39. The South African equivalent of a Tylenol.

40. FGD held on June 11, 2009 in Sol Plaatjie.

41. Thulani Skhosana was my primary informant in Sol Plaatjie. Over the course of the years, I conducted multiple in-depth interviews with him and also accompanied him to his various doctor's and healer's appointments.
42. See Wacquant (1989, p. 27) for this point.

REFERENCES

Abdool- Karim, S. S., Ziqubu-Page T. T., and Arendse R. (1994). *Bridging the gap: Potential for health care partnership between African traditional healers and biomedical personnel in South Africa*. Report of the South African Medical Research Council. South African Medical Journal 84(December Insert): s1–s16.

African National Congress (ANC). (1994). *A National Health Plan for South Africa*. http:// www.anc.org.za/show.php?id=257. Accessed on December 30, 2011.

African National Congress. (2002). Castro Hlongwane, caravans, cats, geese, foot & mouth and statistics: HIV/AIDS and the struggle for the humanisation of the African. Unknown Author. (First posted to the ANC website by Peter Mokaba on March 2002). Retrieved from http://www.virusmyth.com/aids/hiv/ancdoc.htm. Accessed on June 3, 2011.

Anderson, W. (2006). *Colonial pathologies: American tropical medicine, race, and hygiene in the Philippines*. Durham, NC: Duke University Press.

Arnold, D. (1993). *Colonizing the body: State medicine and epidemic disease in nineteenth-century India*. Berkeley, CA: University of California Press.

Asforth, A. (2005). *Witchcraft, violence and democracy in South Africa*. Chicago, IL: University of Chicago Press.

Berman, K. (2008) (March 3–7). *Art saves lives: The creative arts, community engagement, & HIV/AIDS in South Africa*. Creative community partnerships for creative community development: University of Johannesburg-University of Michigan Collaborations. University of Michigan, Ann Arbour, MI.

Bhabha, H. (1994). *The location of culture*. New York, NY: Routledge.

Bourdieu, P. (1962). *The Algerians* (A. C. M. Ross, Trans.). Boston, MA: Beacon Press.

Bourdieu, P. (1977). *Outline of a theory of practice*. (R. Nice, Trans.). Cambridge: Oxford University Press.

Bourdieu, P. (1979). *Algeria 1960: The disenchantment of the world; The sense of honour; The Kabyle house or the world reversed*. (R. Nice, Trans.). Cambridge, UK: Cambridge University Press.

Bourdieu, P. (1984). *Distinction: A social critique of the judgment of taste*. (R. Nice, Trans.). Cambridge, MA: Harvard University Press.

Bourdieu, P., & Richardson, J. G. (Eds.). (1986). *Handbook of theory and research for the sociology of education*. New York, NY: Greenwood Press.

Bourdieu, P. (1989). Social Space and Symbolic Power. *Sociological Theory, 7*, 14–25.

Bourdieu, P. (1990). *The logic of practice*. (R. Nice, Trans.). Stanford, CA: Stanford University Press.

Bourdieu, P. (2000). *Pascalian meditations*. (R. Nice, Trans.). Stanford, CA: Stanford University Press.

Bourdieu, P. (Ed.). (2007). *Sketch for a self-analysis*. Chicago, IL: University of Chicago Press.

Bourdieu, P., & Sayad, A. (2004). Colonial rule and cultural sabir. *Ethnography, 5*(4), 544–586.

Bourdieu, P., et al. (1999). *The weight of the world: Social suffering in contemporary society*. Stanford, CA: Stanford University Press.

Campbell, S. S. (1998). *Called to heal: Traditional healing meets modern medicine in Southern Africa today*. London: Zebra Press.

Chigwedere, P., Seage, G. R., Gruskin, S., Lee, T.-H., & Essex, M. (2008). Estimating the lost benefits of antiretroviral drug use in South Africa. *Journal of Acquired Immune Deficiency Syndrome, 49*, 410–415.

Colvin, M., Gumede L., Grimwade K., and Wilkinson D. (2001). Integrating traditional healers into a tuberculosis control programme in Hlabisa, South Africa. *Medicine Control Council Brief, 4*(December). Retrieved from http://www.mrc.ac.za//policybriefs/tbtraditional.pdf. Accessed on June 20, 2011.

Comaroff, J., and Comaroff J. L. (1991). *Of revelation and revolution: Christianity. Colonialism, and consciousness in South Africa* (Vol. 1). Chicago, IL: University of Chicago Press.

Decoteau, C. L. (2013, Forthcoming). *Ancestors and antiretrovirals: The bio-politics of HIV/AIDS in post-apartheid South Africa*. Chicago, IL: University of Chicago Press.

Delius, P., & Glaser, C. (2005). Sex, disease and stigma in South Africa: Historical perspectives. *African Journal of AIDS Research, 4*(1), 29–36.

Department of Health. (2005). *The traditional Health Practitioners Act, 2004*. Cape Town: Government Gazette (Vol. 476, No. 27275), February 11, 2005. Retrieved from http://www.doh.gov.za/docs/bills/thb.html. Accessed on June 8, 2011.

Department of Health. (2007). *Traditional Health Practitioners Act 22, 2007*. Cape Town: Government Gazette, *511* (42), January 10, 2008. Retrieved from http://www.info.gov.za/view/DownloadFileAction?id=77788. Accessed on June 8, 2011.

Department of Health, South Africa. (2003, November 19). Operational plan for comprehensive HIV and AIDS care, management and treatment for South Africa. Retrieved from http://www.info.gov.za/otherdocs/2003/aidsplan.pdf. Accessed on March 20, 2008.

Derrida, J. (1978). Structure, sign and play in the discourse of the human sciences. In A. Bass (Trans.) *Writing and difference*, (pp. 278–300). Chicago, IL: University of Chicago Press.

Digby, A. (2005). Self-medication and the trade in medicine within a multi-ethnic context: A case study of South Africa from the mid-nineteenth to mid-twentieth centuries. *Social History of Medicine, 18*(3), 439–457.

Digby, A. (2006). *Diversity and division in medicine: Health care in South Africa from the 1800s*. Oxford: Peter Lang.

Digby, A., & Sweet, H. (2002). Nurses as culture brokers in twentieth-century South Africa. In W. Ernst (Ed.), *Plural medicine, tradition and modernity, 1800–2000* (pp. 113–129). New York, NY: Routledge.

Dirlik, A. (1996). The postcolonial aura: Third world criticism in the age of global capitalism. In P. Mongia (Ed.), *Contemporary postcolonial theory: A reader* (pp. 294–320). New York, NY: Arnold.

Doctors for Life International v Speaker of National Assembly and Others. (2006, 17 August). Retrieved from http://www.constitutionalcourt.org.za/uhtbin/cgisirsi/xoSXBfgKRp/MAIN/259070012/9%23top. Accessed on June 8, 2011.

Dugger, C. (2008, November 25). Study cites toll of AIDS policy in South Africa. *The New York Times*.

Dugger, C. (2009, October 31). Zuma rallies S. African to fight AIDS. *The New York Times*. Retrieved from http://www.nytimes.com/2009/11/01/world/africa/01zuma.html. Accessed on June 1, 2011.

Fassin, D. (2007). *When bodies remember: Experiences and politics of AIDS in South Africa.* Berkeley, CA: University of California Press.

Flint, K. E. (2001). Competition, race, and professionalization: African healers and White medical practitioners in Natal, South Africa in the early Twentieth Century. *Social History of Medicine, 14*(2), 199–221.

Flint, K. E. (2006). Indian–African encounters: Polyculturalism and African Therapeutics in Natal, South Africa, 1886–1950s. *Journal of Southern African Studies, 32*(2), 367–385.

Flint, K. E. (2008). *Healing traditions: African medicine, cultural exchange, and competition in South Africa, 1820–1948.* Athens, OH: Ohio University Press.

Gilroy, P. (1994). Black cultural politics: An interview with Paul Gilroy by Timmy Lott. *Found Object, 4,* 46–81.

Gordon, D. (2001). A sword of empire?: Medicine and colonialism in King William's Town, Xhosaland, 1856–1891. *African Studies, 60*(2), 165–183.

Green, E. (1994). *AIDS and STDs in Africa: Bridging the gap between traditional healing and modern medicine.* Boulder, CO: Westview Press.

Green, E. (1999). *Indigenous theories of contagious disease.* London: AltaMira.

Gumede, M. V. (1990). *Traditional healers: A medical practitioner's perspective.* Cape Town: Blackshaws.

Hall, S. (1996a). When was 'the post-colonial'? Thinking at the limit. In I. Chambers & L. Curti (Eds.), *The post-colonial question: Common skies, divided horizons* (pp. 242–260). New York, NY: Routledge.

Hall, S. (1996b). Who needs identity? In S. Hall & P. DuGuy (Eds.), *The question of cultural identity* (p. 1017). London: Sage.

Heywood, M. (2008). *Politics of health.* Online book about the TAC. Retrieved from http://www.tac.org.za/community/heywood. Accessed on June 15, 2011.

Janzen, J. M. (1981). The need for a Taxonomy of health in the study of African Therapeutics. *Social Science and Medicine 15B, 3,* 185–194.

Jochelson, K. (2001). *The colour of disease: Syphilis and racism in South Africa, 1880–1950.* New York, NY: Palgrave.

Johnson, K. (2005). Globalization, social policy and the state: An analysis of HIV/AIDS in South Africa. *New Political Science, 27*(3), 309–329.

Marks, S., & Andersson, N. (1992). Industrialization, rural health, and the 1944 National Health Services Commission in South Africa. In S. Feierman & J. M. Janzen (Eds.), *The social basis of health and healing in Africa* (pp. 131–161). Berkeley, CA: University of California Press.

Mbali, M. (2004). AIDS discourses and the South African state: Government denialism and post-apartheid AIDS policy-making. *Transformation, 54,* 104–122.

McGregor, L. (2005). *Khabzela: The life and times of a South African.* Johannesburg: Jacana Media.

Medical Control Council (MCC). (2011). *National adverse drug event monitoring centre.* University of Cape Town. Retrieved from http://web.uct.ac.za/depts/pha/nademc.php. Accessed on March 28, 2011.

Medical Research Council (MRC), South Africa. (2011). *Indigenous knowledge systems.* Retrieved from http://www.mrc.ac.za/iks/indigenous.htm. Accessed on March 7, 2011.

Mills, E. (2005). HIV illness meanings and collaborative healing strategies in South Africa. *Social Text, 31*(2), 126–160.

Nattrass, N. (2007). *Mortal combat: AIDS denialism and the struggle for Antiretrovirals in South Africa.* Durban: University of KwaZulu Natal Press.

Niehaus, I. (2002). Bodies, heat, and taboos: Conceptualizing modern personhood in the South African Lowveld. *Ethnology, 43*(3), 189–208.

Olumwullah, O. A. (2002). *Dis-ease in the colonial state: Medicine, society, and social change among the AbaNyole of Western Kenya.* Westport, CT: Greenwood Press.

Packard, R. (1989). *White plague, black labor: Tuberculosis and the political economy of health and disease in South Africa.* Berkeley, CA: University of California Press.

Prakash, G. (1999). *Another reason: Science and the imagination of modern India.* Princeton, NJ: Princeton University Press.

Setel, P., Lewis, M., & Lyons, M. (Eds.). (1999). *Histories of sexually transmitted diseases and HIV/AIDS in Sub-Saharan Africa.* Westport, CT: Greenwood Press.

Shohat, E. (1992). Notes on the 'post-colonial'. *Social Text, 10*(31/32), 99–113.

Sidibé, M. (2009). *Speech by director general of UNAIDS on the commemoration of world AIDS day.* Pretoria Showgrounds, December 1. Retrieved from http://data.unaids.org/pub/SpeechEXD/2009/20091201_ms_speech_wad09_en.pdf. Accessed on June 1, 2011.

Singh, J. (2008). The ethics and legality of traditional healers performing HIV testing. *The Southern African Journal of Medicine, 9*(4), 6–10.

Steinberg, J. (2008). *Sizwe's test: A young man's journey through Africa's AIDS Epidemic.* New York, NY: Simon & Schuster.

Steinmetz, G. (2006). Bourdieu's disavowal of Lacan: Psychoanalytic theory and the concepts of 'habitus' and 'symbolic capital'. *Constellations, 13*(4), 445–464.

Steinmetz, G. (2007). American sociology before and after world war II: The (temporary) settling of a disciplinary field. In C. Calhoun (Ed.), *Sociology in America: A history* (pp. 314–366). Chicago, IL: University of Chicago Press.

Sunday Independent. (2004, November 7). *Deputy ministersees traditional healers helping to find a cure for AIDS.* (473), 44

Thornton, R. (2002). *Traditional healers, medical doctors and HIV/AIDS in Gauteng and Mpumalanga provinces, South Africa.* Final Report to the Margaret Sanger Institute. Johannesburg: University of the Witswatersrand (Unpublished: Cited with permission from the author).

Thornton, R. (2008). *Unimagined community: Sex, networks, and AIDS in Uganda and South Africa.* Berkeley, CA: University of California Press.

Thornton, R. (2009). The transmission of knowledge in South African traditional healing. *Africa, 79*(1), 17–34.

van der Linde, I. (1997). Western and African medicines meet. *South African Medical Journal, 87,* 268–270.

Vaughan, M. (1991). *Curing their ills: Colonial power and African illness.* Stanford, CA: Stanford University Press.

Viljoen, M., Panzer, A., Roos, K. L., & Bodemer, W. (2003). Psychoneuroimmunology: From philosophy, intuition, and Folklore to a recognized science. *South African Journal of Science, 99,* 332–336.

Wacquant, L. J. D. (1989). Towards a reflexive sociology: A workshop with Pierre Bourdieu. *Sociological Theory, 7*(1), 26–63.

Wacquant, L. J. D. (2004). Following Pierre Bourdieu into the field. *Ethnography, 5*(4), 387–414.

Xaba, T. (2002). The transformation of indigenous medical practice in South Africa (1985 to 2000). In V. Faure (Ed.), *Bodies and politics: Healing rituals in the democratic South Africa* (pp. 23–39). Johannesburg: Les Cahiers de l'IFAS (No. 2, February).

Xaba, T. (2005). *Witchcraft, sorcery or medical practice? The demand, supply, and regulation of indigeneous medicines in Durban, South Africa.* Ph.D. dissertation, University of California, Berkeley, CA.

THE POSSIBILITIES OF, AND FOR, GLOBAL SOCIOLOGY: A POSTCOLONIAL PERSPECTIVE [☆]

Gurminder K. Bhambra

ABSTRACT

This article addresses the way in which perceptions about the globalized nature of the world in which we live are beginning to have an impact within sociology such that sociology has to engage not just with the changing conceptual architecture of globalization, but also with recognition of the epistemological value and agency of the world beyond the West. I address three main developments within sociology that focus on these concerns: first, the shift to a multiple modernities paradigm; second, a call for a multicultural global sociology; and third, an argument in favor of a global cosmopolitan approach. While the three approaches under discussion are based on a consideration of the "rest of the world," their terms, I suggest, are not adequate to the avowed intentions. None of these responses is sufficient in their address of earlier omissions and each falls back into the problems of the mainstream position that is otherwise being criticized. In contrast, I argue that it is only by acknowledging the significance of the "colonial global" in the constitution of sociology that

[☆] Reprinted from *Postcolonial Sociology*, Political Power and Social Theory, Volume 24, 2013, pp. 295–314.

Postcolonial Sociology
Political Power and Social Theory, Volume 24, 271–291
ISSN: 0198-8719/doi:10.1108/S0198-8719(2013)0000024017

it is possible to understand and address the necessarily postcolonial (and decolonial) present *of "global sociology."*

INTRODUCTION

This article addresses the way in which perceptions about the globalized nature of the world in which we live are beginning to have an impact within sociology such that sociology has to engage not just with the changing conceptual architecture, as Saskia Sassen (2007) calls it, of globalization, but also with recognition of the epistemological value and agency of the world beyond the West, as Leela Gandhi (1998) has put it. The idea of a "global sociology," I shall argue, has been promoted as a way in which sociology can redress a previous neglect of those represented as "other" in its construction of modernity pointing toward a rejuvenation of sociology that is adequate for this new global age. In this article, I shall address three main developments within sociology that focus on these concerns: first, the shift to a multiple modernities paradigm away from earlier theories of linear modernization; second, a call for a multicultural global sociology taking into account the work of scholars from other parts of the world; and third, an argument against the perceived methodological nationalism of much social science in favor of a global cosmopolitan approach. While the three approaches under discussion are based on a consideration of the "rest of the world," usually in response to earlier critiques of a lack of such an engagement, its terms, I suggest, are not adequate to the avowed intentions. My argument will be that none of these responses is sufficient in their address of earlier omissions and that each falls back into the problems of the mainstream position that is otherwise being criticized. To a large extent, these approaches replicate existing divisions and problems as opposed to challenging and resolving them.

Instead, I shall argue that a postcolonial "connected sociologies" approach, with its critique of Eurocentrism and its central concern with histories of colonialism and slavery, provides more adequate resources for making sense of our contemporary global world. It is only by acknowledging the significance of the "*colonial* global" in the constitution of sociology, I suggest, that it is possible to understand and address the necessarily postcolonial (and decolonial) *present* of "global sociology." Recognition of the historical role of colonialism and slavery in the making of the modern world enables us to examine how these world-historical processes have constructed our conceptions of the global in terms of racialized hierarchies embedded both in institutions and in the development of sociological concepts and categories. The re-organization of understanding through the lens of coloniality, I argue, acknowledges the significance of a specific kind of hierarchical ordering that has, for the most part, been implicit to our discipline and remains missing in the three responses under discussion. While the sociological imagination hitherto has been formed around particular transformations of hierarchy – for example, from status to citizenship (and the associated issues of class and gender in that process) – the postcolonial sociological imagination broadens this remit through an examination of the reproduction and transformation of racialized hierarchies on a global scale and the argument that they have similar significance to other hierarchies and are similarly embedded within them.

The emergence and development of postcolonial criticism within the social sciences has led proponents of the "standard" view to make minor adjustments, but then to suggest that this is all now very familiar. The argument is that, while the critique may once have had purchase, its force now is only in relation to positions that have already been superseded. The minor modifications made to existing positions are believed to be sufficient and the focus is generally on changing future applications of sociology in line with these modifications. I argue, however, that the postcolonial critique of sociology has not yet properly been acknowledged, let alone superseded. Further, any proper transformation would require a reconstruction "backwards" of our historical understandings of modernity and the emergence of sociology, as well as "forwards" in terms of how this newly reconstructed sociological understanding would enable us to address present and future issues differently. A parallel that might be useful to think with is that of feminism and its critique of sociology.

The issue within feminist debates in sociology was not simply about a claim that the empirical range of problems that sociology addresses needed to be extended, but also that existing topics needed to be understood in terms of the relation to the issues of gender that were, and are, implicit to them. In its strongest form, feminism introduced a conceptual reorientation of sociology around the idea of patriarchy, and in a weaker form, around the gendered nature of social relations. These critiques did not simply involve statements that at the moment of recognition of gender we had entered a world that was *now* to be understood as gendered and that, *in the future*, sociological categories should address gender issues. Rather, the argument was also that established understandings about *the past* were deficient precisely insofar as gender was an issue of the past (albeit having been unrecognized) as well as of the present and future. The necessity for the reconstruction of sociology's objects was not discernible prior to the impact of feminism upon sociology and sociology has necessarily been reconstructed as a consequence of engagement with feminist critique (Holmwood, 1995, 2001; Jackson 1999; Stanley 2000, 2005). The analogous situation in relation to postcolonial critiques of the social sciences is to argue that colonialism is a social and political structure of modernity that necessarily impinges upon other social structures associated with modernity and that social relations are necessarily racialized or otherwise hierarchized in colonial terms (see Bhambra, 2007b). The remit of "global sociology," properly understood, must be to address problems and issues that cannot simply be seen as a consequence of manifestations of "late modernity." A truly global sociology would need to recognize histories of colonialism and slavery in any attempt to rethink sociology as adequate for our global (postcolonial) age.[1]

MODERNITY, SOCIOLOGY AND POSTCOLONIAL CRITIQUE

Sociology and modernity, as many scholars have argued, need to be understood as co-constitutive (Heilbron, 1995).[2] It was with the emergence of what is understood to be the "modern world" – the combined and cumulative events of the Renaissance and Reformation, the Scientific Revolution, the French and Industrial Revolutions – that a new, "modern," form of explanation, sociology, emerged to make sense of that world. Indeed, setting out the parameters of "the modern" became defined as a key task of sociology, both conceptually and methodologically. Even where sociologists have subsequently disagreed about the nature of modernity, the timing of its emergence, or its later character, they all agree on its central role in the configuration of the discipline (see, e.g., Giddens 1973; Heilbron, 1995; Nisbet, 1966). Further, notwithstanding the many differences between sociologists in their attempts to delineate modernity, they all agree that it is marked by ideas of rupture and difference: a temporal rupture between a premodern past and a modern industrial present, and a qualitative spatial (cultural) differentiation between Europe (and the West) and the rest of the world. With sociology being constituted both in the context of the emergence of the modern world and organized in terms of providing a

modern form of explanation of that world, it is no surprise that sociology
came to be strongly associated with understandings of "the modern." The
"traditional," from which the modern was distinguished, was seen as the
preserve of anthropology, or then area studies (see Steinmetz, 2007).[3] In
this way, the disciplinary divide itself structured a division of the world that
obscured the interconnections constituting the global that was in process of
being divided. Indeed, it re-cast that division in terms of a developmental
process that would resolve differences in the diffusion of a modernity that
was represented as world-historical in its significance.

This division – posited as both explanatory and normative – was carried
through methodologically via the use of ideal types as the basis for
comparative historical analysis. Ideal types necessarily abstract a set of
particular connections from wider connections and, further, suggest *sui
generis* endogenous processes as integral to the connections that are
abstracted (for further discussion, see Holmwood and Stewart, 1991). The
connections most frequently omitted are those "connecting" Europe and the
West (the modern) to much of the rest of the world (tradition). These
connections are thereby rendered exogenous to the processes abstracted
from them at the same time as these processes are represented as having a
significant degree of internal coherence, independent of these wider
connections. In this way, a dominant Eurocentered focus to the analysis is
established, both methodologically and normatively, while relegating non-
European contributions to specific cultural inflections of preexisting
structures that are held to be a product of European modernity (Bhambra,
2007a). This is best exemplified by the continuing belief in the miracle *in*
Europe, if not *of* Europe; that is, following Weber, a belief that modernity
emerged first in Europe and then diffused around the rest of the world.
While the association of modernity and Europe is now less likely to be
presented as a normative exemplar, it is nonetheless posited as historical
fact; and one where there is an elective affinity between the instituted
structures of modernity and Enlightenment values attributed European
origin. In this way, modernity is conflated with Europe and the process of
becoming modern is rendered, at least in the first instance, one of
endogenous European development, followed by diffusion to the rest of
the world.

Industrialization, for example, is seen to be a European phenomenon that
was subsequently diffused globally. However, if we take the cotton factories
of Manchester and Lancaster as emblematic of the industrial revolution in
the West, then we see that cotton was not a plant that was native to
England, let alone the West (Washbrook, 1997). It came from India as did

the technology of how to dye and weave it. Cotton was grown in the plantations of the Caribbean and the southern United States by enslaved Africans who were transported there as part of the European trade in human beings. The export of the textile itself relied upon the destruction of the local production of cotton goods in other parts of the world (Bhambra, 2007a). In this way, we see that industrialization was not solely a European or Western phenomenon but one that had global conditions for its very emergence and articulation. The history of modernity as commonly told, however, rests, as Homi Bhabha argues, on "the *writing out* of the colonial and postcolonial moment" (1994, p. 250; see also Chakrabarty, 2000). The rest of the world is assumed to be external to the world-historical processes selected for consideration and, concretely, colonial connections significant to the processes under discussion are erased, or rendered silent. This is not an error of individual scholarship, I suggest, but something that is made possible by the very disciplinary structure of knowledge production that separates the modern (sociology) from the traditional and colonial (anthropology) thereby leaving no space for consideration of what could be termed, the "postcolonial modern."

Following Bhabha (1994), I argue that the starting point for any understanding of "global sociology" has to be consideration of a history adequate to the social and political conditions of the present. These conditions are not simply informed by understandings of "globalization," but more specifically by an understanding of the postcolonial global conditions which are rarely the starting point for sociological analyses (see Bhambra, 2007b). As Seidman remarks, for example, sociology's emergence coincided with the high point of Western imperialism, and yet, "the dynamics of empire were not incorporated into the basic categories, models of explanation, and narratives of social development of the classical sociologists" (1996, p. 314). Those who defend the dominant approach to comparative historical sociology frequently accept that Eurocentrism is a problem that has sometimes distorted the way in which modernity has been conceptualized within sociology. They also argue that "Eurocentrism" cannot be denied as "fact," that, put simply, the European origins of modernity cannot be denied. However, it is precisely that "fact" that is denied when global interconnections are recognized (see Bhambra, 2007a; Hobson, 2004). In this article I argue that continuing to see Europe as the "lead society," to use Parsons's (1971) significant formulation, albeit the lead society within what is now characterized as a globally constituted plurality of "multiple modernities" (e.g., Beck 2000; Eisenstadt 2000; Wittrock, 1998), keeps in place a problematic (and implicitly normative) hierarchy, based on an historically inadequate account of the emergence of modernity, that does not enable the consideration of a properly *global* sociology. In a properly global sociology, interconnections would be recognized as constitutive of modernity and its institutional orderings and not simply be seen as an aspect of a later phase of globalization.

MULTIPLE MODERNITIES AND GLOBAL CULTURAL VARIETIES

In recent years, modernization theory, with its assumption of unilinear global convergence to an explicitly Western model, has been supplanted by the approach of multiple modernities and its concern with global cultural variations (Eisenstadt, 2000).[4] Within this approach, the modern is understood as encompassing divergent paths, with the global variety of cultures giving rise to a multiplicity of modernities. The shift from earlier modernization theory has come, in part, as a consequence of scholars beginning to appreciate that the differences manifest in the world were not, as had previously been believed, simply archaic differences that would disappear through gradual modernization. Instead, there is recognition that other societies could modernize differently and that these differences, for theorists of multiple modernities, now represent the different ways in which societies adapted to processes of modernization. There is still a belief that modernity was, in its origins, a European (and Western) phenomenon, but now the argument is that in its diffusion outward it interacted with the different traditions of various cultures and societies and brought into being a multiplicity of non-convergent modernities. It is this multiplicity that is seen to set the theory of multiple modernities apart from earlier modernization theory which, it is allowed, *was* Eurocentric in its postulation of a singular modernity to which all other societies were expected to converge. This apparent recognition of difference and the structural inclusion of multiplicity within the conceptual framework of modernity are deemed to be sufficient modifications to answer the postcolonial critique of modernity as Eurocentric.

The argument put forward by theorists of multiple modernities is that, while the idea of *one modernity*, especially one that has already been achieved in Europe, *would be Eurocentric*, theories of multiple modernities must, nonetheless, take Europe as the reference point in their examination of alternative modernities (Eisenstadt & Schluchter, 1998, p. 2). This is as a consequence of their characterization of modernity in terms of a division between its institutional form and a cultural program which, they suggest, is itself "beset by internal antinomies and contradictions, giving rise to continual critical discourse and political contestations" (Eisenstadt, 2000, p. 7). These internal antinomies are regarded as the basis for the variety of forms of modernity – usually pathological – that subsequently come into being, such as the communist Soviet types and the fascist, national-socialist types (see Arnason, 2000). The standard European type of modernity is presented as the exemplary form – in which the tensions between issues of autonomy, emancipation, and reflexivity, on the one hand, and of discipline and restrictive controls on the other, are resolved – and as the basis of critique of other pathological forms. While theorists of multiple modernities point to the problem of Eurocentrism, then, they do so at the same time as asserting the necessary priority to be given to the West in the construction of a comparative historical sociology of multiple modernities.

The suggestion by theorists of multiple modernities that modernity needs to be understood in terms of an institutional constellation inflected by cultural differences, enables them to situate European modernity – seen in terms of a unique combination of institutional and cultural forms – as the *originary* modernity and, at the same time, allows for different cultural encodings that result in modernity having become *multiple*. In this way, Europe becomes the origin of the Eurocentered type and its Enlightenment assumptions (Eisenstadt & Schluchter, 1998, p. 5). Further, those assumptions are argued to be necessary to the critique of pathologies at the same time as they are absolved of implication in the creation of those pathological types. In particular, it is notable that issues of colonialism and enslavement appear *neither* in representations of the exemplary, *nor* the pathological forms and are, in fact, not regarded to be a part of the socio-political or economic structures of modernity. Arguing for the cultural inflection of institutions enables multiple modernities theorists to present the idea that core institutions are not themselves socio-culturally formed. In this way, issues of race and ethnicity, for example, come to be regarded as external limits on, or additions to, market forms, rather than themselves being built into market forms. Whereas one sociological response to conventional accounts of modernization was to argue that core institutional forms should be understood as structured by class or by gender, what remains missing is the parallel criticism that those forms also embed racialized hierarchies (see Bhambra, 2007b; Holmwood, 2001).

As Arif Dirlik has argued, by identifying "multiplicity" with culture and tradition, "the idea of "multiple modernities" seeks to contain challenges to modernity" – and, I would argue, to the substantial reconfiguring of sociology – "by conceding the possibility of culturally different ways of being modern" (2003, p. 285), but not contesting *what it is to be modern* and *without drawing attention to the social interconnections in which modernity has been constituted and developed.* By maintaining a general framework within which particularities are located – and identifying the particularities with culture (or the social) and the experience of Europe with the general framework itself – theorists of multiple modernities have, in effect, sought to neuter any challenge that a consideration of the postcolonial could have posed. In this way, theorists of multiple modernities seek to disarm criticism by allowing for multiplicity at the same time as maintaining the fundamental structure of the original argument. The idea of multiple modernities can be argued to represent a kind of global multiculturalism, where a common (Eurocentered) modernity is inflected by different (other) cultures. In this context, it is significant that other – seemingly unconnected – calls for global sociology have the form of a call for a global multicultural sociology.

GLOBAL MULTICULTURAL SOCIOLOGY

While the argument of multiple modernities provides a critique of linear modernization theory and engages with a re-examination of the substance of sociological categories, what I am calling global multicultural sociology addresses issues of sociological epistemology in the context of multiple modernities. The most recent arguments for a global multicultural sociology have come in the wake of two conferences of the National Associations Committee of the International Sociological Association organized respectively by Sujata Patel in Miami in 2006 and by Michael Burawoy in Taipei in 2009. The discussions from these conferences have been widely reported in journals, edited volumes and other publications (see, e.g., Burawoy et al., 2010 and Patel, 2010b), and they consolidate themes from earlier engagements by sociologists on understandings and delineations of "global sociology." The 1980s, for example, saw extensive debate on the possibilities for the "indigenization" of the social sciences, centered on the arguments of Akinsola Akiwowo (1986, 1988). Akiwowo's project of indigenization was based upon a call for learning from the traditions of various cultures in order to develop, through a process of investigation and argumentation, universal propositions and frameworks that would be adequate for the task in a variety of locations. While calls for the indigenization of sociology opened up "spaces for alternative voices," they were seen to have had little discernible impact on the hierarchies of the discipline more generally (Keim, 2011, p. 128; see also Keim, 2008). The critiques were dismissed as political, or politically correct, and there was little engagement with the epistemological issues being raised (notwithstanding that they raised similar issues to feminist critiques of sociology at more or less the same time (see, e.g., Hartsock, 1984; Smith, 1987)).

The debates on indigenization were followed in subsequent decades with discussions concerning the development of autonomous or alternative social science traditions. These arguments for a newly constituted version of global sociology were put forward by scholars such as Syed Hussein Alatas (2002, 2006), Syed Farid Alatas (2006, 2010), Vineeta Sinha (2003), and Raewyn Connell (2007), and focused on the need to recognize multiple, globally diverse, origins of sociology. The debate, as outlined by S. F. Alatas, focused on two complementary strands: one, "the lack of autonomy" of Third World social science and two, "the lack of a multicultural approach in sociology" (2006, p. 5). The common position among the different arguments put forward by these scholars centered on a belief in the importance of the civilizational context for the development of autonomous, or alternative, social science traditions. With this, they aligned themselves, intentionally or not, with the approach espoused by theorists of "multiple modernities" whereby the Western social scientific tradition, linked to modernity, is given centrality and is regarded, as "the definitive reference point for departure and progress in the development of sociology" in other places (S. F. Alatas, 2006, p. 10).

The autonomy of the different traditions rests on studies of historical phenomena believed to be unique to particular areas or societies. As S. F. Alatas argues, autonomous traditions need to be "informed by local/ regional historical experiences and cultural practices" as well as by alternative "philosophies, epistemologies, histories, and the arts" (2010, p. 37). Western social science, then, becomes a reference point for the divergence (or creativity, as expressed through the *appropriation* of Western traditions read *through* local contexts) of other autonomous traditions, as opposed to the site of convergence (or imitation, as expressed through the *application* of Western traditions *to* local contexts), as was believed to be the case with earlier indigenization approaches (that, it was suggested, simply sought to replace expatriate scholars with "local" scholars trained in the expatriate traditions).

As with multiple modernities, however, there is little discussion of what the purchase of these autonomous traditions would be for a *global* sociology, beyond a simple multiplicity. The most that is suggested is that the development of autonomous traditions would require new attention to be "given to subjects hitherto outside our radius of thinking" and that this "would entail the repositioning of our sociological perspective" (S. H. Alatas, 2006, p. 21). There is little discussion, however, of why these subjects might have previously been outside our radius of thinking or what the process of bringing them inside consists of; the exclusions are naturalized and made issues of identity, not methodology or disciplinary construction. The limitations of existing approaches are seen to reside in their failure to engage with scholars and thinkers from outside the West and the main problem is taken to be one of marginalization and exclusion. The solution, then, is a putative equality, through recognition of difference, and redressing the "absence of non-European thinkers" in histories of social and sociological thought. While this may enable the creation of a (more) multicultural sociology for the future, it does little to address the problematic disciplinary construction of sociology in the past (see, Adams et al., 2005, and for discussion, Bhambra, 2010, 2011a).

Unsurprisingly, the idea of a multicultural global sociology, as with feminist critiques before it (see Stanley, 2000), has generated claims of a problematic relativism which is seen to debilitate sociology. Margaret Archer, for example, in her Presidential Address to the ISA World Congress, criticized the move within sociology toward what she saw as fragmentation and localization. With the title of her address, "Sociology for One World: Unity and Diversity," Archer proceeded to map "the irony of an increasingly global society which is met by an increasingly localized sociology" (1991, p. 132). Piotr Sztompka, another former President of the ISA, followed Archer in arguing strongly against the move to establish a multicultural global sociology. In a recent review of the volumes that came out of the ISA Taipei conference, Sztompka (2011) argues that a particular ideology has pervaded the ISA – one which regards the hegemony of north American and European sociology as problematic; which believes in the existence of alternative, indigenous sociologies; and sees the struggle for global sociology as a way of contesting the hegemony of the dominant forms and creating a balanced unity of the discipline. In contrast, his key concern, following Archer (1991), is highlighting the fact that "there is, and can be, only one sociology studying many social worlds" (2011, p. 389). The place of sociologists outside of the West, according to him, is to supplement the truths of the centre. As he suggests, "the most welcome contribution by sociologists from outside Europe or America is to provide evidence, heuristic hunches, ingenious, locally inspired models and hypotheses about regularities to add to the pool of sociological knowledge which is universal" (2011, p. 393).

There is little understanding that the new knowledges thus generated might in some way call for the reconstruction of existing sociological concepts and categories and thereby maintain a single sociology; that is, one *reconstructed* on the basis of these new insights. This is so notwithstanding the acceptance in the orthodox account of an explanation of the origins of sociology in a moment of "de-centering" of Europe by societies at its North Western edges. A de-centering of sociological epistemologies is taken to be a one-off matter, which is ironic, given that the sociological conditions of present concerns about globalization look very much like a similar geo-political shift in power to that which accompanied the emergence of modernity as presented in standard accounts.

GLOBAL COSMOPOLITANISM

While Archer (1991) and Sztompka (2011) have criticized the move toward a multicultural global sociology from the standpoint of the adequacy of existing forms of sociological understanding, others have done so by outlining an alternative position. Perhaps the most persuasive articulation for an alternative to global multicultural sociology is in the claims for a new universalism of a globally cosmopolitan sociology as put forward by Ulrich Beck (2000, 2006). His argument goes some way toward recognizing the "localism" of the centre, but it does so by casting it as a restriction on future developments (from elsewhere) as we shall see in the following section. For Beck, the problem is how to avoid the relativism of local knowledges, including that of Western sociology, rather than how to learn from local knowledges elsewhere.

Over the first decade of the twenty-first century, Beck (2000, 2006) has argued for the necessity of a cosmopolitan approach to engage critically with globalization and to go beyond the limitations of state-centered disciplinary approaches typical of the social and political sciences.[5] He suggests that sociology delimits the object of its inquiry within national boundaries, displaying an outdated methodological nationalism, rather than in the more appropriate context of "world society." As a consequence, it is less well able to engage with the "increasing number of social processes that are indifferent to national boundaries" (2000, p. 80). This global age, for Beck, is marked by a transition from the "first age of modernity" which had been structured by nation-states, to a cosmopolitan "second age" in which "the Western claim to a monopoly on modernity is broken and the history and situation of diverging modernities in all parts of the world come into view" (2000, p. 87). The global age, then, is necessarily perceived as being a *multicultural* age, given that multiple modernities are said to be the expression of cultural differences. With this, Beck follows the approach of multiple modernities theorists in their general analysis, but his call for a *second age* of modernity, and what follows from this – a call for a cosmopolitan sociology – is distinctive.

Beck (2000, 2006) not only argues that modernity is now multiple, but further suggests that the concepts which had been in use in developing sociological understandings in the first age are now no longer adequate to the task of understanding modernity in its second age. This is primarily a consequence of the fact that the standard concepts of the social sciences were developed to understand a world composed of nation-states. Now that we are in the second, *global*, age of modernity, he argues, these concepts are no longer appropriate. Instead, what is needed is a new set of categories and concepts that would emerge from reflection upon this new cosmopolitan age of modernity as represented by the moves toward world society. While I have also argued that sociological concepts are inappropriately bounded – specifically, that they are "methodologically Eurocentric," rather than methodological nationalistic – this is not something that is *only now* becoming an issue as a supposedly "first modernity" gives way to a contemporary now-globalized world. At a minimum, "first modernity" could be argued to be as much characterized by empires and regional blocs as by nation-states (see also Wimmer & Schiller, 2003). As a consequence, the concepts of the "first age," I argue, were as inadequate in their own time as they are claimed to be today and need more comprehensive reconstruction than is suggested by Beck.

Beck (2002) sees cosmopolitanism – and the reconstruction of sociology through a cosmopolitan paradigm – as an issue of the present and the future. There is no discussion in his work of thinking cosmopolitanism back into history and re-examining sociology's past in light of this. Further, there is little acknowledgment that if certain understandings are taken to be problematic today, they are likely also to have been problematic in the past and thus require a more comprehensive overhaul than he proposes. Indeed, Beck argues that he is not interested in the memory of the global past, but simply in how a vision of a cosmopolitan future could have an impact on the politics of the present. He seems to think that it is possible to discuss "the present implications of a globally shaped future" (2002, p. 27) without addressing the legacies of the past on the shaping of the present. He simply brushes away the historically inherited inequalities arising from the legacies of European colonialism, imperialism, and slavery and moves on to imagine a world separate from the resolution of these inequalities. In contrast, I would argue that any theory that seeks to address the question of "how we live in the world" cannot treat as irrelevant the historical configuration of that world (for discussion, see Trouillot, 1995). In this way, I argue, Beck's cosmopolitan approach is as limited as the state-centered approaches it criticizes precisely in the way that it sanctions the appropriateness of their concepts to the past, arguing that it is simply their application to the present and the future that is at issue (for further discussion, see Bhambra, 2011b; also Patel, 2010a).

Ultimately, Beck's arguments for a cosmopolitan sociology continue to take Western perspectives as the focus of global processes, and Europe as the origin of a modernity which is subsequently globalized. His particular version of cosmopolitanism, I would suggest, is an expression of cultural Eurocentrism masquerading as potential global inclusivity; potential, because this inclusivity is dependent upon "others" being included in the "us" as defined by Beck (2002). It is not an inclusivity that recognizes "others" as having been present, if marginalized and silenced, within standard frameworks of understanding; nor is it an inclusivity that seeks to establish cosmopolitanism from the ground up (for properly cosmopolitan understandings of cosmopolitanism, see Lamont & Aksartova, 2002; Mignolo, 2000; Pollock et al., 2000). Rather, for Beck, a cosmopolitan sociology is a normative injunction determining how others ought to be included and how those others ought to live with us in this newly globalizing age. His hostility to others is nowhere better exemplified than in the title of his article, "Cosmopolitan Society and its Enemies." In contrast, a global sociology that was open to different voices would, I suggest, be one that provincialized European understandings in its address of the global and created a new universalism based upon a reconstructed sociology of modernity.

TOWARD A POSTCOLONIAL GLOBAL SOCIOLOGY

The different approaches discussed above – multiple modernities, multi-cultural sociology, cosmopolitanism – all attempt to grapple with two main issues in their statement of a global sociology. First, how can sociology address the critiques made by postcolonial theorists, among others, regarding its failure to address issues of difference as it is manifest in the world; and second, how can sociology be made relevant to a world newly understood in global terms. The main way of addressing the first issue is through an additive approach that celebrates a contemporary plurality of cultures and voices. The multiple modernities paradigm, for example, recognizes the diversity of globally located cultures and accepts the possibility of culturally diverse ways of being modern. These aspects, of multiplicity (over singularity) and divergence (over convergence), are deemed to be sufficient to address earlier critiques. Yet, there is little acknowledgment of the presence of these "others" in the history of modernity as understood in its originary form. The world-historical events recognized in the constitution of modernity remain centered upon a narrowly defined European history and there is no place for the broader histories of colonialism or slavery in their understandings of the emergence of the modern. This failing of multiple modernities is replicated in the move to multiple, or multicultural, global sociologies where the centrality of the West remains in place and new voices are allowed to *supplement* the already existing truths about a Eurocentered modernity, but not to *reconstruct* them. If the new cosmopolitanism in the "age of second modernity" appears different, it is only by virtue of eschewing multiculturalism, while paradoxically accepting the conceptual and methodological premises of the multiple modernities paradigm. As Holmwood notes, although scholars allow for new (postcolonial) voices within sociology, their understandings of the sociological endeavor are such that these new voices "do not bear on its previous constructions" (2007, p. 55). All reconstruction is to be applied to the future while maintaining the adequacy of past interpretations and conceptual understandings.

In their address of the global, all three approaches regard it as constituted through contemporary connections between what are presented as historically separate civilizational contexts. None of the approaches take into consideration the histories of colonialism and slavery as central to the development of the "global" and, therefore, they work with an impoverished understanding that sees the global only as a phenomenon of recent salience. Beck's global cosmopolitanism, for example, addresses the inadequacy of sociological concepts for the present age, but he does not recognize "the global" as constituted historically. Rather, he is simply concerned with the emergence of a new cosmopolitan global age and a cosmopolitan sociology adequate to new challenges in the future. In a similar fashion, calls for a multicultural global sociology, in which voices from the periphery would enter into debates with the centre, are based on the idea that sociology could be different in the future with little acknowledgment that, in order for this to happen, sociology would also need to relate differently to its past. In contrast, I argue that to address what is regarded as problematic within contemporary understandings of sociology, we need to start by examining the way in which sociology understands the past and how this influences its configuration of categories and concepts in the present. The main issue, I propose, is the failure to address the omission of the colonial global from understandings of how the global came to be constituted as such.

By silencing the colonial past within the historical narrative central to the formation of sociology, the postcolonial present of Europe (and the West) is also ignored. As a consequence, sociological attempts to address the "newly" global are misconstrued and thereby inadequate for a proper address for the problems we share in common. In accepting the adequacy of sociological accounts that exclude considerations of the world from understandings of world-historical processes, a form of ethnocentrism is perpetuated. As Bhabha argues, however, shifting the frame through which we view the events of modernity forces us to consider the question of subaltern agency and ask: "what is this 'now' of modernity? Who defines this present from which we speak?" (1994, p. 244). This provocation calls on us to re-examine the conceptual paradigm of modernity from the perspectives of those "others" usually relegated to the margins, if included at all. The task, as he puts it, is to take responsibility for the unspoken, unrepresented pasts within our global present and to reconstruct present understandings adequate to that past (1994, p. 7); and, I would add, reconstruct past understandings adequate to our shared present.

One example of this would be for nation-states in the West to confront their colonial and imperial histories (and thereby recognize their postcolonial present) by acknowledging the "influx of postwar migrants and refugees" as part of "an indigenous or native narrative *internal to national identity*" (Bhabha, 1994, p. 6, emphasis added; see also Amin, 2004). Just as in standard sociological accounts industrialization is represented as endogenous and its extension as diffusion, so migration has usually been regarded as a process both exogenous and subsequent to the formation of nation-states. The idea of the political community as a *national* political order has been central to European self-understanding, and remains in the three sociological approaches discussed in this article. Yet most European states were colonial and imperial states as much as they were national states – and often prior to or alongside becoming national states – and so the political community of the state was much wider and more (and differently) stratified than is usually now acknowledged. By locating migration as subsequent to nation-state formation, migrants are themselves then located as *newcomers* with their stake within that community regarded as different in relation to those accepted as *native* to it (see Wimmer & Schiller, 2003). In this way, to the extent that migrants are often racially marked, understandings of race and ethnicity become associated with issues of their later distribution within a political community – as "minorities" – rather than an examination of their constitutive role in the formation of those communities. The essential "character" of these communities is argued to be formed independently of the processes by which migrants come to be connected to their places of new settlement. A more appropriate address would locate migrants within the broader systems of nation-state formation in the context of imperial states and colonial regimes and therefore to be understood as *integral* to such processes as opposed to being regarded as subsequent *additions* to them.

The turn to the global, as exemplified by the approaches under consideration here, is presented as a new development within sociology. However, as I have sought to demonstrate, these approaches simply perpetuate earlier analytical frameworks associated with understandings of the Eurocentered modern. Replacing the "modern" with the "global," an increasingly contested sociological history is naturalized, enabling sociologists to sidestep the fundamental issue of the relationship between modernity and sociology. In this way, the global histories of colonial interconnections across, what are presented as, separate modernities continue to be effaced from both historical and analytical consideration. As a consequence, understandings of "global sociology" are seen to emerge through the accretion of "new" knowledge from different places with little consideration of the long-standing interconnections among the locations in which knowledges are constructed and produced. Nor is there recognition that global sociology would require sociology itself to be re-thought backward, in terms of how its core categories have been constituted in the context of particular historical narratives, as well as forwards in terms of the further implications of its reconstruction. A postcolonial approach to historical sociology, in contrast, requires address of histories of colonialism and empire in the configuration of understandings of the global. What is in prospect, is not an embrace of relativism, but a recognition that a truly global sociology with universal claims will derive from reconstructing present understandings in the light of new knowledge of the past and the present.

ACKNOWLEDGMENTS

Thanks to John Holmwood, Ipek Demir, and Vicky Margree for comments and suggestions on this article. Any errors that remain are mine.

NOTES

1. For discussion of sociology's engagement with issues of empire and colonialism, see Magubane (2005) and Go (2009).

2. The arguments of this section are developed in more detail in Bhambra (2007a).

3. In this context, it is significant that Latour's (1993) challenge to the idea of modernity – that we have never been modern – is itself conducted from an "anthropological" perspective, asserting both difference and the lack of fundamental difference between the modern and what preceded it. However, in his elaboration of extended networks in the construction of social phenomena, Latour, himself, does not go beyond the West.

4. For further elaboration of the arguments in this section, see Bhambra (2007a, pp. 56–79).

5. Some of the arguments in this section are further elaborated in Bhambra (2011b).

REFERENCES

Adams, J., Clemens, E. S., & Orloff, A. S. (Eds.). (2005). *Remaking modernity: Politics, history and sociology*. Durham, NC: Duke University Press.

Akiwowo, A. A. (1986). Contributions to the sociology of knowledge from an African oral poetry. *International Sociology*, *1*(4), 343–358.

Akiwowo, A. A. (1988). Universalism and indigenization in sociological theory: Introduction. *International Sociology*, *3*(2), 155–160.

Alatas, S. F. (2002). The development of an autonomous social science tradition in Asia: Problems and prospects. *Asian Journal of Social Science*, *30*(1), 150–157.

Alatas, S. F. (2006). Editorial introduction: The idea of autonomous sociology: Reflections on the state of the discipline. *Current Sociology*, *54*(1), 5–6.

Alatas, S. F. (2010). Religion and reform: Two exemplars for autonomous sociology in the non-western context. In S. Patel (Ed.), *The ISA handbook of diverse sociological traditions*. London: Sage.

Alatas, S. H. (2006). The autonomous, the universal and the future of sociology. *Current Sociology*, *54*(1), 7–23.

Amin, A. (2004). Multi-ethnicity and the idea of Europe. *Theory, Culture and Society*, *21*(2), 1–24.

Archer, M. S. (1991). Presidential address: Sociology for one world – Unity and diversity. *International Sociology*, *6*(2), 131–147.

Arnason, J. (2000). Communism and modernity. *Daedalus: Multiple Modernities*, *129*(1), 61–90.

Beck, U. (2000). The cosmopolitan perspective: Sociology of the second age of modernity. *British Journal of Sociology, 51*(1), 79–105.

Beck, U. (2002). The cosmopolitan society and its enemies. *Theory Culture Society, 19*(1–2), 17–44.

Beck, U. (2006). *Cosmopolitan vision*. Cambridge: Polity Press.

Bhabha, H. K. (1994). *The location of culture*. London: Routledge.

Bhambra, G. K. (2007a). *Rethinking modernity: Postcolonialism and the sociological imagination*. Basingstoke: Palgrave MacMillan.

Bhambra, G. K. (2007b). Sociology and postcolonialism: Another 'missing' revolution?' *Sociology, 41*(5), 871–874.

Bhambra, G. K. (2010). Historical sociology, international relations and connected histories. *Cambridge Review of International Affairs, 23*(1), 127–143.

Bhambra, G. K. (2011a). Historical sociology, modernity, and postcolonial critique. *American Historical Review, 116*(3), 653–662.

Bhambra, G. K. (2011b). Cosmopolitanism and postcolonial critique. In M. Rovisco & M. Nowicka (Eds.), *Companion to cosmopolitanism* (pp. 313–328). Farnham: Ashgate.

Burawoy, M., Chang, M.-K., & Hsieh Michelle, F.-Y. (Eds.) (2010). *Facing an unequal world: Challenges for a global sociology*. Vols. 1–3. Jointly published by the Institute of Sociology at Academia Sinica, Council of National Associations of the International Sociological Association, and Academia Sinica, Taiwan.

Chakrabarty, D. (2000). *Provincializing Europe: Postcolonial thought and historical difference*. Princeton, NJ: Princeton University Press.

Connell, R. (2007). *Southern theory: The global dynamics of knowledge in social science*. Cambridge: Polity Press.

Dirlik, A. (2003). Global modernity? Modernity in an age of global capitalism. *European Journal of Social Theory, 6*(3), 275–292.

Eisenstadt, S. N. (2000). Multiple modernities. *Daedalus: Multiple Modernities, 129*(1), 1–29.

Eisenstadt, S. N., & Schluchter, W. (1998). Introduction: Paths to early modernities – A comparative view. *Daedalus: Early Modernities, 127*(3), 1–18.

Gandhi, L. (1998). *Postcolonial theory: A critical introduction*. Edinburgh: Edinburgh University Press.

Giddens, A. (1973). *Capitalism and modern social theory: An analysis of the writings of Marx, Durkheim and Max Weber*. Cambridge: Cambridge University Press.

Go, J. (2009). The "New" sociology of empire and colonialism. *Sociology Compass, 3*, 1–14.

Hartsock, N. C. M. (1984). *The feminist standpoint: Developing the ground for a specifically feminist historical materialism. Money, sex, and power: Toward a feminist historical materialism*Boston, MA: Northeastern University Press.

Heilbron, J. (1995). *The rise of social theory*. Cambridge: Polity Press.

Hobson, J. (2004). *The Eastern origins of the West*. Cambridge: Cambridge University Press.

Holmwood, J. (1995). Feminism and epistemology: What kind of successor science? *Sociology, 29*(3), 411–428.

Holmwood, J. (2001). Gender and critical realism: A critique of Sayer. *Sociology, 35*(4), 947–965.

Holmwood, J. (2007). Sociology as public discourse and professional practice: A critique of Michael Burawoy. *Sociological Theory, 25*(1), 46–66.

Holmwood, J., & Stewart, A. (1991). *Explanation and social theory*. London: Macmillan.

Jackson, S. (1999). Feminist sociology and sociological feminism: Recovering the social in feminist thought. *Sociological Research Online, 4*(3). Retrieved from http://www.socresonline.org.uk/4/3/jackson.html

Keim, W. (2008). Social sciences internationally: The problem of marginalization and its consequences for the discipline of sociology. *African Sociological Review, 12*(2), 22–48.

Keim, W. (2011). Counterhegemonic currents and Internationalization of sociology: Theoretical reflections and an empirical example. *International Sociology, 26*(1), 123–145.

Lamont, M., & Aksartova, S. (2002). Ordinary cosmopolitanisms: Strategies for bridging racial boundaries among working-class men, Theory. *Culture and Society, 19*(4), 1–25.

Latour, B. 1993. *We have never been modern* (C. Porter, Trans.). Hertfordshire: Harvester Wheatsheaf.

Magubane, Z. (2005). Overlapping territories and intertwined histories: Historical sociology's global imagination. In J. Adams, E. S. Clemens & A. S. Orloff (Eds.), *Remaking modernity: Politics, history, sociology* (pp. 92–108). Durham, NC: Duke University Press.

Mignolo, W. D. (2000). The many faces of cosmo-polis: Border thinking and critical cosmopolitanism. *Public Culture, 12*(3), 721–728.

Nisbet, R. A. (1966). *The sociological tradition.* New York, NY: Basic Books Inc.

Parsons, T. (1971). *The system of modern societies.* Englewood Cliffs, NJ: Prentice-Hall Inc.

Patel, S. (2010a). The imperative and the challenge of diversity: Reconstructing sociological traditions in an unequal world. In M. Burawoy, M.-K. Chang & M. Fei-yu Hsieh (Eds.), *Facing an unequal world: Challenge for a global sociology* (pp. 48–60). Taipei: Academica Sinica and International Sociological Association.

Patel, S. (Ed.). (2010b). *The ISA handbook of diverse sociological traditions.* London: Sage Publications.

Pollock, S., Bhabha, H. K., Breckenridge, C. A., & Chakrabarty, D. (2000). Cosmopolitanisms. *Public Culture, 12*(3), 577–579.

Sassen, S. (2007). *A sociology of globalization (Contemporary Society Series).* New York, NY: W.W. Norton and Co.

Seidman, S. (1996). Empire and knowledge: More troubles, new opportunities for sociology. *Contemporary Sociology, 25*(3), 313–316.

Sinha, V. (2003). Decentring social sciences in practice through individual acts and choices. *Current Sociology, 51*(1), 7–26.

Smith, D. (1987). *The everyday world as problematic: A feminist sociology.* Buckingham: Open University Press.

Stanley, L. (2000). For sociology, Gouldner's and ours. In J. Eldridge, J. MacInnes, S. Scott, C. Warhurst & A. Witz (Eds.), *For sociology: Legacies and prospects.* Durham, NC: Sociology Press.

Stanley, L. (2005). A child of its time: Hybridic perspectives on othering in sociology. *Sociological Research Online, 103.* Retrieved from http://www.socresonline.org.uk/10/3/stanley.html

Steinmetz, G. (2007). Transdisciplinarity as a nonimperial encounter. *Thesis Eleven, 91*(1), 48–65.

Sztompka, P. (2011). Another sociological Utopia. *Contemporary Sociology, 40*(4), 388–396.

Trouillot, M.-R. (1995). *Silencing the past: Power and the production of history.* Boston, MA: Beacon Press.

Washbrook, D. A. (1997). From comparative sociology to Global History: Britain and India in the pre-history of modernity. *Journal of Economic and Social History of the Orient, 40*(4), 410–413.

Wimmer, A., & Schiller, N. G. (2003). Methodological nationalism, the social sciences, and the study of migration: An essay in historical epistemology. *International Migration Review, 37*(3), 576–610.

Wittrock, B. (1998). Early modernities: Varieties and transitions. *Daedalus: Early Modernities, 127*(3), 19–40.

PARAMETERS OF A POSTCOLONIAL SOCIOLOGY OF THE OTTOMAN EMPIRE☆

Fatma Müge Göçek

ABSTRACT

The traditional postcolonial focus on the modern and the European, and pre-modern and non-European empires has marginalized the study of empires like the Ottoman Empire whose temporal reign traversed the modern and pre-modern eras, and its geographical land mass covered parts of Eastern Europe, the Balkans, Asia Minor, the Arabian Peninsula, and North Africa. Here, I first place the three postcolonial corollaries of the prioritization of contemporary inequality, the determination of its historical origins, and the target of its eventual elimination in conversation with the Ottoman Empire. I then discuss and articulate the two ensuing criticisms concerning the role of Islam and the fluidity of identities in states and societies. I argue that epistemologically, postcolonial studies criticize the European representations of Islam, but do not take the next step of generating alternate knowledge by engaging in empirical studies of Islamic empires like the Ottoman Empire. Ontologically, postcolonial studies draw strict official and unofficial lines

☆Reprinted from *Decentering Social Theory*, Political Power and Social Theory, Volume 24, 2013, pp. 73–104.

Decentering Social Theory
Political Power and Social Theory, Volume 25, 293–324
ISSN: 0198-8719/doi:10.1108/S0198-8719(2013)0000025009

between the European colonizer and the non-European colonized, yet such a clear-cut divide does not hold in the case of the Ottoman Empire where the lines were much more nuanced and identities much more fluid. Still, I argue that contemporary studies on the Ottoman Empire productively intersect with the postcolonial approach in three research areas: the exploration of the agency of imperial subjects; the deconstruction of the imperial center; and the articulation of bases of imperial domination other than the conventional European "rule of colonial difference" strictly predicated on race. I conclude with a call for an analysis of Ottoman postcoloniality in comparison to others such as the German, Austro-Hungarian, Russian, Persian, Chinese, Mughal, and Japanese that negotiated modernity in a similar manner with the explicit intent to generate knowledge not influenced by the Western European historical experience.

Due to the traditional postcolonial focus on the modern and the European, pre-modern and non-European empires have been much less studied. And the Ottoman Empire is one such empire: its temporal reign traversed the modern and pre-modern eras, and its geographical land mass covered parts of Eastern Europe, the Balkans, Asia Minor, the Arabian Peninsula, and North Africa. In this article, I approach the Ottoman Empire through the vantage point of postcolonial studies. I first place the three corollaries of postcolonial studies, namely the prioritization of contemporary inequality, the determination of its historical origins, and the target of its eventual elimination in conversation with the Ottoman Empire. I then discuss and articulate the two criticisms that ensue from taking a postcolonial sociological approach to the Ottoman Empire; these concern the role of Islam and the fluidity of identities in states and societies. I argue that epistemologically, postcolonial studies criticize the European representations of Islam, but do not take the next step of generating alternate knowledge by engaging in empirical studies of Islamic empires like the Ottoman Empire. Ontologically, postcolonial studies draw strict official and unofficial lines between the European colonizer and the non-European colonized, yet such a clear-cut divide does not hold in the case of the Ottoman Empire where the lines were much more nuanced and identities much more fluid. Still, I argue that contemporary studies on the Ottoman Empire productively intersect with the postcolonial approach in three research areas, namely, the exploration of the agency of imperial subjects;

the deconstruction of the imperial center; and the articulation of bases of imperial domination other than the conventional European "rule of colonial difference" strictly predicated on race. I conclude with a call for undertaking the postcolonial analysis of the Ottoman Empire in comparison to others such as the German, Austro-Hungarian, Russian, Persian, Chinese, Mughal, and Japanese that negotiated modernity in a similar manner; such a comparison, I contend, would generate knowledge not influenced by the Western European historical experience.

THREE COROLLARIES OF POSTCOLONIAL STUDIES AND THE OTTOMAN EMPIRE

Scholars who cannot often agree on the theoretical lineage of postcolonial studies nevertheless concur on how it is practiced. A postcolonial researcher takes an interdisciplinary approach to critically analyze the connection between power and knowledge, focuses primarily on the adverse impact of eighteenth- and nineteenth-century Western European transformation on the rest of the world, and employs often a cultural lens to destabilize the power-knowledge connection with the political intent to establish a more just and equitable world. As such, I think that the approach of the postcolonial scholar as well as those following in their footsteps reveal what can be termed "the three corollaries of postcolonial studies." These are specifically the following: (i) the prioritization of contemporary inequality: the research focus is on the intersection of power with knowledge that empowers the subject while enfeebling the object; (ii) the determination of its historical origins: the roots of such contemporary empowerment are often traced spatially to Western Europe, temporally to the seventeenth and eighteenth centuries, and culturally to the Enlightenment; and (iii) the elimination of contemporary inequality: the persisting empowerment needs to be eliminated in order to create a common humanity predicated on equality, justice, and world peace. The ensuing discussion of these three corollaries in relation to the Ottoman Empire provides three novel insights. First, the Ottoman Empire has been marginalized due to its demise during the rise of the West; second, the Ottoman Empire's temporal and spatial location traversing the Enlightenment period and the geographical boundaries of Europe provides the perfect vantage point from which to productively question the often unbearable weight of Western domination. And third, the empirical analysis of the Ottoman Empire would help promote the postcolonial vision of eliminating contemporary inequality by destabilizing the Western colonization of knowledge on the one side and the production of an alternate approach on the other.

Prioritization of Contemporary Inequality

The specific focus of postcolonial scholars in approaching contemporary inequality varies significantly. Some deconstruct the subject/scholar in order to destabilize its hegemony over power, others instead concentrate on the object/the studied with the intent to empower the silenced object (Nandy, 1983), while still others undertake both endeavors simultaneously (Magubane, 2004). What unites all postcolonial scholars is their subjectivity: all have either lived in or worked on more than one culture, or have been marginalized in one cultural context due to their religion, ethnicity, race, sexuality, or research topic. Their experiences therefore facilitate the acquisition of a certain critical reflexivity that in turn enables them to better identify, articulate, and analyze the relationship between power and knowledge.

Temporally, many focus on contemporary inequality, but eventually step back into history in tracing its origins to the early modern period and spatially to states and societies that do not starkly signal the connection of power to knowledge on the one side and to the critical analysis of variations within Western European Enlightenment on the other (Mehta, 1999; Muthu, 2003; Washbrook, 2009). As such, recent postcolonial analyses of the early modern Iberian empires of Spain and Portugal, Italian city-states, as well as contemporaneous settlements, colonies, and states in the Americas, Africa, and South-East Asia have all helped alleviate the epistemological stronghold especially Great Britain and India had over the field (Ballantyne, 2003; Pagden, 1995; Subrahmanyam, 2006).

Yet the analysis of the Ottoman Empire still remains in the margins of the field. In discussing the contemporaneous inequality embedded within the Empire, scholars often focus not on internal processes but instead on the empire's escalating interaction with the Western world. The temporal intersection of the loss of Ottoman imperial power with the rise of Western European empires turns into an explanation in and of itself, thereby escaping thorough empirical analysis. And the same faulty logic applies to the German, Austro-Hungarian, Persian, Mughal, Russian, Chinese, and Japanese empires and others that also "lost" during the escalating Western world domination. I would contend, however, that one needs to analyze such "marginalized" cases in order to recover the nature of their resistance to or negotiation with the West on the one side and the dynamics of the local processes independent of the West on the other.

Determination of the Historical Origins of Contemporary Inequality

The European Enlightenment privileged science, rationality, and progress to eventually establish and legitimate Western hegemony over the rest of the world. Such hegemony started to be critically examined initially in the aftermath of World War II, and in earnest at the end of the Cold War. Significant in this examination was the analysis of the intersection of power and knowledge in the construction and practice of the social sciences that came into being during the Enlightenment (Dubois, 2006; Eze, 1997; Linebaugh & Rediker, 2000; Muthu, 2003; Swanson, 2004). Such criticism also entailed a re-examination of the concept of difference through which the Enlightenment marginalized the rest of the world; the nature of the origins and use of the categories of race, ethnicity, tradition, and religion were re-assessed as a consequence (Dubois, 2005; Stoler, 1992). Yet, such an orientation had inherently privileged the eighteenth to the twentieth century temporally and the histories of Western European societies over the rest of humankind epistemologically; some scholars therefore questioned the application of the postcolonial framework to earlier centuries (Seidman, 2005). Others wondered if such an application did not end up reproducing the Western hegemony that postcolonial studies aimed to destabilize and deconstruct (Cooper, 2005b; Dirlik, 2002), or serving as a mere excuse to keep bashing the West (Bayart, 2011).

Spatially, some scholars analyzed the empowered, namely world empires and nation-states with imperial ambitions (Burton, 2003), while others focused on the enfeebled and the colonized (Nandy, 1983). It was in this context that the mission, content, and boundaries of postcolonial studies generated the most debate.[1] While some argued against connecting the disparate strands of postcolonial studies into a single entity lest it turned into a hegemonic tool (Dutton, Gandhi, & Seth, 1999), others defined it as "the academic, intellectual, ideological and ideational scaffolding of the condition of decolonization, [that is], the period following political independence for nations and cultures in Africa, Asia and South America (Nayar, 2010, p. 1)."[2] Such spatial orientation in turn dichotomously privileged past and present states and societies that either wielded visible power or were subjugated by such power. The imperial colonizing Western

European states (especially Great Britain and France) and the United States on the one side, and the colonized India and South America on the other emerged as the prominent political actors of postcolonial analysis.

Studying the Ottoman Empire would positively contribute to settling such debates over the temporal, spatial, and epistemological boundaries of postcolonial studies. The Ottoman Empire's temporal and spatial existence destabilizes the inherent privileging of Western hegemony. Temporally, the Ottoman Empire existed from the thirteenth to the twentieth century thereby covering the pre-Enlightenment, Enlightenment, and post-Enlightenment periods. Spatially, Ottoman rule extended from the Middle East to the Balkans and Eastern Europe in the West, to the Caucasus in the East, to the Crimea in the North and the Arabian Peninsula and North Africa in the South. Such temporal and spatial location thus provides the perfect counterpoint to productively question the often unbearable weight of Western domination in postcolonial studies.

Elimination of Contemporary Inequality

Postcolonial analysis has a political mission in that it endeavors to establish a future where all humans exist on equal terms, where everyone respects difference instead of employing and exploiting it with the intent to establish dominance over others. Hence, such an orientation ethically moves the liberation of all humankind to the forefront (Bayly, 2006; Hasseler & Krebs, 2003, p. 96). Yet, how to proceed in actualizing such a project remains unclear: should one first deconstruct the current Western hegemony or focus on constructing an entirely new approach instead from scratch, one not 'tainted' by the West?

Analyses of empires such as the Chinese, Japanese, Russian, and Ottoman ones that do not fully fit the standard object of postcolonial studies become significant in this context because they enable scholars to engage in both endeavors simultaneously. The non-Western context challenges the inherent Western hegemony over knowledge, and empirical research of local processes enables the construction of a novel approach (Brower & Lazzerini, 1997; Makdisi, 2002c). Of these two endeavors, however, the former is much easier to undertake. It is therefore not surprising that not many scholars have engaged in such activity in the context of postcolonial studies, let alone the Ottoman Empire. The most significant recent work in this context is Raewyn Connell's ambitious book entitled *Southern Theory* (2007).[3] After acknowledging the existing power of the global "Northern theory" constructed by the colonizing West, Connell turns to the colonized local south – specifically to Australia, Africa, Iran, India, and Latin America – with the intent to generate a "Southern theory" out of local texts negotiating Western colonization. Connell specifically attempts to overcome the Western colonization of knowledge by focusing on the works of southern scholars like Ali Shariati of the Middle East, Raul Prebisch of Latin America, Paulin Hountondji of Africa, and Ranajit Guha of India. Connell provides a productive start, yet one that needs to be built upon for decades if not centuries to come. Another significant venue for expanding the boundaries of knowledge beyond its Western colonization is advocated by Walter Mignolo (2009a, 2009b, 2010) who calls for "epistemic disobedience" to generate a de-colonial cosmopolitanism of multiple trajectories. Mignolo engages in such activities with the explicit intent to imagine and build democratic, just, and non-imperial/colonial societies.[4] As such, the empirical analysis of the Ottoman Empire could help challenge the Western colonization of knowledge on the one side and the construction of an alternate approach on the other, thereby promoting the postcolonial project of ultimately eliminating contemporary inequality.

Given the advantages of empirically analyzing the Ottoman Empire in order to advance the three corollaries of postcolonial studies, it is necessary to map out the framework of a postcolonial sociology of the Ottoman Empire. Drawing such a framework provides two insights: first, contemporary practices of postcolonial studies do not adequately take into account the role of religion or the fluidity of identities. Second, contemporary work of scholars in the field of Ottoman studies actually promotes a postcolonial approach in relation to exploring the agency of imperial subjects, deconstructing the hegemony of the imperial center, and articulating the ethnic, religious, and cultural bases of imperial domination and thereby destabilizing the conventional European "rule of colonial difference" strictly predicated on race.

TOWARD A POSTCOLONIAL SOCIOLOGY OF THE OTTOMAN EMPIRE

Like the Russian Empire, the Ottoman Empire was geographically contiguous but never fully a part of what was culturally considered to be the boundaries of Europe; the relations of either empire with the spatially adjacent regions they conquered were not easily definable as colonial. Like the Iberian empires of Spain and Portugal, the temporal span of the Ottoman Empire traversed both the early modern and modern eras, but unlike the former, it did not acquire overseas colonies at any time. What differentiated the Ottoman Empire from all empires of European origin and akin to the Mughal, Chinese, and Japanese empires was that Ottoman rule was predicated on a non-Christian religion, specifically – like the Mughal – on Islam. The Ottoman Empire ruled for more than 600 years (1299–1922) over significant parts of Eastern Europe, the Balkans, Asia Minor, the Arabian Peninsula, and North Africa only to fragment into a multiplicity of nation-states during the course of the twentieth and twenty-first centuries. As such, the Ottoman Empire presents an ideal case not only to test the Eurocentrism of existing sociological theory and practice, but also to provide additional insight into the parameters of postcolonial sociology.

Two Emerging Criticisms

Recent analyses of the Ottoman Empire focusing specifically on inequalities across time and space are much more widespread within the field of history than sociology. Temporally, they tend to gravitate toward two periods in Ottoman history, the early modern period up to the end of the seventeenth century, and the late modern period from the nineteenth to early twentieth century. Spatially, those working on the central Anatolian lands of the empire tend to naturalize the connection between power and knowledge while those concentrating on the peripheral provinces in the Balkans, Arabian Peninsula, and North Africa polarize the same connection instead. While the specific vantage point of scholars thus impacts the nature of their analysis, they do not yet critically reflect upon their particular interpretations. This limitation is further compounded by the scholars' subjectivities: younger generations of scholars are more willing to challenge and replace existing analyses at all costs, while older generations continue to practice history without at all taking the postcolonial approach into account. Still, I concur with Steven Seidman (2005) that the Ottoman Empire continues to provide a significant empirical context for the development of postcolonial studies.[5] The review of recent works on the Ottoman Empire generates two insightful criticisms of postcolonial studies that concern the role of Islam on the one side and the fluidity of imperial identities on the other.

The Role of Islam

The most significant dimension that emerges in the scholarly discussion of any non-Western empire is inadvertently that of difference, that centers around not race, but culture in general and religion in particular. In the case of Islam, this emphasis on religion is often approached critically due to Edward Said's influential works on the Orientalism (1978) and cultural imperialism of Europe (1993). Utilizing Foucault's insight into the colonization of knowledge, Said articulated the manner in which Europe epistemologically colonized the Middle East by defining the parameters of local meaning production (Englund, 2008). Scholars did indeed initially start to address this criticism in their research, only to be sidelined by two recent events that once again typecast Islam. The first event in 1989 comprised Ayatollah Khomeini's issuance of a religious edict calling for the death of novelist Salman Rushdie for the latter's discussion of the prophet Muhammad in his novel *The Satanic Verses* (1988). This religious attack on a work of fiction combined with the unexpected success of the Iranian Revolution led to the regeneration of a predominantly anti-Islamic discourse in the West for infringing on an author's freedom of expression and thought. And the second event took place about a decade later in 2001 when the Twin Towers in New York and parts of the Pentagon were destroyed by a terrorist attack allegedly carried out in the name of Islam. These negative depictions of Islam were further fueled by a third event, namely the cartoon controversy in 2005 when a Danish newspaper printed editorial cartoons on the prophet Muhammad that led to protests by Muslim communities throughout the world.

The ensuing postcolonial criticisms of Rushdie and the fervent reaction of Muslim communities drew attention to political visions that were embedded not only in Islam, but also in the postcolonial rhetoric (Bilgrami, 1990; Brennan, 1992). Even though many postcolonial scholars agreed that cultural hegemonies inherent in religions needed to be destabilized for the liberation of all humanity, it became evident that how this was going to be actualized in the case of Islam was much more ambiguous. Since Islam had not been reformed and secularized like Christianity, the question posed in Western media was whether Islam should go through a similar secularization and, if so, under whose leadership. Posing the question in this manner once again highlighted the existing power inequality between countries with significant Christian and Muslim populations, where the former especially dominated the latter culturally. The scholarly discussion in the West then turned onto the divides within this initially monolithic representation of Islam, highlighting the divide between the reformist and fundamentalist interpretations (Benedict et al., 2007; Dubois, 2005; Erickson, 1998; Majid, 2000). While the moderate forces within Islam were not as well organized or as prone to engage in violent action as the fundamentalist ones, the Western coverage of Islam nevertheless continued to highlight Islamic fundamentalism at the expense of Islamic reformism. The discussion of religion, specifically Islam, thus intersected not only with power, but also knowledge. Soon Western discourse moved to temporally and spatially contextualize Islam as an ideology.

The initial attempt spearheaded by Shmuel Eisenstadt (2003) and Said Arjomand (2011) to comparatively depict Islam as an "axial civilization," and the local changes within the civilization as instances of "multiple modernity" did indeed bring the Islamic world into sociological analysis, but did so under terms that were once again inherently set by the Western European experience of modernity. This traditional sociological approach has been recently challenged by the works of two postcolonial scholars, Walter Mignolo and Madina Tlostanova (Mignolo, 2006; Mignolo & Tlostanova, 2006; Tlostanova, 2006, 2007, 2008, 2011). They approach Islam from the South American (Mignolo) and Russian periphery (Tlostanova), highlighting the racial "other"ing that Islam as a religion and Muslims as believers had been subjected to as a consequence of the historical development and ensuing hegemony of the West since the Renaissance. The initial marginalization of Islam by Christian theology during the Renaissance, Mignolo argues, was reactivated and maintained by secular philosophy during and after the Enlightenment. Racially, especially the emergence and sustenance of the Black Legend by Great Britain excluded the Muslims, Jews, and the Russian Orthodox as well as the Spanish, Portuguese, and Africans as impure. In the ensuing centuries, this exclusion then legitimated the violence of capitalism and imperialism upon these "impure" peoples (Mignolo, 2006).[6] The ensuing epistemic privilege of five countries – France, England, Germany, Italy, and the United States – in defining social theory normalized this inherent exclusion up to the present (Grosfoguel, 2010). As such, knowledge from the borders was inscribed by the three imperial languages of French, German, and English of the second Western modernity,[7] making non-Western knowledge totally irrelevant to the social sciences except as an object of study. Hence in approaching Islam, postcolonial scholars first demonstrate how it had been "other"ed by the West through the centuries. Since such "other"ing of Islam provided insights into the production and reproduction of Western hegemony, the same scholars then started to focus on specific empirical contexts that had been able to withstand and often successfully negotiate Western hegemony.

It is in this context that postcolonial scholars turn to a detailed analysis of the Russian and Ottoman Empires[8] in particular. Mignolo and Tlostanova depict these two empires as "subaltern, Janus-faced, empire-colonies" that were juxtaposed between the dominant Western capitalist empires on the one side and their own colonies on the other. The Russian and Ottoman empires were infected with "secondary Eurocentrism" and with the double consciousness such Eurocentrism induced. This unique synthesis made it ontologically and empirically difficult to conceptualize them within the dominant Western hegemonic discourse. Mignolo and Tlostanova interpret this inherent difficulty with optimism, however, arguing that further postcolonial analysis of such thinking from the "borders of Europe" may generate an alternate to northern theory. Madina Tolstanova specifically locates the Caucasus within the Russian/Soviet ex-colony; by doing so, she is able to develop the parameters of border thinking not only from the periphery in Baku, but also from the standpoint of Islam (Tlostanova, 2006, 2007, 2008, 2011). Tlostanova posits the in-betweenness of the Russian and Ottoman empires with Europe and Asia on the one side and Western modernity and Islam on the other. These empires were indirectly colonized by Western modernity in multiple – epistemic, political, and economic – ways. And the power relations they developed with their subjects were unlike those Western European empires: the colonizers and the colonized had a much more equal relationship in that they were not fully overpowered by the modernized colonizer.[9]

Such postcolonial analyses of Islam and the Russian and Ottoman empires do indeed highlight and nuance the past and present inequalities in the world. Yet they fail to address criticisms especially regarding their employment of history in their analyses (Cooper, 2005a, 2005b). Frederick Cooper states that postcolonial scholars doubly occlude history: they iron out differences within European history while articulating such differences in the histories of those colonized by Europe. He notes in particular that postcolonial scholars "pluck stories" that fit their argument without taking into account the larger historical context, "leapfrog legacies" to build causal arguments without fully articulating the historical process of colonization, and "flatten time" by treating European history only in terms of the negative dimensions of the Enlightenment, thereby not analyzing Europe within its own historical complexity.[10] Perhaps the one postcolonial scholar that attempts to alleviate this criticism is sociologist Syed Hussain Farid Alatas (1981, 2007). Alatas draws on the works of Ibn Khaldun (1332–1406) to generate an alternate historical sociology of Muslim societies, a sociology that does not focus, like Eurocentric analyses do, on what does not work, but instead employs Khaldun's locally generated sociological tools to survey what actually transpires on the ground. Even though Alatas is thus able to demonstrate the inadequacy of Eurocentric analyses, he still has not fully developed an alternate explanation of how Muslim societies form and transform throughout history. Still, the insights relating to the role of Islam in states and societies lead one to query the role religion played in the Western world: specifically, how did variations in the practice of Christianity structure states and societies across time and place?

In all, then, focusing on the role of Islam in shaping states and societies did initially enable postcolonial scholars to criticize the Eurocentrism of existing theories. Yet, the same scholars have not yet been able to fully formulate an alternate approach because they have not yet adequately approached either Muslim empires or the Western empires that eventually dominated them empirically within their own historical complexity. So the first step in developing such an alternate approach is to analyze non-Christian empires in general and Islamic empires in particular through their own archives and processes of local knowledge production such as songs, poetry, literature, and oral traditions.

The Fluidity of Imperial Identities
Postcolonial studies distinctly separate the early modern and modern periods in terms of the emergence of a clear racial difference between the Western colonizer and the non-Western colonized. Such a depiction highlights the modern emergence of inequality with very broad brush-strokes, overlooking in the process those empires that fell in-between for long stretches of time, ones that were neither the colonizer nor the colonized as experienced in Western European history. The Ottoman Empire is one such case in point. Scholars of the Ottoman Empire carefully distinguish the "early modern period" that approximately covers the time span from the successful siege of Constantinople in 1453 to the unsuccessful siege of Vienna in 1683, from the "transition" period encompassing 1683 to the 1839 end of the reign of the reformist sultan Mahmud II, and the "modern" period from 1839 to the dissolution of the empire in 1922. Their analyses reveal that the Ottoman imperial identity remained much more fluid throughout and was often premised on categories like ethnicity, religion, and tribal affiliation.

The intersection of religion, politics, and knowledge emerge as the central focus of scholars focusing on the early modern period (Baer, Makdisi, & Shryock, 2009; Barkey, 2005; Doumanis, 2006; Ginio, 2004; Grillo, 1998; Kunt, 1974, 2003). Two Ottoman institutions are highlighted in the analyses:

devşirme, that is the levy of mostly Christian children of the subjects as the sultan's slaves, and *millet*, that is the corporate communal organization of mostly Christian subjects within the empire. Metin Kunt demonstrates that even though such a levy was executed with the intent to produce officials loyal to the sultan, the slaves often remembered and retain their ethnic, regional origin, native languages, and customs; they also remained in contact with other members of their biological families. Eventually, two prominent factions of solidarity developed among the Ottoman administrative elites, those of the Balkan origin on the one side and the Caucasian origin on the other. Still, their loyalty to the sultan preceded all other forms of social identity. The communal organizations of non-Muslim subjects of the empire were also loosely defined, enabling all subjects regardless of religion to interact with each other on a daily basis. Marc Baer, Karen Barkey, R.D. Grillo, and Nicholas Doumanis all highlight this social accommodation and tolerance between religion and politics, principles that were not at all present in the contemporaneous European imperial counterparts.[11] Such fluidity in identity and flexibility in social boundaries contrasts with the previous Eurocentric binary, the strict postcolonial power divide between the rulers and the ruled. It leads one to surmise that the rigid, invariable, and inviolable Western European depictions probably varied across time and place as well, and often did not distinguish rhetoric from praxis.

This fluidity of identity is indeed the major contribution of scholars employing a critical, if not a postcolonial, approach to the early modern period (Baer, 2008; Dursteler, 2006; Elouafi, 2010; Hathaway, 2003; Philliou, 2011). At the imperial capital during the seventeenth century, Marc David Baer (2008, p. 31) argues that Christians, Jews, and Muslims "interacted on a daily basis, in the tavern, on the street, during public festivals and imperial celebrations, in the Shariah court and other institutions." Likewise, Eric Dursteler (2006, p. 20) studying the Venetians in Constantinople takes a stand against the Orientalist stand of a binary, oppositional, and conflictual relationship between Muslims and Christians, arguing instead that early modern identity was "multilayered, multivalent and composite." Identity construction entailed a socially constructed, contingent, and relational process where even the political and religious identity boundaries of non-Muslims residing at the imperial often shifted depending on the pressures of the particular local context. Even though the idea of a nation existed, it was "notoriously imprecise," referring to "people born in the same city or region" (2006, p. 13); as such, the primary identity among the communities of merchants and diplomats living in the Ottoman Empire was regional, spatial, and geographical. Christine Philliou (2011,

p. xix) reiterates the same argument for the eighteenth century in the context of the Ottoman Balkans, stating that "family and patronage relationships helped forge projects across formal institutions and confessional divides."

Such was the case in Ottoman North Africa as well. In studying Tunisia, Amy Aisen Elouafi (2010) notes that a combination of factors including "religion, ethno-national origin, trade or descent from a prominent family" determined elite status; African slaves were a visible component of elite society as they were incorporated into the households of the wealthy. Race and rank comprised the two components of social identity alongside kinship, occupation, and religion; as such, these differences were recognized, but not politicized. They eventually transformed into a binary relationship under European occupation. In analyzing Ottoman Egypt and Yemen, Jane Hathaway (2003, p. 5) concurs that households, that is conglomerations of patron–client ties under one person in charge, provided the main political organization in these contexts; a broad range of people of various ethnic, geographical, and occupational backgrounds including "Balkan and Anatolian mercenaries, Circassian and Georgian slaves, Bedouin or Turcoman tribesmen, peasants and artisans" coexisted within the political culture of the household where the primary factional alliance provided all household members with an overarching identity. Such depictions of fluidity of identity in early modern Ottoman Empire successfully challenge the Eurocentric, Orientalist formulations that instead reified differences and divides, anachronically mapping onto the empire binarisms introduced much later by European colonial rule.[12]

This epistemological reformulation of early modern Ottoman Empire is also accompanied by a spatial one whereby the empire is not solely analyzed in relation to its connection to Europe, but instead located within the global world, especially including its connections with the Islamic world and Asia through trade and conquest. Linda Darling (1998) challenges the conception of the Ottoman Empire as stagnant and declining, revealing that such terms of difference only became universalized during the age of imperialism with the spread of Western hegemony. It was not the decay of the east in general and the Ottoman, Mughal, and Safavid empires in particular that allowed the European to emerge into global predominance, Darling contends, but instead the development of capitalism through political violence and economic exploitation of the rest of the world. Andrew C. Hess (1970), Affan Seljuq (1980), Abbas Hamdani (1981), Thomas D. Goodrich (1987), and Salih Özbaran (1990) restore the agency of the Ottoman Empire during the early modern era by articulating the empire's extensive trade and political relations with the Orient in general and the Malay-Indonesian

Archipelago in particular. They point out the communication of the Ottoman sultan with the Portuguese king in an attempt to stay active not only in the western Mediterranean and the Indian Ocean, but also to contend for a while in the discovery of the New World. On their maps, the Ottoman officials clearly marked the New World as their administrative province of "Antilia." The Sa'dian regime of Morocco prevented Ottoman access to the Atlantic Ocean, however, and the Ottoman engagement in wars on the European continent thwarted the Ottoman activities against the Portuguese on the Indian Ocean. As a consequence, the Ottoman Empire remained contained within its contiguous territories. This early modern Ottoman narrative recounts the age of discovery not solely from the hegemonic vantage point of Europe, but highlights and brings in the activities of non-Western empires on their own terms, thereby relativizing and provincializing the Western narrative.

In terms of the "transition" period encompassing 1683 to the 1839 end of the reign of the reformist sultan Mahmud II, scholars often debate the nature of the transformation the Ottoman Empire started to undergo mostly in reaction to the rise of Western military and economic pressure. The majority interpret the military, fiscal, and administrative reforms in and of themselves, rather than as harbingers of an inevitable decline. By doing so, they have once again taken the first step in successfully challenging the act of reading history back from the present through a unilinear, predetermined trajectory of decline. Yet the development of a more contextually careful narrative still need to work on the differentiation of form from content: during this time period, even though the Ottoman state and society increasingly appear Westernized in form, how much this change in form also translated to the transformation of content remains unclear. Hence, the issue of how similar and different Ottoman imperial practices were from their Western European counterparts brings back the Saidian anxiety regarding the use of Western categories to explain the rest of the world. In this context, Salzmann and Tracy provide significant nuanced insights. Ariel Salzmann (1993) notes specifically that the modern Ottoman state structure was ushered in the early nineteenth century through two practices, fiscal privatization and administrative decentralization. James Tracy (1994) points out that Mughal and Ottoman trade continued strong during the eighteenth century, thereby putting to rest the previous argument that European powers came to dominate regional commerce right away.

The process of Ottoman imperial change during this transition period is now being carefully analyzed in its own terms, without falling into the historical determinism of escalating Western European hegemony and

ensuing inevitable Ottoman decline. Virginia Aksan reflects on this process
the most (2005/2006, 2007, 2008); she demonstrates that Ottoman fiscal and
military reform impoverished state control over the path of change and
polarized society along religious lines. Gradually, the sense of belonging to
the empire by sharing in its resources became increasingly constricted to
Sunni Muslims – and later to ethnic Turks; this constriction was most
evident in the composition of the reformed military. Reforming the empire
along Western European lines thus started to adversely impact the fluidity of
Ottoman imperial identity. It is therefore no accident that Ussama Makdisi
(2000) discusses the significance of sectarianism in eighteenth century
Lebanon since this period did indeed mark the polarization of boundaries
across communal groups of the empire. Such boundaries had been closely
monitored by the Ottoman state through the legal system and by the
communal leaders who monitored daily practice. Yet as social groups
started to increasingly fight over the distribution of resources, state and
communal leaders could no longer contain the escalating violence. In the
process, the social actors of modernity multiplied, with the actors ranging
from Ottoman reformists officials, to non-Muslims and foreigners engaged
in trade, to missionaries introducing their particular vision through the
schools they founded (Makdisi, 1997, 2002b).

In all then, during the transition period, Ottoman state reforms undertaken after the Western European practices and institutions adversely
impacted the fluidity of Ottoman identity. Initially, many imperial subjects
located in the Ottoman social structure had belonged to intersecting
communities with varying degrees of clout making their identities fluid.
With the Westernizing reforms, identities became more solid and stratified,
introducing publicly visible inequality and enmity among social groups. This
Ottoman analysis generates a novel insight: How can one narrate the
Western European transformation through the vantage point of fluid
identities? Specifically, was there a process through which identities became
solidified in a similar manner or had they been differently constructed all
along?

INTERSECTIONS OF OTTOMAN STUDIES AND
POSTCOLONIAL ANALYSIS: THE MODERN PERIOD

Scholarly work on the Ottoman Empire during its "modern" period from
the end of the reign of the reformist sultan Mahmud II in 1839 to the

dissolution of the empire in 1922 has been most influenced by postcolonial analysis because of the temporal intersection of European and Ottoman modernities. In this context, the debate among scholars once again revolves around interpreting the nature and degree of separation of form from content: adopting Western practices brings the Ottoman Empire much closer to its European counterparts *in form*, thereby enabling many scholars to identify similarities to European colonial rule. Yet the spatial and temporal boundaries of this impact *in content* remain understudied and unclear. How practices predating Westernized ones may have stayed in play in spite of the adoption of new forms needs to be further studied in depth. Still, many scholars of the Ottoman Empire have started to converse with postcolonial studies, bringing the analysis of power inequality to front stage. The predominant scholarly focus on Ottoman formal political power certainly highlights escalating power inequalities within the Ottoman Empire. Once again, however, how these inequalities exist across time and space, that is, how they are negotiated by different imperial communities like the non-Muslims, Kurdish tribes or Chechen, and Circassian immigrants, and how this negotiation differs during the autocratic rule of sultan Abdülhamid II as opposed to the ensuing proto-nationalist rule of the Young Turks are not yet apparent.

The discussion of late Ottoman history in the context of the postcolonial debate has to commence with the scholarly intervention of Selim Deringil (2003). In a seminal article, Deringil argued that during the course of the nineteenth century, the Ottoman administrative elite gradually adopted the mindset of Western imperialism in interpreting their periphery, thereby inadvertently conflating the Western ideas of modernity and colonialism. This "borrowed colonialism" led Ottoman officials to depict the provincial subjects as living in "a state of nomadism and savagery." After identifying the tension within Ottoman modernity through such "borrowed" scale of difference, Deringil extends this argument to the Ottoman state's treatment of nomads in general and those in Tripoli, Hijaz, and Yemen in particular. His intervention builds upon Ussama Makdisi's introduction (2002a, p. 768) of the concept of Ottoman Orientalism, that is, the emergent Ottoman mode of administration of its own Arab periphery "based on a hierarchical system of subordination along religious, class, and ethnic lines." Through the works of Makdisi and Deringil, the postcolonial approach to the late Ottoman Empire thus starts to become articulated.

Most of the recent work employing the postcolonial approach literally focuses on the Ottoman Empire's last three decades from the 1880s to the 1910s. This was the period of rapid land contraction during which the empire literally lost 95% of its land mass (Paker, 2007, pp. 137–140). Given this extremely high rate of social change, it is no accident that identities became increasingly polarized internally and power inequalities in the empire escalated as a consequence. Postcolonial scholars approach this polarization in a manner that constructively overcomes the traditional emphasis on the naturalized power of the imperial center at the expense of the periphery, and on the political rhetoric of the Ottoman state instead of local empirical realities on the ground. They do so through conducting in-depth empirical analyses of especially the periphery with the intent to reveal how imperial power was negotiated across the center-periphery divide. As such, they not only reveal that power binarism did not exist in the Ottoman Empire in a manner similar to Europe, but that people at the periphery had much more agency than previously thought. Yet I would argue that the causal leap postcolonial scholars make from such polarized identities to escalating power inequalities needs to be further questioned. It is still unclear as to whether this renegotiation of power was due to the impact of Ottoman modernity espousing to adopt and apply a Western mode of imperial administration, or the simply empirical consequence of a rapidly shrinking empire, one that would have occurred regardless of the onset of modernity. Nevertheless, postcolonial scholars working on the Ottoman Empire have generated three significant insights in the analysis of inequality in Ottoman history regarding the agency of imperial subjects, the hegemony of the imperial center, and the alternate bases of imperial domination.

Exploring the Agency of Imperial Subjects

Scholars who focus on Ottoman modernity trace its particular character-istics through the travel accounts and memoirs of the officials of Turkish descent serving solely in the Arab and North African provinces. Their studies reveal an increasing divide between the educated, "civilized" officials of the imperial center who attempt to study, discipline, and improve the "colonial" subjects in the periphery (Herzog & Motika, 2000; Provence, 2011). Scholars analyzing the Ottoman provinces of the Transjordan (Carroll, 2011), Yemen (Kühn, 2007), Algeria (Shuval, 2000), and the Balkans (Spiridon, 2006) also empirically substantiate this new polarization between the Ottoman-Turkish officials and their colonial subjects.[13] All agree that the Ottoman "colonial" relationship was much more nuanced than its Western European counterpart: the local was not summarily "other"ed, denigrated, and exploited; instead, it retained its agency and negotiated relations with the Ottoman capital, Western Europeans, and their local counterparts. Yet these postcolonial scholars naturally assume that the origin of this increased inequality was embedded in Ottoman modernity. None critically analyze and deconstruct the imperial center, especially in terms of contextualizing who these Ottoman officials appointed to the provinces were, and how, where, and why they adopted their colonial attitudes. Also lacking are comparative studies of Ottoman officials adopting a colonial attitude with those serving the empire in less peripheral parts of the empire or in capacities other than as governors. After all, the Ottoman "colonial" attitude toward the nomads or ethnic Arabs may be similar to or different from the officials' attitudes toward the Greek Rum, Assyrian, Armenian, and Jewish minorities, Alewites, Kurds, and Circassians of the empire; the nature of this possible difference needs to be analyzed in depth.

A truly postcolonial sociology of the Ottoman Empire needs to apply the critical analysis of the intersection of power and knowledge not only to purposely selected imperial social groups like nomads and Arabs, or deliberately selected imperial provinces such as some in North Africa and the Arabian Peninsula. Transformations in social relations in the currently excluded Caucasus, Anatolia, and the Balkans and among the various officials serving in different capacities at these imperial spaces need to be undertaken as well. Temporally, such transformations in power relations also have to be systematically compared to periods predating the last 30 years of the empire. Only after such spatial, temporal, and epistemological comparisons could postcolonial scholars of the Ottoman Empire conclude that what they observe is indeed a new colonial relationship between the Ottoman imperial center and its peripheries. After all, empires contain within them a spectrum of power relationships predicated on the type of formal political rule, where the imperial attitude toward a chieftainship or an emirate is often primarily shaped by historical legacy that widely differs from a province close to the imperial center. Postcolonial scholarship indeed explains the polarizing changes in some types of Ottoman formal political rule in some empirical contexts, but I do not think such explanations are not yet generalizable to the Ottoman Empire as a whole.

In particular, existing postcolonial analyses of late Ottoman imperial rule have generated an epistemological divide predicated on whether such scholars focus primarily on the subject (the colonizer state) or object (the colonized locals) of their analysis. Makdisi, for instance, prioritizes the imposition of a new reformist Ottoman state ideology in the provinces, thereby privileging the subject. He then argues that this central imperial ideology and practice in generated unequal local relations. Jens Hannsen (2002, 2005) instead focuses on the object; he privileges local relations, recovering the agency of provincial Ottoman subjects in successfully negotiating their relations with the center. In his explanation, it is unequal local relations that impact and fragment the imperial center. Whether the scholar focuses on the subject of the colonizing Ottoman state or the object of the colonized populace makes a difference in the ensuing interpretation: Makdisi traces the postcolonial origins of inequality to the imperial center while Hannsen challenges the same inequality by articulating the power located in the periphery. And it seems that the latter group of scholars is gaining the upper hand in recent academic work. Indeed, Isa Blumi (1998, 2002, 2003a, 2003b, 2011)[14] working on Yemen and Albania, and Beshara Doumani (1992) analyzing Palestine history actually employ the complexity of relations during the Ottoman era to destabilize existing dominant, naturalized, Eurocentric nationalist narratives. In doing so, they restore the power and agency of local actors, but fail to critically reflect on the two other sources of power: first, the power located at the imperial center, and second, the power embedded in the particular standpoint and ensuing empirical focus of the postcolonial scholar. While those scholars like Makdisi and Deringil gazing through the lens of the Ottoman imperial center observe and highlight the unequal relationship between the Ottoman capital and the provinces, others like Hannsen and Blumi who adopt the lens of specific provinces instead tease out the process of negotiation between the imperial capital and the province where local subjects retain their agency. In all, then, exploring the agency of the Ottoman imperial subjects articulates the significance in postcolonial studies of time, place, and meaning in interpreting existing power relations.

Deconstructing the Hegemony of the Imperial Center

It is next important to discuss the works of a group of scholars that has recently started to deconstruct the lens of the Ottoman imperial center (Constantinou, 2000; Gölbaşı, 2009, 2011; Riedler, 2011; Turan, 2009). Costas Constantinou initially focuses on the colonization of the Western European diplomatic imagination at the Ottoman imperial capital, demonstrating how such diplomats viewed and imposed binary interpretations onto the complex process of Ottoman administrative rule.[15] Building upon this initial critical insight, Ömer Turan ingeniously inverts the subject and the object by focusing instead on how the significant Ottoman thinker and statesman Ahmed Rıza criticized the Western civilizational project from the vantage point of its lack of universal morality. Edip Gölbaşı instead approaches possible Ottoman coloniality from the imperial capital institutionally through the practice of military conscription; he reveals that local conditions dictated the Ottoman administrative decision-making as impeiral officials often excluded certain communities like the Yezidis from being conscripted. Florian Riedler further challenges the uniformity of the Ottoman decision-making process at the imperial center by analyzing emergent forms of political opposition in general and conspiracies in particular. He argues that many conspiracies developed in cases where there initially was no space for a loyal opposition, thereby once more articulating the complexity of the imperial decision-making process. Hence, these scholars challenge the conceptual boundaries of late Ottoman coloniality from the vantage point of the center where such decisions were made.

In addition to contesting the hegemony of the imperial center through the analyses of particular officials and institutional practices, scholars of late Ottoman history have also started to question the nature of the impact of the Westernizing reforms. After all, while there has been agreement in the field that there has certainly been a transformation in the empire that could be labeled Ottoman modernity in form, debates continue over the exact content as well as the extent of the transformation. And it is in this context that some scholars have recently started to develop a novel approach to study the Ottoman Empire, one that prioritizes not individuals or institutions, but instead particular sites of modernity. Such sites not only challenge the hegemony of the imperial center, but also identify their often dialectical impact upon Ottoman imperial domination.

Articulating Alternate Bases of Imperial Domination

Scholars working on the Ottoman Empire (Aral, 2004; Bektaş, 2000; Brummett, 2007; Hanssen, 2011) through the standpoint of sites of modernity are able to move beyond the limitations of time and space to capture their impact on Ottoman imperial power. So far, they have employed three cultural sites, namely technology transfer, gender relations, and human rights to reveal how the negotiation of these sites within Ottoman state and society produced complex power transformations. Yakup Bektaş analyzes the 1857–1864 construction of the Istanbul-Fao overland telegraph line that traversed the full length of the Ottoman domains in Asia, thereby uniting

Britain with India. Such technological modernity both empowered, but also eventually weakened Ottoman imperial rule. The sultans initially utilized the advantage of electric communication to consolidate their control over the empire, but eventually sultan Abdülhamid II was removed from power when the Young Turks in opposition employed the same communication channel to actualize their 1908 constitutional revolution. Focusing on the rearticulation of Ottoman gender roles and relations in cartoon space from 1876 to 1914, Palmira Brummett argues that women emerged as new, yet contradictory symbols during this time period: they embodied the empire or its pieces, but were also purposefully left at home. Such experienced contradictions of Ottoman modernity enabled the empire to articulate its exceptionalism vis-a-vis Western Europe, emphasizing four differentiating characteristics, namely its multiethnic, polyglot nature; a long history of cultural achievement; morality (especially female); and Islam. Hence, Ottoman modernity forced state and society to enunciate what made their imperial rule different from their Western European counterparts, thereby emphasizing disparities instead of similarities.

Berdal Aral moves beyond the binarism inherent in modernity in relation to comparing the West with the rest. He analyzes the idea of human rights not in terms of how it was conceived in the West to be then exported to the rest, but instead on how it evolved in the Ottoman Empire on the latter's own terms. The empire employed religious law to ascertain and protect the rights of all subjects, prioritized the benefits of collectivities rather than those of individuals, and emphasized justice rather than freedom. In addition, it did not initially seek to control the "public sphere" unless politics set in, as it did after mid-nineteenth century. Hence, Aral demonstrates that the Ottoman negotiation of human rights singled out particular concepts and practices at different junctures. Finally, in his most recent work, Jens Hanssen takes a different epistemological route by tracing the Ottoman transimperial networks that start to form with the advent of modernity. He studies the rise and fall of the Levantine Malhame family at the Ottoman imperial court by focusing on transimperial networks among Levantine society, late Ottoman bureaucracy, European diplomacy, and capitalist expansion. Through his focus on such networks, Hanssen approaches late Ottoman imperial actors on equal terms with other local and transimperial ones. In all then, studying specific cultural sites of modernity challenges the hegemony of the Ottoman imperial center by demonstrating how such sites both enhanced and undermined imperial power. And it also provides for a new venue through which to introduce Western European empires to the non-Western context, not as monist hegemons but instead as actors that slip in through local contradictions and crises.

CONCLUSION

This extensive review of the intersections of Ottoman studies with postcolonial analysis points to the significance of the initial point of origin of the research: those scholars focusing on the imperial center interpret escalating power inequality within the empire differently than those approaching the empire from the periphery. Also significant is the unit of analysis of the research: scholars often move beyond the contours of formal structural analysis to concentrate on particular individuals, institutions, as well as cultural sites such as informal social networks, human rights, or telegraph technology. In mapping out the possible future direction of the postcolonial studies of the Ottoman Empire, I would propose focusing on social practices rather than the actions of specific social actors located at either the imperial center or the periphery. Such focus has three distinct advantages: it enables scholars to concentrate on the historical process where all actors negotiate with each other on equal terms; it eliminates the epistemological divide privileging either the subject or the object of analysis, and it restores the agency of all parties without prioritizing the standpoint of one over the others.

Such future scholarly emphasis on Ottoman social networks and social practices needs to also incorporate a comparative perspective placing Ottoman imperial history in conversation with other imperial practices. Exemplary is Sanjay Subrahmanyam's (1997, 2005, 2006a, 2006b) con-textualization of the early modern Ottoman Empire through his framework of "connected histories" where he specifically compares the Mughal, Ottoman, and Habsburg Empires[16] with the intent to differentiate the imperial encounters from colonial ones. Even though all three empires covered vast, mostly contiguous territory, Subrahmanyam argues, none has been written into the history of modernity. That history privileged the British, Dutch, and French empires, duly dismissing the Mughal, Ottoman, and the Habsburg as "declining" empires.[17] When he analyzes the latter three empires in detail, however, it becomes evident that the Habsburg Empire, based on the dual principles of settlement and economic exploitation, was the only one that was explicitly colonial from its inception. The Mughal and Ottoman empires instead controlled contiguous territories through compromise and administrative and ideological flexibility, often maintaining the local practices of the newly incorporated territories. These two empires also did not systematically exploit and draw in resources from the outlying territories, attempt to culturally homogenize them or employ race as a cultural marker legitimating exploitation like the Habsburg Empire did; as such, they were not colonial empires. Their systematic exclusion from the history of modernity, Subrahmanyam states, silenced the global and conjunctural nature of modernity, instead giving full agency to Europe as the *sole* producer and exporter of modernity to the world at large. Such a return to the sixteenth century reveals that history was not then and still is not – and ought not be – the monopoly of the single cultural tradition of Europe.

This conception of connected histories has recently inspired many scholars to engage in theoretical and empirical comparisons of the Ottoman Empire during the modern period (Emrence, 2008; Jacoby, 2008; Khoury & Kennedy, 2007; Rogan, 1999). Dina Khoury and Dane Kennedy bring the Ottoman and British Indian empires to the same analytical space, articulating the similarities and differences between the two in relation to the global and internal crises in the nineteenth century in general and the conjunctures of global war (1780–1830), centralization (1835–1775), militant control (1875–1895), and war and nationalism (1905–1916) in particular. Tim Jacoby instead enters into a dialogue with Michael Mann's taxonomy of imperial rule predicated on compulsory cooperation,[18] arguing that the taxonomy privileging Western European empires does not fully hold in the Ottoman case. The Ottoman Empire did not only develop a more benign relationship with its peripheries, but also adopted many local practices in doing so. Cem Emrence adopts a trajectory-specific approach that further articulates the Ottoman imperial structure. During the nineteenth century, the Ottoman coast, interior and frontier, emerged spatially as distinct imperial paths with varying economic, political, and social orders. Emrence thus nuances the existing postcolonial perspective that does not properly take into account the variations of rule in the Ottoman provinces. Eugene Rogan's work further differentiates the nature of Ottoman rule in East Anatolia (Kurdistan), the Transjordan, the Hijaz, Yemen, and Libya, arguing that each region displayed different modes of incorporation into the Ottoman state. Focusing on the Ottoman Transjordan in particular, he then argues that this particular province comprised an Ottoman "frontier," specifically a contact zone between the Ottoman state and tribal society. In general then, such studies point to similarities and differences not only among, but also within empires and do so in a manner that treats each one on equal terms.

I end this article with a call for the comparative analysis of the Ottoman Empire in relation to all those empires that negotiate and adopt elements of Western modernity only to pass them onto their provinces. The German, Austro-Hungarian, Russian, Persian, Chinese, Mughal, and Japanese empires all fall into this category for instance. Yet, to my knowledge, there have not yet been any sustained workshops or conferences that specifically place the scholars working on these empires in conversation with each other. Such imperial comparisons would undoubtedly highlight similarities and differences not only in how these empires negotiated modernity, but also how such negotiations impacted their subject populations. And in doing so, they would generate knowledge that is not overshadowed by the Western European historical experience.

NOTES

1. For the most recent debate in the context of postcolonialism in France, see *Public Culture* 23(1) (2011), especially the criticisms of scholars calling French scholars to acknowledge their colonial heritage and its violence on the one side (Baneth-Nouailhetas, 2011; Bertaux, 2011; Gandhi, 2011; Lazreg, 2011; Mbembe, 2011; Stoler, 2011; Young, 2011) and those resisting such acknowledgement on the other (Bayart, 2011).

2. Nayar (2010, pp. 1–4) also defines *colonialism* as "the process of [actual] settlement by Europeans in Asian, African, South American, Canadian and Australian spaces ... entailing an exploitative political or economic process as well as a cultural conquest of the native," *colonial discourse* as "the construction in European narratives of the native usually in stereotypical ways ... upon which Europeans perceive, judge and act upon the non-European," *imperialism* as "the [Western] ideology legitimating remote governance and control of Asian or African [or other] nations, often entailing economic, political, military domination and exploitation ... without actual settlement in the non-European spaces," *neocolonialism* as "the actual practice of imperialism," *postcoloniality* as "the historical and material conditions of formerly colonized Asian, African and South American nations," and *decolonization* "as the process whereby non-white nations and ethnic groups in Asia, Africa and South America strive to secure economic, political and intellectual freedom from their European masters." Osterhammel (1997, pp. 4, 29–38) likewise defines *colonialism* as "a system of domination established by a society that expands beyond its original habitat" to then further articulate six colonial epochs, namely (1) 1520–1570 construction of the Spanish colonial system in Mexico, (2) 1630–1680 establishment of the Caribbean plantation economy, (3) 1760–1830 onset of European territorial rule in Asia, (4) 1880–1900 with a new wave of colony formation in the old world, especially Africa, (5) 1900–1930 heyday of colonial export economies, as especially the French and British seized former Ottoman provinces, and (6) 1945–1960 period of the "second colonial occupation" of Africa. For additional

discussions of postcolonialism, see Gandhi (1998) and Loomba (2005, 2008) who articulate the new humanities, identities, feminism, and nationalism, Quayson (2000) who emphasizes literature as a politically symbolic act, Young (2001) who analyzes practices of freedom struggles, and Hiddleston (2009) who especially focuses on postcolonial ethics.

3. See also Levander and Mignolo (2011) on the global south, Alcoff (2007) in critically analyzing Mignolo, and Rumford (2006) on theorizing borders.

4. The two other significant works are undertaken by Ann Stoler (2001) who draws on her work on Dutch colonies to then compare it with the condition of Native Americans in North American history and by Bart Moore-Gilbert (2009) who critically studies the colonial activities of his own colonial ancestors in India. Such comparisons across time and space also destabilize the connection between knowledge and power.

5. Seidman traces the origins of the dichotomy of empires and nations to the Enlightenment thinkers who imagined that the early modern era dominated by empires was followed by the modern, unilinear social progress of nations. These thinkers conveniently overlooked the fact that from the sixteenth century through at least World War II empires, no nation-states provided the dominant political framework throughout the world.

6. According to this formulation, the rhetoric of Western modernity could only be sustained through its dark and constitutive side, namely the logic of coloniality (Mignolo and Tlostanova, 2006, p. 206).

7. The first Western modernity was that introduced to the rest of the world by the Iberian empires of Spain and Portugal from the fifteenth to the seventeenth centuries. The ensuing colonization of knowledge especially after the second Western modernity was in turn silenced by the rhetoric of the globalization of culture (Mignolo and Tlostanova, 2006, p. 208).

8. Also included among these empires were that of Japan (1895–1945), but it was not analyzed in as much detail as the Ottoman and Russian empires (Mignolo and Tlostanova, 2006, p. 209).

9. The resulting ambiguity of location leads these regions to highlight their sacred geography or geopolitics in an attempt to recover their lost identity on the one hand and to form alliances with both the North and the South on the other. For another similar analysis of Russia's imperial borderlands, see Brower and Lazzerini (1997).

10. It should be noted that Sankar Muthu (2003) does indeed address the complexity of discourse regarding the non-West within the Enlightenment discourse, but does not necessarily employ the postcolonial approach in doing so.

11. Eyal Ginio (2004) additionally analyzes the place of Gypsies (*kıptı*) in Ottoman society only to reveal that they formulated an ambiguous group that was neither Muslim nor non-Muslim.

12. For additional studies, see also Brummett (1994), Goffman (1998, 2002), and Greene (2000).

13. Lynda Carroll (2011) treats the Ottoman administrative attempts to forcefully settle nomadic tribes in the Transjordan as an indication of this new colonial mentality while Thomas Kühn (2007) nuances the "exclusionary inclusiveness" of Ottoman rule in Yemen by arguing that the locals were included in local administration, but now along sectarian lines. Tal Shuval (2000) articulates the manner in which the local janissary corps sustained their exclusionary Turkishness

through recruiting Turks into the militia and marrying selectively. Monica Spiridon (2006) discusses the coexistence of two sets of local elites in the Balkans, one retaining the traditional Turkish-style hierarchy and the other embracing the social consequences of Western-style education to challenge that hierarchy.

14. Isa Blumi employs the Ottoman experience to destabilize binary nationalist narratives in Yemen and Albania. Viewing the issue of identity formation from the standpoint of the Ottoman imperial subjects, Blumi destabilizes the narratives that assume what was proposed by the Ottoman state and interpreted by Western Europeans in the context of Albanians did not at all capture the complexities on the ground as many Albanians had very disparate views and identities, ones systematically silenced by nationalist historiography.

15. For a similar study on the Enlightenment thinkers' binary images of the Turks, see also Çırakman (2001).

16. Subrahmanyam (2006, p. 69) also mentions the Persian Safavid and the Chinese Ming and Qing empires, but does not analyze these as extensively.

17. Also overlooked in the process were the world-embracing ambitions of the Ottoman and Habsburg empires in the sixteenth century; the former was dismissed as the "Sick Man of Europe" and the latter through the "Black Legend." The Black Legend demonized the Spanish Empire and the Habsburgs that ruled over it for a while in terms of the treatment of the indigenous subjects overseas and religious minorities in Europe.

18. Michael Mann's five part taxonomy of "compulsory cooperation" comprises military pacification, the military multiplier effect, the correlation of authority with economic power, labor intensification, and the coerced diffusion of cultural norms (Jacoby, 2008, p. 268).

REFERENCES

Aksan, V. H. (2005/2006). Ottoman to Turk: Continuity and change. *International Journal*, *61*(1), 19–38.

Aksan, V. H. (2007). The Ottoman military and state transformation in a globalizing world. *Comparative Studies of South Asia, Africa and the Middle East*, *27*(2), 259–272.

Aksan, V. H. (2008). Theoretical Ottomans. *History and Theory*, *47*, 109–122.

Alatas, S. F. (2007). The historical sociology of Muslim societies: Khaldunian applications. *International Sociology*, *22*(3), 267–288.

Alatas, S. H. (1981). Intellectual captivity and developing societies. In A. Abdel-Malek (Ed.), *The civilization project: The visions of the Orient* (pp. 19–62). Mexico: El Colegio de Mexico.

Aral, B. (2004). The idea of human rights as perceived in the Ottoman Empire. *Human Rights Quarterly*, *26*(2), 454–482.

Arjomand, S. A. (2011). Axial civilizations, multiple modernities, and Islam. *Journal of Classical Sociology*, *11*(3), 327–335.

Baer, M., Makdisi, U., & Shryock, A. (2009). CSSH discussion: Tolerance and conversion in the ottoman empire: A conversation. *CSSH*, *51*(4), 927–940.

Baer, M. D. (2008). *Honored by the glory of Islam: Conversion and conquest in Ottoman Europe*. New York, NY: Oxford University Press.

Barkey, K. (2005). Islam and toleration: Studying the Ottoman imperial model. *International Journal of Politics, Culture, and Society, 19*(5), 5–19.

Ballantyne, T. (2003). Rereading the archive and opening up the nation-state: Colonial knowledge in South Asia (and Beyond). In A. Burton (Ed.), *After the imperial turn: Thinking with and through the nation* (pp. 102–124). Durham: Duke University Press.

Bayart, J.-F. (2011). Postcolonial studies: A political invention of tradition? *Public Culture, 32*(1), 55–84.

Bayly, C. (2006). Moral judgment: Empire, nation and history. *European Review, 14*(3), 385–391.

Bektaş, Y. (2000). The sultan's messenger: Cultural constructions of Ottoman telegraphy, 1847–1880. *Technology and Culture, 41*(4), 669–696.

Benedict, P., Berend, N., Ellis, S., Kaplan, J., Makdisi, U., & Miles, J. (2007). AHR conversation: Religious identities and violence. *Amarican Historical Review, 112*(5), 1433–1481.

Bilgrami, A. (1990). Rushdie, Islam and postcolonial defensiveness. *Yale Journal of Criticism, 4*(1), 301–311.

Blumi, I. (1998). The commodification of otherness and the ethnic unit in the Balkans: How to think about Albanians. *Eastern European Politics and Societies, 12*(3), 527–569.

Blumi, I. (2002). The Ottoman Empire and Yemeni politics in the Sancak of Ta'izz, 1911–18. In J. Hanssen, T. Philipp & S. Weber (Eds.), *The empire in the city: Arab provincial capitals in the late Ottoman Empire*. Beirut: Orient Institute.

Blumi, I. (2003a). Contesting the edges of the Ottoman Empire: Rethinking ethnic and sectarian boundaries in Malesore, 1878–1912. *International Journal of Mathematical Engineering and Science, 35*(2), 237–256.

Blumi, I. (2003b). *Rethinking the late Ottoman Empire: A comparative social and political history of Albania and Yemen, 1878–1918*. Istanbul: Isis Press.

Blumi, I. (2011). *Reinstating the Ottomans: Alternative Balkan modernities, 1800–1912*. London: Palgrave Macmillan.

Brennan, T. (1992). Rushdie, Islam and postcolonial criticism. *Social Text, 31/32*, 271–276.

Brower, D. R., & Lazzerini, E. J. (Eds.). (1997). *Russia's Orient: Imperial borderlands and peoples, 1700–1917*. Bloomington, IN: Indiana University Press.

Brummett, P. (1994). *Ottoman seapower and Levantine diplomacy in the age of discovery*. Albany, NY: SUNY Press.

Brummett, P. (2007). Gender and empire in late Ottoman Istanbul: Caricature, models of empire and the case for Ottoman exceptionalism. *Comparative Studies of South Asia, Africa, and the Middle East, 27*(2), 283–302.

Burton, A. (Ed.). (2003). *After the imperial turn: Thinking with and through the nation*. Durham, NC: Duke University Press.

Carroll, L. (2011). Building farmsteads in the desert: Capitalism, colonialism and the transformation of rural landscapes in late Ottoman period Transjordan. In S. K. Croucher & L. Weiss (Eds.), *The archeology of capitalism in colonial contexts: Postcolonial historical archaeologies* (pp. 115–120). New York, NY: Springer.

Çırakman, A. (2001). From tyranny to despotism: The Enlightenment's unenlightened image of the Turks. *International Journal of Mathematical Engineering and Science, 33*, 49–68.

Connell, R. (2007). *Southern theory: The global dynamics of knowledge in social science*. Cambridge: Polity.

Constantinou, C. M. (2000). Diplomacy, grotesque realism, and Ottoman historiography. *Postcolonial Studies, 3*(2), 213–226.

Cooper, F. (2005a). *Colonialism in question: Theory, knowledge, history*. Berkeley, CA: University of California Press.

Cooper, F. (2005b). Postcolonial studies and the study of history. In A. Loomba, S. Kaul, M. Bunzi, A. Burton & J. Esty (Eds.), *Postcolonial studies and beyond* (pp. 401–482). Durham, NC: Duke University Press.

Darling, L. (1998). Rethinking Europe and the Islamic world in the age of exploration. *Journal of Early Modern History*, *2/3*, 221–246.

Deringil, S. (2003). They live in a state of Nomadism and savagery: The late Ottoman Empire and the postcolonial debate. *Comparative Studies in Society and History*, *45*(2), 311–342.

Dirlik, A. (2002). Historical colonialism in contemporary perspective. *Public Culture*, *14*(3), 611–615.

Doumani, B. (1992). Rediscovering Ottoman Palestine: Writing Palestinians into history. *Journal of Palestine Studies*, *21*(2), 5–28.

Doumanis, N. (2006). Durable empire: State virtuosity and social accommodation in the Ottoman Mediterranean. *The Historical Journal*, *49*(3), 953–966.

Dubois, L. (2006). An enslaved Enlightenment: Rethinking the intellectual history of the French Atlantic. *Social History*, *31*(1), 1–14.

Dubois, T. D. (2005). Hegemony, imperialism and the construction of religion in East and Southeast Asia. *History and Theory*, *44*, 113–131.

Dursteler, E. R. (2006). *Venetians in Constantinople: Nation, identity, and coexistence in the early modern Mediterranean*. Baltimore, MD: Johns Hopkins University Press.

Dutton, M., Gandhi, L., & Seth, S. (1999). The toolbox of postcolonialism. *Postcolonial Studies*, *2*(2), 121–124.

Eisenstadt, S. N. (2003). *Comparative civilizations and multiple modernities (two volumes)*. Leiden: Brill.

Elouafi, A. A. (2010). The colour of Orientalism: Race and narratives of discovery in Tunisia. *Ethnic and Racial Studies*, *33*(2), 253–271.

Emrence, C. (2008). Imperial paths, big comparisons: The late Ottoman Empire. *Journal of Global History*, *3*, 289–311.

Englund, S. (2008). Historiographical review: Monstre Sacre: The question of cultural imperialism and the Napoleonic empire. *The Historical Journal*, *51*(1), 215–250.

Erickson, J. (1998). *Islam and postcolonial narrative*. Cambridge: Cambridge University Press.

Eze, E. C. (Ed.). (1997). *Race and the enlightenment: A reader*. New York, NY: Blackwell.

Gandhi, L. (1998). *Postcolonial theory: A critical introduction*. New York, NY: Columbia University Press.

Ginio, E. (2004). Neither Muslims nor Zimmis: The Gypsies (Roma) in the Ottoman State. *Romani Studies*, *14*(2), 117–144.

Goffman, D. (2002). *The Ottoman Empire and early modern Europe*. Cambridge: Cambridge University Press.

Gölbaşı, E. (2009). "Heretik" Aşiretler ve II. Abdülhamid Rejimi: Zorunlu Askerlik Meselesi ve İhtida Siyaseti Odağında Yezidiler ve Osmanlı İdaresi (Heretical Tribes and the Regime of Sultan Abdulhamid II: Yezidis and Ottoman Administration in Relation to the Issues of Mandatory Military Service and the Politics of Conversion). *Tarih ve Toplum*, *9*, 87–156.

Gölbaşı, E. (2011). *Osmanlı Kolonyalizmi Perspektiflerine dair Eleştirisel bir Değerlendirme (A critical assessment of the perspectives on Ottoman colonialism)*. Working Paper.

Goodrich, T. D. (1987). Tarih-i Hind-i Garbi: An Ottoman book on the New World. *Journal of American Oriental Society*, *107*(2), 317–319.

Greene, M. (2000). *A shared world: Christians and Muslims in the early modern Mediterranean.* Princeton, NJ: Princeton University Press.

Grillo, R. (1998). *Pluralism and the politics of difference: State, culture and ethnicity in comparative perspective.* Oxford: Oxford University Press.

Grosfoguel, R. (2010). Epistemic Islamophobia and colonial social sciences. *Human Architecture: Journal of the Sociology of Self Knowledge, 8*(2), 29–38.

Hamdani, A. (1981). Ottoman response to the discovery of America and the new route to India. *Journal of American Oriental Society, 101*(3), 323–330.

Hannsen, J. (2002). Practices of integration: Center-periphery relations in the Ottoman Empire. In J. Hannsen, T. Philipp & S. Weber (Eds.), *The empire in the city: Arab provincial capitals in the late Ottoman Empire* (pp. 49–74). Beirut: Orient Institute.

Hanssen, J. (2005). *Fin de Siecle Beirut: The making of an Ottoman provincial capital.* Oxford: Oxford University Press.

Hanssen, J. (2011). Malhame-Malfame: Levantine elites and transimperial networks on the eve of the Young Turk Revolution. *International Journal of Mathematical Engineering and Science, 43*(1), 25–48.

Hasseler, T. A., & Krebs, P. M. (2003). Losing our way after the imperial turn: Chartering academic uses of the postcolonial. In A. Burton (Ed.), *After the imperial turn: Thinking with and through the nation* (pp. 90–101). Durham: Duke University Press.

Hathaway, J. (2003). *A tale of two factions: Myth, memory, identity in Ottoman Egypt and Yemen.* Albany, NY: SUNY Press.

Herzog, C., & Motika, R. (2000). Orientalism "alla turca": Late 19th/early 20th century Ottoman voyages into the Muslim "outback". *Die Welt des Islams, 40*(2), 139–195.

Hess, A. C. (1970). The evolution of the Ottoman Seaborne Empire in the age of the oceanic discoveries, 1453–1525. *Amarican Historical Review, 75*(7), 1892–1919.

Hiddleston, J. (2009). *Understanding postcolonialism.* Stocksfield: Acumen.

Jacoby, T. (2008). The Ottoman State: A distinct form of imperial rule? *Journal of Peasant Studies, 35*(2), 268–291.

Khoury, D. R., & Kennedy, D. (2007). Comparing empires: The Ottoman domains and the British Raj in the long nineteenth century. *Comparative Studies of South Asia, Africa and the Middle East, 27*(2), 233–244.

Kühn, T. (2007). Shaping and reshaping colonial Ottomanism: Contesting boundaries of difference and integration in Ottoman Yemen, 1872–1919. *Comparative Studies of South Asia, Africa and the Middle East, 27*(2), 315–331.

Kunt, M. I. (1974). Ethnic-regional (Cins) solidarity in the seventeenth-century Ottoman establishment. *International Journal of Mathematical Engineering and Science, 5*(3), 233–239.

Kunt, M. I. (2003). Sultan, dynasty and state in the Ottoman Empire: Political institutions in the sixteenth century. *The Medieval History Journal, 6,* 217–230.

Linebaugh, P., & Rediker, M. (2000). *The many-headed hydra: Sailors, slaves, commoners, and the hidden history of the revolutionary Atlantic.* Boston, MA: Beacon.

Loomba, A. (2008). *Colonialism/postcolonialism.* London: Routledge.

Magubane, Z. (2004). *Bringing the empire back home.* Chicago, IL: University of Chicago Press.

Majid, A. (2000). *Unveiling traditions: Postcolonial Islam in a polycentric world.* Durham: Duke University Press.

Makdisi, U. (1997). Reclaiming the land of the Bible: Missionaries, secularism and Evangelical modernity. *Amarican Historical Review, 102*(3), 680–713.

Makdisi, U. (2000). *The culture of sectarianism: Community, history and violence in nineteenth-century Ottoman Lebanon.* Berkeley, CA: University of California Press.

Makdisi, U. (2002a). Ottoman Orientalism. *Amarican Historical Review, 107*(3), 768–796.
Makdisi, U. (2002b). Rethinking Ottoman imperialism: Modernity, violence and the cultural logic of Ottoman reform. In J. Hanssen, T. Philipp & S. Weber (Eds.), *The empire in the city: Arab provincial capitals in the late Ottoman Empire.* Beirut: Orient Institute.
Makdisi, U. (2002c). After 1860: Debating religion, reform and nationalism in the Ottoman Empire. *International Journal of Middle East Studies, 34*, 601–617.
Mehta, U. S. (1999). *Liberalism and empire: A study in nineteenth-century European thought.* Chicago, IL: University of Chicago Press.
Mignolo, W. (2006). Islamophobia/Hispanophobia: The (re)configuration of the racial imperial/colonial matrix. *Human Architecture: Journal of the Sociology of Self Knowledge, 5*(1), 13–28.
Mignolo, W. (2009a). Dispensable and bare lives: Coloniality and the hidden political/economic agenda of modernity. *Human Architecture: Journal of the Sociology of Self Knowledge, 7*(2), 69–88.
Mignolo, W. (2009b). Epistemic disobedience, independent thought and decolonial freedom. *Theory, Culture and Society, 26*(7–8), 159–181.
Mignolo, W. (2010). Cosmopolitanism and the de-colonial option. *Studies in Philosophy and Education, 29*, 111–127.
Mignolo, W., & Tlostanova, M. (2006). Theorizing from the borders: Shifting to geo- and body-politics of knowledge. *European Journal of Social Theory, 9*(2), 205–221.
Moore-Gilbert, B. (2009). The politics of "postcolonial" memory (extract from My father was a terrorist? A kind of a Memoir – work in progress). *Postcolonial Studies, 12*(3), 341–357.
Muthu, S. (2003). *Enlightenment against empire.* Princeton, NJ: Princeton University Press.
Nandy, A. (1983). *The intimate enemy: Loss and recovery of self under colonialism.* Delhi: Oxford University Press.
Nayar, P. K. (2010). *Postcolonialism: A guide for the perplexed.* London: Continuum.
Özbaran, S. (1990). An imperial letter from Süleyman the magnificent to Dom Joao III concerning proposals for an Ottoman-Portuguese Armistice. *Portuguese Studies, 6*, 24–31.
Pagden, A. (1995). *Lords of all the world: Ideologies of empire in Spain, Britain and France, c. 1500-1800.* New Haven, CT: Yale University Press.
Paker, M. (2007). Egemen Politik Kültürün Dayanılmaz Ağırlığı (The Unbearable Weight of Dominant Political Culture. In M. Paker (Ed.), *Psiko-Politik Yüzleşmeler (Psycho-political encounters)* (pp. 131–152). İstanbul: Birikim.
Philliou, C. M. (2011). *Biography of an empire: Governing Ottomans in an age of revolution.* Berkeley, CA: University of California Press.
Provence, M. (2011). Ottoman modernity, colonialism, and insurgency in the interwar Arab East. *International Journal of Middle East Studies, 43*, 205–225.
Quayson, A. (2000). *Postcolonialism: Theory, practice or process?* Cambridge: Polity.
Riedler, F. (2011). *Opposition and legitimacy in the Ottoman Empire: Conspiracies and political cultures.* London: Routledge.
Rogan, E. L. (1999). *Frontiers of the state in late Ottoman Empire: Transjordan, 1850–1921.* Cambridge: Cambridge University Press.
Rumford, C. (2006). Introduction: Theorizing borders. *European Journal of Social Theory, 9*(2), 155–169.
Rushdie, S. (1988). *The satanic verses.* New York, NY: Picador.
Said, E. (1978). *Orientalism.* New York, NY: Pantheon.
Said, E. (1993). *Culture and imperialism.* New York, NY: Knopf.

Salzmann, A. (1993). An ancient regime revisited: "Privatization" and political economy in the eighteenth-century Ottoman Empire. *Politics and Society, 21*(4), 393–423.

Seidman, S. (2005). Bringing empire back in. *Contemporary Sociology, 34*(6), 612–616.

Seljuq, A. (1980). Relations between the Ottoman Empire and the Muslim kingdoms in the Malay-Indonesian archipelago. *Islam, 57*, 301–310.

Shuval, T. (2000). The Ottoman Algerian elite and its ideology. *International Journal of Middle East Studies, 32*(3), 323–344.

Spiridon, M. (2006). Identity discourses on borders in Eastern Europe. *Comparative Literature, 58*(4), 376–386.

Stoler, A. (1992). Sexual affronts and racial frontiers: European identities and the cultural politics of exclusion in colonial Southeast Asia. *Comparative Studies in Society and History, 34*(3), 514–551.

Stoler, A. L. (2001). Tense and tender ties: The politics of comparison in North American history and (post)colonial studies. *The Journal of American History, 88*(3), 829–865.

Stoler, A. L. (2011). Colonial aphasia: Race and disabled histories in France. *Public Culture, 23*(1), 121–156.

Subrahmanyam, S. (1997). Connected histories: Notes towards a reconfiguration of early modern Asia. *Modern Asian Studies, 31*(3), 735–762.

Subrahmanyam, S. (2005). On world historians in the sixteenth century. *Representations, 91*, 26–57.

Subrahmanyam, S. (2006). A tale of three empires: Mughals, Ottomans and Habsburgs in a comparative context. *Common Knowledge, 12*(1), 66–92.

Swanson, H. (2004). Said's orientalism and the study of Christian missions. *International Bulletin of Missionary Research, 28*(3), 107–112.

Tlostanova, M. (2006). Life in Samarkand: Caucasus and Central Asia vis a vis Russia, the West and Islam. *Human Architecture: Journal of the Sociology of Self Knowledge, 5*(1), 105–116.

Tlostanova, M. (2007). The imperial-colonial chronotope. *Cultural Studies, 21*(2–3), 406–427.

Tlostanova, M. (2008). The Janus-faced empire distorting Orientalist discourses: Gender, race and religion in the Russian/(post) Soviet constructions of the "Orient." *Worlds and Knowledges Otherwise, II*(2), 1–11.

Tlostanova, M. (2011). The south of the poor north: Caucasus subjectivity and the complex of secondary "Australism." *The Global South, 5*(1), 66–84.

Tracy, J. D. (1994). Studies in eighteenth century Mughal and Ottoman trade. *Journal of the Economic and Social History of the Orient, 37*, 197–201.

Turan, Ö. (2009). Oryantalizm, sömürgecilik eleştirisi ve Ahmed Rıza Batı'nın Doğu Politikasının Ahlaken İflası'nı yeniden okumak (Orientalism, colonial critcism and Ahmed Rıza: Revisiting La Faillite Morale de la Politique Occidental en Orient). *Toplum ve Bilim, 115*, 6–45.

Washbrook, D. (2009). Intimations of modernity in South India. *South Asian History and Culture, 1*(1), 125–148.

Young, R. C. (2001). *Postcolonialism: An historical introduction.* Oxford: Blackwell.